The Development of the English Playhouse

The Development

by the same author

CIVIC THEATRE DESIGN
THE THEATRE
THE THEATRE ROYAL, LEICESTER

RICHARD LEACROFT
A.R.I.B.A. M.S.I.A.

of the English Playhouse

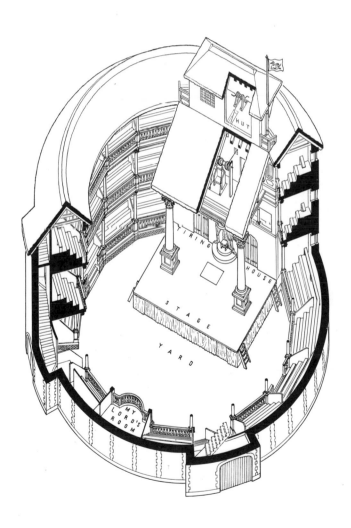

EYRE METHUEN
LONDON

First published in 1973
by Eyre Methuen Ltd., 11 New Fetter Lane, London EC4P 4EE
Copyright © 1973 by Richard Leacroft
Filmset by BAS Printers Ltd., Wallop, Hampshire
Printed in Great Britain by
Fletcher & Son Ltd
Norwich

SBN 413 28820 X

The edition is not for sale in the United States of America,
its dependencies, and the Philippine Republic

To my Mother

Contents

a reconstruction. Saunders' Ideal Theatre – a reconstruction. The study of acoustics. Criticism of the pit doors. Convenience and safety of the audience.

Wyatt's Drury Lane – a reconstruction. His theories on theatre design and the Spectatory. Introduction of the Picture Frame. Study of acoustics and social problems: their effects on auditoria design. The problems of entrances, payboxes and staircases. Fire precautions. Construction and scenic details of the stage. Smirke's Covent Garden – a reconstruction. Use of the proscenium wall as a fire precaution. Old Price Riots and the private boxes. Developing separation of the social classes. Reconstruction of Covent Garden by Albano as the Royal Italian Opera House. Fireproof construction of corridors and staircases. The use of gas lighting and the Theatre Royal, Norwich. Beazley's alterations to Drury Lane – a reconstruction.

The spread of the pit beneath the dress circle. The Theatre Royal, Plymouth – a reconstruction. Use of cast-iron construction. Details of stage machinery. Traps, bridges, barrels, drums and shafts: remains at the Theatre Royal, Bath. The Theatre Royal, Leicester – a reconstruction. The introduction of stalls, and the design problems involved. Further details of the stage machine – sliders, sloats and grooves. Sachs' typical wood stage.

Barry's Covent Garden – a reconstruction. The adaptable auditorium, and adjustable pit floor. Use of fireproof construction and cellular structure. Criticisms by French architect of lack of a proscenium wall, and proper ventilation. Changes in scenic design, and their effects on stage devices. Effects of the 1878 Metropolis Management and Building Acts Amendment Act. Installation of proscenium wall and iron doors. Her Majesty's rebuilt. Criticisms of the enlarged pit. Contemporary comments and criticisms on theatre design. Ventilation of theatres and widespread use of gas. Requirements of the Board of Works for exits, stairs, etc.

Preface

The present tendency to reconsider the design of theatre buildings in terms of the Open Stage and other variants on the 'traditional' picture-frame theatre makes the need for a fuller understanding of the growth and development of this theatre form essential not only to those students of the drama, faced with the need to visualise the varying environments of the eras with which they are particularly concerned, but also to all those concerned in the provision of new theatres and new theatrical forms. This work is designed to present in visual and literary terms the architectural development of the English playhouse from its beginnings in the Christian church to the establishment of the picture-frame theatre in the early years of the present century, together with the social, economic, safety and theatrical conditions which have to varying degrees affected this development.

The visual evidence is primarily presented as a series of cut-open, scale reconstructions which, being all reproduced to a common scale, enable the reader to grasp most readily the changing sizes and forms of the various buildings, or to make direct comparison between, for example, the size of the Globe Theatre and that of today's Drury Lane, and to appreciate at a glance the vast difference between the 'stage of Old Drury in the days of Garrick' and that of Henry Holland's theatre which occasioned Richard Cumberland's comment regarding Drury Lane and Covent Garden that henceforward they must be regarded as 'theatres for spectators rather than playhouses for hearers'.

It will be readily appreciated that this series of drawings has to a large extent conditioned the pattern of the book and, as it was found necessary to limit the preparation of the reconstructions to those theatres for which a reasonable amount of information was available, some buildings whose historical importance would otherwise have justified their visual inclusion have had to be presented only in literary terms. It is perhaps a happy coincidence that so much information is available regarding the two Theatres Royal, so that it is largely through the changing needs and fortunes of Drury Lane and Covent Garden that the developing theme has been viewed once the general playhouse pattern has been formulated. To these key buildings have been added a number of examples of both London and provincial theatres, which have been chosen for the light they throw on particular aspects of theatre design not already covered by the Theatres Royal, with their own particular problems of scale and use. It was also found necessary to include in some detail the development of stage machinery, which a close study of the reconstructions will reveal as conditioning to a high degree the shape and structure of the theatre buildings.

In the preparation of these reconstructions it has been necessary to photograph many original drawings, and, in the case of those buildings still extant, to take photographs and measured details of the many aspects of the structures which escape record on the architect's plans and sections. Much of this work would not have been possible without the help of my son, Robert, to whose patient skill I am much indebted, and to whom I must record my most sincere thanks. I must also express my indebtedness and thanks to my colleague, Mr G. A. Jones, ARIBA, for his part in the preparation of a number of the reconstructions. My sincere thanks are also due to Mr Hope Bagenal, FRIBA, for making available his records of the Westminster Play, and for his critical advice on the preparation of the relevant drawing, to Mr Robert Eddison for his kind help, to Mr Ralph Edwards, FRIBA, for making available his drawings of the Theatre Royal, Bristol, and to Miss K. M. D. Barker for her help and advice concerning the history of this building.

Dr F. H. W. Shepherd, General Editor of the G.L.C. *Survey of London*, most generously made available the researches related to the preparation of the Survey volume on the Theatres Royal, Drury Lane and Covent Garden, without which it would not have been possible to update my reconstructions of the Wren and Adam designs for Drury Lane. I am also grateful to Professor Edward Langhans of the University of Hawaii for his help, advice and generosity with material regarding the Restoration theatres; to The Rt. Hon. Viscount De L'Isle for permission to base material on the Baron's Hall of Penshurst Place; to Dr V. Mowry Roberts of Hunter College, New York, and Mr Paul Myers for their help in obtaining material from the New York Public Library; to Professor Rand Carter of McGill University for material relating to the Theatre Royal, Drury Lane; and to Mr Eliot Walker for his help in obtaining material relating to Wren's Drury Lane.

Thanks are also due to Mr Michael Kissaun of the Manoel Theatre, Valetta, Malta, for his permission and help regarding the recording of the scenic machinery of his theatre; to Mr George Hoare, Manager of the Theatre Royal, Drury Lane, for the loan of material; to Mr T. Benton of the Archive Office, The Royal Opera House, Covent Garden; to Mr P. Selby, Manager of the Palace Theatre; to Mr Howard, Manager of the Duke of York's Theatre; to Mr Baily, Manager of Her Majesty's Theatre; and to Mr B. Chitty, Manager of the Theatre Royal, Bristol, for their help and co-operation in permitting me to photograph and record their buildings.

My thanks are also due to the Editor of *Building* for permission to quote from the *Builder;* to the Editor of the *Architect and Building News* for permission to quote from both the *Architect* and the *Building News;* to the Editor of *Engineering* for permission to quote from the magazine; to Mr Charles Rigby and to the Librarian of Mount St Bernard Abbey for their translations of the descriptions of the Swan Theatre and the 1566 performance in the Hall of Christ Church College, Oxford; to Mr John Harris of the R.I.B.A.; to Mr S. Webb, Librarian of All Souls College, Oxford; to Dr R. A. Sayce, Librarian of Worcester College, Oxford; to Mr Bourne and the staff of the G.L.C. Department of Architecture and Civic Design, and Miss Mercer and the staff of the G.L.C. Records Office; to Mr Neil Beacham of the National Monuments Record; to Mr J. Farrell, Sub-Librarian of the University, Bristol; to Miss Dorothy Stroud, Assistant Curator of Sir John Soane's Museum; to Mr G. W. Nash and his staff at the Victoria and Albert Museum; and to Mr Best Harris, Librarian to the City of Plymouth and his staff, for their invaluable help in preparing extracts from their local papers regarding Foulston's Theatre Royal. Particular thanks are also due to the Staff of the City of Leicester Polytechnic Library for their continued help throughout the period involved in the preparation of this work.

My thanks are also due to Mr John Cullen and the staff of Eyre Methuen for their help and advice in the preparation of the book, and finally my most sincere thanks are due to my wife for her continual help, advice, solace and encouragement throughout the years of preparation.

'Keven Lodge'
Countesthorpe, Leicester.
1963–1970

1 Medieval origins and Renaissance influences

Existing buildings, erected for other purposes, have influenced the shape and form both of playhouses and theatrical presentations through the centuries, and it is not surprising that this study should start in the church. Although there are remains of Roman theatres and amphitheatres, and of structures possibly influenced by them, such as the fan-shaped timber seating at Yeavering in Northumberland[1] dating from the first half of the 7th century AD, or the various rounds found in different parts of the country[2] which may, or may not, have theatrical origins, early references to the drama in this country come from a Benedictine monastery. Indications of the dramatic presentation of the Easter ceremony, the *Quem Quaeritis*, are recorded in the *Regularis Concordiae* written by Ethewold, Bishop of Winchester, in the late 10th century. From these early beginnings further portions of the services were dramatised until plays evolved which were performed within the churches, for which simple scenic devices, such as a practical lidded sepulchre, probably sufficed[3] The prologue to a 12th or 13th century French play of the Resurrection first of all details 'Tus les lius et les mansions' (All the places and the houses). These include the crucifix, the sepulchre, a prison cell, Heaven and Hell, a place for Pilate and his six or seven courtiers, Caiaphas on a chair, the Jewish folk and Joseph of Arimathea with Nicodemus in the fourth place, then the disciples and in the sixth place the three Marys. Provision was to be made in the middle of the place for Galilee, and also for Emmaus.

These we may note were differently described as 'places' and as 'houses', the definition perhaps permitting a difference between those areas of church floor where persons were to stand or sit without any special provision – the 'places' – and those requiring some form of scenic construction, perhaps an indication of a building – the 'houses' (fig.1a.b.). Galilee was, however, to be in the middle of the place, which suggests that the term place could also be used to refer to the open space, in this instance, of the nave. As the choir of a church was not normally entered by the laity, and was indeed screened off from the public areas of the church by rood or parclose screens, it may perhaps be assumed that such performances would have been given within the nave.

Fig.1.a.b. Capitals in the cloister of Monreale cathedral, 12th century

The decorated pulpitum or rood screen, like the later screens of the medieval hall (fig.9), immediately suggests itself as a backing to a playing area, possibly even with a raised stage built in front, with Heaven to one side and Hell to the other. The processional nature of the Christian ceremony would suggest an open space down the centre of the nave, with further stations set to either side, or like Galilee in the middle (on the centre line) of the place – the nave (fig.2). The standing congregation could gather to either side of the nave, milling around and moving through the nave arcades, and along the backs of the congregation overflowing into the aisles as the players advanced from station to station.

If the actors were to be seen at the stations then these would need to be raised so that they could be viewed down the length of the nave above the heads of the congregation. Drawings of the Mystery of Lucerne,[4] presented in the open market square in the late 16th century, probably retained the pattern of these earlier performances presented in the churches, and show raised stages at either end of the open place, suggesting that there could well have been a second raised stage built across the west end of the nave. There are many instances, as at Melbourne in Derbyshire, where the nave was joined across the west end by a gallery, which could have provided an upper, and, in the vaulted space beneath, an inner stage. Wickham[5] has suggested the use of the triforium and clerestorey for the accommodation of spectators, and the former could have provided a suitable position while it was still the tribune of the Norman church. During this period, with semi-circular arches most nave arcades were comparatively low, providing a very reasonable view of the action in the nave, particularly when this was on a raised stage, but with the development of the pointed arch, nave arcades grew in height and the angle of vision correspondingly deteriorated. At the same time the tribune, as a walking way, gave place to the triforium, which was little more than the roof space over the aisle, and, as such, access was restricted by the roof timbers. By the time this transition had been made, however, it is highly likely that the plays were already on their way out of the church to join the processions and secular players in the streets and market places.[6]

Descriptions of such 'mansions' are to be found in the 12th century play of *Adam* which required that 'Paradise be set up in a somewhat lofty place' surrounded by 'curtains and silken hangings, at such a height that those persons who shall be in Paradise can be seen from the shoulders upward . . . Fragrant flowers and leaves are scattered there; in it are divers trees with hanging fruits so as to give the impression of a most lovely place.' In this particular play the performance was given outside the church, probably before the west doors, as one character is required to go 'back into the church.'[7] Hell would appear to be an enclosed place into which Adam and Eve were to be dragged, where 'they shall make a

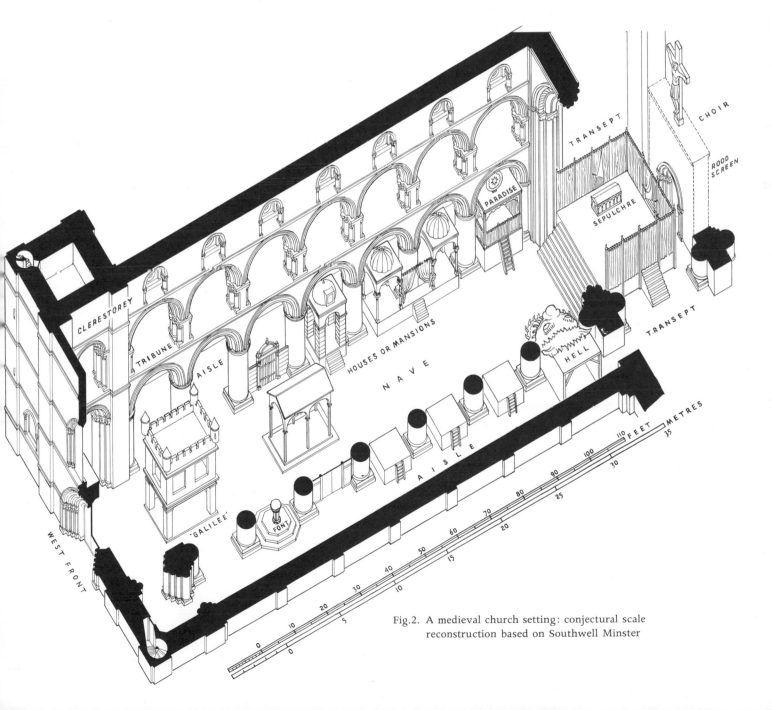

Fig.2. A medieval church setting: conjectural scale reconstruction based on Southwell Minster

great smoke arise, and they shall shout out to each other in Hell in jubilation, and clash their pots and kettles, so as to be heard without' and 'the devils shall go forth, and shall run to and fro in the square.' From which it would appear that the horrors of hell were to be imagined rather than seen.

Examples of the arrangement of mansions around a raised reactangular stage may be seen in the Valenciennes Passion Play (1547), where the varying forms and shapes adopted by the practical mansions attained a reasonable degree of verisimilitude,[8] and the drama of St Laurentius, Cologne (1581),[9] where the audience are assembled before the long side of a rectangular stage raised on barrels and enclosed by decorative walls against which are ranged various mansions, with further pieces of scenery adjoining two trees around which the stage appears to have been built.

A further variation on the theme may be seen in the mid-15th century illustration of the Martyrdom of St Apollonia (fig.3). Here the various houses are raised above the ground and are depicted grouped around one half of a circular 'place'[10] which appears to be occupied alike by players and performers, the former acting either on their own particular raised stage or making their way through the crowd to a central space which, like the open market place, could either retain its negative character or be mentally related to the mansion from which the actors had descended. The mansions here, with the exception of Hell, show few realistic features but are all variations on a simple canopied booth. Two of these are generally considered to be occupied by important members of the audience, whilst a third houses the 'orchestra'. In this example the circle is enclosed by a wattle fence and hedge, possibly provided to prevent unauthorised entry to the 'theatre', which suggests that a system of payment for the actors could have been based on a charge for entry.[11]

A diagrammatic arrangement of such mansions as are described above is illustrated in the manuscript of the *Castle of Perseverance,* dating from the early 15th century,[12] in which the 'place' is shown enclosed by a ditch filled with water, with the castle of Perseverance situated at the centre of the circle. Just such an arrangement could have been provided for in rounds similar to those already mentioned. Examples may still be seen and used at St Just and Perranzabuloe in Cornwall, where a circular space, in the former case having a diameter of some 126 feet, is enclosed by a bank.[13]

The use of such a round is described by Richard Carew in his *Survey of Cornwall* (1602), where he tells us:

> 'The Guary miracle – in English a miracle play – is a kinde of Enterlude, compiled in Cornish out of some Scripture history . . . For representing it they raise an earthen Amphitheatre in some open field, having the Diameter of his enclosed playne some 40 to 50 feet; The country people flock from all sides, many miles off, to hear and see it; for they have therein devils and deviccs, to delight as well the eye as the eare. . . .'[14]

Such rounds could well be relicts from the Roman occupation, if not directly in their material form, at least in the continuity of arena and theatre ideas disseminated by the

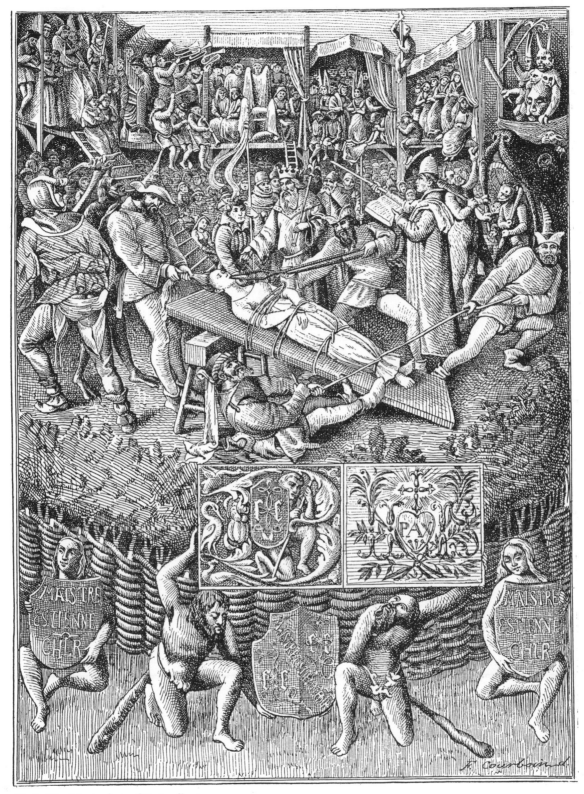

Fig.3. The Martyrdom of S. Apollonia

Fig.4. Temporary stage for phylax comedy

Romans throughout the country, while the use of the mansions and booths could have been a development of half-forgotten ideas inspired by the booths of strolling players, similar to those used by the 'phylax' players of Ancient Greece (fig.4),[15] or by the strolling players of the Roman period, who could have performed in theatres and arenas such as those at St Albans and at Silchester and Caerwent.[16]

A further variant, probably derived from secular and civic pageantry[17] on the mansion principle found in this country, was the mobile mansion built on wheels so that it could be moved from place to place within a town or city (fig.5). These pageants, according to the 16th century Archdeacon Robert Rogers,

'weare a high scafolde with two rowmes, a higher and a lower, upon four wheels. In the lower they apparelled them selves, and in the higher rowme they played, beinge

Fig.5. Corpus Christi play, Coventry

all open on the tope, that all behoulders mighte heare and see them. The places where they played them was in every streete . . . to se which playes was great resorte, and also scafoldes and stages made in the streetes in those places where they determined to playe their pagiantes.'[18]

Each pageant was provided by one of the trade guilds who were responsible for the presentation of the plays on the appropriate holy day, and it would appear that the pageant was built or adapted to represent the setting, e.g. Noah's Ark or Hell's Mouth. It has been suggested[19] that as the plays normally lasted several days, the wagons could have been shared by different guilds and adapted by them, each on its own day, to its own particular purpose. Starting from in front of the abbey, cathedral or main church, the pageants were drawn from place to place in the town, and at each place a performance of the play was given to the audience standing around, seated on specially built scaffolds, or leaning from surrounding windows. How exactly these scaffolds were arranged is not known, but it has been suggested that each pageant was drawn up in turn at the points of performance in the town, after which it moved to the next position, making way for the following pageant.[20] From the make-up of some of the plays, however, it would seem possible that several pageants might have been grouped around an acting area, possibly even the stages mentioned by Archdeacon Rogers, in an open square at one and the same time for a performance of one part of a play, all of which would move on together to replace a similar set of pageants in its turn.[21]

There are indications that in more than one instance upper and lower stages were used with vertical movement between them in the form of angels ascending to, or descending from, Heaven, and with similar movement between earth and Hell. As early as 1903 Streit[22] published a reconstruction showing just such a triple arrangement of stages, but this would almost certainly have had to be a permanently built rather than a mobile stage, set up in the market place in a manner similar to the settings for the Lucerne play.[23] In the Coventry plays there are references to a 'wynd' and a 'windlass',[24] which may have been required for hoisting angels aloft, and the Chester plays require that Christ ascend to the Heavens on a cloud. Salter draws attention to the need for 'a pit or trap in the floor of the stage' and the use of curtains permitting the discovery of a character, and Wickham[25] notes that the York pageants of 1486 describe similar ascents and descents from overhead, and an ascent through the floor. In these cases, however, there may have been only the one visible stage, the ascent from below being from the 'dressing room', and the movement above into a roof space of sufficient size to receive an ascending angel (fig.6). Wickham has suggested a machine room above the stage, but this is unnecessary, and indeed in a mobile pageant which must not be top-heavy, unlikely. The weight of the windlass and its operators, most likely one on either side,[26] would obviously be placed at or near ground level, with ropes to pulleys in the upper structure. This upper space would be just large enough to accommodate an ascending angel, and could be provided in the pitch of a roof, in a decorative turret or in some similar architectural feature.

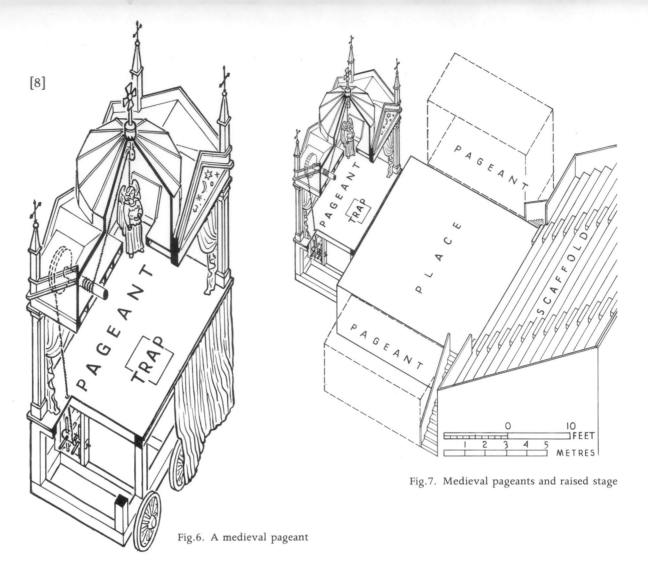

Fig.6. A medieval pageant

Fig.7. Medieval pageants and raised stage

The use of a raised stage has been an essential feature of the presentation of drama from early Greek times, wherever a standing audience surrounds the players who must be raised for all to see, and this in turn suggests the raising of the more important personages of the audience on scaffolds to a level with the raised stage, so that they may have a natural view of the players without the need to crane their necks.[27] It is just such an arrangement that is suggested by Archdeacon Rogers' comments, with the raised stage open all round to be seen by a maximum number of the audience. Open all round does not, however, preclude the use of a ceiling and roof supported on four corner posts, although these would curtail the view from the upper windows, balconies and roofs of surrounding buildings. Nor does it preclude the use of curtains for concealment or discovery. A stage direction from the *Ludus Coventriae*: 'then shall the place where Christ is in shall suddenly unclose round about',[28] suggests that curtains were drawn back on all four sides to reveal the occupants. Such a scene of 'Christ sitting at the table and his disciples each in their degree' implies, however, a directional pattern in the nature of the production which is always difficult in 'theatre-in-the-round', and it may be assumed that any such direction would be aimed at the important personages seated on the scaffold, or at the lord of the manor in later 'hall' productions. If an open playing space, the 'place', is to be provided adjoining the decorated pageant, then the directional nature of the actor-audience relationship must be accepted as this 'place' must of necessity be largely on the side of the pageant closest to the seated spectators, and as a result the view of the performance on this open playing space by any audience on the other side will be interrupted by the pageant itself. The 'place' could have been at ground level or been raised at pageant level (fig.7). Wickham's suggestion that each pageant may have had its own mobile 'acting area' seems unnecessarily cumbersome and repetitive. Such an unlocalised playing area would obviously be better provided as a permanent structure built at each performance station in proper relationship to the scaffolded seating, and it may well be just such a pattern that Rogers was describing when he mentioned 'the scafoldes and stages made in the streetes in those places where they determined to playe their pagiantes', the pageants, singly or in groups, tying up alongside the stage when their turn came.

These plays were presented with great attention to realistic detail. Earthquakes, thunderbolts, miracles and fires were normal features and the Mouth of Hell (fig.3) was contrived with massive jaws that opened and closed to permit the passage of many devils who prodded the damned into hell amid the smoke and flames which belched forth. Although Herod 'ragis in the pagond & in the strete also'[29] and the devils ran among the audience and played practical jokes on them,[30] suggesting that the 'place' may in some instances have been the open street, such activity does not preclude the existence of a raised 'place'.

Although no payment seems to have been required from the audience, there are records of persons leasing the performing rights of the plays so that they should be sited near their houses, when they could hire places out in their balconies, windows or on specially erected scaffolds.[31] Payments were, however, made to many of the actors.

Some lords had among their servants persons who performed in the lord's house, or in the homes of adjoining landowners. No doubt their performances, like those outlined above, were given in the open air when the weather was suitable, but for performances at such times as the Christmas festival a warm and weather-proof interior was essential. In general the medieval manor house centred around a hall in which the whole establishment of the estate gathered for meals and social functions. At one end a raised dais, lit by an oriel window, carried a table across the width of the hall at which the owner and his family sat. Along the length of the hall further tables housed the retainers, with the hearth in the centre of the hall floor, later to be replaced by a fireplace in one or both of the side walls. At the end of the hall, opposite to the dais, a passageway from an outer to an inner court was screened by a partition generally containing two openings, which later were equipped with doors (fig.8). The height of the hall was such that it dominated the adjoining one – or two – storey buildings, but the passageway was usually ceiled just over head-height, leaving a space above which could be, and often was, used as a gallery. Beyond the 'screens' passage, doorways led to the buttery and pantry, which in turn connected with an external kitchen and the servants' quarters.

This large hall provided an excellent setting for any form of theatrical performance (fig.9), with an ideal geographical location of the parts. The family, raised on the dais, looked down the length of the hall, while the trestle tables, pushed back to the side walls, provided at least three levels of seats: benches on the floor, the edge of the tables, and benches set on the tables. The open space of the hall floor provided the same kind of acting area — 'place' — as was to be found in the church and the rounds, here approached by the two doors in the screens from the servants' rooms, which could be used for dressing. The doors could serve as mansions, but simple free-standing pieces of scenery could have provided additional stations if or when required by the action of a particular performance.

The actor-audience relationship for these varying medieval arrangements was here dictated by the architectural limitations of the enclosing roofed hall, and a strong rectangular pattern emerged, which in the larger halls would be emphasised in length, but in the smaller ones could approximate more nearly to a square. Points of entry to the acting area would appear to have been dictated by the position of the screen openings, but this does not necessarily follow if the conventions of the period permitted an actor to remain 'invisible' in his progress from these openings to a particular position allotted to him, from which point he could make his 'visible' entry when his cue fell due.

The guild plays were still performed out of doors on their pageants until well into the second half of the 16th century, and variations on these plays were doubtless performed indoors in the halls. Other entertainments were devised for indoor performance during the intervals of a feast. At court they took differing forms known under titles ranging variously between Interludes, Masks or Masques, and Plays. Exactly what constituted an Interlude is difficult to define, but it would be feasible to relate it to some form of short 'one-act' play, although in some respects the term is used to indicate something more closely related to the word Mask, a form of embryonic ballet with music, song and dance. The Tudor Interludes were often associated with banquets[32] and as a result the hall fulfilled the double purpose of dining hall and playhouse.

Many Interludes were written for indoor production[33] and needed no other setting than that provided by the architecture of the hall, its open 'place' enclosed by an audience seated on the side benches, and by the serving and kitchen staff pressing in from their quarters beyond the screens, to find seats on the floor in front of the side benches, or crowding around the screens but leaving narrow gangways from the doors to the central acting area. Such passages were not always wide enough for some self-important characters in the plays, who called for room and space in which to move.[34] As with the guild plays, the audience was drawn into the action, particularly by the comedians.

Not all Interludes could, however, be so easily presented, many requiring the use of scenic devices such as the centrally placed structure noted in the *Castle of Perseverance,* in addition to mansions set around the acting area. In some instances actual pageant wagons were used within a hall, as on the occasion of the wedding of Prince Arthur and Katherine of Aragon in 1501, when three great pageants were wheeled into Westminster Hall.[35] The first was a castle on wheels drawn by four men disguised as animals, eight 'goodly and fresshe ladies, lokyng owt of the wyndowes' and four small boys dressed as maidens, sitting and singing in the four turrets, one at each corner. Following this was a fully rigged ship which appeared to be sailing on the sea, and when it arrived before the King alongside

Fig.8. Performance in a medieval hall

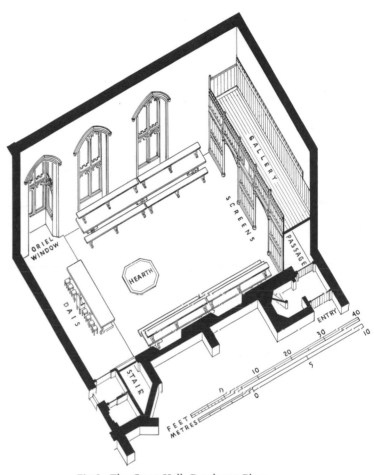

Fig.9. The Great Hall, Penshurst Place

the castle, two 'goodly persons' descended by ladders. The third pageant was 'in liknes of a great hill' containing eight 'goodly knights' who dismounted and danced with the ladies. While the dancing continued the pageants were removed.[36]

Such pageants provided a raised stage with curtains which could be drawn to reveal the performers, who could both descend from it and return to it. As has already been noted, many pageants were also equipped with such mechanical devices as traps and upper structures permitting appearances from below or ascensions to and descents from the heavens. It does not seem possible that such pageants could have been wheeled into the normal hall, as the limitations of the screens passage and entry doors would have prevented it. It may be that they were built in the hall and hidden until required, as is suggested by a device used in 1511. This was screened from the view of the spectators, or at least from the royal personage, by a 'great cloth of Arras' until its part in the performance came due, when the curtain was displaced and the pageant brought 'more nere'.[37] In the same year a castle of timber was built to be used in the hall at Eltham Palace, but where this was placed is not stated. It could well have been built as a permanent setting against the screens, incorporating within its design the two entry doors.

Two pageants, one representing a castle and the other a rock and fountain for Apollo, the latter measuring 14 feet by 8 feet,[38] were built in 1572 for a mask presented at Whitehall before the Duc de Montmorency, but this performance was given in a pavilion built for the purpose, 'decked with birch and ivy under a canvas roof' and referred to as 'the Banquetting Howse'.[39] Special provision for the entry of such vehicles could have been made in a pavilion, but where it was not possible to bring in a pageant the mechanical devices which they provided had to be made available in some other way. The introduction of some form of fixed stage, however small, could provide the revealing, or concealing, curtains and permit the use of trap doors and ascents to, and descents from, heaven.

In 1527 an entertainment given in a specially erected banqueting house at Greenwich[40] had a setting 'at the nether ende' which was revealed 'by lettyng doune of a courtaine' and represented 'a goodly mount, walled with towers . . . with all things necessary for a fortresse' and a cave from which a number of ladies emerged.[41] Nevertheless movable scenery remained a necessary part at least of some mask productions, and throughout the 16th century we have much mention[42] of chariots, sea monsters, movable towers, and a 'castell for Lady peace to sytt & be browghte in before the Queenes Maiestie'.[43] In addition a cloud piece was adapted for the 1578–79 season at court: 'A hoope & blewe Lynnen cloth to mend the clowde that was Borrowed and cut to serve the rock in the plaie of the burnying knight and for the hire thereof and setting vpp the same where it was borrowed'.[44] This was made of 'linen blue & hoops' and was drawn up and down by means of pulleys, its progress being controlled by long boards made into a 'stere', presumably some sort of guiding rail. There was also a sun which moved across the heavens.

A description of a similar arrangement in operation in 1565 provides some indication of the complicated nature of the entertainments: 'a travers slyded away; presently a cloud was seen move up and downe almost to the top of the greate chamber, upon which Cynthia was discovered ryding: The Moon Goddess was then joined by Ariadne, who floated up towards her on a cloud from the lower end of the hall'. Later 'the travers that was drawn before the Masquers sanke downe'[45] to reveal eight knights beneath a great oak.

The continuing use of existing architectural features in the form of the doors is suggested by arrangements made for the entertainment of Elizabeth I at King's College, Cambridge, in 1564, with a performance of the *Aulularia* of Plautus.[46] On this occasion the whole width of the chapel (fig.10) was fitted with a raised platform some 5 feet high, set near to the rood

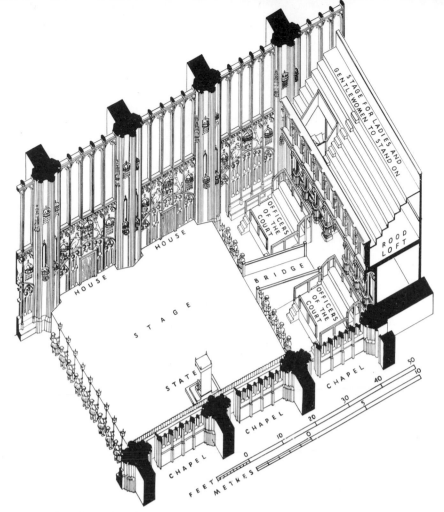

Fig.10. Stage in King's College Chapel, 1564

screen with a bridge from the choir door, and of such a width that two of the chapels on the north side could be used as 'houses', while the south wall was 'hanged with cloth of state'. The 'state' for her majesty was placed on the same raised platform as the players. Standing room for the ladies and gentlewomen of the court was provided on the rood loft, and for the 'choyce officers of the Court' in the space between the rood screen and the platform. Some of the audience were permitted to stand on the platform at the players' end, while guards holding torches stood on the floor alongside the platform. As the existing doors to the north chapels would have been largely covered by the 5 feet high stage, it has been assumed in their construction that, as the Queen's Surveyor had broken through 'the East window of the North Vestry door' to provide a 'privy way' for the Queen,[47] he could as easily have broken through the windows of the chapels adjoining the stage to provide adequate doors to the 'houses' at stage level.

The use of built 'houses' is, however, indicated by the Revels Accounts for the Christmas entertainments at Court for the same year which include payment for 'canvas to couer diuers townes and howsses and other devisses and Clowds ffor a maske and a showe and a play by the childerne of the chaple', and in the following year 'canvas to couer the Townes with all and other provicions for A play maid by Sir percivall hartts Sones with a maske of huntars & diuers devisses and a Rocke, or hill ffor the ix musses to singe vppone with a vayne of Sarsnett Dravven vpp and downe before them'.[48] In addition to hand torches the entertainments were lit by chandeliers hung on wires stretched across the hall. Candles were used individually in metal lanterns, especially when placed near walls or scenery.[49]

Throughout the 1580s the Master of the Revels' accounts continuously record such features as 'a city and a palace . . . a great curtain, a mountain and a great cloth of canvas . . . a city and a Battlement . . . a city and a town . . . a great city and a senate house . . . a great cloth, a battlement, wall and mount of canvas'. Such palaces and senate houses were probably similar to that designed by Garret Christmas for Dekker's *Londons Tempe,* 1629, (fig.11)[50] which shows a rectangular curtained room some 18 feet wide by perhaps 6 feet deep. From further descriptions such structures were built sufficiently strongly to support actors or musicians on an upper storey, presumably a development of the traditional

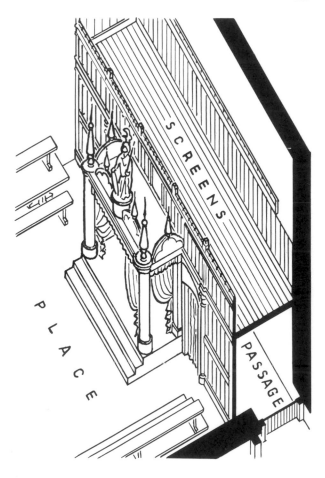

Fig.11. A stage erected against the screens

Fig.12. A city erected against the screens

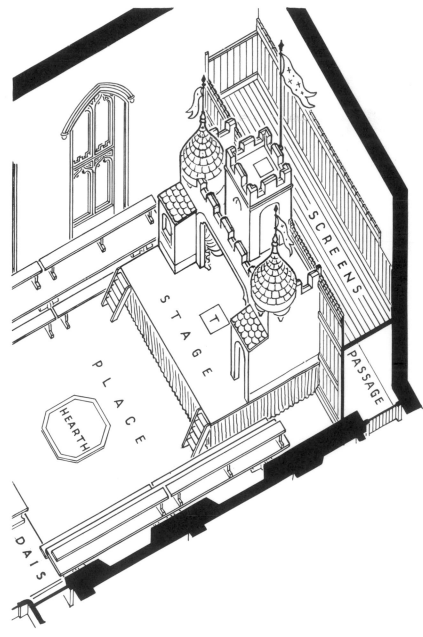

mansions. A city may have been presented in a manner similar to that illustrated here (fig.12) as a castle with a central arched opening and flanking side towers, developed perhaps from medieval pageants. Such features could have had a raised stage set against the screens end of the hall, and would at the same time have provided a curtained recess at the back of the stage for interior scenes and discoveries. Variations on the central pavilion theme recur in paintings and illustrations throughout the 14th and 15th centuries. Fabriano's *Presentation in the Temple* (1423)[51] illustrates just such a central pavilion flanked by practical mansions arranged across the back and sides of a rectangular space, and the same can be seen in the 15th century painting by Neroccio, *Episode from the Legend of St Benedict*.[52] In its simplest form the central pavilion is represented by a curtained dais with a throne set before a curtained backing to a raised stage, such as continued to be used by such companies of actors as the Italian Commedia dell'arte, and illustrated as the setting for foreign performers in a Dutch engraving of 1635.[53] A throne of the sort shown in this drawing is indicated on the reconstruction of the Swan Theatre (fig.23).

While the scenery for the masks was derived from the earlier medieval mansions, both had been influenced by ideas emanating from Renaissance Italy. Here interest in the classical arts, literature and architecture was of paramount importance, and the discovery in 1427 of a manuscript including comedies by Plautus and Terence stimulated investigation into the correct methods of staging these plays. In his *Fifth Book of Architecture* the Roman architect, Vitruvius, described at length the Greek and Roman theatres, and their methods of scenic production, but to people unfamiliar with the actual appearance of the classical theatres, his descriptions were not easy to follow, and even today, with our greater archaeological knowledge, many aspects are still unclear. He described, for example, the use of three kinds of scenes which he called the 'tragic', the 'comic' and the 'satyric'. Tragic scenes were 'delineated with columns, pediments, statues, and other objects suited to kings' and 'comic scenes exhibit private dwellings; satyric scenes are decorated with trees, caverns, mountains, and other rustic objects delineated in landscape style'.[54] Regarding the actual scenery used, Vitruvius tells us that in the centre of the 'scaena' there were 'double doors decorated like those of a royal palace. At the right and left are the doors of the guest chambers. Beyond are spaces provided for decoration.' In these spaces are placed periaktoi, 'triangular pieces of machinery which revolve, each having three different faces . . . Beyond these places are the projecting wings which afford entrances to the stage, one from the forum, the other from abroad.'

Illustrations to publications of the works of Terence and Plautus indicate the varying attempts made to understand the Vitruvian descriptions. The Lyons *Terence* of 1493 shows an arrangement having a raised platform backed by a series of openings. Each opening was curtained and had a name displayed above it indicating the place it was intended to represent. Where curtains are shown open it would appear that each interior was decorated to represent its locale, and actors are shown within, at least one being in bed. In its simplest form these openings were arranged in a straight line across the rear of the stage, as indicated in the settings for the *Andria* (fig.13a), but variations include a straight-sided centrally placed bay projecting forward on to the stage, with a single opening in the advanced face in the setting for the *Adelphoe* (fig.13b), a double opening in the setting for the *Heautontimoroumenos* (fig.13c), and in one instance a rectangle set diagonally on the stage.

(a) *The Andria*   (b) *The Adelphoe*   (c) *The Heautontimoroumenos*

Fig.13. Stage settings for the plays of Terence, 1493

Although the Terence illustrations suggest a stage of limited size, this may be due to lack of skill on the part of the artist. In at least one example, a performance of the *Poenulus* in Rome in 1513, the stage was 'almost a hundred feet wide, twenty-four feet deep, and about eight feet high'. At the back of the stage was a highly decorated arcade screen divided into five sections by columns with gilded bases and capitals, each section framing a doorway covered with curtains of gold cloth. Above was a frieze of beautiful paintings and a gilded cornice. At the two ends of the screen were two great towers with doors, one marked 'via ad forum'.[55] Similar classical columns may be seen in the settings for the *Heautontimoroumenos* and the *Adelphoe*, but in the *Andria* setting the columns are replaced by medieval-type buttresses. In direct contrast, the illustrations to the *Terence des Ducs*[56] show actors performing in and before practical three-dimensional houses of the medieval pattern bearing little relationship to the formal architectural environments of the Lyons settings.

The architect, Sebastiano Serlio, writing in the second book of a *Treatise on Architecture*,[57] dealt with perspective painting with particular reference to its place in the theatre. He illustrates a temporary theatre to be constructed in an existing hall, which combines the Vitruvian principles of theatre design with the contemporary use of perspective scenery. The illustrations (figs.14,15) clearly define the three elements considered essential for theatrical productions. Within the rectangular building Serlio shows timber scaffolding arranged concentrically around a semi-circular, slightly raised, orchestra – E, with individual seats for the important personages on the circumference of the orchestra. Beyond this is a rectangular space – D, at floor level, with a raised level stage – C, adjoining, both of which extend to the full width of the hall.

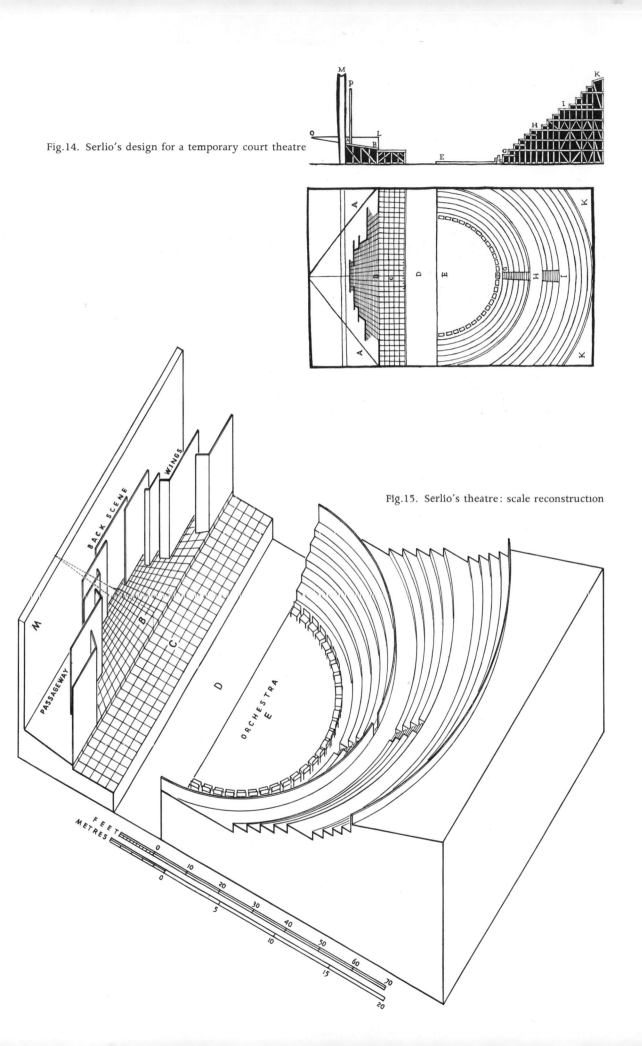

Fig.14. Serlio's design for a temporary court theatre

Fig.15. Serlio's theatre: scale reconstruction

BACK SCENE

WINGS

PASSAGEWAY

M

B

C

D

ORCHESTRA
E

FEET
METRES

0

10

20

30

40

50

60

70

0

5

10

15

20

'The scaffold or stage is built in two parts, the front part – C raised as high as the level of a man's eyes and built firmly and strongly and on a level. The second part – B is raised by one-ninth of its depth above the first scaffold and is built on an incline, so that the scenes, which are arranged on this scaffold, may be the more easily seen. The back wall of the stage is to be built at a distance from the wall of the hall sufficient to make possible the passing back and forth of the "personages" behind the scenes without their being visible to the audience.'[58]

The scenes which stand on this rear sloping stage take the form of a flat back scene, flanked on either side by further panels to each of which is attached a narrower panel on the centre stage edge like an open book. These wings are arranged in such a way as to enclose the view of the audience within the scene, which extends in this manner to the full width of the hall. Behind these wings and back scene is a flat wall – M, which probably gave an impression of the sky seen above the tops of the side wings. There are four sets of wings, but only the front two have an open space between them which could have provided any form of entry for the actors.

The wings and the back scene were to be painted in perspective to provide the three settings mentioned by Vitruvius – the tragic, the comic, and the satyric – for each of which Serlio illustrated perspective scenes making use of the wings discussed above. It will readily be appreciated that the use of the perspective scene, in which the parts are distributed on a series of receding wings, limits the use of this scenic area by actors who cannot decrease their size to conform to the rapidly diminishing size of the perspective buildings. It is not surprising, therefore, that Serlio permitted no space between the second, third and fourth pairs of wings, on which the reduction would be too great for direct comparison with the living actor. It can therefore be safely assumed that the actor did not normally venture on to this sloping stage where even the 'paving stones' are represented in perspective, but remained either on the raised flat stage – C, or on the two areas – D, E, at floor level. Unfortunately Serlio does not indicate points of entry for either actors or audience into the hall,[59] but the actors' entrances must have been made through doors at either end of the rectangular acting areas, or, as has been suggested above, they may have entered the hall out of view of the audience, that is at some point behind the front pair of wings, and then gained access to the stage through the spaces between the first and second pairs of wings, or through openings in the wings themselves.[60] Movement between the upper and lower stage levels is facilitated by the provision of steps, shown in each of the three scene drawings, but not in the general plan of the theatre. Their omission from the latter drawing is probably due to their being considered by Serlio as part of the perspective scene, as architectural steps are indicated in both the tragic and the comic scenes, but steps of a rock-cut variety are indicated in the satyric scene.

In the earlier return to classical conditions the mansions of the Terentian stage permitted a continuance of the medieval relationship between mansions and 'platea' (place), or general acting area. The introduction of the perspective vista of houses, vanishing towards a central back screen, reduced the practicability of the houses to, at the most, the first two pairs of screens, and it would therefore appear that we are now facing a major change in the relationship of scenic items to the actor.

In the classical theatre each architectural doorway, entry way or ramp had its own recognised scenic location, known alike to actors and to audience. The central door represented the royal palace, the other doors the homes of lesser characters and the entry ways led from, and to, accepted places. Further enlightenment as to the exact location of a scene was provided by the periaktoi and other painted scenic devices. It would, however, appear that a greater degree of realism was involved in the medieval presentations, where the individual practical 'mansions' replaced the architectural doors and presented the actor with additional, often raised, acting areas. These were constructed and decorated to provide a high degree of realism and verisimilitude, even though in some instances their proportions and size might bear little relation to what they represented, doors and windows being nevertheless of sufficient size to be usable by the actors when so required. This practical character was no longer possible when the parts of each 'house', except perhaps the foremost pair, had to conform to the degree of reduction required within the general pattern of the overall perspective scene. Doubtless, however, both practical mansions arranged in a street, and perspective scenic vista, continued in use, individually and in combination, in much the same unsophisticated way that the new Italian architectural details were mixed with the vernacular methods of building throughout the whole of the 16th century.

It should be realised, however, that Serlio's houses were not just flat painted panels as the plan perhaps suggests, but had cut-out pieces added to give an irregular outline, and sections could be removed so that it was possible to see through to the 'house' behind. His drawings also indicate the possibility of smaller houses at the front, over which the house behind might be viewed.

Among the many performers at Court were the children of the choir schools who performed plays in the Latin manner, and these companies had their own theatres in the school buildings. Plays were also performed by the students of the universities, and by schoolboys as part of their grammar school education. At Westminster, from as early as 1413,[61] the acting 'of classical dramas was traditionally regarded as the best method by which to give students facility of speech and familiarity with common Latin idiom.'[62] It would be natural to expect that such plays would be set in the Roman manner noted above. In 1528 the boys of Paul's School acted the *Phormio* of Terence at a banquet given by Cardinal Wolsey[63] and it could have been on a similar occasion in the previous year that the Italian ambassador spoke of 'a very well designed stage,'[64] which suggests perhaps that the setting may have been in the Italian manner.

When Paul's boys acted before the King and the French Ambassador in the same year, 1527, the great chamber was arranged with a central fountain surrounded by benches[65] and with a silken hawthorn tree set to one side and a mulberry tree to the other. The habit of including a mask, a show and a play as entertainment for a single evening makes it difficult to differentiate between them when it comes to determining if the setting described belonged to one, and if so to which, or if it could be adapted for all. This pattern of entertainment probably required a great deal of interchange between the various theatrical devices which could be made available for any form of production. An item concerning the Westminster scholars records that payment was made to 'a painter for drawing the cytee and temples of Jerusalem, and for paynting towres,'[66] which suggests the introduction by that date of scenery on the Terentian method, and in 1580 there are references to houses used in the play in the Westminster School hall itself.

When Elizabeth visited Oxford in 1566[67] the arrangement of the Hall in Christ Church differed from anything that has previously been noted in that for this performance the stage appears to have been erected at the dais, or upper end, with the state in the middle and seating for the noblemen and ladies built up along the walls. As a result the great crush of students and others were able to make their way direct from the stairs, through the entry doors, into the body of the hall. The Queen made her approach by a specially built and decorated bridge leading directly from her lodgings to an opening cut in the side wall. The hall itself was decorated with a gilded and vaulted ceiling which in size and grandeur was comparable with a Roman palace of the ancient world. The theatre is described as large and lofty, raised on many steps, and one is tempted to think in terms of the Serlian scaffolded arrangement (fig.15) of stage and cavea, were it not for the mention of balconies and scaffolding built along the side walls. The stage was further described as being flanked by 'magnificent palaces and mansions for the players', while a throne 'was fixed in a lofty position, adorned with cushions and tapestries and covered with a canopy of gold' for the use of the Queen.

The raised stage was equipped with at least one trap-door through which Diomedes rose up from the depths of the infernal regions below. The radical change in building the raised stage at the west, or upper end, of the hall was probably occasioned by the fact that had it been placed at the normal screens end it would have blocked the entry ways for the very large audience, who would have had to make their way across the stage itself to reach their seating, or standing, places, thus destroying any surprise or illusion from the effects to be revealed. Normally the entrances in the hall screens could be used by both actors and audience, as the earlier medieval scenic arrangements contained no unusual surprises, or complicated machinery, but with the advent of the new Italian ideas, particularly of perspective scenery, the need to keep this area hidden from view became more important. On two further occasions in 1605 (p.52) and 1636 (p.56) the same hall was arranged with the stage at the upper end, presumably for the same reasons.

While such classical arrangements for plays might be found in the educational centres, the use of mansions distributed around the open floor of the hall continued for masks at Court, and an illustration (fig.16) of the *Balet comique de la Reyne* as performed in the Petit Bourbon in Paris on 15th October, 1581, shows clearly how these were arranged. The King

Fig.17. Setting for a play by Plautus, 1518

Fig.16. A ballet in the Petit Bourbon, Paris, 1581

is seated on the central axis of the hall, flanked by ambassadors, his state presumably being set within the great apse at the end of the hall. On either side are two raised galleries which were permanent architectural features. The hall was in fact a great deal wider than is suggested by this illustration,[68] permitting those members of the audience seated along the sides at floor level to be accommodated on raised tiers of seats. Set amid these spectators, on either side, are two mansions, the one depicting a cloud, the other a wood, although we are told[69] that 'On the left of the hall was a Gilded Vault for musicians, on the right the Grove of Pan, and at the foot the Garden of Circe, both veiled by curtains.' The cloud hung centrally 'between the Vault and the Grove' in the roof. The Garden of Circe may be seen centrally placed at the opposite end of the hall to the state, and is defined as an enclosed stage area by a low rail or balustrade. Within this open space are a number of animals and the whole is backed by a distant view, possibly in perspective and most likely painted as a single cloth, or panel, set in an arched recess behind the central opening of a triple arched trellis covered with foliage. The two side arches provide access for the performers entering the main acting area. General illumination of the hall is indicated by two hanging fittings supporting candles.

In view of what so many scholars have said about members of an audience being able to see all the action in performances during these early periods, it should be noted that the arrangement of the side mansions here is such that few persons on the same side of the hall could have seen much of any action contained within them, the whole performance being aimed at the noble patron whose sight lines were the only ones taken into account. In addition to these stationary pieces of scenery there was also a mobile fountain on which maskers entered, as well as the Chariot of Minerva.

The arrangement illustrated here was equally typical of the English mask. Even early in the 17th century a mask, *The Vision of the Twelve Goddesses*,[70] staged before the Queen at Hampton Court in January, 1604, had a great mountain standing at the end of the hall before the screens with 'a winding stayre of breadth for three to march' where the musicians and a whole bevy of ladies were placed. At the upper end of the hall 'stood another rock-like structure, wrought to reveal a cave', and on the left-hand side of the hall the removal of a small curtain showed a temple. In this case the scenic devices took up so much space that only a limited audience could be admitted.

In 1581 a temporary Banqueting Hall was erected at Whitehall, on the site of the present Banqueting Hall, which was to last until 1606 when it was pulled down.[71]

> 'Ther was a banquet howse made in manner & fourme of a long square 332 foot in measure about; 30 principalls made of great masts, being xl foot in length apeece, standing upright; betwene every one of theis masts x foot a sunder & more. The walls of this howse most arteficially wth canvas, and painted all the out sides of the same howse most arteficially wth a worke called rustick, much like unto stone. This howse hath 292 lights of Glas. The sides w^thin the same howse was made wth x heights of degrees, for men & weomen to stand upon; and in the top of this howse was wrought most cuninglie upon canvas works of Ivie & holy, wth pendants made of wicker rods, & garnished wth baies, Rue & all manner of strang flowers, and garnished wth spangs of gould, as also garnished wth hanging Tuscans made of holly & Ivie, wth all manner of strang fruits, as pomegarnetts, orrengs, pompions, . . . Betwene thes works of baies & Ivie were great spaces of Canvas, wch was most cuninglie painted, the cloudes wth the starrs, the sunne and sunne beames, wth diverse other coats of sundry sorts belonging to Qs ma^tie, most ritchlie garnished wth gould.'[72]

Von Wedel, writing of his visit to Whitehall in 1584, described the Hall as 'a high and spacious house with many windows, and inside full of seats and benches one above the other, so that many people may be seated there. The ceiling is hung with leaves and thick bushes.'[73]

We have no further information as to the arrangement of the acting area, but it is possible that some form of raised stage was provided, as during the period when this building was in use there are entries in the Revels accounts of 'a city, . . . a Battlement; a town; . . . a house:' as well as a great curtain, a great cloth of canvas, and a great cloth,[74] the latter features possibly suggesting the arrangement of mansions behind a painted or concealing curtain set at the front of a stage. A description of Queen Elizabeth's reception of Francis de Bourbon mentions 'a kind of stage (theatre)' set at the end opposite to the entrance where the Queen sat under a canopy, which may have been a permanent raised stage.[75]

As late as 1518 the Venice edition of Plautus indicates the continuing use of the arcaded

Fig.18. Plan of Westminster dormitory, 1718

background flanked by practicable mansions, albeit apparently of the Serlian form (fig.17). The background too has altered in that the individual compartments earlier sited here are now replaced by a series of arched openings through all of which may be seen the same landscape vista. We may perhaps assume that scenes such as that depicted here provided the scenic locale for the school theatres. The earliest visual record that we have, however, would at first sight seem to refute this suggestion. A plan of 'Part of ye Dormitory allotted for the Acting part' dated December, 1718,[76] depicts an area 28 feet 3 inches wide and side walls of 73 feet 5 inches and 65 feet 6 inches respectively, the difference being reflected in a sloping wall at the stage end. This plan (fig.18) shows ten rows of benches facing the stage, the rear eight rows being elevated successively. There could be an indication of a raised stage, some 2 feet 6 inches high, with five pairs of diagonally placed wings and a back scene enclosing a vista area. The whole is enclosed at the front by larger diagonal wings reaching to the side walls which may be presumed to form part of a framing element. Against these wings, and enclosing an area of stage, are further benches parallel with the side walls, two on one side and three shorter lengths on the opposite side, where they are cut back to permit entry from the dormitory doorway. The main set of benches facing the stage are cut back at this side to leave an entrance passageway some 3 feet 9 inches wide, and a further approach is made to the rear of these raised benches by means of a set of steps apparently set in the adjoining room.

It seems likely that this is a survey drawing of existing facilities prepared when Wren was working on a proposed design for the new dormitory, and if this were so it would indicate no more than that the school was keeping up to date with the latest scenic inventions, the use of diagonal wings (fig.67); if, however, it is a sketch of proposed alterations then they were presumably never instituted, as Wren's schemes for the dormitory were passed over in favour of designs by Lord Burlington or Henry Flitcroft.[77]

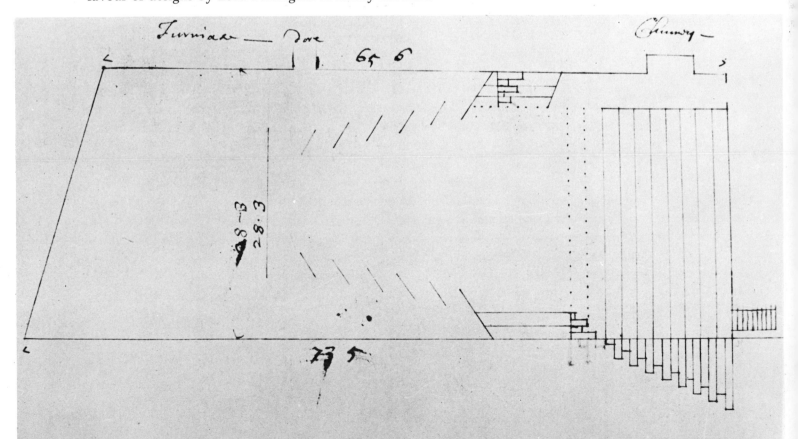

[24]

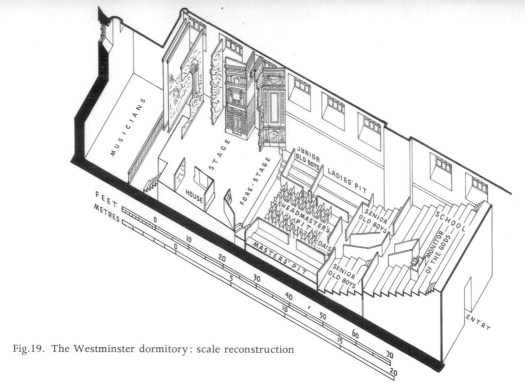

Fig.19. The Westminster dormitory: scale reconstruction

Whatever the situation in the early 18th century, the arrangement which persisted down to the present century, and which was surveyed by Mr Hope Bagenal at a performance of Terence's *Phormio* in 1938, indicates (fig.19) a layout of stage and seating conforming closely to the arrangement of degrees and state around an open floor space for dancing such as has already been noted, and which will be discussed in greater detail below (p.60ff). Here, however, the dancing space has been filled with rows of chairs as the performance of a play did not require its use. The raised stage filled the full width of the dormitory and was flanked by angled wings, beyond which were two practical houses with doors and windows above, arranged one on either side in the Serlian manner. They were backed, however, by a pair of flat wings, beyond which was a cut-cloth and two alternative back-cloths, one of which, the City of Athens, was painted in 1858.[78]

In discussing the development of the neo-classical theme in this country Wickham has argued that no academies like that in Vicenza, Italy, (p.65)[79] existed in this country for the investigation and propagation of new scenic ideas, but it may surely be argued that their equivalent was to be found in the schools with their private theatres where 'the theories formulated out of earlier Graeco-Roman traditions' may be presumed to have been known, discussed, put into practice and disseminated in the various performances that the students gave of their plays outside the school premises. He further suggests that architectural theory was not 'sufficiently advanced or appreciated for anyone to argue with or contradict Inigo Jones', and the same premise may be taken regarding Jones' introduction to the fully developed Serlian methods of scenic staging. But in architecture the way had been prepared for the acceptance of Jones' architectural theories for 100 years, through the writings of such men as John Shute and later Sir Henry Wotton. In the same way it may be argued that Jones' use of the neo-classic perspective scene as a full-blooded entity was only made possible by earlier use of the individual features, understood and misunderstood, in such centres as the schools.

2 The emergence of playhouse forms

From the 14th century[1] onwards, performances, besides those presented by the guilds, had been given by companies of players under the patronage or protection of a lord, noble or gentleman, or even the king himself. There are many records[2] of performances by such players, for example the monks of Selby Abbey[3] were entertained by the King's Players between 1450 and 1483, and during the 16th century the records show that such companies varied from six to eight players, but the normal company was made up of four men and a boy who played all the women's parts.[4] Their performances may not, however, have consisted exclusively of plays. These companies performed, as already noted, in such halls and spaces as were available, which would have included the manor hall, the guild hall, and the large hall contained in many inns. In summertime they could also have made use of the inn yard or any other convenient enclosed space where it would have been possible to control the entry of an audience, making sure that only those who had paid could gain access to the 'theatre'.

In addition some companies may have set up their stages on the village green, in the market place, or on the fair ground, where it would have been necessary to carry the hat round among the audience for payment. They also on occasion played in the church, as many documents affirm. The Leicester Borough Accounts for 1551 mention 'the play, that was in the church'.[5] By 1595 the churchwardens of Winslow[6] were being fined for permitting the performance of an interlude in their church, and in 1602[7] the churchwardens of Syston were paying the visiting players not to use the church for their play.

For the performance of plays by such companies, the scenic equipment was likely to be light, limited by their need to travel from place to place, but even for performances at Court[8] the money spent on plays was far less than that spent on Disguisings or Masks, suggesting that even here the play leant more heavily on its verbal content than on scenic contrivings. It might be argued that the Interludes could and did make use of the same scenic devices provided for the other spectacular entertainments which made up the evening's fare.

Wherever they presented their plays the arrangements would have been affected by the prevailing conditions, and for indoor performances the environment would usually have been the rectangular manor hall, where they would normally have performed before the screens. Records suggest, however, that this end of the hall was not always used, the actors setting up their stage at the upper, or dais, end.[9]

That some degree of contrivance was to be found among such travelling companies may well be suggested by Sir Philip Sidney's comments on current theatrical procedure in his *Defence of Poesie, c.* 1584:

> 'The Player, when he commeth in, must ever begin with telling where he is, or els the tale wil not be conceiued. Now ye shal haue three ladies walke to gather flowers, and then we must beleeue the stage to be a Garden. By and by, we heare newes of ship-wracke in the same place, and then wee are to blame if we accept it not for a Rock. Vpon the backe of that, comes out a hidious Monster, with fire and smoke, and then the miserable beholders are bounde to take it for a Caue. While in the meantime two Armies flye in, represented with foure swords and bucklers, and then what harde heart will not receiue it for a pitched fielde?'[10]

He also mentions the use of notices to name the place of the stage, or the function of a particular door, a device already noted in the illustrations (fig.13a.b.c.) to the plays of Terence and Plautus.

By the middle of the 16th century, laws were being passed to control the movement of vagrants around the countryside, and to force them to return to their places of origin and take up work there. Such ordinances could be used against travelling players unless they showed themselves to be the legitimate servants of some town council, gentleman, or lord, who could vouch for them. From 1572, however,[11] the privilege of raising a company of players was strictly limited to persons of the highest rank. Throughout the remainder of the century increasing legislation both controlled and limited the number of players touring the country, and led to the surviving companies settling in permanent homes in the capital, from which they made tours of the provinces at such times as their houses became untenable owing to outbreaks of plague or puritanism or the controls of local authorities. So we find companies settling in those inns which had previously been used temporarily, notably at such places as the Cross Keys, the Bull, the Bel Savage and the Bell.[12]

By the 1570s we find such existing premises being taken over by the players and adapted as theatres, and new buildings being erected for use as theatres which took the shape of premises that had previously served various uses as well as those of the players.[13] In 1574 the Queen had granted a licence 'in favour of a James Burbage and four fellows of the company of the Earl of Leicester to exhibit all kinds of stage-plays during the Queen's pleasure in any part of England "as well for the recreation of her loving subjects as for her own solace and enjoyment" '.[14] In 1576 when James Burbage came to build a permanent home for his company he chose a site outside the limits of the City of London, in Shoreditch, where he and what was now the Lord Chamberlain's company could perform free from the ever-increasing restrictions of the City authorities. Here he built The Theatre in the open fields. This was an unroofed theatre whose form was adapted from the bull and bear baiting yards sometimes used as suitable enclosures by the players. This 'plaiehowse' proved so successful that Burbage built another close by called The Curtain, both companies of players being under the protection of the Lord Chamberlain. (The term 'unroofed' is applied to the open yard public theatres, as distinct from the wholly roofed private theatres.)

In the same year Richard Farrant, the master of a group of choirboys, the Children of the Chapel, leased six rooms in an old monastic building in the Blackfriars, which, although within the City, was by nature of its ecclesiastical foundation exempt from its jurisdiction, and these he converted to 'a continuall howse for plays'.[15] The Blackfriars had for some time been used by the Master of Revels as offices and a store for mask equipment. It is to be presumed that each school of choirboys had its own theatre, but the Blackfriars Theatre is notable in that Farrant opened it to the public, or at any rate to the courtier class. Little direct evidence is available as to the shape or form of this theatre, although it is suggested that it must have occupied one or two areas at first floor level, the one 46 feet 6 inches by 25 feet, the other 110 feet by 22 feet,[16] the two separated by a staircase. The latter area would appear to be the more feasible possibility. Although narrower by some 6 feet than the dormitory at Westminster (fig.18), the length was more than adequate by the standards illustrated there, where the overall length is no more than 75 feet 6 inches. This area was composed of four rooms, and Farrant had permission to remove one partition in the area leased: in fact he removed more.

The arrangement of the auditorium could well have followed the pattern indicated in the sketch plan of the Westminster dormitory, with side benches flanking an open area of floor, and a main body of stepped benches beyond this facing the stage. It has been claimed[17] that Farrant had instituted the feature of a seated 'pit', as compared with the standing groundlings who we shall note (p.32) were a feature of the open-air theatres, and if this is true it can only mean the provision of additional benches on the open area. This is precisely the arrangement noted for the Westminster play (fig.19), an arrangement which could well have come into being by this early date. There was certainly classical precedence for using the 'orchestral', or dancing, area for seating: Vitruvius tells us that the senators sat there, and Sabbattini[18] suggested that the young and beautiful ladies of the audience should be seated here protected from the gallants by a ring of older women. Although this advanced area was used for dancing in the masks, it may well have been losing its importance as an acting area, particularly where a raised stage was given added importance by the Serlian or Terentian setting. In the cramped surroundings of the Blackfriars it would certainly seem sensible to fit in additional benches in this position.

The use of this advanced area for seating may well have been no sudden innovation, but could have come about gradually by the slow incursion of stools and benches around the edges, as the managements of such restricted playhouses squeezed in a few additional customers. Indeed the habit of seating members of the audience on the stage, which lasted until Garrick's time (p.118), could have developed from the gradual constriction of this advanced area. These seats right next to the actors would be the best from which to see and to be seen, and it would inevitably follow that higher prices could be charged for slipping a customer into a front position. As the orchestra, or acting area, was filled up and the actors were forced to remain on their raised stage, so the desirability of slipping in still more customers, at a price, would lead to an incursion on to the sides of the stage itself. When James Burbage adapted a theatre in these premises (p.42) the advanced acting area had been wholly given over to the audience. The Prologue to Shirley's *Doubtful Heir*, written for the Blackfriars and performed at the Globe, has a line which suggests that the audience should sit 'As you were now in the Black-Fryers' pit'; which is the term later applied to this area.[19] There were also 'stooles standinge vppon the stage'.[20]

Unfortunately the only illustrations which are generally related to roofed theatres all date from the 17th century. Nevertheless these well known *Messalina* and *Roxana* illustrations (figs.20a.b.) can hardly be said to present a particularly complicated arrangement. Both illustrations show what could well be interpreted as an open, but curtained, area at the rear of a raised stage, with in one case a single opening at first floor level, and in the other two openings. In both the stage is wedge-shaped and railed. This could be an arrangement which had persisted from the earlier 16th century roofed theatres under discussion, but if we are to consider the arrangements indicated in the Swan Theatre (fig.21) then it would seem possible that any backing to these earlier stages related more closely to the hall screens, with their two doors and balcony over. There is, however, a distinct flavour in these two illustrations of a Terentian setting, which could have found favour in such educational premises as the Blackfriars.

The later replacement of the doors in a permanent wall by a continuous, but curtained,

Fig.20. Early 17th century indoor stages
(a) *Roxana,* 1632

(b) *Messalina,* 1640

opening could be looked on as an advance in technical design, in that it would then be possible to vary the stage backing to form continuous alcoves, entry doors, or any other scenic arrangement that the play might require. The back wall to *Messalina* would appear to follow the wedge-shaped plan of the stage, and may well represent a permanent development of the temporary pavilions of the medieval period (p.15), or be an adaptation of Terentian ideas (fig.13b.c.). Study of the plays performed at the first Blackfriars[21] has suggested the use of mansions and a curtained recess, but whether this was provided by a movable pavilion or similar structure, or was an actual opening in the rear wall of the stage, it is not possible to say. The use of triangular periaktoi, as described by Vitruvius, is attributed to the Blackfriars,[22] set to either side of the stage in the position of the Serlian mansions seen at Westminster, and these could well indicate a change in locale related to permanent doors and the curtained recess.

The stage must have been sufficiently raised to permit the use of trap doors, as the stage directions for one play call for the emergence of a 'Tree of gold' which rose from the stage floor and sank back, and for the ascension of Pluto 'from below in his chaire'.[23]

It is unlikely that the unroofed theatres built at this time were consciously based on the circular plan of the Roman theatre,[24] the shape being undoubtedly derived from the bull and bear baiting yards. These were readily adaptable to dramatic use, by players setting up their portable stages and tiring tents, or houses, against one side of the open arena.[25] That such buildings resembled in some degree the auditorium of an ancient Roman theatre, or amphitheatre, was probably largely coincidental. At least one of the unroofed theatres, the Fortune, was built with a rectangular plan,[26] a shape which would at first sight seem to have been based on the private halls and roofed theatres of the period with which the players were familiar, but Wickham[27] has most probably put his finger on the core of the matter when he suggests that the circular shape was used so that the buildings could readily be adapted to gaming houses should their use for plays be restricted at any time by the authorities, thus insuring the owners against loss by the multi-purpose nature of the building design.

Few details concerning these early theatres are available, although we do know that the Theatre had three galleries, a yard and an 'Attyring howse or place where the players make them ready'.[28] According to Chambers 'the building was constructed mainly of timber with some ironwork' and he further suggests that at least one of the galleries was divided into upper rooms where the audience could sit or stand. 'The stages, galleries and roomes that are made for people to stand in' are mentioned in a privy council order of July, 1597, for the pulling down of the 'Curtayne, Theatre or anie other common playhouse'.[29] Both the Theatre and the Curtain were used for 'bear-baiting, fencers and profane spectacles' in addition to plays, according to a petition of the Lord Mayor of 3rd May, 1583, and Ordish suggests[30] that the stage was removable to make provision for these activities.

In 1587 the Rose was built by Philip Henslowe[31] on the south bank of the Thames at Southwark. With the Rose we come to one of the theatres which are variously illustrated on contemporary, or near contemporary, maps. Both this theatre and the nearby Beargarden are illustrated by John Norden in 1593[32] as cylindrical buildings, whereas the *Civitas Londini*[33] map of 1600, from the Royal Library in Stockholm, shows it as six-sided. This confusion of circular and straight-sided buildings is reflected in most of the views of the south bank theatres, and can perhaps only be resolved in relation to the materials used in the construction of the exterior walls. If the theatre was built wholly of timber framing then a straight-sided plan is most likely, but where a conglomerate material such as flint was used for the wall structure then a circular plan would have been most natural, at any rate for the outer wall, the inner, timber-framed structure being straight-sided. The Rose is referred to as 'a playe howse now in framinge & shortly to be erected & sett vppe vpone the same'[34] and this would seem to suggest a wholly framed structure, which was being pre-fabricated in the builder's yard, a method commonly used in Elizabethan times in the construction of timber houses, and equally applicable to any other timber structure. Records of purchases made in 1592[35] are probably materials required for additions or repairs to the building; they include lime, sand, chalk and bricks. The work included painting the stage and installing ceilings to 'my lord's rome' and also the 'Rome over the tyerhowsse',[36] and carpenters, painters, and a thatcher were required for the work. In 1595 Henslowe did the theatre about with 'ealme bordes'[37] and according to Chambers the various building accounts suggest a timber building on a brick base. Carpenter's work included 'mackinge the throne In the heuenes.'

The Swan theatre, built between 1594–6 by Francis Langley, was situated in Paris Garden, Southwark. It is illustrated diagrammatically on a map of the Paris Garden Manor of 1627, with three concentric circles.[38] A small central circle surrounded by two closely related circles is subdivided by radial lines into eight parts, and on the N.E. side is a rectangular projection overlapping two of these segments. In Norden's updating of his 1593 map in 1600[39] he shows the Swan as a circular building. Norden's map is inset in the *Civitas Londini* mentioned above, and this shows all the theatres, which Norden depicts as round, to be straight-sided. Visscher, in his map of *c.* 1616, shows a straight-sided theatre, but his map is considered to be inaccurate, indeed he sites the Swan too far north on the bank of the river: once again the exterior views available tend to confuse the issue.

From records[40] we know that by 1602 there were hangings and curtains, a throne in heaven and a stage raised sufficiently high for the emergence of damned souls from beneath. In addition, however, we have a sketch of the interior of the Swan which was copied by a Dutchman named van Buchel from a drawing sent to him by his friend de Witt (fig.21) on a visit to London *c.* 1596. De Witt also described the Swan[41] thus:

> 'the most outstanding and also the most spacious of the theatres is the one whose emblem is a swan (commonly called the Swan Theatre). It can seat three thousand persons and is built of a concrete of flint stones (which are plentiful in Britain) and supported by wooden pillars painted to imitate marble so as to deceive even the most prying. Its form shows a trace of the Roman style as I have depicted above.'

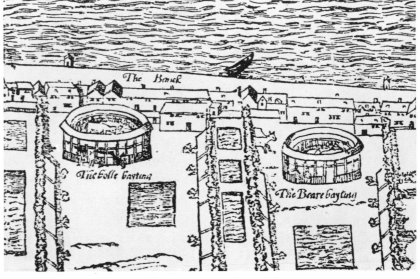

Fig.21. The Swan Theatre, *c.* 1596, after de Witt　　Fig.22. Amphitheatres on Bankside, *c.* 1560, after Ralph Aggas

With this drawing before us we are able to make some sense of the various items noted above in the different theatres: three galleries; a yard; a tiring house; my lord's room; and a room over the tiring house. All these features, with the exception of my lord's room, are shown, and the stage arrangements depicted are precisely those we would expect to find when we realise that the pattern for stage presentations had been formulated in the years spent by the players performing in the rectangular halls before the screens. A rectangular raised stage is backed by a wall containing two doors and a balcony above, an arrangement clearly derived from the rectangular acting area before the hall screens. This stage is set within an amphitheatre of three galleries, a clear development of the timber bull and bear baiting yards.

A map of Bankside published between 1560-90 includes two of these structures illustrated in some detail (fig.22), and in it we see that an open circular yard was enclosed by a roofed ring where spectators might stand or sit. The buildings appear to be only one storey high and are constructed of timber, fenced within and without to handrail height. Both buildings are drawn as if circular in spite of the timber construction being clearly evident, suggesting that in fact the 'circle' would have been contrived from a large number of straight or near-straight sides. The development of these single-storey structures to a height of three galleries would be an obvious improvement, whether the buildings were to be used for plays or for other forms of amusement. It has been suggested that the stages of the Theatre and the Curtain were removable to permit alternative uses of the buildings, and it is therefore natural that the players should set up a stage whose shape conformed – limiting as they may have been – to the acting areas to which they were accustomed, whether they were playing on the floor of a hall, or on the boards of a demountable scaffold. We have no evidence as to the stage furnishings of the earlier theatres, but by the time the Swan was built the players had already had some eighteen years of performing in their evolutionary playhouses, and had therefore had ample time to make some simple improvements to the original arrangements. If the stages of the Theatre and the Curtain were removable then it is unlikely that provision was made for any permanent upper structure above the stage from, or to, which descents or ascents could be made: when needed these could have been built up in a temporary fashion similar to that already in use for interior productions (fig.12). The Rose, however, built some ten or eleven years after the first two theatres, had a room above the tiring house, and, as may be seen in de Witt's drawing, a similar arrangement existed at the Swan, but here there is an additional feature in the form of a roof over the rear portion of the stage supported on two columns. The rear wall of the stage, or front of the tiring house, would appear to be a straight line forming a chord across the circle of the galleries, but it is quite obviously a structural part of the building, and may well have been similarly treated in earlier buildings. Here, however, it is unlikely that the stage was removable, although there is in fact no reason why it should not have been so long as the columns remained in situ on their bases, built presumably solidly to stage height.

De Witt has named the tiring-house 'mimorum ades', or house of the actors, whilst to the stage he has given the correct classical name of 'proscanium' for a raised stage before the 'scenae'. This he has done to underline his view that the Elizabethan theatres resembled those of ancient Rome.

A visitor to England in 1599, one Thomas Platter of Basle, described the theatres open at the time in the following terms:

> 'And thus every day at two o'clock in the afternoon in the city of London two and sometimes three comedies are performed at separate places, wherewith folk make merry together, and whichever does best gets the greatest audience. The places are so built, that they play on a raised platform, and every one can well see it all. There are, however, separate galleries and there one stands more comfortably and moreover can sit, but one pays more for it. Thus anyone who remains on the level standing pays only one English penny: but if he wants to sit, he is let in at a further door, and there he gives another penny. If he desires to sit on a cushion in the most comfortable place of all, where he not only sees everything well, but can also be seen, then he gives yet another English penny at another door. And in the pauses of the comedy food and drink are carried round amongst the people, and one can thus refresh himself at his own cost.'[42]

De Witt shows entry ways leading from the level standing or, as he terms it, the 'planities sive arena', to the lowermost gallery which he calls the 'orchestra'. From here stairs led to the upper galleries, which de Witt terms the 'sedilia', and the 'porticus', thereby likening the topmost gallery to the colonnaded walking way around the top of a Roman theatre (fig.41). From the drawing it would appear that the galleries had stepped floors or were equipped with benches, or both, and that all the roofs were thatched or tiled. There is no indication of 'my lord's room' and it may well be that this was placed in the same relation to the stage as was the state or dais in the Court, and hall, theatres, being centrally situated on the axis of the stage in the lower gallery which de Witt named the orchestra, or the place where Vitruvius says that places were reserved for the seats of the senators. The phrasing of the term 'my lord's room' would suggest that this was an area set aside for the use of the lord under whose patronage the players performed, and whose servants they were. The contract for the Hope, built by Philip Henslowe in 1613, stipulates that it should be built[43] 'of suche large compasse, fforme, widenes, and height as the Plaie house Called the Swan in the libertie of Parris garden', and further requires that the builder, Gilbert Katherens, 'shall also make two Boxes in the lowermost storie fitt and decent for gentlemen to sitt in; And shall make the particions betwne the Rommes as they are at the saide Plaie house called the Swan'.

The single 'lord's room' at the Rose was most likely used by the gentlemen when not required by his lordship, and could have been the place mentioned by Platter where for a third penny one might sit on cushions in the most comfortable place of all, and from which one might not only see well but also be seen. Such a place was apparently partitioned off from the remainder of the gallery, probably to the full height, as in this central position the walls would not have interfered with the other spectators' view of the stage. The room was finished with a plastered ceiling. The higher revenue obtained from the sale of seats in this room doubtless led to the duplication of such space in the manner mentioned as a requirement for the Hope, which may or may not already have been incorporated in the Swan. Ordish[44] suggested that the room over 'the tyerhowsse' at the Rose was 'a room reserved for visitors of position', and by this he would appear to be relating it to the position of the first floor gallery which de Witt shows above the two doors of the tiring house. Such a gallery would obviously have played a useful part as an upper acting level, but could equally well have been used to bring in extra revenue if seats were sold to additional members of the audience at such times as the gallery was not required by the actors, and, indeed, if later fashions are anything to go by, there is every possibility that spectators might have been accommodated here even when the space was in use by the actors.

In attempting a reconstruction of the Swan and the second Globe it was necessary to make certain assumptions regarding the possible dimensions of the building. It may not be too far-fetched to assume a certain pattern in the internal dimensions of the playhouses, based originally on a possible standardisation in the requirements of the gaming houses and repeated in those playhouses which served a dual purpose. The known internal dimension of 55 feet for the Fortune Theatre was therefore taken as a basis for both the reconstructions included here (figs.23,29), with an 8 feet 6 inch maximum width for the lowermost gallery in the Swan, an overall diameter for the building including outer walls of 76 feet, a 12 feet maximum width for the Globe gallery, and an overall dimension of 83 feet. Both buildings were based internally on a 16-sided figure, as this not only provided a reasonable

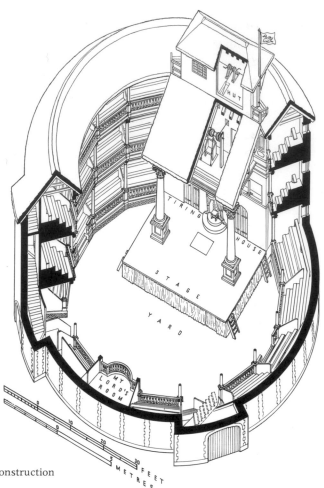

Fig.23. The Swan Theatre, c. 1594–96 : scale reconstruction

approach to a circle, but at the same time made use of timber beams of an acceptable 10 to 11 feet length.

In the Swan reconstruction (fig.23) three facets have been taken as the width of the stage and tiring house, which provides a relative proportion of these parts to the enclosing galleries consistent with the appearance of the building as depicted by de Witt. In both reconstructions the size of timbers and the overhang of galleries have been based on those given in the Hope and Fortune contracts, but taking into account that the timbers for the Fortune were to be 'lardger and bigger in assize Then the Scantlinges of the Timber of the saide newe erected howse Called the Globe'.[45] The tiring house is seen in de Witt's drawing to project in front of the adjoining galleries, a feature which is found to be consistent with the recession of the lower galleries behind a tiring house façade set to line with the facets of the upper gallery.

It is difficult to tell from de Witt's drawing how the stage was supported, but it would appear to be raised some 4 feet above ground level, if the size of the figures is to be relied on, and it has been argued[46] that these may not be reliable. Argument has centred around the vertically hatched areas beneath the front edge of the stage, and these have been interpreted variously as openings to the under-stage area, or as supports for the two columns or even the stage. The reconstruction has inclined to the first interpretation, thereby providing openings from which the damned souls could emerge (p.30); and there may have been additional openings at the sides of the stage. With a slight excavation of no more than 1 foot 6 inches to 2 feet very limited headroom could have been found beneath the stage, and provision could also have been made for the working of the traps set either in the rear, covered, part of the stage, in the front, or even in both (but excavation could only have taken place in those theatres where the stage was not removable). Removable steps have been shown providing access from the yard to the stage for use as and when necessary.

In spite of attempts to place the upper room, or hut, directly above the stage, it was found that in this position the practical and structural value of the projecting roof was invalidated. As a result it was accepted that the two free-standing columns were in fact supporting the front edge of this roof, which is then seen to have meaning as a protection to the rear stage. It has been argued[47] that the use of elaborate scenic pieces acquired or derived from Court productions needed protection from the weather. It is to be presumed, however, that the Heavens were by now an essential piece of scenic architecture, and as such required a limited area of roofing within the otherwise unroofed space. The viewpoint of de Witt's drawing precludes a view of the Heavens from which Ben Jonson's 'creaking throne' could descend, but it would seem reasonable to place this ceiling at a level where it might be attached to beams supported at one end on the framing of the tiring house front, and at the other on the great cross beam spanning between the two columns. The ceiling was possibly boarded and painted[48] to resemble the heavens with clouds, moon, sun and stars in the manner of such church ceilings as may be seen at Muchelney (fig.25), and at Staunton Harold. De Witt draws this roof with a steep enough pitch to permit headroom for the working of the throne, providing that the opening for this is situated within close working distance of the front of the tiring house. Access to this area could have been from a room behind, above which would have been the actual machine room, or hut, where the windlass for the throne might have been situated, with cables passing through a hole in the floor. It seems likely from a constructional aspect that this machine room would have been built as a direct extension upwards of the tiring house frame in the manner indicated in the reconstruction. This room provided access to the flagpole for hoisting the performance flag, and also, it is claimed, for sounding the commencement trumpet from a position of advantage above the roofs of the galleries.

De Witt's drawing indicates very clearly the internal appearance of an 'unroofed' theatre of the end of the first phase of theatre building, and there is no reason to quarrel with any of the features which he depicted; they are precisely what one would expect at the end of a period of consolidation in which existing acting habits have been married to a spectator frame developed for the viewing of such three-dimensional activities as bull and bear baiting. Even as late as 1603, a patent or licence was granted under the Great Seal of James I to the King's Players, Lawrence Fletcher, William Shakespeare, Richard Burbage, and others their associates, to play 'Comedies, Tragedies, histories, Enterludes, moralls, pastoralls, Stage-plaies, and Suche others like', either at their usual house called the Globe, in Surrey, or 'within anie towne halls or Moutehalls or other conveniente places' throughout his dominions.[49]

Seating, similar to that provided later by Inigo Jones in one of his buildings (figs.47,48), has been shown on all three tiers of the Swan reconstruction, with standing room behind on the upper floors. Working on a basis of 18 inches width of seating per person, and $1\frac{1}{2}$ square feet of standing space, and allowing for six persons to be seated in my lord's room, some forty in the gallery in the tiring house, and an additional twenty-four seated on the stage, we arrive at an approximate capacity for the house of 2,726, a figure which could no doubt be improved on for a popular production. Taken together with the inevitable coming and going of some sections of the audience, it can be seen that de Witt's figure of 3,000 could well be accommodated in a full day's attendance.

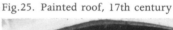

Fig.24. The Swan Theatre

Fig.25. Painted roof, 17th century

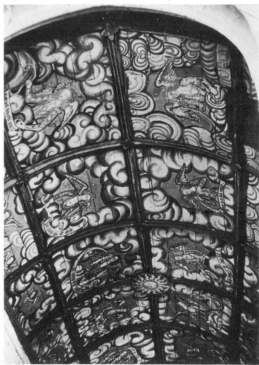

Inevitably the relationship between the actor and his audience would, in many instances, have been far from perfect; a fair percentage of the audience standing or seated in the galleries adjoining the tiring house would have had difficulty (fig.24) in following the action developing in, or immediately adjoining, the tiring house façade, and for many the columns and their massive bases must have blocked their view of parts of the stage. Such imperfections must, however, be expected of a building that has not been specifically designed for its purpose, and if we are correct in placing 'my lord's room' in the position of the state or dais in relation to the stage then this frontal view, from time-honoured usage, would have been the only one that really mattered. Sufficient imperfections are to be found in modern theatres designed specifically by architects for the purpose, and with all their attention directed to the provision of good sight lines.[50] Why then should we expect the Elizabethans to have solved this problem, when for them it was not of paramount importance? Indeed, if we are to believe the objections of the Puritans, plenty of use could be found for those areas not occupied by spectators wishing to give their full attention to the show, and from what we shall see later (pp.46,128,174) of the Georgian and Victorian theatres there is really no reason to cast doubt on the Puritans' condemnations. For the Elizabethans the rectangular stage and circular, or near-circular, auditorium worked, but nevertheless they may have been only too aware of the limitations which this relationship imposed, and, as will be suggested later (p.41), they may well have attempted to overcome at least some of these problems as each new theatre was built.

After 1597[51] the Privy Council limited the public companies in London to those of the Lord Chamberlain and the Lord Admiral. The former, under Burbage, had played at the Theatre and the Curtain, but in 1599 they pulled down the Theatre and used its timbers to build the Globe on the south bank. The Lord Admiral's men, under Henslowe, played at the Rose until 1600, when they moved to the newly built Fortune in Golding Lane, Cripplegate. Our knowledge of these two theatres is contained in a contract[52] for the building of the latter. This theatre differed from the other unroofed theatres in having a rectangular rather than a circular shape for the surrounding galleries. This shape does not seem to have been as satisfactory as the circular plan, in that the audience seated in the corners of the galleries were not so well placed in relation to the stage as they would have been if seated in one of the facets of a many-sided 'circular' amphitheatre, where all would be facing more directly towards the stage. One can only assume that the square was chosen in that it conformed more closely to the arrangements of the roofed theatres, and this, in turn, could suggest that the later unroofed theatres were incorporating features already developed in the roofed buildings. On the other hand a square building would have held more audience than a similarly sized 'circular' building, and so the choice of shape may merely have been a matter of greater receipts.

Nevertheless, in many aspects, notably in the divisions of the various rooms, in the stairs and the stage, the Fortune was to be built and decorated in 'the manner and fashion of the saide howse Called the Globe.' These comparisons are useful in determining the similarities between the two buildings, but unfortunately still leave in doubt their exact constitution. What the contract does do, however, is to give exact information regarding the dimensions of one such theatre. The open yard was to be 55 feet square, surrounded by galleries of a width of 12 feet 6 inches, giving an overall dimension to the building of 80 feet square. The timber frame of the galleries was to be carried on brick piles to a height of at least 1 foot above ground, and was to be three storeys high, the first or lowest being 12 feet high, the second floor being 11 feet, and the third or upper gallery, 9 feet. Each of the upper storeys was to 'juttey forwarde' 10 inches beyond the floor below. The stage was to project to the centre of the house and was to be 43 feet wide. The 1613 contract for the Hope Theatre provides further information regarding the structure of the galleries. Here the ground floor posts were to be 10 inches by 10 inches by 12 feet high. The posts of the middle gallery on the inside were to be 8 inches by 8 inches and in the top storey 7 inches by 7 inches. The intermediate (prick) posts of the ground floor, 8 inches by 8 inches; in the middle storey 7 inches by 7 inches; and 6 inches by 6 inches in the top storey. The 'brest sommers', or main bearing beams, on the ground floor storey were to be 9 inches by 7 inches; in the middle storey 8 inches by 6 inches. The 'byndinge' joists—presumably those on the radius of the circle of the theatre – of the ground floor storey 9 inches by 8 inches; of the middle storey 8 inches by 7 inches. In this building the brick foundations were to be built to a height of at least 13 inches above ground level. All the upper roof was to be of tiles: the word roof is used in the singular as in this theatre the stage was to be removable, 'a stage to be carryed or taken awaie, and to stande vppon tressells', and as a result there was no separate stage roof supported on pillars. This theatre appears on a contemporary sketch by Wenzel Hollar, and in *The Long View of London*, published in 1647 (fig.26), for which the sketch was prepared. Although wrongly named the Globe in *The Long View*,[53] the theatre is clearly depicted as having a swept-up roof which attains to a greater height over the tiring-house portion of the theatre, as a result, presumably, of an extension at this point of the roof span either by cantilevers or bearer beams to enable the heavens 'to be borne or carryed without any postes or supporters to be fixed or sett upon the saide stage'.

Fig.26. The second Globe Theatre (*left*) and the Hope or Bear Garden (*right*), after Hollar

The Fortune contract required four divisions for, on the basis of the Hope, presumably two 'gentlemens roomes and other sufficient and convenient divisions for Twoe pennie roomes, wth necessarie Seates to be placed and sett Aswell in those roomes as througheoute all the rest of the galleries of the saide howse.' These roomes were also to be ceiled with 'lathe lyme & haire'. A 'Stadge and Tyreinge howse' were 'to be made erected & settupp wthin the saide fframe wth a shadowe or cover over the saide Stadge wch Stadge shalbe placed & sett' in the manner indicated on a plan originally attached to the contract, which suggests that the stage may have been more complicated in shape than the simple rectangle suggested by the quoted dimensions. The stage was to be 'paled in belowe wth good stronge and sufficyent newe oken bourdes And likewise the lower Storie of the saide fframe wthinside, and the same lower storie to be alsoe laide over and fenced wth strong yron pykes.' In all other respects the stage was to be proportioned and fashioned like that at the Globe 'Wth convenient windowes and lighte glazed to the saide Tyreinge howse.' These glazed windows may have been on the exterior of the building to light the rooms, or, since the lighting of rooms might well be taken for granted as an essential feature of any building, this particular reference could have alluded to additional scenic devices in the stage wall of the tiring house (p.43). Here also the frame (presumably the galleries), the stage, and the staircases, were to be roofed with tile, unlike the roofs of the Globe and the Rose which were to be thatched. From this it may be assumed that the stairs projected from the main body of the building and needed an independent roof.

The posts of the Fortune were to be square and treated as pilasters unlike those of the Globe, which must therefore have been rounded and turned like those of the Hope, which was to have 'turned cullumes vppon and over the stage'. The Fortune pilasters were also to be decorated at the top with 'Satiers' or human heads and trunks forming the upper part of the 'square columns', and supporting at least a part of a capital on their heads (fig.27). These, like the columns at the Swan, were probably painted in excellent imitation of marble, in addition to being richly decorated and coloured.

The Globe was destroyed by fire on 29th June, 1613, during a performance[54] of *Henry viii*, when the firing of cannon set fire to the thatch. According to Sir Henry Wotton, the whole house burnt to the ground in less than an hour. The Globe was rebuilt in 1614, and a view of the exterior is also seen in Hollar's *Long View of London* (fig.26). This shows a circular building with two projecting staircases, and a ring of windows around the main body of galleries. The most distinctive feature of the theatre is the machine room, which is here shown to be much larger than that depicted by de Witt at the Swan. It has a double-pitched roof with an ogee-shaped Tudor turret set in the roof valley at the outer end of the machine room. The machine room now reaches forward to the centre line of the theatre, and spreads across this diameter to reach the inner face of the galleries on either side.

This marked change in the position, size and width of the machine room must surely reflect some changes in the stage beneath. The stage of the Fortune also extended to the centre of the building, and since the width of the Swan stage was reflected by the width of the Heavens

Fig.27. 'Satier' or 'Therme'

above, so one may expect the stage of the second Globe to reflect the Heavens in a similar manner, and extend the full width of the yard to the galleries on either side. If this is so then the stage now filled one half of the enclosed space, leaving the other half as the 'level standing' or yard.

The tiring house of the Swan, with its two doors of entry, could not permit a wide range of movement for appearances or exits. It may be, of course, that these doors gave entry on to the stage for actors who then took up their positions in some form of practical mansion which could be introduced on to the stage for a specific play, or even for a specific scene. We know, for instance, from Henslowe's inventory[55] of properties at the Rose that such scenic devices as a rock, a cage, a tomb, a Hell's Mouth, a tomb of Guido, a tomb of Dido, a bedstead, a pair of stairs, various trees, moss banks and a wooden canopy, were available for use in the manner suggested in Robert Greene's *King James the Fourth* (c.1591): 'Enter ASTER OBERON, King of the Fairies; and ANTICS, who dance about a tomb placed conveniently on the stage.'[56] 'Invisible' movement around the stage to the required point of entry is an accepted convention in some forms of drama, and may well have been an accepted feature of the Elizabethan stage. William Poel[57] has suggested that

> 'There are instances in the First Folio, and elsewhere, I believe, where either actors are shown, in the stage-directions, to enter some lines before they speak, or to be given two entrances, one, let us say, in the rear of the stage, and the other from the side where the gallants are seated, and the actor is waiting for his cue to take up his dialogue within the ring.'[58]

It has already been suggested that the central pavilion of hall performances (figs.11,12) may have been used as a feature of such stages as the Swan[59] and Chambers suggests that the actual number of points of entry from the rear wall could have been extended by hanging curtains right across the width of the façade so that actors could appear through the curtains directly in front of the doors, or by moving behind the curtains appear at any other point where a joint was made in the fabric. It has also been suggested[60] that the door openings, with the doors opened wide back on either side against the wall, could have been used as discovery spaces (on the lines of the Greek thyromata[61] or the Terentian arcade-mansions) by the drawing aside of the curtains at these points. Florio's description of 1598[62] of the word *Scena* as 'a skaffold, a pavillion, or forepart of a theatre where players make them readie, being trimmed with hangings, out of which they enter upon the stage,' suggests that curtains or tapestries were used as decorations at least if for no other purpose. The use of black hangings for tragedies[63] could have applied here, although it has been suggested that such hangings may have been used around the sides of the stage to conceal the underside.

The discovery space could contain any person, object or piece of furniture which was to be suddenly revealed or even concealed, and as such would normally be provided with curtains as the easiest method of making the discovery possible, a use which has already been noted as standard theatrical practice throughout the middle ages and into the hall performances; similar curtains appear in all the other views of 16th and 17th century stages noted above (figs.20.a.b.). Such a discovery space may have been equipped with some form of scenic illusion, even though it may not have provided what some authorities have regarded as an additional acting area or inner stage.[64] The decoration, seen earlier (fig.13.a), of the interior of the mansion for the *Andria* of Terence suggests that such illusions were considered possible for these productions, although the apparent size of the individual mansion made its use as a place of action difficult. Decoration, in the form of perspective scenery, may also be seen behind the central opening of the post-Elizabethan playhouse, the Cockpit-in-Court (figs.53–4).

Examples of the thrusting out of a bed with its occupant on to the stage occur. A play, Middleton's *A Chaste Maide in Cheapside*, performed at the Swan, required a 'bed thrust out upon the stage; Allwit's wife in it'.[65] This suggests that where action was required, particularly if a number of people were involved, then such pieces of furniture, or properties, or the actors themselves, would move, or be moved, out on to the main stage where a greater number of the audience could see them than if they had remained within a recess in the tiring house façade. The main stage, or at least that part of it with which they were directly concerned, could then have taken on the locale and characteristics of the inner space.

Stage directions concerning the use of an upper acting area appear in many plays; sometimes the action concerns no more than a single performer looking down from a window or gallery, to or from which ascents or descents might be made by ladder or basket. In some cases windows are defined as bay-windows, and in at least one instance in Ben Jonson's *The Devil is an Ass*, performed at the Blackfriars in 1616, two adjoining windows were required.[66] There are also many instances in which a number of persons appear 'above'. Walter Hodges has quoted the instances of Christopher Sly's prologue to the *Taming of the Shrew* and the monument in *Antony and Cleopatra*[67] and has argued from these that such an undoubted upper scene must have been performed in a more generally visible position than would have been provided by the use of such a space as the gallery depicted by de Witt at the Swan. To fulfil these requirements he suggests the introduction of what we might define as a pageant stage, set in the central pavilion space between the two doors, open above and curtained below, and of such a height that it could be entered from the tiring house gallery. It is, however, highly likely that the relationship of the audience to both stage and tiring house had not remained that illustrated by de Witt, and indeed it is to solve these very problems that the pattern of the theatre may well have changed by the time the second Globe and similar theatres were built, so that, with the majority of the audience occupying positions from which they could view the tiring house wall, the use of structural galleries in this position would have been a practical proposition. The often repeated suggestion that actors in this position would have been too far removed from their audience for the appreciation of intimate scenes may be seen to be a fallacy when the exact physical relationship is studied, as it may be in the reconstructed Shakespearean theatre at Ashland in Oregon (figs. 32a.b.).

There was most probably a music room at the Swan, as a stage direction from the Swan play *Chaste Maid* mentions, and from other sources we hear of, the music 'within' and 'above'. It has been suggested that the tiring house gallery served this purpose.[68]

In 1596 James Burbage acquired premises in the Blackfriars,[69] which was adapted for use as a theatre but leased to boy companies until the King's Company moved in in 1608, and used this theatre concurrently with the Globe until 1642. Little is known of the appearance of this building, except that it was 66 feet by 46 feet and had a stage, boxes, galleries, and seats.[70] It must have occupied the same block as Farrant's theatre, but whether it was at ground level or on the first floor is not really known.[71] The stage was smaller than that of the Globe, and Armstrong has suggested that it may have been wedge-shaped on the lines of the *Messalina* and *Roxana* drawings (figs 20a.b.). By 1609, when Thomas Dekker wrote *The Gull's Horne Booke*, the custom of the audience sitting on the stage was recognised both for the unroofed and the roofed theatres. A three-footed stool set among the rushes with which the stage was strewn provided accommodation for the gentlemen, who, having waited until the Prologue was ready to begin, crept from behind the arras 'as though you were one of the *Properties*, or that you dropt out of the *Hangings*'.[72] The arras and hangings may well have formed a rich decorative backing to the stage, perhaps painted to accord with the play, but they could also have concealed a discovery space. Although it has been suggested that such a space may have been built before the tiring house, in these later theatres it seems likely that such features, if considered essential, would have been incorporated into the structure of the tiring house and surroundings of the stage. Armstrong[73] notes that a Blackfriars' play, Fletcher's *A Wife for a Month*, required a discovery space behind a curtain capable of accommodating at least twelve characters. Further evidence led him to consider it as an additional acting area, capable, in a Phoenix theatre play, of accommodating a table, a bed, and a cupboard, and the action concerned with these fittings; at the same time it is suggested that the habit of coming out of this area to perform on the main stage, which then took on the locale of the inner area, was still in use. It is, however, hardly surprising that such inner areas should be used for action in the private theatres, as all were adapted within the limited space of existing buildings, the rectangular nature of which (with the possible exception of the Phoenix) would have placed the majority of the audience in a frontal position to the stage in which they could look into such recesses. Once this convention had developed in the roofed theatres, it would have been hard to transfer plays to the unroofed theatres if their actor-audience relationship had not undergone a similar change.

In 1616 a cockpit in Drury Lane was converted by Christopher Beeston into a theatre, which was rebuilt the following year after fire damage, and then called the Phoenix.[74] It was probably the only one of the roofed theatres that was not rectangular. Salisbury Court was converted from an old barn.[75] In most cases the total width of the buildings available for stage and side galleries together was no more than that specified for the Fortune stage alone, so that every inch of playing space would have had to be developed to its limit (Salisbury Court was equipped with seats, boxes, viewing rooms, and galleries[76]). There would have been little space on the stage itself for Serlian style mansions with practical doors (fig.28), which could more readily have been provided in the side walls of the stage itself. Such practical doors, providing access to the main stage of these roofed theatres, were large enough to admit a sedan chair, and were equipped with knockers, locks and bolts.[77] Stage directions mention doors being 'opposite', and it is likely that with the limited width available for the stage it would have been found necessary to set these in the enclosing side walls, leaving space between, across the rear of the stage, for the discovery space or inner stage. Above this area was a further room with a balcony at the front in the Phoenix and Blackfriars theatres at least. Flanking the central area were practical windows, which, at the Blackfriars, were bay windows (p.41). There were also windows in the external walls which could presumably have been used for lighting the theatre during daylight performances; these had to be 'clapped down to give the illusion of night scenes'[78] when candlelight was used.

The enclosed space of such a chamber playhouse provided better acoustics than did the unroofed open space of the larger public playhouse, and this apparently affected the actor's style of delivery in that the Blackfriars did not require the company 'to break our lungs' as did the Globe.[79] A comparison of the two theatres is not just one of size, but as a result of the more cramped conditions at the Blackfriars the audience in the equivalent of the 'yard' are known to have been seated on benches in what was now called (p.28) the 'pit',[80] an arrangement probably necessitated by the need for the audience, seated in the lower side galleries and in the gallery facing the stage which existed at the Blackfriars, to be able to see over the heads of the occupants of the pit. Height limitations in the existing halls possibly controlled the level to which such galleries could be raised. At Salisbury Court[81] 'the upper room (sic) . . . in the said theatre were framed and fixed so low that the spectators on the second seats could not discern the actors on the (st)age.' It should be noted that, whereas the yard of the unroofed public theatres was occupied by groundlings, the seated pit of the roofed private theatres was 'for the Gentry'. The groundlings, it would seem, had now become the gods.

The internal arrangements of these indoor theatres may well have had some effect at least on the arrangements of the stages and tiring houses of the unroofed theatres built during the early years of the 17th century. The Red Bull, built by 1605-6, was an unroofed theatre[82] which, Reynolds has deduced from a study of the plays performed there, must have had a raised stage covered by a heavens, above which there would have been a machine room, where ascents and descents could be controlled. There was a curtained stage balcony and a curtained space at stage level, which may have been built as part of the tiring house structure, or may have been a temporary feature set up before the tiring house wall; this he conceives as being wedge-shaped after the fashion of the rear wall indicated in the *Messalina* frontis-piece (fig.20b.). There were doors giving access to the stage which provided at least three separate points of entry, and on the evidence of the frontispiece to a Red Bull play, *Swetnam*, he suggests windows at the lower level, at least two leaded lights being shown in this illustration. Although there is no evidence for them in the Red Bull plays, Professor Reynolds

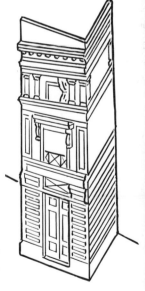

Fig.28. Serlian type mansion

suggests the possibility of obliquely placed doors with balconies above them, and a third storey opening in the tiring house.

In attempting the reconstruction of the second Globe theatre (figs.29,30) use has been made of some of the features known to have existed in the roofed playhouses, many of which were already incorporated in the Red Bull. The narrow width of the Swan stage limited the number of doors and openings that could have been accommodated in the tiring house wall, and the need to make provision for such additional features could have been a good enough reason for widening the stage in such later buildings as the second Globe. It was noted earlier that such a widening is suggested here by the extension of the machine room at the Globe to the full width of the yard, unlike that at the Swan which was only as wide as the stage itself. The size of the machine room as indicated on Hollar's *Long View* (fig.26) is now so considerable that it seems unlikely to have contained no more than the machinery for the 'creaking throne'. Consequently in the reconstruction (fig.31) it has been suggested that the upper gables of the machine room shown on the view provided space for a grid from which might depend a variety of painted cloths or scenes, mainly, no doubt, in the form of clouds which could accompany the descending throne in a similar manner to those in use at court (pp.52, 64): a proposal that takes into account some of the elaborate scenery which Wickham

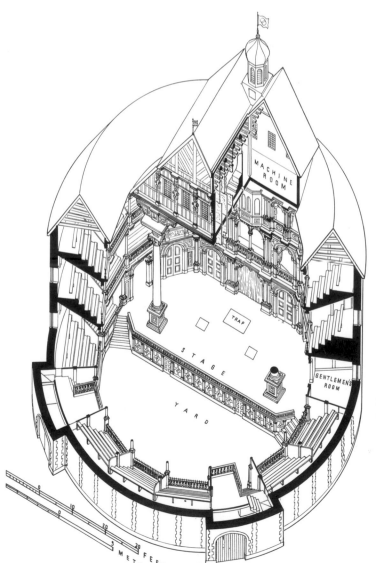

Fig.29. The second Globe Theatre, 1614: conjectural scale reconstruction

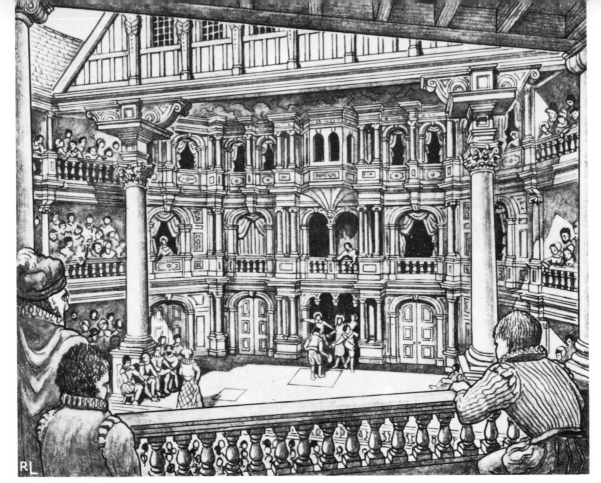

Fig.30. The second Globe Theatre

suggested[83] may have been acquired, or derived, from court performances. These, it has been assumed, would descend through slots contrived in the Heavens painted on the underside of the machine room floor, the openings being filled, when not in use, by hinged flaps. The use in this manner of the area of the machine room directly above the stage would still leave considerable space behind for the storage of scenes and properties, which could easily be lowered to stage level when their use was required.

The extension of the stage to the full width of the yard[84] permitted the introduction of a central curtained opening which would be an essential feature of any symmetrically designed Renaissance building, and in particular of a theatre with its implications of a neo-classical frons scenae. Doors are set on either side of this in the tiring house wall, and in addition two further doors are set obliquely in the adjoining facets of the sixteen-sided amphitheatre.

The idea of setting doors obliquely at the rear of the stage could have been instigated by the adaptation of the cockpit in Drury Lane into the Phoenix theatre, which if it was anything like the Cockpit-in-Court (fig.51b) in shape, could have had a stage backed by a straight face and two oblique facets. The Lord's room had by 1609 become 'the Stages Suburbs',[85] suggesting that it was now associated with the 'two Boxes in the lowermost storie fitt and decent for gentlemen to sitt in' mentioned in the Hope contract. In the reconstruction they have been placed in the two remaining facets of the amphitheatre directly connected with the stage. In front of these boxes the gentlemen could sit on their stools on the rush-

Fig.31. The second Globe Theatre: detail of Fig.29

strewn stage, the gentlemen's rooms themselves having become the dark places where 'much new Satten is there dambd by being smothred to death in darkness'.

Above the gentlemen's rooms could have been the two-penny rooms, whilst further space would have been provided above the oblique doors, usable either by the audience or the actors, or both, as the play demanded. A curtained space or balcony has been shown over the centrally placed stage-level curtained area, with curtained openings, or windows, over the flanking doors. Such curtains could well have had a decorative character of their own, those at the Fortune being, according to Tatham's Prologue for the Fortune players in 1640, only of worsted, while the curtains at the Red Bull were of 'Pure Naples silk'.[86] Reynolds has suggested the possibility of an upper balcony, or curtained space, at third floor level just below the painted heavens, where an actor might 'prefigure passion, he raves, rages, and protests much by his painted Heavens, and seems in the height of this fit ready to pull Jove out of the garret, where perchance he lies sleeping on his elbow or is employed to make squibs and crackers to grace the play'.[87] The space is obviously there to be used, as the heavens must have been above the third gallery of the amphitheatre if it was to be viewed from there, and galleries placed here may have provided not only additional acting levels, but a room that could have housed the musicians. As will be seen later (p.86), a similar raised position was almost certainly used by the musicians in the Restoration playhouse, The Duke's Theatre in Dorset Gardens. The curtained and windowed gallery provided there may well have been a continuation of theatrical practices developed during the early years of the century. It is noticeable in all stages of architectural development that neither client nor architect find it easy to break free from conventional practices; even at such times of architectural upheaval as the Renaissance, conventional building patterns and methods persisted in spite of the new architectural forms and styles, and it is unlikely that in accepting the new scenic methods, which will be discussed later, the players could have freed themselves from all existing conventions. One feature which continued into the Restoration era was the use of entry doors on to the stage, and their placing in the side walls of the Restoration stage may also lead to acceptance of the suggestions for oblique doors and a central space in these early 17th century playhouses under discussion.

All these doors have been shown on the reconstruction as double doors,[88] in order to provide openings of sufficient width for the passage of such items as a sedan chair, or similar properties, on to the stage, or even the riding of an ass or mule through the opening.[89] Traps are shown in the stage, but there is no evidence for their positions, and in basing their positions on those in the 18th century playhouses, one may perhaps be placing too much reliance on the persistence of tradition. As in the Swan reconstruction (fig.23), two entrances are shown leading from the exterior directly into the yard, which in the earlier theatres must have been of sufficient size to allow the passage of large animals, so permitting easy adaptation of the theatres to bull and bear baiting yards. Here the first penny would have been paid for entry to the yard. Leading from the yard are two flights of steps, similar to de Witt's *ingressus*, giving access to the two projecting staircases shown by Hollar in his *Long View of London*. A further penny paid here permitted access to the scaffold where 'he may stand or sit'.

The Fortune contract required divisions for the gentlemen's rooms and the Twopenny rooms, which may represent an extension of Platter's places where one can not only see well but be seen, and in the reconstruction the gentlemen's rooms have been shown adjoining the stage with the Twopenny rooms above; both sets of rooms have been partitioned off from the remainder of the galleries and ceiled. Doors in the partitions permit the collection of the extra payment involved in their use. Unlike the earliest theatres where the galleries were probably provided only for standing, and perhaps for the use of stools, the Fortune contract specifically required seats to be placed in all the galleries as well as in the private rooms, probably leaving the rear portion of the galleries unseated as a promenade and standing space (the practice of standing in theatres was an accepted feature down to the present century). Such space could be no more than a walking way round the rear of the stepped seats in the lowest gallery, widening on each of the upper floors as it became increasingly difficult to provide proper sight-lines for seated spectators.

If one works on a similar basis to that used to determine the seating capacity of the Swan (p.36), the capacity of this theatre would appear to be roughly identical, and it would seem as though the increase in the overall size of the building had been largely taken up by the greatly extended stage facilities. It is, for example, of interest to note the decrease in the size of the yard as compared with that at the Swan, with a, presumed, consequent movement of the groundlings to the increased standing areas at the back of the seating on the upper tiers; a move which would confirm the metamorphosis of the groundlings into gods noted earlier in the indoor theatres (p.43).

Each facet of the amphitheatre has been divided into individual boxes by low partitions, which would not interfere with sight-lines from any of the seats in the half of the amphitheatre facing the stage. The gentlemen's, and Twopenny, rooms are so related to the stage, however, that the use of full height partitions here, whilst providing privacy for the occupants and their lady friends, would not have interfered with anyone else's view of the stage. The stage front, and the lower levels of the bottom gallery, have been boarded in as was required for the Fortune theatre, and topped with iron spikes to prevent the groundlings from climbing into the more expensive areas. Access doors have been provided from the understage area to the yard, and steps to the stage set in the corners. Both features are provided for use by the devils, and other underworld characters of the play, who, while the traps are in use by the important characters, may come out from under the stage and clamber up at each corner in the manner suggested by Professor Nicoll[90] as an interpretation of the stage directions from *The Silver Age* and *The Golden Age* where 'Divels' are required to 'appear at every corner of the stage with severall fire-workes' and four winds must 'Enter at 4 severall corners'. Both these plays were originally performed at theatres which are generally thought to be the Rose, the Curtain, the Red Bull or the Cockpit[91] and the four corners may therefore have been referring to a free-standing stage of the Swan pattern, which could also have been the arrangement in these earlier theatres. Access to such Swan type stages was provided by ladder-like steps set against the corners of the stage when required by the action of the play. No permanent steps are shown by de Witt, but if such points of entry were found necessary, they may well be assumed to have become a permanent feature of later theatres.

The columns supporting the heavens and machine room would still have blocked out the view of some spectators to parts of the stage, but 'sitting behind a column' is not by any means confined to these Shakespearean theatres. A theatre based on the dimensions of the Fortune is the Shakespeare Festival Theatre at Ashland in Oregon. Similar, but more slender, pillars are used here for the same purpose, and as a result obscure less of the stage

Fig.32. The Shakespeare Festival Theatre, Ashland, Oregon, 1959.
The stage from the positions of
(a) the upper gallery
(b) the lower gallery of the original Fortune

than would those included in the second Globe reconstruction. Two views of this stage photographed from what would have been the positions of the upper and lower galleries (figs.32a.b.) in the original Fortune, show that in fact they interfere very little with the view: indeed in some respects they make a positive contribution to the stage space by emphasising the three-dimensional relationship of the various portions of the stage around these vertical elements. This Ashland reconstruction has interpreted the Fortune stage as partly wedge-shaped, projecting the stipulated 27 feet 6 inches forward, and being 42 feet wide at the base of the wedge, with extensions outwards to the surrounding walls – an interpretation of the contract dimensions that might well have been covered by the plan of the stage originally attached to the contract. The tiring house façade at Ashland was designed so that there is an inner stage some 23 feet wide at stage and first floor levels, capable of being readily adapted to accommodate two doors with windows above and a projecting balcony between. This arrangement suggests that there is no reason why the original theatres may not have been equally adaptable, making use of Reynolds' suggested curtained discovery space built within the tiring house frame for one production, and with the addition of his wedge-shaped pavilion, or balcony, before it for another. Oblique doors with bay windows over are here set diagonally across the corners of the square gallery frame, and a third stage level is incorporated in the tiring house façade directly beneath the heavens.

The introduction of the additional points of entry on to the Globe stage would have permitted a much wider variation of movement across the stage than was possible at the Swan with its two points of entry, although, as was suggested earlier, greater use may have been made there of scenic devices to which the two doors gave access. The limited size of the roofed theatres, however, would have made it difficult to continue the use of such scenic devices and still have room on the stage for the actors and their movements, and as a result it would have been found not only possible, but advisable, to make full use of the doors, windows, or curtained recesses and balconies instead. These could readily be incorporated in the essential stage surrounds as part of the architecture, especially when such changes conformed to the new Italian principles, so leaving the stage itself free for the action and movement of the actors. On the very much larger stages of the unroofed theatres it would still have been possible to make use of the scenic devices in conjunction with the permanent architectural features on which the actors were now coming to rely. Reynolds has shown in his study of the Red Bull that the doors were now used as a conventional representation of a change of scene in that an actor having made an exit through one door would be accepted as being in a different place on his return to the stage through another: and, similarly, an exit through a trapdoor with the immediate return of the actor to stage level was taken to represent a change of stage locale from Earth to Hell.[92] So the doors became an essential feature of any theatre, and had to be incorporated in reconstructions or new buildings.

The Fortune theatre was burnt down in 1621, and was rebuilt as 'a large round brick building' in 1622,[93] to be dismantled in 1649 and totally demolished in 1662. The Globe was pulled down in 1644.

3 Actor, audience and the perspective scene

In the study of the Court masks the introduction of cloths which could have been painted in perspective has been noted, and at Christ Church, Oxford, and in other educational premises, there were indications of what may have been Serlian-type houses arranged on either side of a perspective vista. For Ben Jonson's *Masque of Blackness*, presented in the temporary Banqueting Hall at Whitehall in 1604–5 on a stage 'xl foote square and iiij^{or} foote in heighte with wheeles to goe on,' Inigo Jones devised a curtain painted to represent a landscape of woods with hunting scenes. This fell and 'an artificial sea was seen to shoot forth . . . the *Scene* behind, seemed a vast sea (and vnited with this that flowed forth) from the termination, or *horizon* of which (being the leuell of the *State*, which was placed in the vpper end of the hall) was drawne, by the lines of *Prospectiue*, the whole worke shooting downwards, from the eye'. The movement of the sea was presumably contrived by 'a great Engine at the lower end of the Roome, which had Motion, and in it were the Images of Sea-Horses with other terrible Fishes, which were ridden by Moors, . . . At the further end was a great shell in form of a skallop, wherein were four seats.'[1] As indicated, the scene was drawn in perspective, and was presumably enclosed by Serlian book wings on either side. Although the scene had movement it did not itself change: 'the Moon was discovered in the upper part of the house, triumphant in a silver throne . . . The Heaven about her was vaulted with blue silk, and set with stars of silver, which had in them several lights burning,' probably in the manner suggested by Sabbattini for 'Divided Heavens' (fig.33[d]).[2] The audience was arranged in the normal mask pattern, with the state centrally placed at the upper end. This, however, had to be raised so that the King's eye was on a level with the scene's horizon, for only at this level and from a central position in front of the scene's vanishing point could the picture painted on the succeeding wings– houses – be viewed as a complete and continuous perspective. The maskers were revealed in the scene, and then, coming forward off the raised stage, they danced in the orchestral area between the state and the stage. The following year Jones designed *The Masque of Hymen* in which a great globe rotated, and clouds moved forward carrying gods and ladies. Two great 'golden' statues held up the clouds, presumably at the front of the scene where they could hide the machinery responsible for the movement of the clouds, which opened to reveal the three regions of the air from which further clouds descended carrying eight ladies.[3]

For the Twelfth Night mask in 1607 two stages were erected at differing levels,[4] the higher for the scene and the lower for the dancing. The scene had 'nine golden trees of fifteene foote high, with armes and braunches very glorious to behold'. From these trees the maskers appeared:

> 'That part of the stage whereon the first three trees stode began to yielde, and the three foremost trees gently to sincke, and this was effected by an Ingin plac't under the stage. When the trees had sunke a yarde they cleft in three parts, and the Maskers appeared out of the tops of them, the trees were sodainly conuayed away, and the first three Maskers were raysed agine by the Ingin.'[5]

The simple exhange of one vista for another was unlikely to satisfy the audience's tastes for long. As has already been noted, spectacle plays an important and recurring part in popular drama, and Renaissance designers, their inventive genius stimulated by Vitruvius's mention of the provision of machinery for festivals, were not slow to take up the challenge. It is not necessary to go into detail here as to the exact nature of the various machines and effects, it is their effect on the theatre structure with which we are concerned. In Serlio's stage (figs.14-15) the scenery visible to the audience was arranged so as to conceal from view the areas of stage not included within the vista, thus providing areas of stage to either side where actors might congregate prior to their appearance on or before the scene. Provision was also made so that movement from one side of the stage to the other might be made out of sight of the audience. Above the vista, the view of the audience was limited by the enclosing arch of the sky, but when it was necessary to admit the descent of clouds and actors, gaps had to be provided in such a way that audience vision was still contained within the scenic vista. The introduction of elaborate machinery around the visual area complicated the problem of concealment, and an element became necessary which not only masked the 'invisible' portions of the stage, but at the same time 'framed-in' the perspective vista of the visible stage. Such frames were made from similar materials to those used for the construction of the scenery, and in the temporary court theatres they would have been designed to conform to the setting of the particular production for which provision was being made.

Movement within the scene was only a first stage. As early as 1605 Inigo Jones had experimented with a change of scene at Oxford where he erected 'a false wall . . . . close to the upper end of the Hall . . . . fair painted and adorned with stately pillars – which pillars, would turn about, by reason whereof, with the help of other painted clothes, their stage did vary three times in the acting of one Tragedy'.[6] Since three changes of scene were presented it has generally been assumed that the 'false wall' was composed of periaktoi. A perspective scene was used here, as is indicated by an argument concerning the positioning of the King's chair, which the university had placed at the point where he would best see the perspective. It was, however, moved some feet from the stage to a point where the King could best be seen by the audience, but where he was no longer set at the correct viewing point for the perspective scene. This argument suggests that the use of perspective vistas required a movement of the state from its customary position at the upper end of the hall, to one more closely associated with the stage. It is of interest to note that the university was not impressed with what Inigo Jones had to offer in the way of new inventions, which suggests that these were already accepted and in use in this educational establishment.

The Hue and Cry after Cupid, presented in 1608, made use of an arrangement apparently based on the classical *scenae ductilis* (fig.33[b]). Behind a 'high, steepe, red cliffe, advancing it selfe into the cloudes' were more clouds from out of which appeared the chariot of Venus drawn by two swans, together with a vision of the Three Graces. The cliff then 'parted in the midst and discovered an illustrious Concave, fill'd with an ample and glistering light, in which an artificiall *Sphere* was made of silver, eighteene foot in the *Diameter*, that turned perpetually'.[7] *Tethys' Festival*, performed in 1610, appears to have made use of a combination of periaktoi and scenae ductilis, the whole set behind a decorated frontispiece, the changes of scene being contrived undetected by dazzling the spectators' eyes with moving lights.[8] In 1613 the scene for the *Lords Masque* was divided into an upper and lower scene hidden behind separate curtains, changes of scene being effected behind clouds which descended across the stage, and on their removal the new scene was revealed. In the 1631 *Albion's Triumph* some five changes of scene were presented.

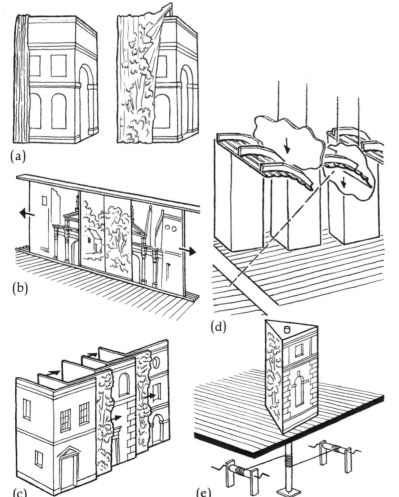

Fig.33. Methods of changing scenery, 1638, after Sabbattini
(a) changing the appearance of book-wing
      by drawing a cloth across it
(b) back scene drawn apart to reveal another scene
(c) second set of wings hidden within a first set
(d) sky divided to permit the passage of clouds or gods
(e) triangular *periaktoi* worked from beneath the stage

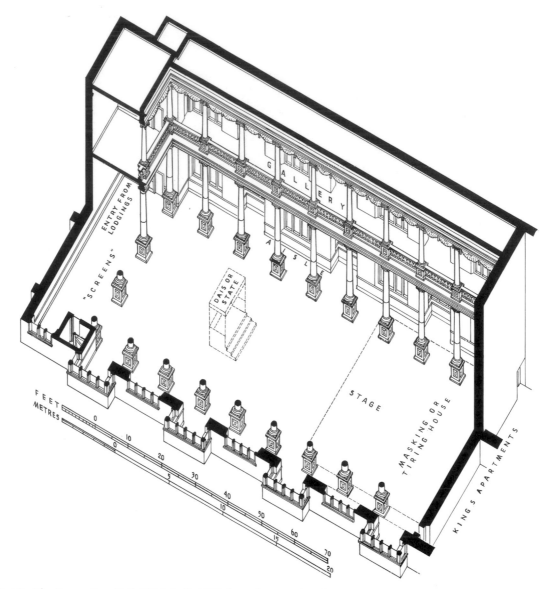

Fig. 34. The Banqueting Hall, Whitehall, 1606–7: scale reconstruction

These masks may well have been presented in the new Banqueting Hall built in 1606-7. A plan drawn by John Smythson[9] shows it to have been 120 feet long by 53 feet wide (measurement of the plan shows the former figure to be overall the end walls, while the latter figure is the width of the hall within the walls, the other figures on the plan being correctly noted) with eight pillars down each side of the hall and four across the entry end, replacing the traditional screens (fig.34). These columns made of wood, carved and gilded, were of the Doric order at floor level and the Ionic above, and supported galleries and the ceiling of the hall. The interior is described by Orazio Busino, Almoner to the Venetian embassy, who visited it in 1618 when the hall was arranged for a mask by Jonson, *Pleasure reconciled to Virtue*, with scenic devices by Inigo Jones:

Fig.35. Hammerbeam roof, with decorative angels

'A large hall is fitted up like a theatre, with well secured boxes all round. The stage is at one end and his Majesty's chair in front under an ample canopy. Near him are stools for the foreign ambassadors . . . Whilst waiting for the King we amused ourselves by admiring the decorations and beauty of the house, with its two orders of columns, one above the other, their distance from the wall equalling the breadth of the passage, that of the second row being upheld by Doric pillars, while above these rise Ionic columns supporting the roof. The whole is of wood, including even the shafts, which are carved and gilt with much skill. From the roof of these hang festoons and angels in relief with two rows of lights . . . every box was filled notably with most noble and richly arrayed ladies, in number some 600 and more according to the general estimate:

'. . . On entering the house, the cornets and trumpets to the number of fifteen or twenty began to play very well a sort of recitative, and then after his Majesty had seated himself under the canopy . . . he caused the ambassadors to sit below him on two stools, while the great officers of the crown and courts of law sat upon benches. The Lord Chamberlain then had the way cleared and in the middle of the theatre there appeared a fine and spacious area carpeted all over with green cloth. In an instant a large curtain dropped, painted to represent a tent of gold cloth with a broad fringe; the background was of canvas painted blue, powdered all over with golden stars. This became the front arch of the stage.'[10]

Both plan and description point to a break from the normal theatrical arrangement for such halls, in particular the replacement of the screens entry, with its two doors, by an open colonnade. Were the problems created by the new staging methods now being taken into consideration in the design of this hall? Examples have been noted (pp.20,26) of stages set at the upper rather than at the lower end of halls, most notably on the occasion of Elizabeth's visit to Christ Church, Oxford, in 1566. If the placing of the stage for this performance is still in doubt, then Inigo Jones's setting of 1605 at Oxford (p.52) can be quoted, to which may be added a later use of Christ Church hall on 29th August, 1636, for a performance before Charles I when there was

> 'a goodly stage, reaching from the upper end of the Hall, almost to the hearth place, and had on it three or four openings on each side thereof, and partitions between them, much resembling the desks or studies in a Library, out of which the Actors issued forth. The said partitions they could draw in and out at their pleasure upon a sudden, and thrust out new in their places according to the nature of the Screen, whereon were represented Churches, Dwelling-Houses, Palaces, &c.'[11]

The new scenic arrangements required concealment from the audience until called into action, and it obviously became increasingly difficult to place such stages at the entry end of the hall as in the past, where they impeded the flow of the audience. It may be argued that the setting for *Florimene*, designed by Inigo Jones for performance in the Tudor Hall on 31st December, 1635 (fig.38), shows an example of the new stage set at the lower end of the hall before the screens, but here the screens entries were blocked off and closed to all but the players, while the audience entered either through the door in the upper end wall of the hall, or through the door in a partition erected across the western window. At Christ Church no such alternative entry for the audience existed to this first floor hall, and the stage of necessity had to be moved. It may therefore be reasonable to assume that the advantages of separating the actors from the audience by placing the stage at the opposite end from the entries was appreciated when the new Banqueting Hall was designed. Sir John Summerson[12] suggests that Inigo Jones was the designer, but Professor Per Palme[13] quotes a reference to 'the L^d architect' in connection with the design, which is hardly a term that would have been applied to Inigo Jones, even after he became Surveyor in 1615.[14] Since Jones was concerned with the design of masks performed at court at this time, he may have been consulted regarding the design, which Summerson suggests was derived from Palladio's Egyptian Hall,[15] of which Jones would have had knowledge. Unlike the Egyptian Hall with its single-storey aisles and double-storey nave, the hall under consideration has been reconstructed as having an upper gallery on either side. Posts for such galleries on a smaller scale are indicated on the *Florimene* plan (fig.36), and galleries were included, albeit cantilevered, by Jones in his 1619 design for the present Banqueting Hall, which replaced the old hall when it was burnt down in that year.

First attempts at a reconstruction of this building were made in which the orders were given their correct classical proportions according to Palladio, but these looked incongruous alongside the 'perpendicular' windows, which are clearly indicated on the plan. These

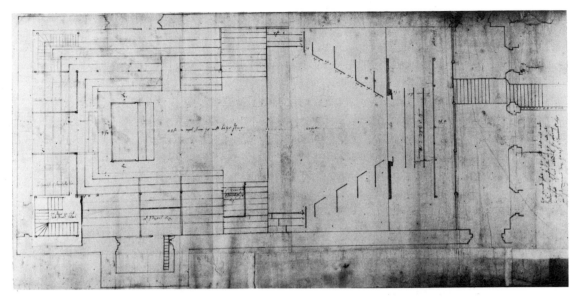

Fig.36. Plan of Tudor Hall, Whitehall, adapted for performance of *Florimene*, 1635

windows, and window bays, suggest that the hall had not fully broken with convention, but retained the characteristics and appearance of earlier halls, to which had been introduced the colonnades and galleries. Indeed the derogatory comments of the King concerning the obstruction of the windows by the rows of columns[16] would suggest that these were not fully integrated into the design as they would have been if the Egyptian Hall design had been correctly carried out, in which case the windows would not have had the form indicated on the plan. Mention of angels in the roof calls to mind the decoration of such hammer-beam roofs as may be seen in East Anglian churches (fig.35), and if we assume an adapted traditional pattern for this hall, it may not be too far-fetched to picture such a roof spanning it. It also seems more sensible to base the orders on proportions according to John Shute,[17] which not only produces columns of a size more suited to timber construction, but also provides bases which raise the columns at ground level at least partly above the level of any temporary scaffolding which must have been introduced for seating, and permits the introduction of balustrading at gallery level.

Unfortunately Smythson gives no indication of the staging arrangements in this hall, nor does he indicate any dais, but leaves the upper end of the hall completely free, even the doors to the King's apartments being set to the sides at the end of the aisles. In the reconstruction the place 'that the Masquers come out of', mentioned by John Chamberlain[18] as being the starting place of the fire which destroyed the 'faire Banquetting howse', has been indicated as occupying, with the stage, the end three bays at the upper end. Raised stages were undoubtedly used for plays at court, as is suggested by the Office of Works Accounts for 1601-2: 'Making readye the Haull with degrees, with bourdes on them and footpaces under the State, framing & setting up a broad Stage in the middle of the

Haull, & making a standing for the L. Chamberlaine, framing & setting up of viij partitions within the Haull end and entryes';[19] an entry which is repeated in 1604.

In 1635 the pastoral *Florimene* was staged in the Tudor Hall at Whitehall, and for this we have a plan (fig.36) showing not only the staging arrangements, but also those for the audience. Among the many drawings prepared by Inigo Jones for scenes and costumes are an almost complete set of drawings for scenes designed for this production, together with a plan and elevation of the scenes, and a section through the stage.[20] From these we can see that a stage was built to the full width of the hall against the screens, and projecting forward some 40 feet 6 inches into the hall, or nearly half the total length from the screens to the upper end. As the whole structure of stage and auditorium had to be built up within the hall, and then removed without damaging the fabric, it would have been necessary to build such stages to a sufficient height to provide space beneath for the working of the various machines and the mechanics involved in their operation. This production required no sub-stage work, but was nevertheless 4 feet 6 inches high at the front, sloping up for a distance of 23 feet to a height of 5 feet. At this point the stage stepped down some 5 or 6 inches to a level platform extending approximately 13 feet to the screens. 7 feet 1 inch back from the front of the stage was fixed the 'frontispiece' or 'ornament which serv'd as a Bordure to enclose the Scene', decorated at the sides with two figures standing on pedestals and two cupids above each. Across the horizontal border at the top were further cupids supporting a central shield inscribed with the name *Florimene*. Some 18 inches behind this, and set inward on a line joining the inner edges of the frontispiece to the centre of the backcloth, is the first of four pairs of Serlian wings. These book-like wings were difficult to change, except by the laborious process described by Sabbattini of dragging painted cloths over the soaped frames with a pole (fig.33[a]). As a result it is not surprising to find that these wings were not changed, but that the changes of scene took place on the flat area behind the sloping stage. We have 'that kind of sceane with triangular frames on ye sydes where there is but one standing sceane and ye sceane changes only at the Backshutters'.

The backshutters are set at that point in the stage where the front sloping part finishes, and there is a step down to the rear flat portion of the stage. At this point grooves, formed from battens, supported a backshutter. This was a framed piece of scenery made in two halves which, when they met at the centre of the stage, formed a single painted background to the scene displayed in perspective on the permanent side wings. The two portions of this shutter could be drawn apart to either side of the stage, where they were hidden from sight behind the side wings, and they could then, if necessary, be withdrawn from the ends of the grooves and be replaced by a second pair to present a differently painted scene. The upper part of the scene was completed by horizontal lengths of canvas spanning the stage, and painted as sky or clouds. Thus the front, sloping, portion of the stage could present a complete, enclosed picture in perspective.

But the scene could be further extended in depth. When the backshutter was opened the audience could see through the resultant opening, which was framed on either side by small

Fig.37. Interior of Tudor Hall during performance of *Florimene*

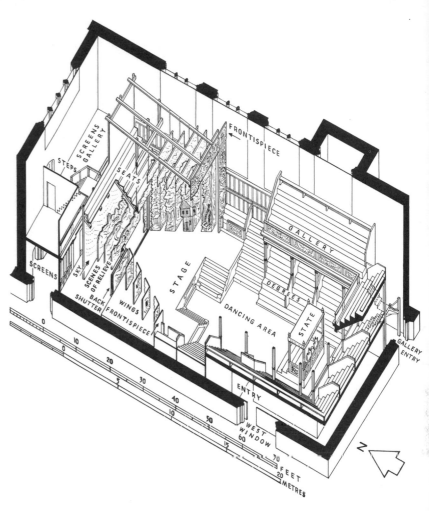

Fig.38. Tudor Hall arranged for production of *Florimene*: scale reconstruction

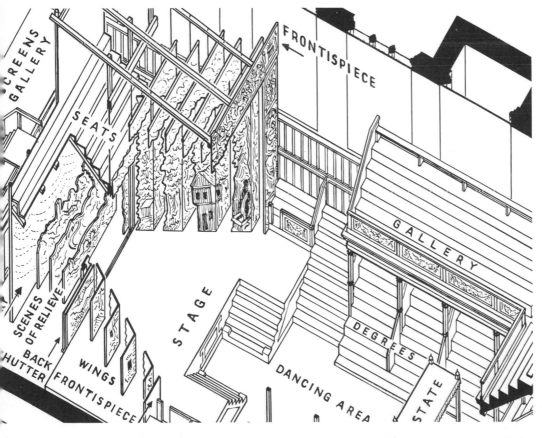

Fig.39. Tudor Hall: detail of stage area of Fig.38

pieces of scenery cut out in profile, or relieve, and attached on either side to the vertical supports which helped to carry the groove structure in which the backshutters slid. A timber framework, on which a cloth was stretched to represent the distant sky, was erected some 3 feet 4 inches in front of the hall screens, the space behind permitting movement across the stage out of sight of the audience. In the space between the backshutter and the sky cloth were set further pieces of scenery, also cut out in relief. For the production of *Florimene* these varied between an interior view of the Temple of Diana, in which the spaces between the columns were probably cut out to permit a view through to the sky cloth beyond, and landscapes representing the differing seasons, in which the foreground, middle and far distances would have been represented on three pieces of scenery set one behind the other before the furthest distance of the sky cloth. The performers made use of the front portion of the stage, where the perspective scene could be kept in proportion to their size, and from here they advanced down steps on to the orchestral or dancing area at hall floor level, between the stage and the state (fig.37).

In preparing the reconstruction (fig.38) of this production a further drawing of an 'un-identified section of the stage'[21] was used to provide the vertical dimensions for the stage and screens. Southern notes a 'rough correspondence' between the *Florimene* plan and this section, but in fact its parts correspond closely to the plan's dimensions, and in one further aspect there is a close correspondence. The drawings of the various 'scenes of relieve' are squared off for enlargement with 1 foot squares, and may be seen, some[22] exactly, others very closely, to measure 13 feet in width and 10 feet in height, and two[23] show a line of clouds across the top presumably hiding the beam supporting the upper grooves. The width of these scenes on plan is noted as 13 feet, and the height as scaled from the section corresponds almost exactly. Above the area allocated for scenes of relieve the section indicates tiers of seats, similar to those seen on the later section by John Webb for the production of *Mustapha* in 1665, which E. Boswell[24] has noted as being the place where 'the Musick playes'. This may also have been the case here, the musicians being concealed behind an upper, cloud-painted shutter when they were not required to be visible to the audience. The presence of these tiers of seats for use either by the musicians, or possibly by the Queen and her ladies as part of the performance, could answer one problem which exists on the *Florimene* plan, where a flight of steps with 11 risers is shown leading up to an opening in the westernmost of the two screens doors, which, with the exception of this one small opening, were blocked off from the passage. The number of steps is far more than is necessary to rise the 4 feet 6 inches from the screens' floor to stage level. The plan, however, could at this point be indicating steps at a higher level, that is, rising from the screens' gallery to just such a high point as is indicated by the topmost tier of seats, and it is this arrangement which has been shown on the reconstruction. The upper works of the stage are hung from a light grid (fig.39), which could have been supported from the timber roof of the hall in a manner similar to that carried out by Webb when the Great Hall was converted into a play-house in 1665.[25] There is a note relating to 'making a floor over the Stage 43 foot long 39 foot wide for ye hanging up of the workes & frames of ye sceenes'.[26]

The audience was accommodated on eight tiers of steps or degrees arranged round the remaining three sides of the hall not already occupied by the stage, further accommodation being provided in raised galleries. Certain sections of the degrees were partitioned off from the remainder to provide boxes for particular personages, as is indicated by notes on the plan: 'ye lady marquis her box' and 'The Countess of Arundell's box'. The width of these degrees varies from approximately 13 inches for those directly adjoining the stage for a length of some 8 feet 6 inches, to 18 inches for the remainder. While it would have been possible to sit on these 18 inch-wide degrees, there would have been very little knee or foot room. It has already been noted that the ladies and gentlewomen of the Court were only provided with standing room in the 1564 adaptation of the rood loft in King's College Chapel, and that in the 1581 Banqueting Hall (pp.13,22) there were 'degrees for men & weomen to stand on', although this is contradicted by von Wedel when he described the same degrees as 'seats and benches' for people to sit on. Busino's description of the 1606 Hall mentions only stools for the ambassadors and benches for the officers of the crown and courts of law, so it is quite possible that the audience had to stand.

On either side, at the front of the stage itself, there were three degrees which may have been used by the musicians. Campion in his *Description of a Masque* tells us that on the right-hand side of the dancing place

> 'were consorted ten Musitions, with Basse and Meane lutes, a Bandoras, a double Sack-butt, and a Harpsicord, with two treble Violins; on the other side somewhat neerer the skreene were plac't 9 Violins and three Lutes, and to answere both the Consorts (as it were in a triangle) six Cornets, and six Chappell voyces, were seated almost right against them, in a place raised higher in respect of the pearcing sound of those Instruments'.[27]

Lines on the eastern musicians' degrees may be intended to represent section lines indicating the height of the degrees, which would then measure some 1 foot 4 inches. If this was the height for all the degrees, the main entrance for the audience could have been through the doorway in the partition blocking the former western window opening, passing along beneath the three rear degrees, and through the recess formed in the western degrees on to the flat 'dancing' area of the hall floor. Entry could also have been made by the old access door from the dais to the private apartments beyond. It is in this corner that a flight of stairs is drawn firmly on an overlay, presumably replacing the stairs sketched lightly in the southwest corner, the dais door now being used as the entrance for the audience in the galleries.

This reconstruction of an existing hall adapted to theatrical purposes illustrates the basic arrangement on which future playhouses were to be formed, with only minor changes, during the following two centuries, but to this must be added one vital factor: the effect on the existing actor-audience relationship occasioned by the introduction of the new feature – the perspective scene. While the limitations of the existing hall had of necessity formulated the pattern shown here (fig.38), it may be noted that Inigo Jones was not entirely happy with this arrangement. An unidentified plan (fig.40) from the same collection of drawings by

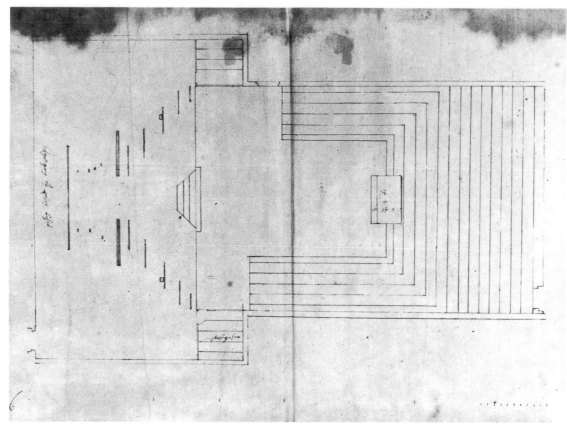

Fig.40. Plan for a mask

Inigo Jones and his nephew John Webb,[28] appears to illustrate an arrangement of stage and degrees within a hall that must have been designed specifically for the purpose of presenting such mask spectacles. If this is so then it is of value to see what changes Inigo Jones made when he was not restricted by existing conditions. The plan differs from that for *Florimene* in showing a T-shaped hall, and it is surely too much of a coincidence to believe that an existing hall had this exact shape. Jones had been commanded in 1637, when it became apparent that the use of the present Banqueting Hall for theatrical purposes was resulting in damage to the Rubens painted ceiling from blackening by candle smoke, to build a new 'Maske-Roome', which was eventually erected with weather-boarding and 'slightly covered'. According to drawings prepared for Davenant's *Salmacida Spolia* which was given in this hall, the dimensions would appear to have been some 112 feet in length, 57 feet in width, and 59 feet high,[29] which in no respect conform to those of the T-shaped hall: this drawing could, however, have been a preliminary design for this building.

The first major point of difference from the *Florimene* plan is the extended width of the stage, which occupies the 47 feet 6 inches width and 31 feet 6 inches depth of the head of the T. This greater width provided additional space at the sides of the stage which could have been used for the congregation of maskers prior to their entries, and for the movement and storage of scenes, such as the scenes of relieve and the shutters which had to be drawn off to the sides to be replaced by other scenes. It had also been found possible to fit the musicians' degrees into the recesses of the T on either side at the front of the stage, and access to them from the back-stage area was now provided by openings in the frontispiece.

The dancing area and degrees for the audience were arranged within the 34 feet wide and 47 feet 6 inches deep tail of the T, which was approached by a door, at floor level, in the side wall, and a further door at high level in the rear wall (surely a further indication that this was not an existing hall). It is in the arrangement of the degrees, as contrasted with those for *Florimene*, that the most important change is indicated. It would seem that the raised galleries have been omitted, but far more degrees have now been placed directly facing the stage, permitting the occupants a greatly improved view of the scenic picture. The masks, at this period, presented a complicated design problem in that there were now two differing forms of theatrical expression contained in the one production. On the one hand there was the scenic picture, with its moving parts within which the maskers appeared, which was best viewed from positions situated directly in front of the scene. On the other hand the maskers, having advanced out of the picture, then danced at floor level, and here they would best be viewed by an audience enclosing them, at least on three sides. Maskers and scenery were not, however, the only things the audience came to see, as Busino so graphically described (p.55). They also found excitement and interest in viewing, and discussing, the rest of the audience, as Pepys has indicated: 'By and by the King and Queene, Duke and Duchesse, and all the great ladies of the Court; which, indeed, was a fine sight . . . The sight of the ladies, indeed, was exceedingly noble; and above all, my Lady Castlemayne.'[30] The three-sided arrangement of the degrees greatly contributed to this.

The T-shaped plan presented a solution which combined the two, retaining the side degrees defining the 'dancing area', but at the same time indicating most clearly where Jones's priorities lay in that he placed the majority of the audience in positions where, after the King, they could obtain the best possible view of his scenes and scenic devices, an arrangement which clearly indicates the nature of the additional factor mentioned above.

This plan also shows a further change from that for *Florimene*, as here the Serlian book wings have been replaced by flat wings, set parallel with the front of the stage. This permitted the side wings to be changed in a similar manner to the backshutters, an arrangement put into effect in a plan and section for *Salmacida Spolia*,[31] presented on 21st January, 1639-40. The section shows a stage built in one continuous slope from front to rear with an approximate height of 7 feet at the front rising to 8 feet at the back. A frontispiece framed the scene, with the horizontal member across the top sloping forward into the open hall, possibly to provide additional space behind for positioning a roller on to which the front 'curtayne could fly up'. Four sets of wings flanked the front vista leading to the backshutters, and each set had grooves at top and bottom with four channels, in each of which a wing could be set. The grooves are longer than the wings they support so that the front pair of wings in each set could be 'drawn off' to disclose a second pair, and so to the fourth. The movement of the side wings made a great many changes of scene possible, and gave greater flexibility to the use of this front area of the stage. John Webb has noted on the sectional drawing 'Profyle of ye sceane when ye sceane doth wholy change as well on ye sydes as at ye back shutters, & when ye sydc peeces are made to change by running in groves.' The grooves for the backshutters are here increased from two channels to three, making it possible to simplify the scene changes here as well.

Above each side wing there was a horizontal top 'border', and 'peeces of Clouds which came downe from ye roofe before ye vpper part of ye syde shutters whereby ye grooves above were hidden & also ye howse behind them'. These cloud pieces were also capable of movement in their own upper grooves and further clouds went 'crosse ye sceane & were hung betwixt the Clouds of ye sydes whereby it appeared but one sole heaven'. Behind the second set of wings were two posts with ropes worked on a windlass beneath the stage which provided the means 'by which Deityes ascend and discend'. Behind the backshutters was the 'space for Releives betwixt ye backshutters & backcloth' and here the section shows two 'great vpright gr--es by which ye seates were lett vpp and downe'. These seats, some 16 feet wide, could rise to the full height of the scenery and sink beneath the stage out of sight. The backshutters were 14 feet high, but above them was a further set of backshutters, presumably painted as clouds, which on opening could reveal the gods on their thrones descending before the full-height backcloth through the very heavens themselves. The upper grooves of the backshutters were concealed by a line of clouds in relieve.[32] This use of the two levels for the inner scene is to be seen in other drawings as well, and helped to provide for a wide variety of scene changes which could be introduced on these stages.

The hall and the scene were lit by candle or oil light, the former as chandeliers, perhaps the normal hall lighting, while special effects could be contrived by the use of lamps placed behind the scenery. The accounts for a mask of 1670-1 have an entry 'for making a trough at ye foote of the stage for lights to stand in'. A further entry of 1679 mentions 'putting vp a long trough to sett the Lamps in, at the end of the staige against the Pitt there'.[33]

4 The elements of a developing playhouse

Inigo Jones was in Italy in 1613-14 where, among other places, he visited Vicenza, the birthplace of the architect Andrea Palladio. Here, in 1580, Palladio had designed a reconstruction of a Roman theatre for the Olympic Society where they could portray their interpretations of Roman plays, and plays written in the correct classical style. The contemporary state of knowledge regarding the remains of Roman theatres enabled Palladio to design a passable facsimile, the main difference from the general form of Roman theatres (fig.41) being that it was designed to fit into a rectangular roofed hall. The limited area of the site led Palladio to interpret the semi-circular Roman auditorium and orchestra as an ellipse, enclosed within an elliptical porticus, free-standing in the corners of the hall and with attached columns where it approached the side and rear walls. A raised stage is backed and flanked by a frons scenae and side walls, richly decorated with painted columns, statues, niches and openings taking the form of entry doors, with open balconies above those in the side walls (figs.42a.b.). The central opening is increased beyond the normal size of the Roman door, and is here treated as an arched opening.

The ceiling over the stage is coffered to represent the timber roof to the Roman stages, while the auditorium ceiling is thought to have been painted to represent a velarium. Behind the frons scenae is a further stage area with a sloping floor, and a domed plaster ceiling beyond is painted to resemble the sky. Palladio died before the building was finished, and it was completed under the control of Vincenzo Scamozzi, who designed the scenic vistas which still back each opening, permitting every member of the audience to have a view down at least one of the streets. These streets were built in perspective of timber and plaster, with three-dimensional statues, columns and mouldings, and with pierced doors and windows. Each street ends in a painted panel which extended the vista into the far distance (fig.43). Both theatre and scenery still stand and are used for annual festivals.

The actors performed on the proscenium, or raised stage, approached through the openings in the scene wall. Movement was, and is, occasionally given to the scenic area by dressing small children as adults and permitting them to move across the streets at points where their size is relative to the scale of the perspective vista. Serlio had suggested a similar device for bringing realism to his perspective scenes by the use of cut-out figures related in size to the scale of the buildings, which could be pushed across the street at appropriate points. As in the original Roman theatres the orchestra here may be used by the actors, or may provide additional space for seating.

This theatre, however, represents only one facet of the theatre development of the period: that is, the provision of as realistic a Roman setting as it was possible to achieve for the academic portrayal of Roman or neo-Roman plays. Already, however, the perspective setting had become an important and integral part of the performance, and in the Serlian theatre the scenery played a more important part in the production than was possible in the archaeological reconstructions of the Roman theatres where the permanent architectural frons scenae dominated the perspective scene. Scamozzi designed such a theatre for Vespasiano Gonzaga, 1st Duke of Sabbioneta,[1] in 1588, and this too can still be used and visited. The building is a rectangle 117 feet long by 40 feet 6 inches wide, containing both auditorium and stage. The gradines – stepped seating – are arranged in a semi-circle, with their ends curving out

Fig.41. Theatre of Pompey, Rome, 55 BC

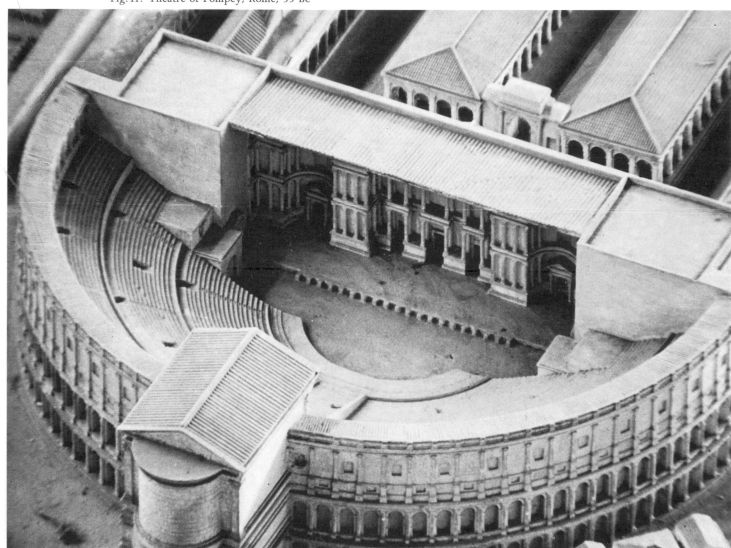

(a) frons scenae and scenic vistas

Fig.42. Teatro Olimpico, Vicenza, 1580

(b) stage and auditorium

Fig.43. Teatro Olimpico: backstage view of permanent scenery

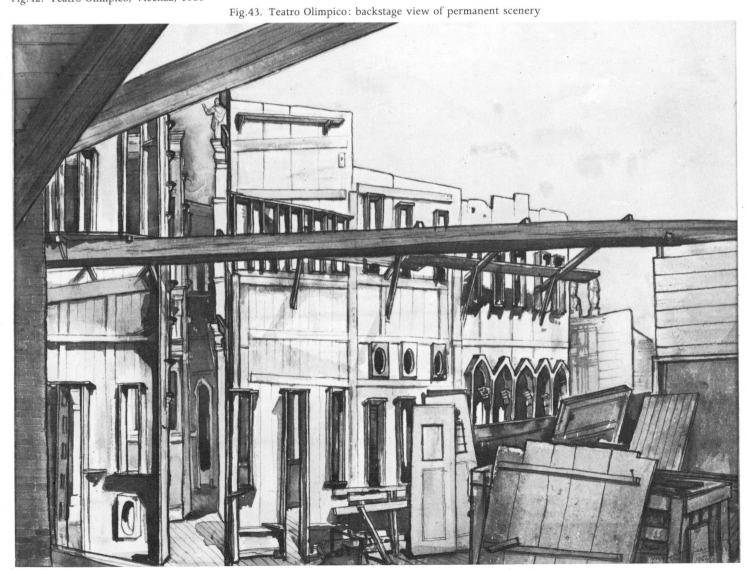

as further semi-circles to the side walls, enclosing a slightly sloping orchestral area which flows into, and is unified with, a rectangular acting area at floor level, similar to that seen in the Serlian plan (fig.14). Adjoining this is a raised stage or 'proscenae' for the actors, beyond which is a sloping stage where a vista of houses leads to a single back panel. A drawing made by Scamozzi in 1580 shows that the actors' stage was also enclosed by a pair of screens painted to fit into the perspective scene, but containing practical doors through which the actors might approach, or leave, the stage (fig.44). The orchestral area was presumably approached by steps from the raised stage, or by a door in the side wall of the theatre. Out of sight of the audience, in the corners of the stage behind the scenic vista, stairs led down to the space beneath, and to rooms at ground level behind the rear wall of the stage. There were also further rooms above, all of which presumably served as dressing rooms for the actors. On Scamozzi's plan the width of the theatre is subdivided at this point into two rooms.

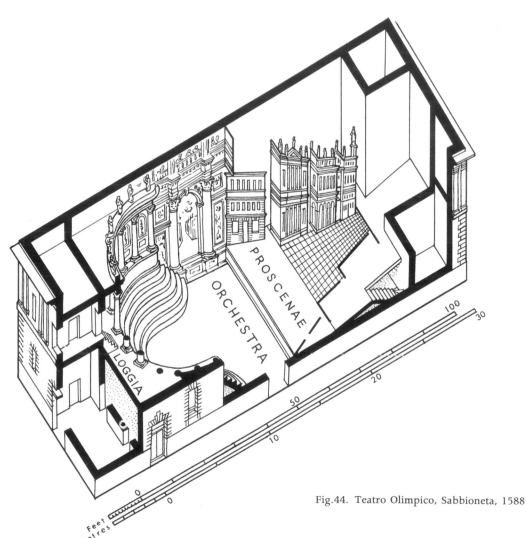

Fig.44. Teatro Olimpico, Sabbioneta, 1588

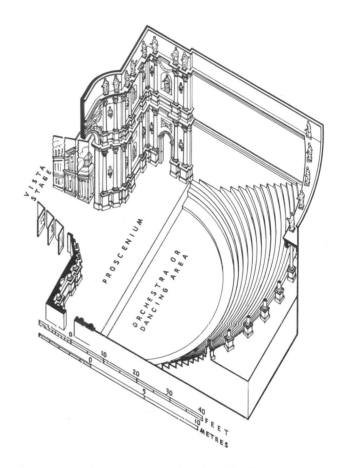

Fig.45. Theatre design by Inigo Jones

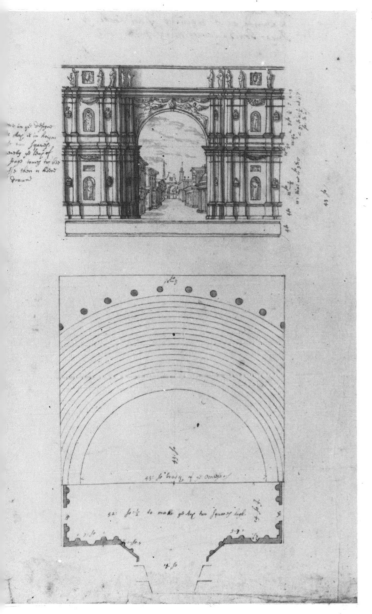

Fig.46. Scale reconstruction based on Fig.45

Mural paintings on the side walls continue the architectural colonnade which surmounts the gradines, and the manner in which this stops on the line of the stage front suggests that the cornice at least was continued across the hall at this point on a painted panel, as suggested in the reconstruction, and possibly in the manner described by Vasari for the performance at the wedding celebrations of Don Francesca of Tuscany in 1565-6 with its 'vast and most lovely canvas painted with various animals hunted and taken in various ways, which upheld by a great cornice, and concealing the prospect scene'.[2]

In the collection of drawings by Inigo Jones and John Webb at Worcester College, Oxford, are two folded sheets of drawings, one set by Inigo Jones, the other a copy of the first by John Webb.[3] On the right-hand side of the sheets are two drawings, one above the other, each representing half of an elevational drawing of a frons scenae with a section through the seating and porticus of an auditorium. W. G. Keith[4] has shown that these two drawings are copied from the original design by Palladio for his Teatro Olimpico, which Inigo Jones obtained on his visit to Vicenza. One half of the original Palladio drawing shows the design more or less as carried out, the other indicates possible variations with an overall greater height to the frons scenae which is reflected in the height of each order, and the replacement of the attic storey of the accepted design by a third order on the upper storey. These two drawings were copied, as indicated above, by Inigo Jones and John Webb, presumably as an investigation of Palladio's design methods and his system of proportions.

On the left-hand side of the Jones and Webb sheets is a plan of a theatre, and an elevation of a frons scenae (fig.45). The design is for a theatre on the Vicenzian theme, but here the rectangle into which the theatre fits is on the opposite axis to the Teatro Olimpico. The stage is correspondingly narrower, about half the width, and has only a single large arch at the centre, with a single door in either end wall. Beyond the central arch a vista of Serlian houses is indicated on both plan and elevation. In front of the rectangular raised stage within the hall is a semi-circular orchestra, with a single tier of semi-circular gradines surrounding it, reminiscent of Serlio's theatre (see footnote 57, p.308).

A note on the top left of the sheet tells us: 'Me in ye designe this Arch is in heigns most two squares: whereby ye length of ye stage seemes to bee lesse then is heere drawne.' This would seem to suggest that the design, which differed from this drawing, had been carried out; alternatively, it could suggest that the drawing was an amended adaptation by Jones of an existing building, even perhaps one measured on his Italian tour. The arch as drawn is one and a half squares high, but a further note written across the stage indicating an increase in stage width from a scaled dimension of approximately 50 feet 6 inches to '52 fo $\frac{1}{2}$ to make ye arch two squares high' suggests alternatively that this could be a preliminary sketch design to which the annotations are amendments. As Keith has indicated,[5] the depth of the stage is also noted as being increased from a scaled 13 feet to a noted 14 feet 9 inches. The overall height of the elevation scales 38 feet (Keith gives 37 feet), but is annotated as 43 feet, while the column spacing which scales 6 feet is noted at 7. If this is a design for a new theatre, or the adaptation of existing premises, we unfortunately have no indication as to which it could be.

However, even if the design was never carried out it does indicate the sort of theatre that Jones was interested in, and it is therefore important as an example of avant garde thought at the time. The reconstruction (fig.46), ignoring the written comments, shows the theatre with all the parts scaled off the actual drawing, the scale having been prepared, as was Keith's, on an acceptance of the 43 feet width indicated for the orchestra.

In the same collection of drawings, inspected by the author in September, 1967, are two further sheets catalogued under the general heading of the Barber-Surgeon's Hall, but the elevation and plan shown on one (fig.47a.b.), and the two cross-sections shown on the other (fig.47c.d.), bear little relation to the remaining drawings for the Hall, and have presumably been incorrectly catalogued under this heading. These drawings show a free-standing building that has all the characteristics of a theatre, and one which retains something of the form of an Elizabethan unroofed playhouse. The auditorium is arranged with semi-circular balconies and straight extended arms enclosing a flat pit, equipped with steps following the

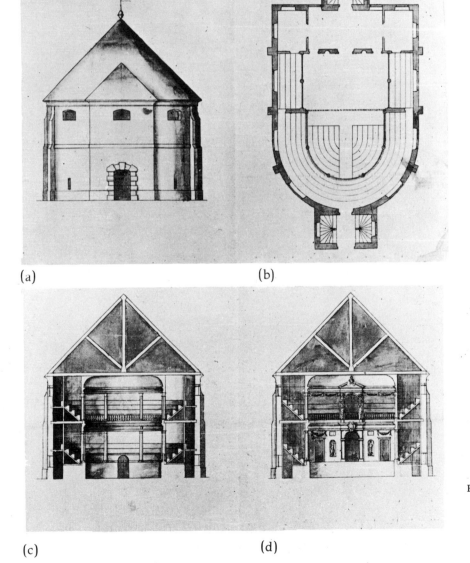

(a)   (b)

(c)   (d)

Fig.47. Unidentified theatre by Inigo Jones
        (a) elevation
        (b) plan
        (c) cross-section through auditorium
        (d) cross-section through stage

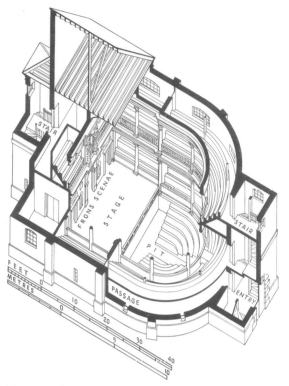

Fig.48. Scale reconstruction based on Fig.47

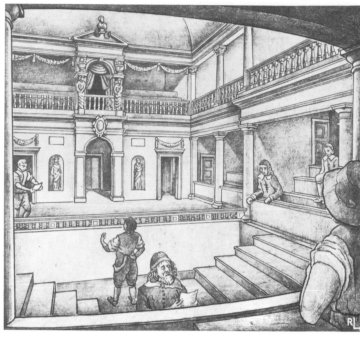

Fig.49. Interior based on Fig.48

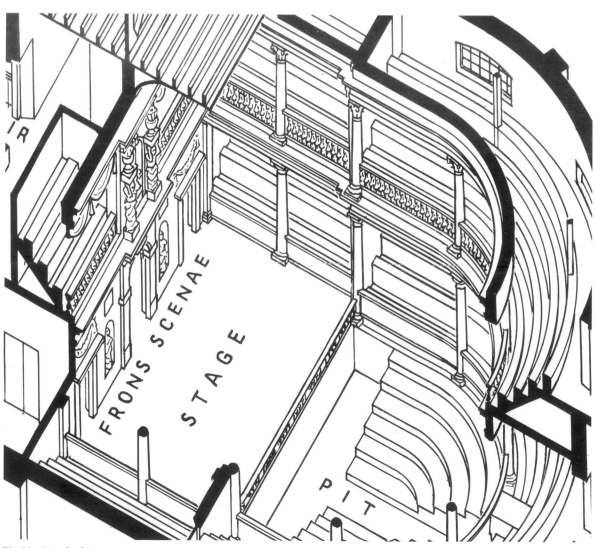

Fig.50. Detail of Fig.48

same curves as the surrounding balconies. This pit is reached by an arched opening beneath the lower balcony, an ill-contrived arrangement where the arch appears to cut through the front rows of benches. A cross wall separates the balconies from a rectangular extension of the building containing a raised stage, with further balconies on two levels at either side. The stage is backed by a classical frons scenae with a central arched opening flanked by small niches with statues and two rectangular doorways, all three openings leading into an inner room beyond. Above is a further arched opening enclosed within a pedimented frame supported by thermes, with two open balconies with benches on either side. Beyond these, in the corners of the building, are further rooms, presumably at two levels. Two staircase towers at front and back provide access by newel stairs on either side of a central landing to the upper levels, the towers projecting outside the main building in a similar manner to those of the Elizabethan playhouses.

The reconstruction (figs.48-9,50) based on these drawings underlines the resemblance in the arrangement of balcony seating, and even the frons scenae with its strong Palladian features recalls the doors and open gallery of the Swan theatre (fig.23). The original drawings suggest that this is possibly a proposed design rather than an executed structure, in that many small features have not been worked out in detail: for example, no allowance has been made for the projection of the column bases, and the consequent incursion of the wall supporting these into the pit interrupts the pattern of the gradines there, which incidentally are shown on plan but not on section. The arched entry into the pit has already been mentioned, and this would surely have required further thought, as would also the floor levels of the back-stage rooms in relation to the passageway beneath the first balcony, which can only have been introduced to provide access to them.

Plays were performed in the Barber-Surgeons' Hall,[6] and Wickham records such an occasion in 1562, but whatever its attribution this design certainly indicates a most interesting adaptation of the earlier playhouses to a smaller, roofed, example. From the draughtsmanship the drawing would appear to be by Inigo Jones rather than by Webb.

A further Inigo Jones drawing of 1639 is a quick sketch of a proscenium arch enclosing a perspective scene.[7] This is entitled 'for ye cokpitt' and it has been suggested that it refers to the Cockpit-in-Court, but, as can be seen from the reconstruction of this theatre (fig.53), the central arch of the frons scenae is extremely small, little more than a normal doorway, whereas the arch shown in the sketch is of considerable size. It has been suggested that this depicts the proscenium arch of the other cockpit in Drury Lane, the Phoenix,[8] but the size of the opening and the amount of scenery depicted are more suited to the scale of either of the unknown theatres (figs.45,57.p.85) than they are to that of an adapted cockpit.

The Cockpit-in-Court has now been proved to have been converted to the designs of Inigo Jones[9] in 1629-30, and a record from the Works Accounts describes precisely the appearance of the frons scenae backing the stage. This description agrees in all respects with the drawings of this building which are also to be found in the Worcester College collection, and include a plan of the whole building, and a detailed plan and elevation of the stage (fig.51a.b.).

These drawings have been ascribed to Webb, who came to work with Jones in 1628, and are in a similar hand to the copy of the Teatro Olimpico, mentioned earlier, with its line hatching replacing Jones's washes for tones, which is inscribed precisely 'This drawing was by Mr. Webb.''

It is now argued that these drawings were prepared for the original conversion, whereas previously the argument has been advanced in favour of a post-Restoration reconstruction by Webb.[10] If any reliance may be placed on a bird's-eye map of London by Faithorne, published in 1658, the Cockpit at this date, according to W. G. Keith, still retained its octagonal external form. If this was so then the plan, which shows the octagonal cockpit squared off, cannot have been made in 1629, but must have been prepared for later alterations carried out after 1658. The Works Accounts record such alterations in November, 1660, for

> 'makeing of v large boxes wth seuerall degrees in them at ye cockpitt and doores in them, taking vp the floore of ye stage and pitt and laying againe the floore of the stage & pitt pendant, making of seuerall seats round and in ye pitt making of two ptitions in the gallery there for the Musick and players setting vp a raylc & ballisters vpon the stage making two other seats for ye gentlemen Vshers a (sic) Mr Killigrew cutting out a way and making a paire of Stayres cont.   stepps to goe into ye Gallery ouer the stage & incloseing the said stayres wth a doore in it Cont. about one square, making of two new doores goeing vnder the degrees and bourding vp one doore vppon the degrees setting vp xj squares of ptitioning vnder the degrees wth vj doores in them.'[11]

A close study of these drawings suggests that they are incomplete, and if this is so it lends credence to the suggestion that they are adapted survey drawings of the existing structure as designed by Inigo Jones, prepared to permit alterations to be considered. Preliminary construction lines are indented with a sharp tool, and only inked in when approved. These include such features as the spiral stairs shown on the reconstruction in the bottom corner, only hinted at on Webb's drawing by a circle pressed into the paper prior to inking in, but shown on such plans as Vertue's *Survey of Whitehall*, 1747.[12] Minor alterations are also pencilled in, notably some unworkable steps in the triangle adjoining the steps down to the stage, and amendments to the two windows and the door in the wall at the rear of the stage. The most convincing argument for incompleteness, however, is the omission of the inking in of the scale for the general plan. While the scale for the stage details is clearly indicated (it is unfortunately omitted from most photographic reproductions of this drawing), that for the general plan is only pricked in.

Whichever argument is correct, the drawings indicate most clearly that the neo-Roman theatre with its entry doors in the frons scenae was in use concurrently with the scenic form of stage. This classical revival would have sanctified the use of doors of entry such as have already been considered in the earlier roofed theatres. But even in this theatre it has been suggested that the central arched opening at least was backed by scenery. Three drawings in the Chatsworth collection conform to the shape of the arched opening, but measure 9 feet in height by 6 feet in width, whereas the opening in the theatre measures 8 feet in height by 4 feet in width.[13] What is surprising, however, is the indisputable fact that the four side doors measure only 5 feet in height, and as such can hardly have been used as entry doors for the actors. If these drawings represent a survey, were the doors wrongly measured and drawn, or, if an original design, were they still in process of alteration? It may be noted that in the central opening (fig.51a) there is the suggestion of a lower arch springing from the line of the present door heads, a relationship which one would have expected to find in the finished design. The doors could well have been raised to conform to the amended springing point of the arch, with a consequent – acceptable – reduction in the height of the panels above the doors. This seems to be the most likely solution, providing doors for the entry of actors on either side of the central perspective scene. If, however, the drawing is accepted at its face value, and the doors are taken to be only five feet high, then it is possible that they may have been used, as indicated on the reconstruction (figs.52,54), as positions for periaktoi, in which case all entrances must have been made through the central opening. I am inclined to the former view, however, that the doors were in fact taller, and so provided entry ways for the actors on to the stage as depicted in the perspective view of the interior (fig.53).

The main stage is shown as level on the elevation, and has been so indicated on the reconstruction, although the rear stage behind the frons scenae has been assumed to slope. The alterations of 1660 included taking up the stage and pit, and rebuilding both 'pendant', which may reasonably be assumed to mean sloping.

It is obvious that Jones was attempting to fit two storeys of orders into an extremely limited height, and as a result was involving himself in problems of scale which were reflected in the height of the door openings. It would have been more satisfactory if he had treated the frons scenae with a single, full-height order, but this would have meant too drastic a break with the Palladian ideals that he was earlier seen to be investigating, and to which he would naturally have wished to aspire in spite of the limitations. It may be assumed from this that the height within which he was working was a structural limitation of the building, controlling the height of the two galleries of seating with which the auditorium was already equipped. It would seem at first sight as though the cornices of the frons scenae would have been lined with the levels of the gallery fronts, but further consideration leads to an acceptance of the fact that it is unlikely that the proportions of these orders would have conformed to the already existing levels of the cockpit galleries. In arriving at these levels one link between the stage and auditorium may be assumed, and that is the need to place the king's eye on a line with the eye-level of the perspective scene. From the prison scene[14] this may be assessed as 3 feet above the level stage. Firm, but not ink, lines at the doors connecting the side galleries with the royal dais suggest the possibility of a step at this position, and with these points in mind it is possible to arrive at levels which not only permit reasonable access by two steps from the dais to the pit floor, but also allow limited headroom for the steps leading down from the pit on either side adjoining the stage front. In attempting to

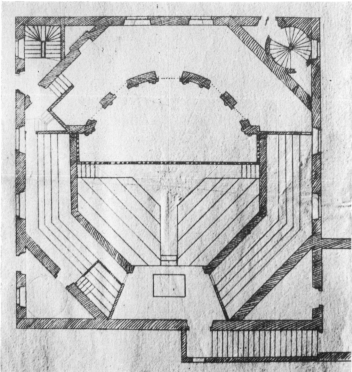

Fig.51. The Cockpit-in-Court by Inigo Jones and John Webb, 1660
(a) detail plan and elevation of stage and frons scenae
(b) general plan of building

understand the seating arrangement indicated on the plan, the 'Barber-Surgeon' drawings (fig. 47b.c.d.) proved invaluable. A comparison of this plan with its sections shows that where Jones used a single line on plan to indicate the rise of a stepping, in section this was translated as an 8 inch-wide seat raised slightly above a narrow footway. The sections also show that these gradines were all 1 foot 6 inches in height. The gallery sections for the Cockpit were therefore worked out on this basis, and took into account the levels of the windows, in relation to building heights, indicated on the Danckert's painting of Whitehall.[15] In both these buildings it would appear, however, as though less comfortable accommodation was provided in the pit area, where there is only height for a series of low gradines, which could, however, have provided space for the use of individual chairs or at least of stools.

It has been assumed that a solid floor existed to the turret room above the cockpit, as this was provided with windows in addition to the glazed lantern. Such a room could have housed the throne, lowering mechanism and a trapdoor in the floor, the floor itself being concealed behind the 'callicoe' covering, adorned with stars of silver foil, which opened, possibly in the manner suggested by Sabbattini, to permit the passage of the throne.[16]

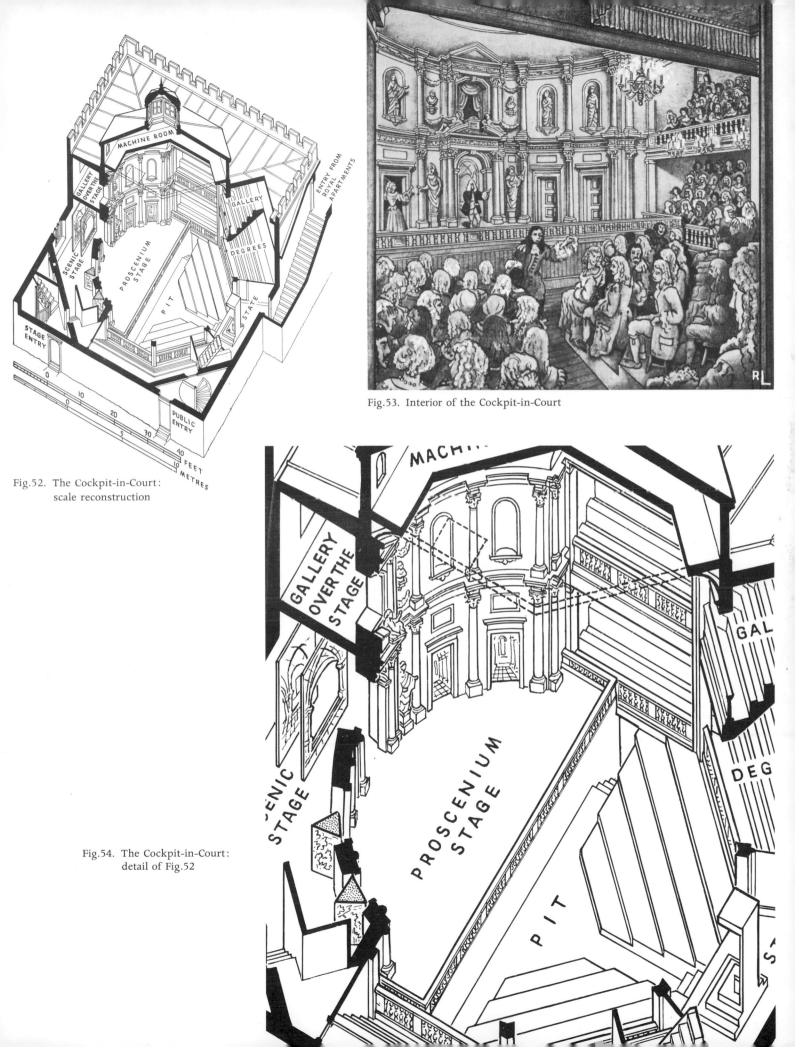

Fig.52. The Cockpit-in-Court:
scale reconstruction

Fig.53. Interior of the Cockpit-in-Court

Fig.54. The Cockpit-in-Court:
detail of Fig.52

The outbreak of the Civil War in 1642, and the resulting Commonwealth, led to the suppression of the theatres, and the dismantling of the Globe, the Blackfriars and the Fortune, as well as the taking down by an order of 26th July, 1648, of 'the Stages, Boxes, Scaffolds, Seats and Forms, in the several Playhouses within the County of Middlesex',[17] and the removal of the 'Boarded Masquing House at *Whitehall*, the Masque House at *St. James*; and the Courts of Guard.'[18] The stages, boxes, seats and galleries of the Cockpit, the Fortune and Salisbury Court were dismantled by the Cromwellian soldiery,[19] whilst at Salisbury Court 'On March 24, 1649, divers soldiers by force and arms entered the said playhouse, cut down the seats, broke down the stage, and utterly defaced the whole building.'

The actors were scattered at home and abroad, and in an order of 9th February, 1648,[20] they were branded as rogues who could be fined and imprisoned for a first offence and publicly flogged for a second. Nevertheless there were illicit performances in the remaining playhouses, but these were subject to constant raids and fines.[21] In May of 1656, Sir William Davenant presented an '*Entertainment by Musick and Declarations after the manner of the Ancients*',[22] for which he charged an admission fee of 5s. This was staged in a long narrow room in his home at Rutland House. At one end there was a stage and on either side were two railed-in places 'Purpled and Guilt, The Curtayne also that drew before them was of cloth of gold and Purple'. 'The Musick was above in a loover hole railed about and covered wth Sarcenetts to conceale them.'[23]

In the autumn of that year Davenant presented *The Siege of Rhodes*, which is generally considered to be the first English opera. This was presumably performed in the same room with scenes designed by John Webb on the lines of those prepared by Inigo Jones for the earlier court performances. Because of the limitations of space and funds the production was extremely simple, lacking the use of those scenes and engines that had provided spectacular action in the earlier shows. The lack of space prevented Davenant from using dancers, suggesting that the remainder of the hall not occupied by the stage was wholly taken up with seating for the paying spectators. Several drawings by Webb exist for this production, including a plan and section of the stage (fig. 55a. b.). From the plan it can be seen that the hall was 22 feet 4 inches wide and that the stage occupied a depth of 18 feet. The front half of the stage sloped upward some 4 feet in 8 feet 6 inches, in a manner similar to that noted for *Florimene*, and stepped down to a flat rear half of the stage. Owing to the limited height of the room, some 13 feet 6 inches, the height of the rear stage and stage front was limited to 2 feet. A frontispiece, similar to that for *Salmacida Spolia*, framed the scene, with three pairs of flat wings supported on vertical posts projecting up through the stage. Behind these were grooves for three pairs of backshutters, beyond which were two scenes of relieve in front of a backscene supported on four posts set 2 feet from the rear wall to leave passage space from one side of the stage to the other. Sky borders crossed the stage on the line of each pair of wings, and a further border masked the upper grooves of the backshutters from the view of the audience.

Unfortunately we have no real knowledge of the arrangements made for seating the audi-

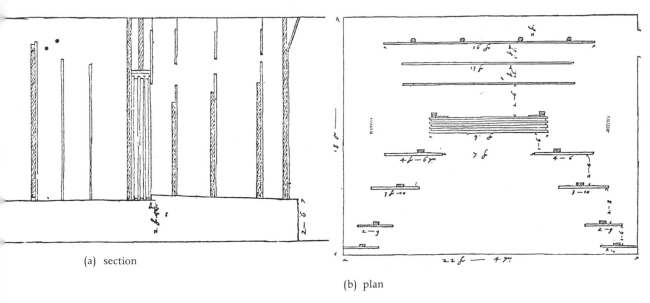

(a) section

(b) plan

Fig.55. Stage for *The Siege of Rhodes,* 1656

ence, but the really important thing is that here we have a performance provided with the same form of movable perspective scenery as was previously used for the court masks.

Davenant was instrumental in presenting an opera, *The Cruelty of the Spaniards in Peru,* publicly at one of the pre-interregnum theatres, the Cockpit or Phoenix in Drury Lane – '*Exprest by Instrumentall and Vocall Musick, and by the Art of Perspective in Scenes, &.*'[24] For these performances, given before July, 1658, he was able to make use of engines and machines which were missing from the performances at Rutland House.

In 1659 General Monk granted John Rhodes a 'Tolleration to erect a playhouse or to haue a share out of them already Tollerated',[25] and he 'fitted up a House then for Acting call'd the *Cock-Pit in Drury-Lane*'. Mr Freehafer suggests that the other tolerances may have gone to the 'Old Actors' to perform at the Red Bull, and to William Beeston at Salisbury Court, sometimes known as Dorset Court.

With the Restoration, Davenant and Killigrew were granted patents permitting them to present plays. Davenant opened with his Duke's Players, basically John Rhodes' company of actors, at the Salisbury Court playhouse, while Killigrew took his King's Players, formed largely from the 'Old Actors,' to the Red Bull, which they used for three performances from the 5th to the 9th November, 1660, when they moved on the following day to the Vere Street Theatre, which had been converted from a covered tennis court, originally built in 1633-4. This building had been used for illicit performances, as it was raided in March, 1653, but it was still in use for its original purpose of tennis, bowls and dinners, so that its suitability for plays was presumably made possible by temporary adaptation. Its size is quoted by Hotson[26] as being 23 feet wide by 64 feet long. When it was, however, adapted by Killigrew it received the commendation of Pepys when he visited it on the 20th November, 1660, and described it as 'The finest playhouse, I believe, that ever was in England.' On the 29th November, 1661, Pepys again visited the theatre, this time with Sir W. Penn who 'went up to one of the boxes, and I unto the 18d places'.[27] But even so it is generally acknowledged that this theatre was designed on the lines of the earlier Elizabethan indoor theatres, with no allowance for the use of the perspective scene, but with a platform stage hung with tapestries, perhaps similar to those illustrated on the frontispieces (figs.20a.b.) of *Roxana*, 1632, *Messalina*, 1640, and *The Wits*, 1662.

Davenant presumably adapted Salisbury Court, stripped of its interior, to his particular needs, but only on a temporary basis, as the agreement with his company suggests that they would act at 'Salisbury Court or elsewhere' . . . 'until he provides a new theatre with scenes'.[28] The same agreement tells us that a band of musicians was required at the theatre, and that actresses had joined the company. There was at least one box in the theatre, to which Killigrew was to have free access, capable of seating six persons, and arrangements were made for payment for costumes, properties, scenes and scene-frames.

The new theatre with scenes was opened in June, 1661, as the Duke's Playhouse, also called the Lincoln's Inn Fields Theatre, which was an adaptation of Lisle's Tennis Court, (Cibber speaks of it as a 'Tennis *Quaree* Court, which is of the lesser sort'),[29] first built between 1656-7. The building was approximately 75 feet in length and 30 feet wide, with two houses or wings projecting from the northern side.[30] The easternmost of these projections was removed by Davenant and replaced by a scene room, presumably adjoining the stage, which would therefore also have been at the east end.

Such tennis courts were normally 110 feet long for a full-size court, by 31 feet 8 inches wide. These rectangular roofed buildings had a range of windows on each long side in the upper part of the walls, and sometimes also across one end. Internally the building was a single great hall with a roofed corridor, the penthouse, which ran along one side and the two end walls, and was separated from the main hall by a waist-high partition, usually with two openings to the court, and the roof supported on a series of posts.

While Davenant made provision for the new perspective scenes and machines in his theatre, it was not possible to break completely free from the normally accepted acting requirements, and it was therefore necessary to make provision for both actors and scenes.[31] The actors were by now used to making their entries to and exits from the stage through the doors in the enclosing walls, in addition to appearing at balconies and windows, the latter being both at ground and upper levels. The limitations of the existing form of the rectangular tennis courts necessarily imposed their own pattern on this theatre, and particularly on its stage. We noted earlier the possible arrangement of the doors surrounding the Elizabethan stage (pp.45,50), both flanking the stage and set obliquely across the corners furthest from the open court, on either side of a central curtained projection, recess or opening. The narrow width of this building would not have permitted doors to be placed obliquely if the central opening was now to be sufficiently wide to accommodate the changeable scene; as a result the necessary doors would have been ranged on either side of the stage with balconies above, and possibly with windows at both levels adjoining both doors and balconies. The Serlian idea of scenery as a backing on a sloping stage to the actor on a flat stage in front, together with the mask combination of dancing area and raised scenic stage, could have led to the acceptance of a double stage in the new theatre: an actors' stage entered by the side doors, and beyond this a further stage, probably sloping, for the scenic devices and machinery, the two separated by a curtain which marked the division between the auditorium and the scenic area, as well as dividing the actors from the scenery. This actors' stage directly related to the audience was still the proscenium of the classical and neo-classical stage set before the frons scenae, and, like Palladio's Olimpic theatre and Jones's Cockpit-in-Court, was within the confines of the auditorium or audience chamber.

In Davenant's theatre there were at least two doors on either side of the stage, with one, and possibly more, traps in the stage floor, and it is quite possible that a music room was placed above the scene opening, as was certainly the case in the Dorset Garden Theatre.[32]

The arrangement of steps, or gradines, familiar in the adaptation of halls for masks or dramatic activities, most probably set the pattern of seating within the existing tennis court. Possible adaptation of the existing penthouse along one side may have been reflected by a similar structure on the opposite side providing seating on two levels, similar to that noted in the Tudor Hall for *Florimene* (fig.38), and these seats could have been subdivided by low partitions into boxes. The side boxes would probably have been continued across the width of the hall facing the stage, again in a similar manner to the *Florimene* arrangement. Contained within these surrounding boxes would have been a rectangular pit, possibly with benches on a stepped or sloping timber floor. If the pit was so stepped up, then the first level of surrounding boxes would have had to be raised sufficiently high to permit the occupants to see over the heads of the back row of the pit. If this were the case, the front of the pit could have been entered from passages beneath these side boxes. Professor Langhans has argued in favour of three tiers of such boxes, on the grounds that there would have been sufficient height for them, but this would probably only have been the case if the lower tier was set sufficiently near to ground level. A Prologue to a play performed in this theatre mentions 'th'upper Box, Pit, and Galleries',[33] which would suggest two tiers of boxes and open galleries above. An alternative interpretation could be for two tiers of side boxes, and a gallery above the front boxes – those facing the stage – with a further gallery above this set into the roof space across the width of the hall. Langhans further quotes references to 'the upper gallery' and 'the Eighteen pence Gallery'.

Pepys, visiting the theatre on Thursday, 7th November, 1667, was 'forced to sit in the side balcone over against the musique-room', and again on Wednesday, 12th May, 1669, he and his wife had to sit 'in the side balcony, over against the musick, did hear, but not see, a new play, the first day acted, "The Roman Virgin", an old play, and but ordinary, I thought; but the trouble of my eyes with the light of the candles did almost kill me.'

This theatre opened on the 28th June, 1661, with *The Seige of Rhodes* and scenes by John Webb, a second part being added to the original production and given the following evening. Meanwhile the success of Davenant's more spectacular productions led Killigrew to consider the need for providing similar attractions for his performances, and as a result he purchased ground in the 'Riding Yard' between Drury Lane and Bridges Street, and opened a theatre there on the 7th May, 1663, as the first Theatre Royal (fig.56). The site was described as measuring 112 feet in length by 59 feet at the east end and 58 feet at the west end. Later plans show, however, that the site was more complicated in its form than the simple rectangle suggested by these dimensions, but the theatre itself was only 100 feet long, with a 10 feet wide yard at one end.[34]

Although there are no illustrations of the interior, we have a number of comments. On the 25th April, 1669, Cosimo III of Tuscany visited the King's Theatre and sat in the Royal box, which would undoubtedly have occupied the same relation to the scene as did the earlier states, being centrally placed opposite the stage in the first level of boxes. He described the interior as being 'nearly of a circular form, surrounded, in the inside, by boxes separated from each other, and divided into several rows of seats, for the greater accommodation of the ladies and gentlemen, who, in conformity with the freedom of the country, sit together indiscriminately; a large space is left on the ground floor for the rest of the audience. The scenery is light, capable of a great many changes, and embellished with beautiful landscapes. Before the comedy begins, that the audience may not be tired with waiting, the most delightful symphonies are played; on which account many people come early to enjoy this agreeable amusement'. On a further visit on the 3rd May, he comments on the lighting 'on the stage and on the walls' which was sufficient for 'the spectators to see the scenes and the performances'.[35] A further visitor, Balthazar de Monconys, on Friday 22nd May, 1663, commented on the pit where the benches, rising one behind the other like an amphitheatre and covered with green cloth, were resorted to by persons of quality. Pepys visited the theatre on Friday, 8th May, 1663, and thought that

> 'The house is made with extraordinary good contrivance, and yet hath some faults, as the narrowness of the passages in and out of the pitt, and the distance from the stage to the boxes, which I am confident cannot hear; but for all other things, it is well, only, above all, the musique being below, and most of it sounding under the very stage, there is no hearing of the bases at all, nor very well of the trebles, which sure must be mended.'

On the 1st May, 1668, he was again at the theatre when he records 'a disorder in the pitt by its raining in, from the cupola at the top, it being a very foul day and cold'.[36] This cupola presumably crowned the circular part of the auditorium and could have admitted light for afternoon and similar daytime performances, as did also the windows (from which Pepys took a chill 'sitting sweating in the playhouse, and the wind blowing through the windows upon my head' in June, 1663),[37] with a possible consequent saving in candles.

This cupola may be seen on a map of London by Morgan and Ogilby, 1681-2,[38] which shows the theatre to be a long low building with windows to an upper storey, a high pitched roof with three dormer windows, and the great cupola occupying a central position (fig.56). A further view appears in George Foster's *New and Exact Plan of the Cities of London and Westminster*, 1738.[39]

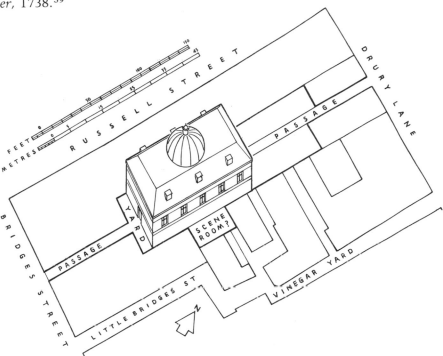

Fig.56. The first Theatre Royal, Drury Lane, 1663: scale reconstruction

In addition to the pit and boxes there is mention of the uppermost galleries and the lower rooms[40] with prices quoted as pit, half-a-crown; middle gallery, one shilling and six pence; upper gallery, a shilling; and boxes at four shillings.[41] Summers suggests that the proscenium, or actors' stage, was here provided with six doors of entry,[42] three on either side, and in this theatre there is again mention of stage windows, including a 'low window', but how these features were arranged is not known.

In March, 1666, while the theatres were closed during the plague, Killigrew took the opportunity to make alterations to the stage, and Pepys had a look round when he found 'the King's play-house, all in dirt, they being altering of the stage to make it wider. But god knows when they will begin to act again; but my business here was to see the inside of the stage and all the tiring-rooms and machines: and, indeed, it was a sight worth seeing.' It was probably as part of these alterations that the musicians were moved from their position partly under the stage to an upper room. No architect's name is directly associated with this building, but it is obvious that here was a more imaginative design than was apparent in the adapted tennis courts, and from the descriptions it would seem that some attempt

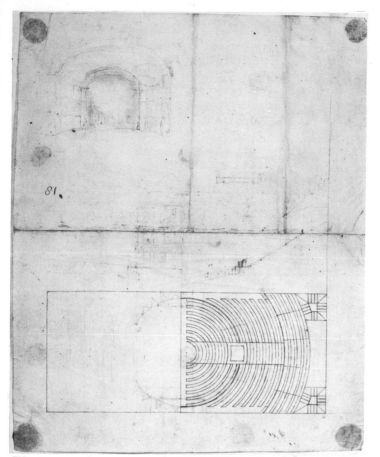

Fig.57. Unidentified theatre design, possibly an adaptation of the Tudor Hall

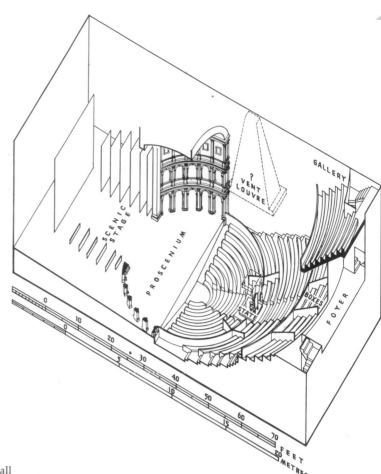

Fig.58. Scale reconstruction based on Fig.57

was being made to design a theatre which reflected the semi-circular cavea of the classical and neo-classical theatres.

It has been suggested that a sketch (fig.57) in the Wren collection at All Souls, Oxford, catalogued as a 'Lecture Theatre Repository for the College of Physicians',[43] could have been a preliminary sketch for this theatre, but it seems more likely that it was a sketch for a possible adaptation of the Great, or Tudor, Hall at Whitehall. The design consists of a plan, the auditorium half inked in, a lightly sketched pencil section and a thumb-nail pencil sketch of the stage area. Although there is no indicated scale it would seem reasonable to assume a scale of 10 feet to 1 inch, which gives a height of approximately 1 foot 10 inches for the benches, comparable to that shown on the Wren section for the Theatre Royal (fig.60), which are then also spaced at similar 2 feet centres. To this scale the plan measures 38 feet 9 inches in width, and 89 feet 6 inches in length, which corresponds to the internal measurements of the Tudor Hall.[44]

The auditorium is arranged with seven semi-circular tiers of benches on a shallow slope rising at 1:5, beyond which the slope increases to $1:2\frac{1}{2}$ for a further eleven stepped seats, the rearmost four rows being partitioned into five boxes. Beyond is a small foyer flanked by two stairs providing access to an upper gallery, the front of which lines with the box fronts below and stretches to the rear wall. Markings on the section suggest that this gallery has eight rows of seats spaced more closely than those below at approximately 1 foot 8 inches. Centrally placed in the auditorium is a flat dais, 1 foot above the level of the stage, with a state, before and behind which is a 7 feet 6 inch wide flight of steps. Flanking the state are two more areas partitioned off as boxes. All this portion of the plan works satisfactorily, as may be seen from the reconstruction (fig.58), and it is of interest that it is this area which has been inked in on the drawing. The stage area, however, is left in a state of pencilled indecision, and the preparation of the reconstruction makes obvious the reason. Within an overall height of 21 feet an attempt has been made to introduce three levels of orders, with a resultant maximum height for the lower arched openings of 6 feet. So out of scale is the resultant design that one was tempted to reconsider the assumed scale for the drawing, but any scale which makes these orders acceptable makes nonsense of the seating dimensions. As a result it is not surprising to find that this area had not been inked in as satisfactory, and this particular scheme was presumably abandoned. It may well be, however, that the ideas expressed, particularly in the auditorium, were put to better use in a design for the first Theatre Royal.

The three-storey frons scenae of the sketch was arranged on an approximately 34 feet 6 inch semi-circle, with its centre on the stage front, reflecting the semi-circle of lower benches with its own centre on the line of the bench ends. A central arch, some 14 feet wide, is flanked by five sub-divisions on either side, each with its own arch, backed by triangles which it has been suggested[45] represented periaktoi. Variations on this arrangement are pencilled in, and an alternative arrangement of the proscenium area shows rectangular areas spanning both stage and auditorium. The whole stage area slopes up at approximately 1:14, and the central opening is backed by a perspective vista. There is a distinct resemblance between this central arch, with its perspective vista, and the sketch by Inigo Jones annotated for 'ye cokpitt,' even the proportions being closely related – indeed one is tempted to wonder if the theatre design under consideration could in fact be a sketch by Inigo Jones acquired by Wren when he was associated as Surveyor with the Tudor Hall. A further feature of the sketch is a pyramidal form suspended some 27 feet above the dais, and reaching up a further 22 feet. If this is in fact a possible suggestion for adapting the Tudor Hall, then this could well be a ventilation louvre carried up from a false ceiling to the roof ridge.

Davenant died in 1668, but sometime in 1669-70, consideration was being given by his wife, who had taken over the company, to the provision of a new theatre for the Duke's company. The 'garden plot behind Salisbury House in the Strand' was first looked at, but a more southernly part of the Gardens, fronting on the Thames at Dorset Stairs, was decided on, and here the new theatre, reputedly designed by Sir Christopher Wren, was erected, and opened on the 9th November, 1671. Its dimensions have been computed by Hotson[46] as 140 feet in length by 57 feet wide, and by Langhans[47] as approximately 147-8 feet long by 57 feet wide, including a 10 feet deep porch. Numerous illustrations of the main frontage to the river show the upper storeys supported on columns and divided into two apartments,

one of which was occupied by Thomas Betterton, who was both manager of the acting and
'keeper' of the playhouse.[48] Illustrations to Settle's *The Empress of Morocco,* 1673, (fig.59)
show the proscenium stage of this theatre, together with a variety of scenes on the scenic
stage beyond. These indicate that a great moulded frame surrounded an opening separating
the two stages, above which was a room projecting forward with a central curtained opening
flanked by figures, and further curtained openings set in the obliquely concave sides. This
was presumably the music room, as the panels beneath the side openings were decorated
with musical instruments in relief. For operas, when an increased orchestra was required,
the musicians could be accommodated on the proscenium stage or were 'plac'd between
the Pit and the Stage'.[49] At these times it is suggested that an advance frontispiece and a
curtain were sometimes set at the front of the proscenium stage to hide the side doors, which
were only required as a feature of the dramatic stage. Here the proscenium was flanked by
arched entry doors, Summers[50] claims there were four doors, two on each side, but
Langhans[51] suggests there may have been only one on each side, on the strength of a stage
direction in a play performed at this theatre which reads 'Enter Mrs Woodly at the door on
the right hand of the stage' and 'Enter Bevil and Carolina at the door on the left hand'.
Above were further arched openings or balconies with balustraded fronts, separated by a
giant pilastered order running through the two storeys, above which a further order was
related to an attic storey enclosing panels decorated in base relief. The whole was richly
decorated with gilded carving ascribed to Grinling Gibbons.

Fig.59. The Dorset Garden Theatre, 1671:
proscenium stage and scenic vista

The auditorium is described by François Brunet[52] as being 'infinitely more beautiful and functional than those in the playhouses of our French actors. The pit, arranged in the form of an amphitheatre, has seats, and one never hears any noise. There are seven boxes, holding twenty persons each. The same number of boxes form the second tier, and, higher still, there is the paradise.' Summers tells us on the authority of Congreve, writing to a friend in 1701, that the stage 'ran out beyond the proscenium arch far into the pit, was in front convex in correspondence with the concentric semi-circles of the seats on the ground floor', and rising, presumably, to the level of the boxes so that Congreve was also able to speak of the pit and boxes at the performance which he attended as being 'thrown into one, so that all sat in common'.[53] He may, however, have been referring to the occasional later practice of charging the same price for pit as for boxes, when the same class of audience would have occupied both parts.

The two levels of boxes probably conformed to the levels of the proscenium doors and their balconies over, while the paradise, or gallery, would presumably have been at the level of the attic storey. There was, as one might now expect, a royal box[54] centrally placed opposite the stage in the lower tier of boxes, probably decorated above with the Royal Arms to indicate its character. If the boxes followed the rectangular pattern noted earlier, then the royal box was probably flanked by a further box on either side facing the stage, with two further pairs of boxes facing each other across the amphitheatre of the pit. This grouping of 2-3-2 boxes would presumably have been repeated on the second or middle tier, with side galleries above flanking the main gallery facing the stage. However, taking Congreve's semi-circles at face value, an arrangement might be assumed more nearly related to Wren's design for the second Theatre Royal (fig.63), or even to the sketch discussed earlier. In this latter case, however, as also in Vanbrugh's Opera House (fig.69), the line of the stage front does not correspond to that of the seats. Possibly an intermediate stage may be assumed between the sketch and the later developed pattern of the second Theatre Royal. This design, as will be seen later, is so polished that it suggests a previous attempt to conform to the neo-classical theme, before Wren achieved the brilliant compromise solution between the reactangular tennis-court, mask type of theatre, and the ideal classical semi-circle.

A curtain separated the actors' stage from the scenic stage beyond, and may be seen in one of the *Empress of Morocco* drawings to have been divided in the middle, and drawn up in a festoon at either side of the top of the opening. With few exceptions this main curtain, once drawn after the delivery of the Prologue on the proscenium stage, remained up and open until the Epilogue. The scenery, consisting of side wings and shutters running in grooves, was moved and changed in full view of the audience, both stage and auditorium being illuminated by daylight or candlelight. Machinery was presumably also provided on the lines of that used by Jones and Webb for the ascent and descent of gods and goddesses amid moving clouds. There is mention in an early 18th century poem[55] of 'those that swing in Clouds and fill Machines', and also of 'Trap-doors and Pit-falls'. One version of this poem, dated 1706, is entitled *A Description of the Play-House in Dorset Gardens*[56] and it may therefore be reasonable to assume that the stage of the Dorset Garden Theatre had such openings. Summers suggests that some of these may have been large enough to permit the passage of 'pieces of scenery of some size, often with characters grouped upon them . . . within the curtain line,'[57] while smaller traps were installed in the proscenium stage through which characters such as the Prologue and the Epilogue could sink or rise.

Although Davenant and Killigrew possessed the only patents permitting them to operate theatres, the King had further licensed in 1660 an actor, George Jolly, who had spent considerable time touring the Continent during the Commonwealth, to purchase, build, or hire a theatre for his company.[58] Jolly made use of both the Cockpit or Phoenix and the Salisbury Court until such time as the machinations of Killigrew and Davenant put him out of business on his own account. Both Killigrew and Davenant sought to extend their empires by creating nursery theatres for the training of young actors for their companies. Killigrew created a nursery in Hatton Garden in 1667, and in 1669 he moved this company to his old Vere Street Theatre in Gibbon's Tennis Court where they remained until 1671.[59]

In 1671 a certain Duckworth was permitted to build a booth or playhouse on a piece of ground in Finsbury Fields called Bun Hill, which was 60 feet long and 40 feet wide.[60] This was pulled down the same year. About the same time Lady Davenant set up a nursery theatre in the Barbican, 90 feet long by 45 feet wide. These two theatres are mentioned here to draw attention to the overall size and proportion of their respective plans, showing the general pattern of the time.

5 The fan-shaped auditorium

In January, 1672, the Theatre Royal was burned down in a fire[1] which is thought to have started in the orange woman's store under the stairs at the back of the playhouse. As a result the King's Players were forced to move to Lisle's Tennis Court, which they occupied for two years, while their new playhouse was being erected on the same site as the first to the designs of Sir Christopher Wren. A longitudinal section through a playhouse (fig.60) designed by Wren[2] has a measured length of approximately 113 feet, which is sufficiently close to the known length of the site of the first theatre, including the open yard, to be generally accepted as being a design for the new theatre.[3] Whether it is the design finally adopted is not known, and it has been argued that as the drawing had been twice torn across it had been discarded, but at least some of the features shown appear in later authenticated drawings of this theatre, and it may by now be safely assumed that, even if the precise details are not as built, in the main this section can be taken to indicate the general appearance of Wren's Drury Lane as finally constructed in 1674. Drawings of the exterior show a rectangular building. A map of 1720[4] shows it divided into six bays each with a tall rectangular window, the whole covered with a hipped roof, and the same features are seen in a map of 1686.[5] The site was still the same enclosed court approached from Bridges Street and Drury Lane by two narrow passages. Additional land to the south of the theatre connected with Little Russell Court and Vinegar Yard had been leased, c. 1662-4,[6] on which was erected a scene-room 'for the mekeing and providing of Scenes, Machins, Cloathes, apparell, and other things to be used in or relating to the acting of Comedies, Tragedies, and other Interludes at the said Theatre, or in any other place where the company . . . shall act.'[7]

A drawing of the frontispiece to the play of *Ariadne*, as published in 1674, shows the stage opening[8] separating the proscenium and the scenic stages, flanked by coupled Corinthian pilasters, and with a curved stage front – both features which can be reflected in the Wren section.

The section (fig.60) shows most of the features which so far have only been surmised in

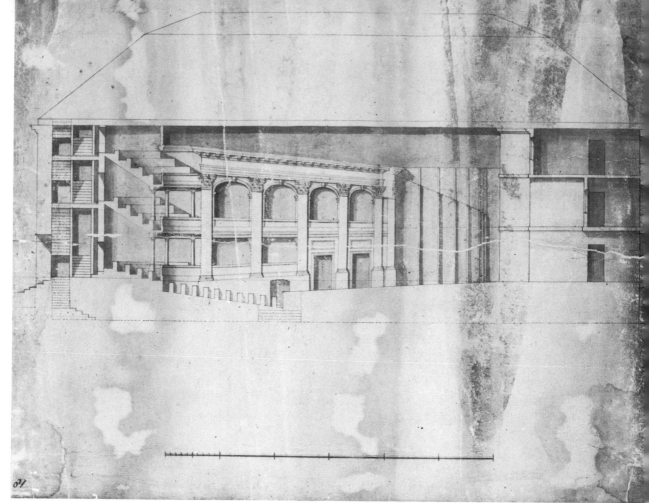

Fig.60. Longitudinal section through a playhouse by Wren

the previous theatres: the sloping pit entered by a door from a passage beneath the side boxes; the two tiers of boxes and the upper gallery, as well as the proscenium doors. The stage combined both proscenium and scenic areas together with what may reasonably be interpreted as a rear vista area flanked by backstage rooms, presumably dressing rooms and a green room, or the actors' social room. Both actors' and scenic stages are on one continuous slope, the rear vista area only being flat. One distinctive feature that is immediately notice-able is the manner in which the side wall of the auditorium was designed to be built in perspective, reducing in height as it nears the scenic area. Here is valuable evidence of the appearance of these various features, which it would be useful to expand if possible; and once again there is written evidence which helps towards this end. By 1696 alterations were made to the building by the management which were described by Colley Cibber in his *Apology* of 1740 as follows:

'It must be observ'd, then, that the Area, or Platform of the old Stage, projected about four Foot forwarder, in a Semi-oval Figure, parallel to the Benches of the Pit; and that the former lower Doors of Entrance for the Actors, were brought down between the two foremost (and then only) Pilasters; in the Place of which Doors, now the two

Stage-Boxes are fix't. That where the Doors of Entrance now are, there formerly stood two additional Side-Wings, in front to a full Set of Scenes, which had then almost a double Effect, in their Loftiness, and Magnificence.

'By this Original Form, the usual Station of the Actors, in almost every Scene, was advanc'd at least ten Foot nearer to the Audience, than they now can be; because, not only from the Stage's being shorten'd, in front, but likewise from the additional Interposition of those Stage-Boxes, the Actors (in respect to the Spectators, that fill them) are kept so much more backward from the main Audience, than they us'd to be:

'But when the Actors were in Posession of that forwarder Space, to advance upon, the Voice was then more in the Centre of the House, so that the most distant Ear had scarce the least Doubt, or Difficulty in hearing what fell from the weakest Utterance: All Objects were thus drawn nearer to the Sense: every painted Scene was stronger; every grand Scene and Dance more extended; every rich, or fine-coloured Habit had a more lively Lustre: Nor was the minutest Motion of a Feature (properly changing with the Passion, or Humour it suited) ever lost, as they frequently must be in the Obscurity of too great a Distance: And how valuable an Advantage the Facility of hearing distinctly is to every well-acted Scene, every common Spectator is a Judge.'[9]

Colley Cibber's comments describe changes that took place prior to 1696, and these as we have seen included the removal of the front four feet of the stage to increase either the size of the pit, or to create an orchestral area, and the consequent replacement of the 'lower Doors of Entrance' by stage boxes. It may also be noted that Wren's side walls had been drastically altered earlier by the removal of the heavy pilasters, which undoubtedly occupied valuable space into which additional audience could be squeezed, retaining only those 'two foremost (and then only) Pilasters' which had flanked the now removed stage doors. This assumption is warranted by the descriptive comments on the later Adam alterations of 1775 that the feeling of lightness achieved at that time was made possible by the removal of 'the old heavy square Pillars on each Side of the Stage.'[10] If this was the case it would set the pattern for the inclusion of pairs of giant orders flanking the prosceniums of such theatres as Shepherd's Covent Garden (fig.74) and the Bristol Theatre Royal (fig.79). The side walls of the proscenium, incorporating the replaced doors of entrance, had presumably been extended back on to the stage to the position of those 'two additional Side-Wings' which had stood in front of the 'full Set of Scenes'.

A visitor to England in 1698 described the pit as

'an Amphitheatre, fill'd with Benches without Backboards, and adorn'd and cover'd with green Cloth. Men of Quality, particularly the younger sort, some Ladies of Reputation and Vertue, and abundance of Damsels that hunt for Prey, sit all together in this Place, Higgledy-piggledy, chatter, toy, play, hear, hear not. Farther up, against the Wall, under the first Gallery, and just opposite to the Stage, rises another Amphitheatre, which is taken up by Persons of the best Quality, among whom are generally very few Men. The Galleries, whereof there are only two Rows, are fill'd with none but ordinary People, particularly the Upper one.'[11]

This theatre lasted until 1791, but a major alteration was undertaken in 1775, when the Adam brothers completely remodelled the interior, as may be seen from the engraving which they published in their *Works of Architecture*.[12] Three scale drawings relating to this alteration exist in the Soane Museum. The first (fig.61) is titled 'Design of a Ceiling for the Theatre Royal, Drury Lane . . . July 19th, 1775'.[13] The second is a rejected design for the ceiling[14] and the third a section through the side boxes showing the 'Method proposed for finishing the Front of the Stage which covers the first Curtain and is never changed. The Apotheosis of Shakespear by the Tragic and Comic Muses . . . May 8th, 1775'.[15] All these drawings will be discussed in greater detail when the Georgian theatre is considered. Their

Fig.61. Design for ceiling of Drury Lane, by Robert Adam, 1775

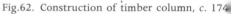

Fig.62. Construction of timber column, c. 174

present value is in providing the additional information which was required before it was possible to attempt a reconstruction (fig.63) based on Wren's longitudinal section.

It will be noted that the plan (fig.61) shows only the ceiling of the auditorium within the limits of the side boxes, the front walls of which splay outwards so that the auditorium increases in width as one moves away from the stage, the boxes growing correspondingly narrower until, some 36 feet into the auditorium, they curve round to meet the outer walls of the theatre. At this point the ceiling measures an overall width of 53 feet 2 inches, which, when taken with the thickness of the walls indicated on the Wren section, would neatly fit the known width of the site. It has already been noted that the Corinthian order which decorates the side walls of Wren's auditorium decreases in size as it advances towards the stage, providing an illusion of perspective that would be more complete if the walls at the same time sloped inward to the distant vanishing point towards which the vertical lines are converging. Baroque examples of architecture follow this rule[16] and it would be most natural for Wren to design in this manner, indeed it is hard to imagine him designing in any other way given the opportunity to create a complete architectural environment around the perspective scene. This is precisely the arrangement which the Adam ceiling shows, but if Robert Adam was making such sweeping changes as his interior view (figs.81,82) suggests, how can we be sure that his box fronts were built on the same lines as those of Wren's earlier boxes?

In the late 18th century theatres there was an independence of design between the enclosing walls of the pit, which were normally of masonry or brick (fig.104), and the upper structure of boxes and galleries, which were normally of timber. The Guildhall at King's Lynn was adapted in late Restoration times into a playhouse, and until 1949 the structural remains of the proscenium stage could be seen supporting its own plaster ceiling[17]. In this example the proscenium ceiling was separate from the ceiling to the rest of the auditorium, which was arranged at a slightly higher level. Three timber posts on either side marked the divisions between a wide box and a narrower proscenium door, and marks on the ceiling indicated that these posts were covered by classical pilasters of timber or plaster similar in their size and form to those indicated by Wren.

It is possible, therefore, that Wren's Corinthian pilasters were built around similar timber posts (fig.62), standing on a solid structural wall separating the pit from the passage beneath the side boxes. An opening in this wall is seen on the section giving access from the pit down steps into the side passage. If one looks carefully at the Adam interior similar entry doors may be noted on either side, although now placed further to the right than is indicated on the Wren section. These, however, stand out as the one feature which is out of accord with an otherwise pleasantly co-ordinated design, intrusively cutting into the rhythm of the box front decoration. Robert Adam is hardly likely to have created such a botched-up job if he had been starting his design completely from scratch, and one is led inevitably to the conclusion that he was attempting to assimilate existing features into his own design, accepting the *fait accompli* of the existing pit wall and passage, as the previous designers had done before him, when much of Wren's upper structure had been removed, leaving only the two pairs of pilasters flanking the proscenium stage. Adam now replaced this upper structure and 'the old heavy square pillars on each side of the stage' by his own much lighter design. If this is so then we have a link between the earlier and later box fronts, and may assume that Wren's auditorium walls followed the same lines as those indicated on the Adam ceiling plans.

By relating the ceiling plans to Wren's section it is possible to develop a ground plan of his theatre. In preparing earlier reconstructions of this building[18] it had been assumed that the Adam auditorium would have stopped on the same line as that indicated on the Wren section, on the upstage edge of the upper of the twin pilasters. The discovery of a plan of 1778,[19] by Dr Sheppard, showing the enclosing walls of the theatre at that time and the surrounding buildings, also indicates the line of the 'Frontispiece' as being 68 feet from the inside of the west wall on the centre line of the theatre, or 5 feet 3 inches further east than Wren's, a position which makes a great deal more sense of Cibber's comments than did the previous assumption.

This new position for the ceiling plan, when related to the Wren section, makes only slight differences in the positions of the side walls on plan, but these slight variations are sufficient to permit all the curves on the plan to be struck from a single centre, in place of the numerous centres used in the previous reconstruction. Cibber mentioned that the semi-oval stage front was parallel to the benches of the pit, and, as was noted earlier (fig.57), any informed designer creating a theatre in the classical manner would have attempted to incorporate the closest possible approximation to a semi-circular cavea. The *Ariadne* drawing shows a curving stage front flanked by straight faces, and in this new reconstruction the dotted line behind the stage front on the section has been interpreted as representing this straight section of stage front, an assumption that permits the curve of benches and stage front to approximate a little more closely to a semi-circle than did the previous arrangement.

The amphitheatre and gallery fronts were used as the datum for all the curves, as their centre and ends are clearly defined on the section, and the benches and rear wall are concentric with them. The omission of the side passages at upper levels leading from the ends of the foyers to the side boxes – as indicated on the previous reconstruction – permits the bench ends to strike the side walls in the exact positions indicated on the section, with the exception of those in the front boxes where the variation shown on the section is so extreme that it can only be assumed that here there was an error of draughtsmanship on Wren's part. As before, the columns, when transposed from the section, are found to fall into place on the line of the front bench as indicated on the section, and to be spaced regularly across the total distance, so that each column is well positioned to support a structurally feasible section of gallery approximately 10 feet wide. If the end columns appear to play a less constructional part, nevertheless their accuracy of positioning appears to be vouched for by the angle and positioning of the corbel bracket supporting the projecting front of the galleries, one over each column, which may be seen to align with the edge of the outermost of the great pilasters.

The removal of the side passages, included in the previous reconstruction, appears at first sight to leave the side boxes without access, but two other theatres indicate how Wren may have made provision for this. In both Covent Garden (figs.73,74) and the Bristol Theatre Royal (figs.76,79) narrow stairs with straight flights and winders may be seen built into the thickness of the outer walls. Bristol, as will be noted later (p.112), incorporated many features from Drury Lane, and the stairs that are still to be seen (fig.64) and used there may well be one of them.

When Drury Lane was adapted by the Adam brothers 'A Spectator'[20] commented that 'The Stairs to the second and third tiers of Boxes I found were projected out of the House beyond the Old Walls, which gives a space to make them much wider and more convenient'. At this time extra space had been acquired outside the theatre, and so it is likely that Wren's boxes were approached in a similar manner to those at Bristol, and such stairs have now been included in the revised reconstruction, providing access to a narrow passage. However, even the improved stairs mentioned above were not acceptable to Tate Wilkinson when he commented:

Fig.63. The Theatre Royal, Drury Lane, Wren, 1674: scale reconstruction

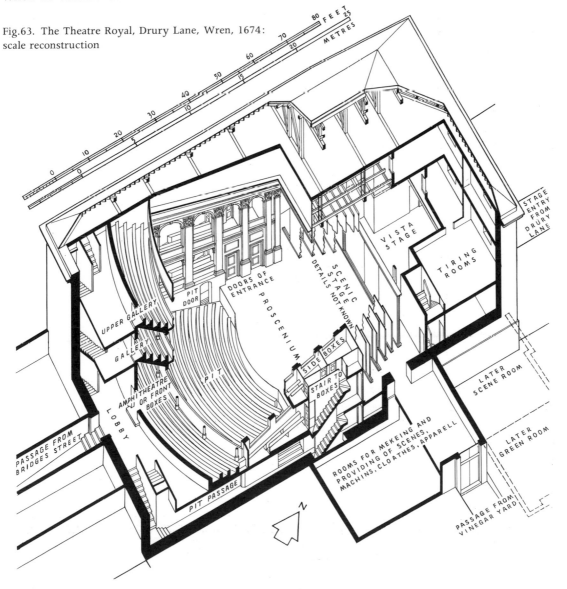

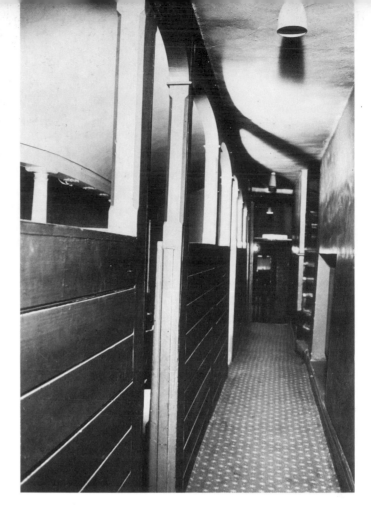

Fig.64. The Theatre Royal, Bristol:
passage at rear of side boxes

'at present the stair-case to the *Upper boxes* at Drury Lane is so narrow, that should an alarm of fire happen, the persons in the two upper tiers of boxes would be thrown into such confusion, should they open at the same time the different doors, the passage is so strait and they would so effectually block up each other, that not one single soul could escape.'[21]

Wren's suggestion on the section of four side wings and a set of backshutters has been interpreted on the reconstruction to require grooves for these features, with a space beyond for scenes of relieve and a skycloth, and a central bay at stage level running back to the rear wall to provide greater depth when required for special vista effects. Tiring rooms, and no doubt the green room, were probably arranged in the corners of the stage and above the vista area, with stairs, the exact position of which has had to be assumed, leading up to them. The space under the stage must have been used as a machine room from which the stage traps could be worked, together with any other machinery necessary for special effects and the movement of scenery.

The reconstruction (fig.63) illustrates well the various features of a Restoration playhouse, and its development from the court and public theatres of the late 16th and early 17th centuries. The proscenium, or actors' stage, is seen to be completely within the limits of the auditorium, and is approached by four proscenium doors, one pair on either side. The scenic stage is set beyond the limits of the auditorium, from which it is separated by the

Fig.65. Interior of
Drury Lane, 1674

front curtain, drawn up on either side behind a painted frontispiece, possibly depicting the Corinthian pilasters shown on the *Ariadne* drawing, and continuing the lines of the Corinthian entablature across the stage. The auditorium, divided into pit, boxes and gallery, arranged in a fan-shape with its side walls built in perspective, illustrates Swift's description of 1704: 'The Contrivance and Structure of our Modern Theatres . . . the Pit is sunk below the Stage . . . the Boxes are built round, and raised to a Level with the Scene.'[22] The majority of seats were admirably placed for viewing and hearing the actor situated on the stage proper within the limits of the auditorium, with the scenery forming a background feature. If the side boxes did not see the scene too well, they were reasonably placed for viewing the actor on his stage. Wren may have considered that their occupants came to be seen rather than to see, and perhaps sacrificed ideal conditions here in order to provide what he obviously considered to be a far more important feature, namely, the continuance of the perspective of the scene into the auditorium so that one would link with the other, especially when viewed from the position of the royal box, which was centrally placed on the axis of the stage in the first tier of boxes, as were the royal boxes in the previous theatres, with the royal crest displayed above. The placing of seats in these side positions would anyway have been an acceptable continuance of the conditions already in existence. One feature that has had to be omitted from the reconstruction is the nature, and exact position, of any openings in the stage floor, which is known from *The Tatler* of the 26th November, 1709, to have been 'full of Trap-Doors'.[23]

The perspective drawing of the interior (fig.65) shows that the view from the extreme side boxes was not so bad as might have been expected from the plan, and it underlines the manner in which the single curve of the amphitheatres gives the majority of the audience perfect viewing conditions of both actor and scene. One can appreciate Cibber's glowing appreciation of this playhouse with the voice of the actor centrally placed in the house, so that the most distant ear could hear the weakest utterance. Indeed, by extending the perspective lines of the scene into the shape of the auditorium Wren managed to arrange his seating with the ideal sight-lines for the maximum number of persons.

During the reign of Charles II, the habit of seating people on the stage appears to have been controlled,[24] probably by direct command of the King. Nevertheless it was the habit of gentlemen of quality to make their way backstage to the Green Room and the tiring rooms, where the actresses were no doubt the main attraction. This suggests that there must have been a direct means of access from the auditorium to the backstage, shown on the reconstruction as an extension of the passages serving the boxes. By the end of the century the audience were back on the stage, and in spite of royal decrees that 'no person of what quality soever presume to go behind the scenes, or come upon the stage, either before or during the acting of the play'[25] the nuisance continued unabated, so that in 1709 *The Tatler* said of Drury Lane that 'There has not been known so great a Concourse of Persons of Distinction; the Stage itself was covered with Gentlemen and Ladies, and when the Curtain was drawn, there appeared also a very splendid Audience.'[26] William Hogarth, illustrating John Gay's *The Beggar's Opera* (fig.66), shows the audience confined behind low walls or screens, probably of canvas painted to resemble draperies with fringes and tassels.

Fig.66. Audience seated on either side of stage: *The Beggar's Opera* by Hogarth

In 1682 the two companies of the Duke's and King's Men were merged into one which performed at the Theatre Royal under the control of Christopher Rich. Under Rich the old system by which the company shared the profits was superseded by the payment of salaries. The older actors were dissatisfied with Rich's management, and they broke away to form a new company under Thomas Betterton, in 1695 moving into Lisle's Tennis Court. By 1696, as has already been noted, Rich had cut some four feet from the front of the Drury Lane stage, and the lower doors, which were now moved into the scenic area, had been replaced by boxes providing additional seating for the audience. Stage and auditorium were lit by six rings of candles, each candle set in a brass socket, which were suspended above the stage, with a great central chandelier in the auditorium.[27]

In 1692 Andrea Pozzo published his *Rules and Examples of Perspective Proper for Painters and Architects*,[28] an English translation of which was published in 1707, with the approbation of Wren, Vanbrugh and Hawksmoor. In this Pozzo included a diagram of a theatre in which a rectangular hall is shown equally divided into stage and auditorium (fig.67). Directly adjoining the stage is a railed-off area for the musicians, beyond which is an area of flat floor for the use of standing spectators, contained by a horseshoe of boxes – loges – arranged on five levels. The partitions separating the boxes are all aligned on the distant vanishing point of the scenes on the raised stage. The side scenes are here set in oblique grooves in what Pozzo calls the Italian manner, and he admits that it is more difficult to paint the scene for grooves placed thus, indeed he suggests the difficulty 'may be avoided by fixing the Grooves parallel to the Poscene; as is usual in some Places, especially in *Germany*, Nevertheless, the *Italian* Manner has this Advantage, That those who are employ'd to prompt the Actors, and shift the Scenes, &c, are less expos'd to sight, in the Performance of their Business'.

In 1704-5 Vanbrugh designed and built the Queen's Theatre[29] in the Haymarket for Betterton's players, the company continuing meanwhile 'to Act at the Theatre in Little Lincoln's Inn Fields till Her Majesty's Theatre in the Hay-Market be intirely finished'.[30] Vanbrugh's design was built of brick of 'an Excessive Largenesse' and 'very different from any Other House in being,'[31] and was some 130 feet long by 60 feet wide. Unfortunately no plans of this theatre as originally designed exist, as it was considerably altered after it had been open for only two or three years; it has, however, been possible to prepare a tentative reconstruction (fig.68) based on later evidence. A plan and section of the theatre (fig.69) exists as altered,[32] and from this it may be surmised that Vanbrugh used a plan which conformed in many respects to the sketch plan (fig.57) ostensibly prepared by Wren. The pit seating was arranged in a semi-circle centred on the front partition of the large orchestra, 11 feet deep by 36 feet wide, with eleven rows of benches enclosed by a slightly higher amphitheatre of six rows of benches facing the stage. Eight columns supported an upper tier of the same size and seating as the amphitheatre, and above this again was a deeper gallery spread back over the lower access vestibules, with its front supported on further columns set behind the third row of benches of the second tier. Dumont's plan shows

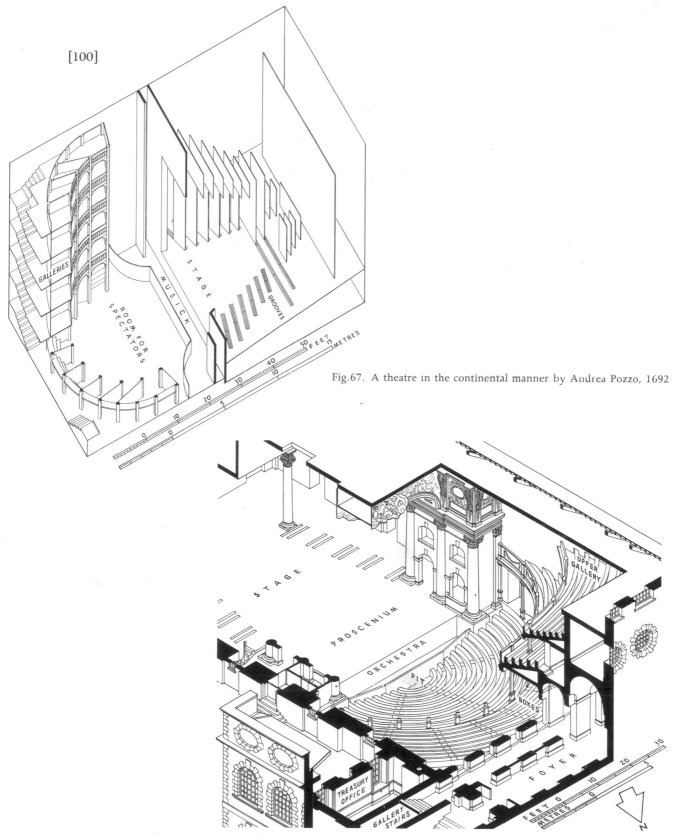

Fig.67. A theatre in the continental manner by Andrea Pozzo, 1692

Fig.68. The Queen's Theatre, Haymarket, by Vanbrugh, 1704–5: scale reconstruction

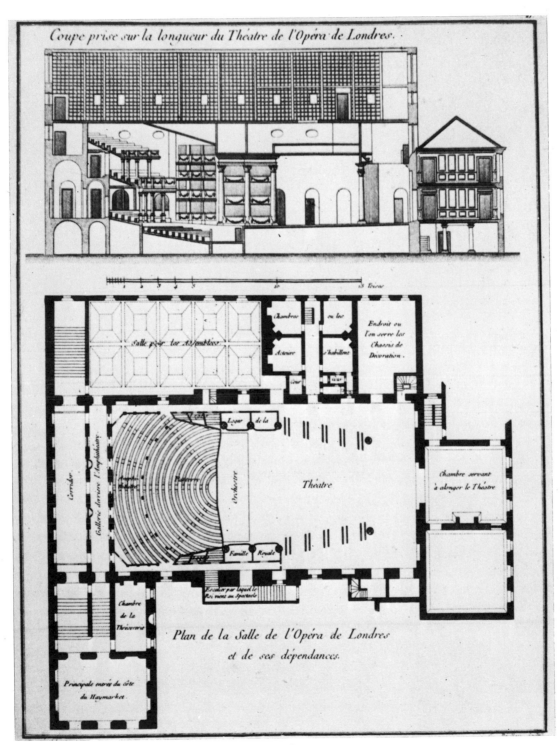

Fig.69. The Queen's Theatre in 1764: plan and section by C. P. M. Dumont.

three tiers each of two boxes on either side of the stage supported between a total of six giant Corinthian columns. The front of the stage lined with the centre columns, and projected some 11 feet into the auditorium, to make a total depth of 60 feet. At 41 feet back from the stage front there was an upper wall supported on two free-standing columns, some 30 feet apart. There was a gallery on either side some 25 feet above the sloping stage. The width of the proscenium stage was 39 feet, with a total width of the main stage between the side walls of 56 feet. A property plan of 1777[33] shows the introduction of a proscenium door on either side, which increased the depth of the proscenium stage by some 8 feet. An early alteration increased the depth of the rear vista stage by some 30 feet, when an arched opening was made in the rear wall of the stage permitting access into a room in the building adjoining the south end of the theatre.

The concentric pattern of the pit did not permit 'normal' entries from beneath the side boxes, such as were seen in Wren's Drury Lane. Instead, it appears to have been approached from its upper level at the point of juncture with the first tier of front boxes and amphitheatre. Colley Cibber in his critical description of the building, written in 1740, gives an idea of the original building which he claims had sacrificed or neglected

> 'every proper Quality and Convenience of a good Theatre . . . to shew the Spectator a vast triumphal Piece of Architecture! And that the best Play, for the Reasons I am going to offer, could not but be under great Disadvantages . . . . For what could their vast Columns, their gilded Cornices, their immoderate high Roofs avail when scarce one Word in ten could be distinctly heard in it? Nor had it, then, the Form it now stands in, which Necessity, two or three Years after, reduced it to: At the first Opening it, the flat Ceiling that is now over the Orchestre was then a Semi-oval Arch that sprung fifteen Feet higher from above the Cornice: the Ceiling over the Pit, too, was still more raised, being one level Line from the highest back part of the upper Gallery to the Front of the Stage: The Front-boxes were a continued Semi-circle to the bare Walls of the House on each Side: This extraordinary and superfluous Space occasion'd such an Undulation, from the Voice of every Actor, that generally what they said sounded like the Gabbling of so many People in the lofty Isles in a Cathedral – The Tone of a Trumpet, or the Swell of an Eunoch's holding Note, 'tis true, might be sweetn'd by it, but the articulate Sounds of a speaking Voice were drown'd by the hollow Reverberations of one word upon another. To this Inconvenience, why may we not add that of its Situation.'[34]

A water colour in the British Museum is said to represent this theatre.[35] It shows a semi-oval arch, such as Cibber mentions, springing apparently from projecting coupled Corinthian columns, which are matched by the scenic wings behind on the main stage. These in no way reflect the giant columns already mentioned, but it has been suggested that this is nevertheless a drawing of this theatre, with the proscenium sides and boxes hidden behind an advanced pair of wings set on either side of the proscenium stage, and masking the stage doors in the manner noted earlier at Dorset Gardens (p.86). Such an arrangement was sometimes used for the performance of operas, to bring the proscenium more into line with the continental opera houses, where the scene came much closer to the audience than was permitted by the English proscenium stage and doors. On these occasions the front curtain too could be advanced to the front line of the stage.

The four tiers of three boxes on either side which form the fan-shaped sides of the pit shown in the Dumont (fig.69) and 1777 plans, were presumably further additions filling in the empty spaces previously occupied by the pit seating, and the ends of the first tier of seats. The decoration of the fronts of these boxes corresponds with that on the front of the first and second galleries, as well as on the fronts of the boxes contained between the Corinthian columns. Two paintings of c. 1724[36] show the theatre in use for a masquerade, for which it was presumably more suited than for the operatic and dramatic performances for which it was originally intended. For these masquerades the pit was floored over level with the stage, and the latter was enclosed by a painted (canvas) ceiling and side hangings. A letter describes such an occasion in the theatre: 'The floor of the pit is on this occasion raised to a level with the stage, and the whole forms a grand and beautiful Saloon. There is also another room behind this, which is hung with light blue damask, bordered with gold and in a very elegant design. There are no windows to be seen, which produces a singular effect.'[37] These paintings show the flat ceiling of the Dumont section, mentioned by Cibber, and we can see that it was painted to represent what may perhaps be taken to be a view through a circular balustraded opening into a cupola above. Flanking the opening can be seen the expected Corinthian columns, but there would appear to be only two tiers of boxes on either side, the upper of which has a semi-oval arch with decorations in the space above, suggesting that the three tiers of the 1774 section were a later addition. An engraving (fig.70) by Hogarth of 1724 shows the outside of Vanbrugh's theatre, with a banner depicting the interior. The shafts of tall columns are shown on either side, and

Fig.70. The Queen's Theatre, from an engraving by Hogarth, 1724

between the upper pairs, there is the suggestion of a tall arched opening, with a smaller box-like opening above, seeming to suggest that at that date proscenium doors were incorporated in the scheme, the architectural character of which has a strong flavour of Vanbrugh's design. The façade shown by Hogarth was presumably that of the entrance wing giving on to the Haymarket, with its three rusticated arched openings at ground level, rusticated arched windows at first floor level, and similarly treated oval windows above, which accord with the oval windows shown opening into both auditorium and stage on the Dumont section. The main building appears on a *Bird's Eye View of London* of 1710 by Kip[38] and is here shown as a tall rectangular block with a pitched roof, crowned by finials at either end, and with three lighting or ventilation flèches on the ridge. The same arrangement of windows is shown, but with the addition of an attic storey with horizontal windows or panels inserted.

Taking the various sources mentioned above, and working backwards from the reconstruction based on the Dumont drawings (fig.71), it has been possible to prepare the reconstruction of Vanbrugh's original design (fig.68). Although Cibber speaks of the 'flat ceiling that is now over the Orchestre' being previously a 'Semi-oval Arch', the whole of the flat ceiling shown on the Dumont drawings as covering the orchestra and the stage has not been interpreted as having such an arch, but only that portion over the stage related to the upper side bays. This is so that it may conform to the break in the entablature shown on the Dumont section, which has no meaning there, but could have had earlier meaning if related to the arch. The corbelled design of the attic storey has been suggested by the British Museum water colour, as have also the details of the arch, which on comparative measurements were found to fit very closely to the dimensions of the building recorded on the Dumont drawings, when the 'Ceiling over the Pit' is carried through on 'one level line from the highest back part of the Upper Gallery.'

Arched proscenium doors with arched openings above on the lines of the Hogarth sketch are included between the giant orders, and on removal of the four tiers of boxes on either side of the auditorium it was found possible to continue the line of the frontboxes and the middle gallery above in a 'Semicircle to the bare walls of the House on either side.' The oval windows in the side walls of the building, although hidden by the ceiling on the reconstruction, have been continued to form decorative features in the attic storey over the giant orders. In view of Cibber's mention of 'bare walls', no attempt has been made to show decoration at this point, although in view of the widespread use of architectural mural painting as carried out by such artists as Thornhill, Laguerre or Verrio at this time, it is highly likely that Vanbrugh's architectural details were continued on the side walls in paint, like those at Sabbioneta (fig.44).

It is of some interest that Vanbrugh did not follow Wren's perspective pattern, and placed the giant orders on either side of the proscenium parallel to one another, rather than fan-shaped, and yet when the tiers of boxes were introduced on either side of the auditorium, they were, for no good perspective reason, arranged opening out on a splay in what was obviously by then the accepted pattern for an auditorium.

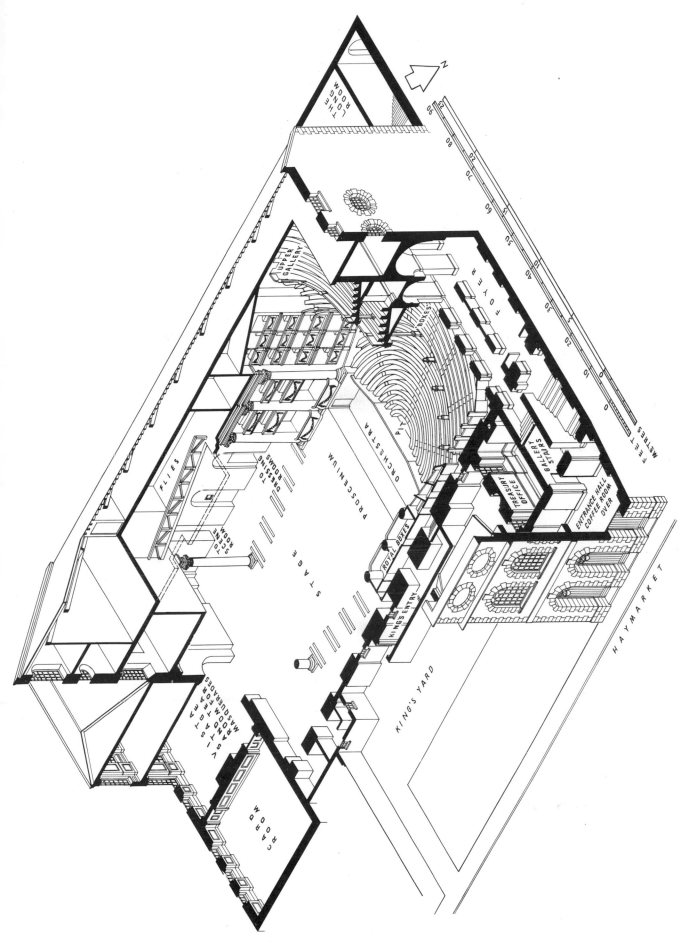

Fig.71. The Queen's Theatre after the alterations of 1707–8: scale reconstruction

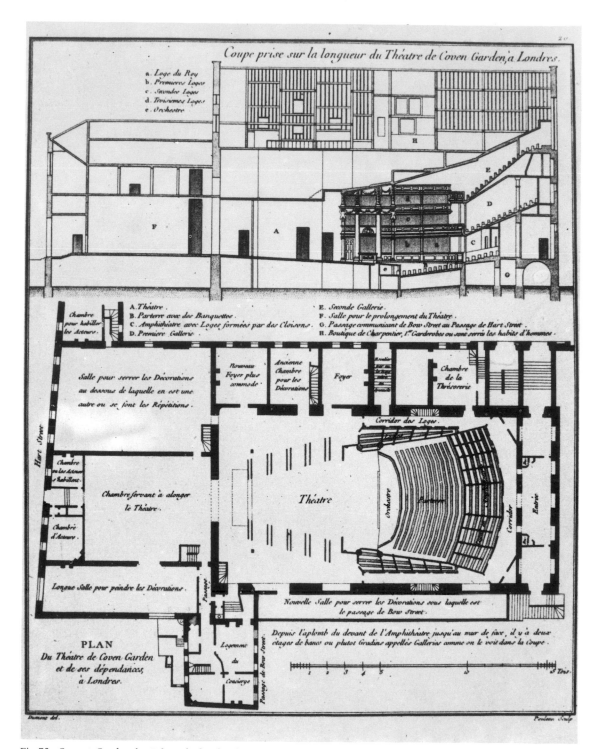

Fig.72. Covent Garden by Edward Shepherd, 1731–2: plan and section by C. P. M. Dumont

In December, 1732, John Rich, son of Christopher, moved his company to a new theatre designed for him by Edward Shepherd in Bow Street, Covent Garden. Dumont also recorded this building (fig.72) and from the plan the site appears to have measured some 175 feet from north to south by 95 feet from east to west, with projections both to east and west. The stage, auditorium and foyer, occupied a block some 119 feet long by 64 feet wide, with a 21 feet wide wing along the west side, which is shown on Dumont's plan as containing stairs to the first and second galleries, manager's offices, and the entrance to the Royal Box. Adjoining the stage is a room designated in French as 'Foyer', which was presumably the Green Room, with next to this the 'Old Scene Room' and then a further Green Room, described as more commodious. Presumably the first was for the lesser actors, the second for the more important members of the company. 'A Carpenters Workshop a Painteing Roome Such Wardrobes and other conveniencys' were to be made 'in the roofe of the said intended Theatre.'[39] These rooms were later supplemented by those shown on Dumont's plan to the north of the stage. Behind the stage, through an opening some 13 to 14 feet wide, was a large vista area, beyond which was the stage entrance from Hart Street, flanked by dressing rooms. To the east was a large scene room, some 35 feet by 51 feet, beneath which was a rehearsal room, and to the west a scene-painting room, 15 feet wide by some 51 feet long.

According to the articles of agreement between Shepherd and Rich 'the Stage the Front and Side Boxes Gallarys and Benches'[40] in this theatre were to be 'finished in as good a manner in all respects as those at the Theatre in Lincoln's Inn Fields', which has been interpreted as meaning that the new theatre should be modelled on the interior of the Lincoln's Inn Fields theatre as rebuilt by Rich, c. 1713-4, but which seems to refer not so much to its form as to the quality of the materials and finishes. Whatever its source, however, we may once again note the preference for the fan-shaped auditorium, with the lines of the box fronts throughout continuing the diminishing perspective scene.

As may be seen from the reconstruction (fig.73) based on Dumont's drawings, the front 12 feet of the stage formed a proscenium area within the auditorium, with a proscenium door and stage box on either side. These latter projected forward on to the stage, and were flanked by Corinthian columns similar to those used by Vanbrugh, on whose theatre this was originally reputed to be based.[41] These stage boxes are referred to in the original agreement, where it is specified that 'the Boxes over the Stage Door and the Boxes over the two Side Boxes adjoyneing to the Kings and Princes Boxes should be ornamented with Entabliture'. This suggests that although a large 'King's front box' was provided, additional royal boxes were also situated in the French manner, adjoining the proscenium doors, in the position they will now occupy in the majority of subsequent theatres. These were presumably decorated when needed for the royal occupants, as an inventory includes 'Three canopys to the Kings and Princes boxes.'[42]

This ornamentation applied to the three tiers of boxes flanking the proscenium stage, the boxes flanking the Corinthian columns being themselves enclosed by minor Ionic orders

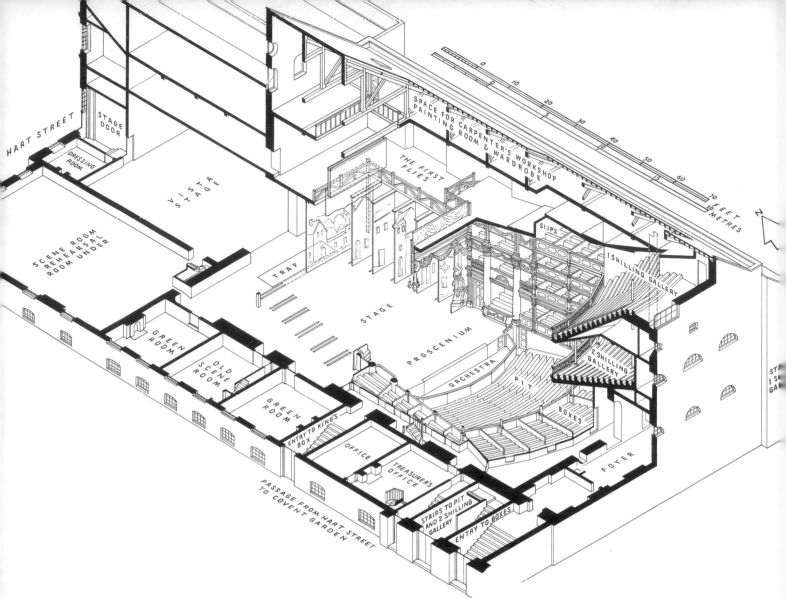

Labels within the illustration: HART STREET · STAGE DOOR · DRESSING ROOM · VISTA STAGE · SPACE FOR CARPENTER'S WORKSHOP PAINTING ROOM & WARDROBE · THE FIRST FLIES · SCENE ROOM REHEARSAL ROOM UNDER · TRAP · SLIPS · 1 SHILLING GALLERY · STAGE · PROSCENIUM · 2 SHILLING GALLERY · GREEN ROOM · OLD SCENE ROOM · GREEN ROOM · ORCHESTRA · PIT · BOXES · ENTRY TO KING'S BOX · OFFICE · TREASURER'S OFFICE · FOYER · PASSAGE FROM HART STREET TO COVENT GARDEN · STAIRS TO PIT AND 2 SHILLING GALLERY · ENTRY TO BOXES · 0 10 20 30 40 50 60 70 FEET · 5 15 25 METRES

Fig.73. Covent Garden: scale reconstruction

at the lower levels and by thermes above. The whole of this three-bay area was reflected by a sloping ceiling, or sounding board, richly decorated with painting. The fronts of these balconies (those over the proscenium doors and opposing box were decorated with balusters) are horizontal. Beyond this proscenium area the box tiers continue at the same levels, but now rise gently as if continuing the practice set in Wren's Drury Lane without the under-standing of its original perspective purpose. The ceiling to the auditorium was raised above that of the proscenium, and permitted the introduction of additional seats above the side boxes, known later as 'slips'. These side boxes were serviced by narrow winding stairs built into the thickness of the wall (fig.74).

Doors on either side beneath the boxes gave entry to the pit, Separated from the stage by a large orchestral area, the pit, containing twelve backless benches, sloped upward towards the front boxes. Here the wide central box was flanked by four narrower boxes on either side, divided by low partitions and fitted with six rows of benches. A more

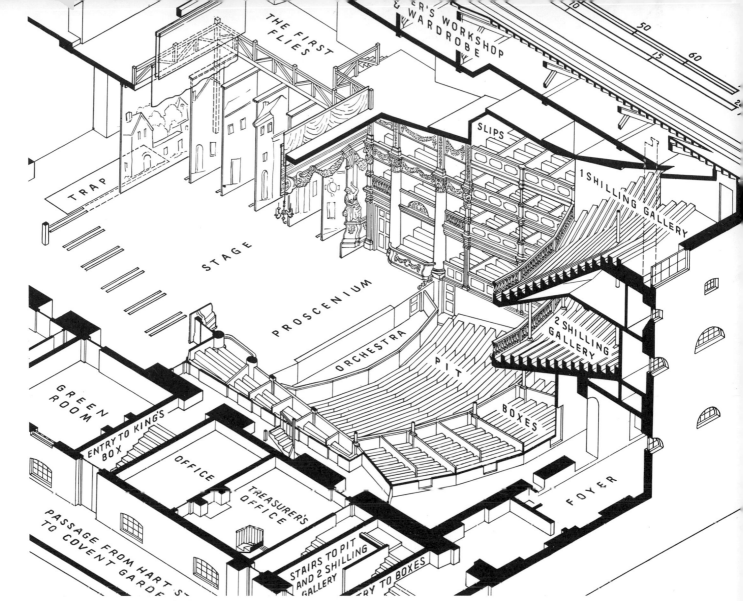

Fig.74. Covent Garden: detail of Fig.73

economical use of timber may be noted in this building, the wasteful curved shapes of benches and partitions in the earlier buildings being here replaced by straight lengths. The middle gallery, at the level of the second tier of boxes, extended over the ground floor foyers and contained fourteen rows of benches, while the upper gallery, set midway between upper side boxes and slips, extended even further back to accommodate sixteen rows. Both galleries were constructed of wood, raking joists resting on timber posts with iron cores at the front, and the brick wall of the great lobby behind.[43]

It will be appreciated that, although the playhouse area is very little larger than that of Wren's Drury Lane, a great many more seats have, nevertheless, been crowded into the space. This has been accomplished by omitting the large classical order, with the exception of the two columns adjoining the stage area, thus gaining considerable space which in Wren's design had been taken up by solid areas of timber and plaster. Further galleries had been fitted into the height of the auditorium, and the space occupied on all floor levels in Wren's design by foyers behind the front galleries was here taken over by additional depth for the galleries themselves. The orchestra was apparently large enough to seat friends of the company, visiting theatre managers, or actors not appearing in the current production, in addition to the musicians. By 1763, however, an illustration depicting the Fitzgiggo Riot[44] shows a much reduced orchestra, leaving room at either end for benches set at right angles to the stage, where these persons might presumably be seated instead. In this illustration the theatre is shown as illuminated by candles set in a central chandelier, and on four hoops similar to those already described at Drury Lane. Further illumination was provided by candles in brackets on the walls and by individual candles provided for the musicians.

The whole stage, excluding the rear vista area added later, was built on a slope. Lines indicating side wings (p.154) are shown on the Dumont plan grouped in pairs, with five pairs on either side. The tops of the side wings were supported in upper grooves, '12 top grooves with 6 iron braces and ropes',[45] presumably attached to the underside of galleries on either side of the stage, called in the original agreement 'the Lodgements over the Stage for the flyings' and 'the first flies', and known today as the fly floors or galleries. These were to be 'framed with good yellow Joysts to be Seven Inches by Nine Inches and the Common Joysts Seven Inches by Three Inches covered with Yellow Deals without Sap on each Side of the Stage fifteen foot wide'.[46] They were fixed some 20 feet above stage level. There were traps, 'the grave trap and 3 others'[47] in the stage floor, but the only one for which there is visual evidence is the large trap at the back of the stage for scenes.

Both the space above the stage and below was filled with machinery for working the scenes. The inventory lists among other items 'the great wheel and spindle, a small wheel and barrel to the circular fly . . . 4 barrels, weights and ropes to the flies . . . The barrel to the Stages with ropes, weights, etc; . . . the scene barrel fixt with cog wheels . . . 6 borders and 6 pair of cloudings fixt to battens with barrels, wts, and ropes, . . . the great counterpoize to all the traps'.[48] On these features we have no visual evidence, but later drawings will show some of these items as more information becomes available in chronological sequence.

Shepherd also designed a theatre in Goodman's Fields, which opened in October, 1732.[49] Although only Covent Garden and Drury Lane held patents to perform plays, numerous other theatres were opening during the 18th century, getting round the restrictions on the performance of plays in various ingenious ways. Goodman's Fields was a much smaller theatre, measuring only 88 feet by 46 feet 6 inches, but it would appear from a plan made in 1786 by William Capon that once again Shepherd had used the fan-shaped auditorium, which we now see to have been a feature of all the theatres so far examined in this period. When Capon investigated this theatre[50] (fig.75) there were seven benches in the pit, six 1 foot wide, while the rear seat set against the box front was 1 foot 6 inches. Here the foot space was 1 foot 6 inches, as was also the foot space between the front bench and the orchestra rail. Unlike the benches and box fronts at Covent Garden, which were in five straight facets, the benches and box fronts here followed the same curve as the orchestra rail. The front of the stage was, however, straight, and lined with the lower edge of the single proscenium door on either side. The orchestra was 5 feet wide.

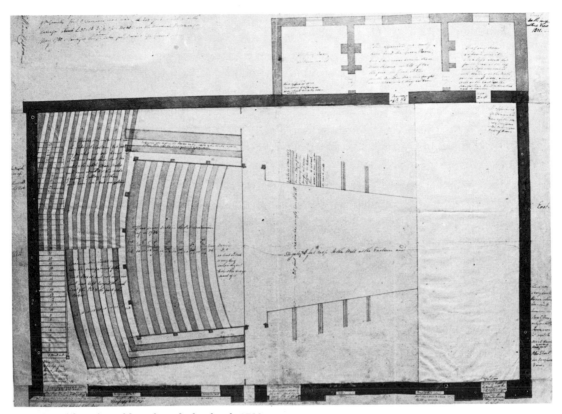

Fig.75. Goodman's Fields, Edward Shepherd, 1732

The fan-shaped auditorium was a valid form as used by Wren, and in using it he placed the majority of the audience in pit, amphitheatre and gallery in the best viewing position in relation to the stage. Indeed it will be seen that by splaying out the side walls the numbers of persons accommodated in the amphitheatre and gallery may be increased. The placing of the side walls so as to create a rectangular pit may slightly improve the sight conditions for those seated in the side boxes, but it does so at the expense of the number of persons who could be seated in more ideal conditions. It is quite possible that Wren thought on these lines, and noted that the fan-shape not only gave him near ideal conditions for the greater part of the audience, but at the same time added the bonus of enclosing the audience within an architectural environment which would make them fully conscious of participating in the perspective scene.

Looked at in this way, the fan-shape is an ideal auditorium form, for the sound spreads out, the vision narrows in, and it will be seen (p.252) that in the end it is to a variant of this form that auditoria eventually return when architects begin to give more detailed consideration to the problems of sight lines and acoustics. Obviously the fan-shape is only valid when a minimum of persons are seated in the side boxes; but even these are not too badly placed while the stage still projects as far into the auditorium as did Wren's, and the emphasis is on the actor, and the voice. But alterations such as were described by Cibber (p.90) changed this delicate balance. In the first place, the stage and actor were drawn back, only four feet to begin with, but even so, far enough to make it that much more difficult for persons in the far side boxes to view the actor, and at the same time their number was doubled if not trebled. The balance of criteria had been changed but was not taken into consideration, the main aim now being to accommodate more audience within an existing structure by 'winding in' (p.164) as many persons as possible. The alterations carried out to Vanbrugh's theatre underline this attitude; here the fan-shape was the only answer as a means of filling in the odd corners of Vanbrugh's auditorium without losing too many seats in the front boxes and galleries, and here, as we have seen, four galleries of spectators were introduced in a position where they actually looked away from the stage, partly hidden anyway by the lower pair of giant columns flanking the proscenium stage. This arrangement was, however, presumably accepted as completely valid. Cibber does not specifically criticise the altered auditorium, unless it is possible to read criticism into the comment on the form in which it then stood which 'Necessity, . . . reduced it to'. Only the original form was criticised, with its superfluous spaces which were now advantageously filled with paying customers.

Although London was the centre of theatrical activity, the provinces were not neglected. The earliest of these provincial theatres which still remains today is the Theatre Royal, Bristol. Building was started in November, 1764, and the theatre was opened on the 30th May, 1766. The architect was James Paty,[51] who appears to have based his design on 'an Elevation Ground Plan and Section of a Theatre Drawn by Mr. Saunders Carpenter of Drury Lane Play House' which were produced at a meeting of the proprietors on 3rd December, 1764.[52] Although representatives of the proprietors 'surveyed and have taken the Measurements of both the playhouses in London, and have also engaged a draft of Drury-lane hᵒ and consulting a very ingenious Carpenter Mr Saunderson the carpenter of the hᵒ'[53] and had also sent for a Model of Drury Lane,[54] it is not clear if the drawings sent by Mr Saunders were measured drawings of Drury Lane in its then condition, or designs for a theatre prepared by him. The phrasing of the minute 'of a Theatre' and the fact that Saunders, the following year, designed a New Theatre (p.116) at Richmond, Surrey, which differed from the fan-shaped plan of both Covent Garden and Drury Lane in that its boxes formed a kind of crescent, suggests the latter. Nevertheless, in size the Bristol theatre must have been based on Drury Lane, as we learn from a contemporary comment[55] that a miscalculation on the part of the workmen engaged in setting out the foundations would have meant that 'the House would have been 8 feet larger in the Clear, than the Theatre Royal in Drury-Lane.' In fact the approximate overall dimensions of the main building, 122 feet by 55 feet, do exceed those of Wren's original building by some 10 feet in length, but are some 2 feet 6 inches to 3 feet narrower in width. The backstage areas at Bristol are very similar in their general arrangement, of a vista stage flanked by dressing rooms, to that noted in Wren's building.

The reconstruction of the theatre shown here (fig.76), represents the building as it was

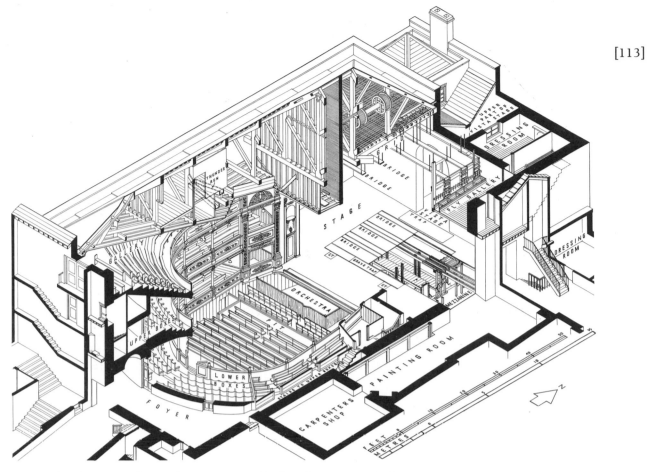

Fig.76. The Theatre Royal, Bristol, James Paty, 1764–6: scale reconstruction

Fig.77. The Theatre Royal, Bristol: auditorium 1943

Fig.78. The Theatre Royal, Bristol:
the gallery before the alterations of 1948

prior to the alterations of 1948, and as such it does not show it in its original form. Some features from the original building are, however, immediately apparent, the most notable being the four great pilasters flanking the sides of what would originally have been the proscenium stage, which projected some 9 feet further into the auditorium from the present stage front. This feature reflects the pattern already noted at this date in both the Covent Garden and Drury Lane theatres, and such an arrangement was to be expected in any theatre with pretentions to grandeur.

In view of the interest in these London theatres it is not surprising to find this feature here, nor is it surprising to note that these pilasters splay outwards so that those at the front of the former stage were 4 feet further apart than the upstage pair. Beyond this point, however, the line of the box fronts changes direction and the outward splay is considerably reduced. At a distance some 2 feet 3 inches short of two bays width, the box fronts curve around on a semi-circle to enclose the pit. At first sight the lines of the box fronts might have been expected to continue the extreme fan-shape set by the first – proscenium – bay, which would then more nearly have accorded with the plan shape to be seen at both London theatres, but this arrangement may by now have been considered one of the imperfections of the London theatres which Saunders improved on when he designed the Richmond, Surrey, theatre 'as a kind of crescent' (p.116), an idea which he may have introduced to the Bristol proprietors. The suggestion has been advanced that this could well be the first use of the continental type of horseshoe auditorium (fig.67) in this country,[56] although it is possible that it is antedated by the Frankfort Gate Theatre, opened in Plymouth in 1758.[57]

The pit would no doubt have been fitted with benches, but at this time they would almost certainly have been backless. It was entered through side doors set sufficiently far from the then stage front to permit the introduction of an orchestra pit some 4 feet wide. When originally built the theatre had nine lower or dress boxes encircling the pit, above which were six upper boxes, three on each side of a central gallery. It is suggested[58] that there was originally no third tier or upper gallery, but if this was the case then the springing line of the roof trusses seems to have been unnecessarily high, being some 6 to 7 feet above the point where a ceiling might reasonably be assumed to have been situated. In 1779 alterations were carried out when additional boxes were introduced into the second tier to form upper front boxes. A writer of the period described how, prior to these alterations, he used to wait 'at the Gallery door and when the door opened scampered up the stairs and then down a long row of benches for the pleasure of sitting exactly over the King's Arms, thinking it delightful to be there one hour before the candles were lighted and two before the performance began!'[59] It would seem from this description as though the centre box at the lower level was designated as the Royal Box with a coat of arms displayed above. At some later date this box front was broken through to provide a more direct access to the pit. During these 1779 alterations 'a large Commodious Scene Room', an elegant tea room and other accommodation were all added. Access to the side boxes was by a passage along the back from a foyer situated beyond a solid curved wall enclosing the rear of the audi-

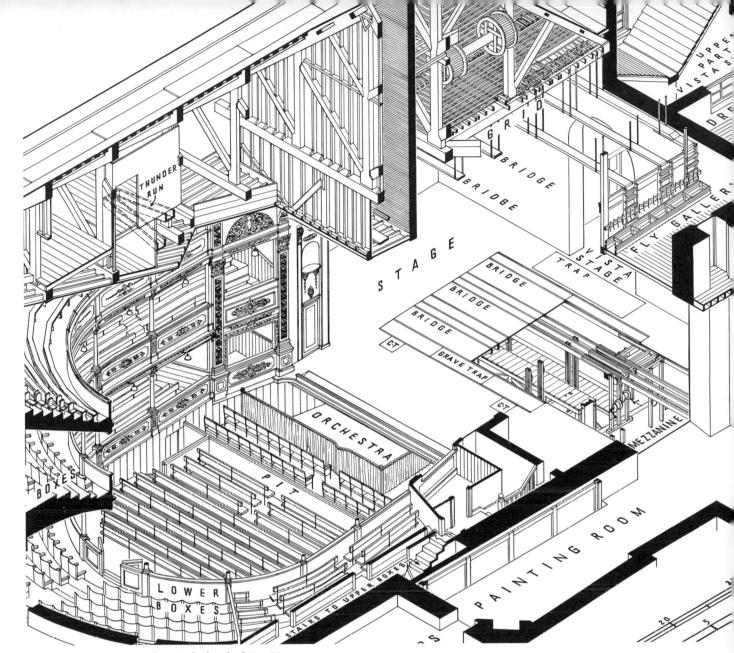

Labels within figure: THUNDER RUN, GRID, BRIDGE, BRIDGE, FLY GALLERY, STAGE, VISTA STAGE TRAP, BRIDGE, BRIDGE, BRIDGE, C.T, GRAVE TRAP, C.T, MEZZANINE, ORCHESTRA, PIT, BOXES, PAINTING ROOM, LOWER BOXES, STAIRS TO UPPER BOXES, 20

Fig. 79. The Theatre Royal, Bristol: detail of Fig. 76

torium, the two tiers of side passages being linked by winding stairs (fig. 64) built into the thickness of the side walls. In 1800 further alterations included the raising of the ceiling to permit the introduction of the present gallery, and presumably the slips. In 1831 a new stage was installed, the wing space enlarged, and a new staircase built to the upper circle, together with improved access to the side boxes and slips.

There are a few spaces in the roof which were floored in, presumably for use as store rooms of one kind or another, and attached to the central roof truss over the auditorium is a thunder run, consisting of wooden channels in which cannon balls could be set running to shake the house with their movement and noise. It is highly possible that until the re-construction of the stage in 1831, the whole of the roof space throughout the length of the building would have been used as a carpenter's shop, as was the normal practice (p.190).

There was a single fly floor, or gallery, on either side of the stage, sloping up parallel with the stage. Some of the items mentioned in the Covent Garden inventory (p.110), which could not be shown on the reconstruction of that theatre for lack of visual evidence, may now be seen here (fig.79). The grave trap and two corner traps (C.T.) are clearly indicated, as are also the wheels and barrels shown above the open grid floor attached to the roof trusses over the stage. This grid, and the nature and purpose of the other openings in the stage floor, dating as they most probably do from 1831, will be discussed when buildings of that period are dealt with (p.208).

Saunders' New Theatre at Richmond, in Surrey, was opened on Saturday, 15th June, 1765.[60] It

'was considered to be a marvel of elegance and completeness. "In it", says a newspaper of the day, "every imperfection in either of the Royal theatres of Drury Lane or Covent Garden is carefully avoided, and every advantage retained; the boxes form a kind of crescent, which renders them commodious; the lobby is as spacious as either of the above theatres; there is but one gallery, which, however, turns out to the advantage of the audience, as it prevents the necessity of having pillars which obstruct the view. The pitt is small, but that seems no inconveniency, as the principal part of the spectators occupy the boxes; a handsome space is allowed for the orchestra; and the panels, in place of being ornamented with a ginger-bread stucco, are painted of a dark colour, which gives the stage an additional degree of light when the curtain is drawn up. The scenes are elegant, and by the connoisseurs the whole is reckoned for its size to be much the best constructed theatre in the British dominions." '

Drawings of the theatre (figs.80a.b.), presumably prepared shortly before its final demolition in 1884, suggest that the auditorium had changed little from the above description. The boxes were separated by the usual low partitions, and those facing the stage each had its own door, as did also the side boxes. On a visit of George III and Queen Charlotte, who would presumably have been seated in one of the stage boxes, those members of the public unable to obtain a seat in the auditorium, which was crowded to excess, were charged by an enterprising management 'for a peep at the august party through the small, glazed, circular apertures of the opposite box-door.'

A pair of proscenium doors faced each other across the stage, each set obliquely to the box fronts, and constructed under an arch of the same width as the pilastered walls containing the doors. A further drawing[61] shows a pit passage beneath the side boxes, with a door at the end leading to the understage areas, and with an indication of an adjoining door on the left which would have led up into the pit.

A further provincial theatre which it is claimed[62] was based on Wren's Drury Lane 'at least as far as the interior is concerned', although the exterior is perhaps more reminiscent of Vanbrugh's Opera House, was the Theatre built in 1757 in Norwich. This building was opened in 1758. In 1800 it was thoroughly adapted, with a number of external additions providing for greater width within the building. The boxes and gallery were rebuilt on an oval plan, with four private boxes next to the stage. The stage too, was rebuilt with the scenes 'worked on an improved principle, by which all the wings are moved at once. Within the first entrance are inward wings which hide the actors from the view of the spectators in the boxes till they make their appearance on the stage.' A description, following further re-decorations carried out in 1813 and 1819, shows that the pit was bounded by three tiers of boxes arranged in an elliptical curve, the centre tier being the dress boxes.

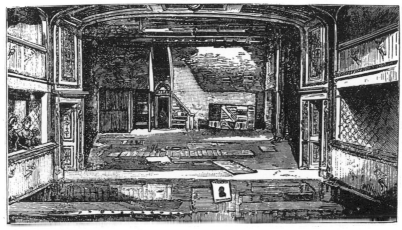

(a) stage from auditorium

(b) auditorium from stage

Fig.80. The New Theatre, Richmond, Surrey, Saunders, 1765

6 The retreat from the proscenium stage

In 1747, David Garrick, who had joined the management of Drury Lane, made further alterations to the building when he enlarged the first gallery. The gradual acquisition of land
surrounding the theatre enabled minor adjustments to be made, such as the formation of a
new entrance to the boxes direct from Russell Street in 1750.[1] Land had earlier been acquired
at the east end behind the stage, and the buildings on it had been used for such purposes
as a wardrobe. At this time Garrick is credited with making alterations to the lighting,
replacing the 'six chandeliers hanging over the stage' and illuminating both stage and
auditorium by lights concealed behind the scenes. He also introduced footlights to the
theatre, first noted in 1670 (p.64), which could be raised and lowered through an opening
at the front of the stage. Such devices seem, however, to have already been in use at Covent
Garden in 1743, when the inventory[2] taken there included such items as the 'counterpoize
to front lamps 170 lbs', which suggests movable footlights, and also '41 sconce candlesticks . . . 5 tin blinds to stage lamps . . . 115 three corner tinn lamps . . . 12 pr. of scene
ladders fixt with ropes . . . 24 blinds to scene ladders, 192 tinn candlesticks to do', which
further suggest that vertical strips of 8 candles each were hung behind each set of side
wings. It is thought that Garrick may have been looking for more efficient methods of
lighting the stage, and had sent to France for samples of their equipment.[3]

Possibly Garrick's most important move, however, was to clear the audience from the
stage. Not only were they now occupying positions on either side of the proscenium stage,
but were ensconced on the scenic stage itself. A description by Tate Wilkinson gives a clear
indication of the situation at this period.

> 'The following advertisement appeared at the bottom of each playbill on any benefit
> of consequence:—"Part of the pit will be railed with the boxes; and for the better
> accommodation of the ladies, the stage will be formed into an amphitheatre, where
> servants will be allowed to keep places." . . . But, my kind reader, suppose an audience
> behind the curtain up to the clouds, with persons of a menial cast on the ground,
> beaux and no beaux crowding the only entrance, what a play it must have been when-

ever Romeo was breaking open the supposed tomb, which was no more than a screen on those nights set up, and Mrs Cibber prostrating herself on an old couch, covered with black cloth, as the tomb of the Capulets, with at least (on a great benefit night) two hundred persons behind her, which formed the background, as an unfrequented hallowed place of *chapless* skulls, which was to convey the idea of where the heads of all her buried ancestors were packed. . . .

'Nay, the stage, which was not thirty years ago near so wide as at present, also the stage-doors, (which must be well remembered) and the stage-boxes, before which there were false canvas, inclosed fronts on each side of two or three seats, on to the lamps, for ladies of distinction, which rendered it next to impossible for those ladies in the stage-boxes to see at all; but still it was the fashion, and therefore of course charming and delightful. – and whenever a Don Choleric in the Fop's Fortune, or Sir Amorous Varnict, in Woman's a Riddle, or Charles in the Busy Body, tried to find out secrets or plot an escape from a balcony, they always bowed and thrust themselves into the boxes over the stage-door amidst the company, who were greatly disturbed, and obliged to give up their seats.'

For a Mr Ryan's benefit on Monday, 19th March, 1753,

'The stage was at 5s. – Pit and Boxes all joined together at 5s. There was only one entrance on each side the Stage, which was always particularly crowded. . . .

'The Stage Spectators were not content with piling on raised seats, till their heads reached the theatrical cloudings; which seats were closed in with dirty worn out scenery, to inclose the painted round from the first wing, the main *entrance* being up steps from the middle of the *back scene*, but when that amphitheatre was filled, there would be a group of ill dressed lads and persons sitting on the stage in front, three or four rows deep, otherwise those who sat behind could not have been seen, and a riot would have ensued: So in fact a performer on a popular night could not step his foot with safety, least he either should thereby hurt or offend, or be thrown down amongst scores of tipsy apprentices.'[4]

If Garrick was to undertake reforms there, it was obvious that the auditorium itself would have to be increased to accommodate the spectators without any loss of revenue:

'The comedians, by waving (sic) the advantage of an amphitheatre on a benefit night, would be considerable losers; and, to remedy that evil, Mr. Garrick very judiciously observed, that the plan of reformation must be preceded by a considerable enlargement of the playhouse; and if it could be contrived, that the space before the curtain might contain as many persons as had formerly filled the pit, boxes, galleries, and the stage, nobody could have any pretence to murmur. Mr. Lacy was of the same opinion, and he concurred with his partner in the prosecution of his scheme; and having a taste for architecture, he took upon himself the enlarging of the theatre, which was com-

Fig.81. Interior of Drury Lane, Robert Adam, 1775

pletely finished in the year 1762. From that time scarcely any but the performers were permitted to visit the scenes of the playhouse.'[5]

As to what these amendments were we have no further information, but, as has already been noted (p.92), we do have visual evidence of the alterations considered necessary in 1775, when Robert Adam was called in to reconstruct the building.

Working on the premise that both Lacy and Adam retained the existing foundations and structural walls enclosing the pit, Adam, with the examples of Covent Garden, Goodman's Fields and the Queen's Theatre before him, would have had no valid reason for changing the fan-shaped auditorium, and he designed his side boxes on the line, but set forward to the face, of the existing pit walls. This gained extra space for the box seating and passages, which were now arranged on three levels in place of Wren's original two. From the 1778

Fig.82. Interior of Drury Lane, with figures corrected to Adam's scale section.

plan (p.94)[6] we know the Adam placed his frontispiece some 5 feet 3 inches further east of Wren's. His proscenium stage was now curtailed from its original depth of some 21 feet to an approximate 11 feet, containing in its depth a single proscenium door on either side, and some two-thirds of the width of the stage boxes. It is of interest to note that in Adam's ceiling plan the area related to the proscenium is defined with an individual panel of decoration, separate from the treatment of the remainder of the auditorium. While Wren's musicians were probably housed in one of the side boxes, Adam now followed the current trend, again as seen at Covent Garden (fig.73), by providing a railed enclosure at lower pit level directly adjoining the stage, and probably approached by entry ways from beneath the stage.

Unfortunately no detailed plan or section of Adam's alterations exists, apart from those already noted (fig.61), and it is on a combination of these and the interior view (fig.81), published by Adam, that the reconstruction (fig.83) has been based. When the sectional elevation of the frontispiece is compared with this view it may be noted that it differs in detail, and it must therefore be assumed to be an abandoned sketch. Nevertheless the overall height as indicated on the section may reasonably be accepted, and if this is applied to the interior view a set of heights may be obtained for the side boxes and their architectural details. It was just such a comparison, made for the original reconstruction, that revealed that the figures depicted in the view had all been drawn to approximately half their correct size, thereby creating an illusion of vastness quite out of character with the actual size of the building. The same view with the figures corrected for size (fig.82) reduces the apparent proportion of the auditorium to a size more compatible with the descriptions of intimacy recorded for this building.

The view of the interior shows that the three tiers of side boxes were subdivided by low partitions with narrow pilasters supporting the tiers. The fronts of the first gallery and the front boxes lined with those of the two lower tiers of side boxes, while the top of the upper gallery front appears to have lined with the underside of the top to the upper side boxes. The abandoned ceiling plan was subdivided into compartments corresponding to the spacing of the side boxes and their pilasters, and from this it is possible to scale off their dimensions and apply them to the reconstruction. Assuming a hidden bench behind the fronts of the first gallery and the front boxes, it would appear that there were eleven benches in each area, with six benches in the upper gallery. This gallery was supported on six equally spaced columns which stood between the fifth and sixth benches of the first gallery, and were continued upward beyond the main ceiling to support an upper ceiling cut through the earlier roof space to provide headroom for the gallery. One would expect these columns to be carried down through the front boxes, and it can only be assumed that they were omitted from the illustration by the engraver. Structurally they would have been necessary at this point, and they have therefore been included in the restoration.

In spite of moving the frontispiece eastwards, it would seem that, either now or at some previous time, possibly during Lacy's alterations, it had been found necessary to remove the rear curved wall of Wren's auditorium at all three levels, and the space gained was now used to accommodate the depth of the eleven benches at the lower two levels. It is, however, possible that the wall was still in position at least at the lower levels after Lacy's alterations, as a very similar wall was incorporated in the design of the Bristol Theatre Royal which was based on the Drury Lane of 1764. The Wren foyers and stairs were also presumably removed, and were now replaced by a narrow lobby across the rear of the auditorium, which has been assumed to be similar to that at Covent Garden. *The Public Advertiser* of 30th September, 1775,[7] describes 'The Lobby behind the Front Boxes' as being

'well and agreeably contrived, and is now kept clear of servants by an adjoining Room being prepared for their Attendance: This is an elegant improvement. The Passages to this Lobby are also much mended, but particularly next to Bridges Street, where the Company are received by three large Arches into a vestibule, or Hall which communicates with the great passage leading to the Boxes.'

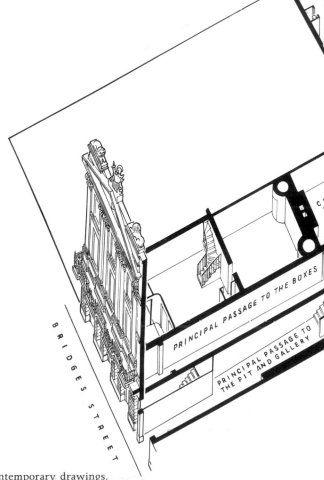

Fig.83. Drury Lane, 1775: scale reconstruction based on contemporary drawings.

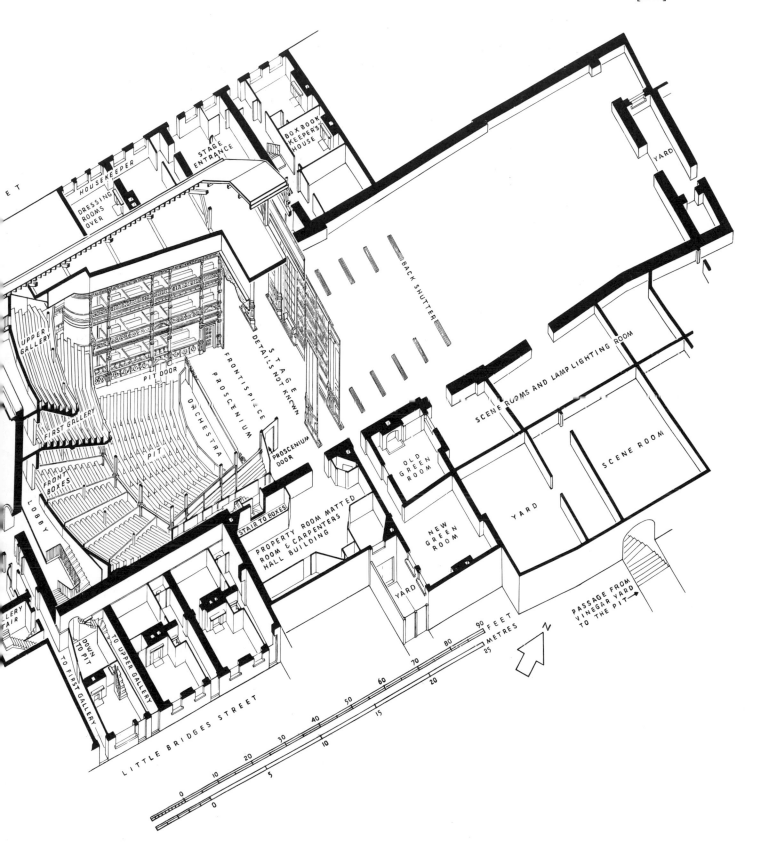

HOUSEKEEPER

DRESSING ROOMS OVER

STAGE ENTRANCE

BOX BOOK KEEPERS HOUSE

YARD

BACK SHUTTER

SCENE ROOMS AND LAMP LIGHTING ROOM

UPPER GALLERY

FRONTISPIECE

STAGE DETAILS NOT KNOWN

PROSCENIUM

FIRST GALLERY

PIT DOOR

ORCHESTRA

OLD GREEN ROOM

SCENE ROOM

FRONT BOXES

PIT

PROSCENIUM DOOR

YARD

LOBBY

STAIR TO BOXES

PROPERTY ROOM MATTED ROOM & CARPENTERS HALL BUILDING

NEW GREEN ROOM

YARD

GALLERY STAIR

DOWN TO PIT

TO UPPER GALLERY

PASSAGE FROM VINEGAR YARD TO THE PIT

TO FIRST GALLERY

90 FEET
80
25 METRES
70
60   20
50
40   15
30
20   10
10   5
0
0
0

LITTLE BRIDGES STREET

The extra height of the lobby floor occasioned by the additional benches in the front boxes raises this floor well above the level of the 'Principal passage to the Boxes'[8] and it has therefore been assumed that the wider ends of this lobby accommodated open stairs from a further lobby at the lower level, an area which could have been considerably enlarged by extension beneath the front boxes.

Whereas in Wren's theatre all the audience appear to have used a single entrance door, with stairs leading indiscriminately to all parts of the house, we now note from the 1778 survey that social distinctions required that each portion of the auditorium, with its own class of occupant, should be approached by its own separate entry way and stair. Exits for escape from the now overburdened building may also have prompted the increase in the number of approach ways. From Bridges Street, with its new and elaborate façade, there was a second passage leading to the pit and gallery. A further entry for box patrons had been provided from Russell Street as early as 1750, and an entrance to the pit was contrived from Marquis Court – Vinegar Yard – beneath the scene rooms and the stage to a side passage situated below the south side boxes. From Little Bridges Street there were separate entrances to the first and upper galleries, each of which was approached by stairs in the premises immediately adjoining the playhouse. These entries too were in existence at an earlier date, as they appear on a map of 1748.[9]

In spite of the comments quoted earlier (p.95) regarding the 'Stairs to the second and third Tiers of Boxes' being 'projected out of the House beyond the Old Walls', it would appear from the 1778 survey that this improvement was only included on the north side of the building. On the south there is no indication of any such arrangement, and so, on the re-construction, the stairs have been shown as indicated on the Wren reconstruction (fig.63). In view of Tate Wilkinson's comments (p.96), the box passages have been reconstructed as no more than 2 feet 6 inches in width, leaving sufficient space to the side boxes which were 'much improved by the additional Height given to each Tier, which admits of the seats being raised considerably above each other, and consequently gives a much better View of the Stage. The Boxes are now lined with Crimson spotted paper and gilt Border which makes a fine Back Ground to all the Decorations.'[10] Commenting further on the interior, *The Public Advertiser* speaks of 'the *Sounding Board*' which 'was much raised on the Part next the Stage and that the Height given to it increased greatly the Appearance of Magnitude in the House,' suggesting that a portion of the Wren ceiling might earlier have been retained in conjunction with the remaining Wren pilasters, two on either side, while the rest of the ceiling had been raised above this. We also learn of the richness of the Adam decoration, with glazed panels, backed by coloured foil, inset in the face of the pilasters with their gilded capitals. Candle brackets were mounted on the two levels of side box pilasters, and on the first gallery front. Adam's design for the ceiling (fig.61) shows a circular painted panel at the centre, but the same source speaks of the Ceiling or Sounding Board, which consists of Octagon pannels, rising from an exterior circular frame to the opening, or Ventilator, in the Center. The diminishing of these Pannels towards the Center, and the shade thrown next to the exterior Frame give the Ceiling the Appearance of a Dome, which has a light and airy Effect.' The mention of the ventilator suggests that Adam had adapted his design to introduce a feature which now became essential with the gradual increase in the size of auditoria, and in particular the increased numbers of people now being packed into the buildings. The 1778 site plan shows that the building was extended to the east to an overall length of some 194 feet, with a distance of 53 feet from the frontispiece to the rear shutter, compared with 55 feet 4 inches in July, 1791,[11] when the overall depth of the stage was given as 130 feet. Thomas Davies tells us in his *Memoirs of the Life of David Garrick* that this great depth was used for processions, and describes one occasion on which the doors at the rear were opened 'into Drury Lane; and a new and unexpected sight surprised the audience, of a real bonfire, and the populace huzzaing, and drinking porter to the health of Queen Anne Bullen. The stage in the mean time, amidst the parading of dukes, duchesses, archbishops, peeresses, heralds, &c. was covered with a thick fog from the smoke of the fire, which served to hide the tawdry dresses of the processionalists . . . the actors, being exposed to the suffocations of smoke, and the raw air from the open street, were seized with colds, rheumatisms, and swelled faces.'[12] Davies, however, would appear to be incorrect in stating that the doors opened into Drury Lane, for the bonfire must have been in the yard at the rear of the building (fig.83). Presumably the dressing rooms flanking Wren's vista area had by now been removed – hence Tate Wilkinson's comment of c. 1790: 'the stage, which was not thirty years ago near so wide as at present' (p.119) – and were now provided on the upper floors of the premises adjoining Russell Street, where the stage door was situated, replacing the earlier entrance through the passage from Drury Lane.

The old scene room on the south side had been rebuilt, and is shown on the 1778 survey as the 'Property Room, Matted Room and Carpenter's Hall', and alongside were the 'Old . . . and New Green' rooms adjoining the 'Scene rooms and Lamplighting room' flanking the south side of the stage. Presumably the roof space of Wren's playhouse had been used as a carpenter's shop, and may well have continued in this use, although we have no knowledge as to the nature of the roof construction at this period. On the reconstructions the roof trusses have been based on other Wren details.

A further view of the Adam interior is seen in the well known *School for Scandal* engraving of 1778 which depicts the details in a clumsier and cruder manner than in the previous engraving, but which nevertheless confirms the general features of the Adam drawings, with the exception of the stage front, which here projects much further into the auditorium than was possible, owing to the position of the pit entry doors, beneath the first narrow bay. It is nevertheless of value in indicating the screened footlights in the centre of the stage, with the decorative wrought iron scrolls filling the remainder of the space, and protecting the stage from those who might wish to climb up out of the pit. These scrolls are also seen on the Adam view, where additional scrolls protect the side boxes from the incursions of the first gallery occupants. The *School for Scandal* drawing also shows the fronts of the stage boxes protected by iron spikes, an arrangement also to be noted in the picture of the Fitzgiggo Riot (p.110) at Covent Garden.

This form of protection does not in fact appear to have been very effective in controlling the more determined, or less controlled, elements of the audience, as the following descriptions, two of many, suggest: 'A young gentleman, on the nineteenth of January, 1746-7, went, enflamed with wine, to the Pit (an Indecency at the Time too frequent there) and climbing over the Spikes on the Stage, very soon made his way to the Green Room.' On another occasion 'almost fifty of the Party, with the young Hero at their Head, rose in the Pit, and climbing over the Spikes on the Stage, ran directly to the Green Room'.[13]

Further evidence as to the abandonment of the sectional elevation may also be gained from the *School for Scandal* engraving, as the central decorative panel shown on the section is here omitted, and the curtains are festooned in the normal way rather than in the somewhat contrived manner indicated on the section. Some of the actors are seen performing on the scenic stage, where they are enclosed by two pairs of wings, and a set of backshutters placed at the second wing position (fig.84).

Fig.84. Drury Lane, 1775: detail of Fig.83

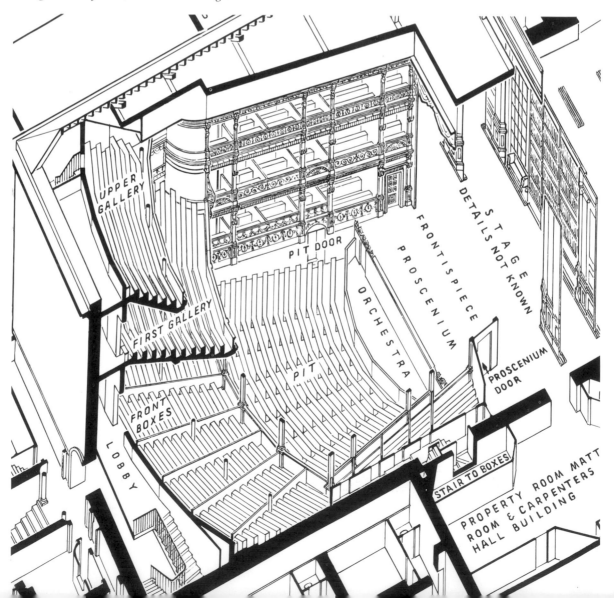

Fig.85. Drury Lane: interior, 1783

The theatre was altered again in 1783 by Thomas Greenwood and William Capon, and their treatment is seen in an interior view prepared by Capon (fig.85). They removed, or painted out, much of the Adam decoration, which had been criticised in some quarters as distracting attention from the scenes by its richness: an argument which may perhaps have had some validity if one thinks of the reflections and highlights occasioned by the glazed pilasters. By modern standards the sober decorations of the Richmond, Surrey, theatre (p.116) seem more appropriate. Although dated 17th September, 1782, it may be that Oulton was describing these alterations when he said

> 'This theatre was very much improved now; the Boxes neatly papered with a light pea grccn, and ornamented with crimson curtains to all the doors; the seats covered with baize of the same colour. His Majesty's box and the opposite one were rather more advanced than before, and the side scene lights were much encreased.'[14]

As at Covent Garden, His Majesty's box now adjoined the stage, a position noted by Adam on his abandoned ceiling drawing, rather than in its previous position in the centre of the front boxes. It would appear that the six rear benches of the front boxes were removed, and a wall inserted in line with the columns over. This may suggest that there were in fact columns at this point in the front boxes, or that if the upper columns had previously been supported on beams from the rear wall to the front pilasters, then this method was now found to be inadequate and extra support was needed which led to the introduction of this feature. There were six doors in this wall leading to private enclosures, perhaps on similar lines to those retiring rooms which caused so much trouble when introduced at a later date at Covent Garden (p.184). Those under consideration here also caused trouble as they 'became a nest for prostitutes of both sexes'[15] and as a result the wall was presumably removed to permit the seats to be 'formed into recesses which communicate with the other boxes', an arrangement which suggests the basket boxes that Holland was to introduce into his designs for both Covent Garden and Drury Lane. There is, incidentally, a mention in this description of iron columns in the back boxes, which could be a reference to the doubtful columns at the rear of the front boxes.

Covent Garden was enlarged in 1782 within the limits of the existing walls by a Mr Richards. From plans prepared by William Capon[16] in 1791 he would appear to have increased the length of the auditorium, and at the same time to have opened up the rear wall of the original stage, so that the earlier vista area and paint and scene rooms were now open to the stage proper. The fan-shaped auditorium was by now coming under criticism, and, with the new criteria involved (p.112), quite rightly so. The fronts of the side boxes were some 45 feet overall in length, as compared to the 39 feet of the previous theatre, and to this must be added the depth of the oblique facets containing the proscenium doors, so that a member of the audience seated at the extreme end of the side boxes was some 11 feet further from the scene than he would previously have been, and some 14 feet from the nearest point of action on the stage. Added to this was the considerable increase in seating capacity in these side areas, so that there were now far more persons who had cause to complain of the poor sight lines involved. Richards greatly reduced the fan-shape of the auditorium, so that the side boxes were nearly, but not quite, parallel with each other across the width of an approximately rectangular pit.

In his *Treatise on Theatres*[17] Saunders described the pit as an 'oblong, 36 feet 6 inches from the front of the stage-floor, and 56 feet from the scene to the opposite boxes, and 38 feet 6 inches wide between the boxes.' The new pit floor was raised to provide a better view of the stage, the side gangways being sunk one step below this level, so that the audience standing here would not obstruct the view from the side boxes.[18] The pit benches were increased in number from twelve to seventeen, and both they, the orchestra rail and the box fronts, were concentric in place of the earlier faceted pattern. Both pit and orchestra were entered from the space beneath the side boxes, some 9 to 10 feet in width. According to Saunders the front boxes were '18 feet deep from the front to the back, the first gallery 30 feet 6 inches, and the second gallery 21 feet 6 inches.' There was an increase in the number of benches in the first – two shilling – gallery from fourteen to sixteen, the gallery continuing through to the rear wall. The second – one shilling – gallery was not so deep as formerly, so that it no longer overhung the front rows of the first gallery. The proscenium doors, too, had undergone a change in that they were now arranged on an oblique angle to the front of the stage, thus advancing them within the sight of a greater number of the audience than had been possible in their previous position. Above the side boxes were 'slips', which were reached from the new lower gallery entrances in the Piazza and Bow Street.[19] A new entrance to the upper gallery was provided within three yards of the gate in the Piazza.

The first tier front and first and second tier side boxes are shown on plans published by Saunders in his *Treatise* as being arranged in pairs, but on the Capon drawings on which the reconstruction (fig.86) is based the second tier side boxes are shown as single boxes. The boxes are separated by a widely spaced colonnade of the Ionic order, these pilasters supporting a balustrade which formed the first gallery parapet. Pilasters of the Corinthian order were similarly used to divide the upper tiers of side boxes, and the slips were 'bounded in front with a ballustrade'. The ceiling was painted to represent a 'serene sky, in imitation of the Roman theatres'.[20]

Nevertheless Saunders was still critical of this arrangement when he commented:

> 'If the sides of a square be ill adapted for viewing . . . the sides of an oblong must be proportionably worse: it is impossible to view the actor from the distant end of the side boxes without great pain, and even then he must be seen very imperfectly, and those seated behind cannot see at all. But the distance occasioned by this form is not the only defect; a considerable one arises from the great depth of the front boxes and two galleries over them. The fronts being low, necessarily obstruct the sound: the little that enters is presently attracted and absorbed by the persons, clothes, &c. of the spectators in the foremost rows'.

Saunders further criticises the unwholesome character of the air when so many people and lights are confined within such deep recesses. Richards had presumably attempted to improve the earlier conditions, when he cut back the upper gallery from its former position with its front directly above that beneath, and carried its front on a row of columns below. If he did, he got little thanks from Saunders for his efforts.

From further comments it appears that Richards had used mouldings and balusters to decorate his box and gallery fronts, as may be seen in a Rowlandson drawing of the interior,[21] which also shows the pilasters and festoons of drapery to the front of the boxes. By the time Saunders was writing in 1790, it would seem as though the divisions between the boxes might well have been in the nature of separating walls, rather than the former low partitions, as these were apparently lined with paper. The balusters may, however, have been survivals from the earlier interior where they can be seen in prints of the period[22] decorating the fronts of the upper stage boxes. Saunders comments on the seating by saying that 'The public should not submit to be crowded into such narrow seats: 1 foot 9 inches is the whole space allowed for seat and void; though a moderate-sized person cannot conveniently sit in a less space than that of 1 foot 10 inches from back to front, nor comfortably in less than

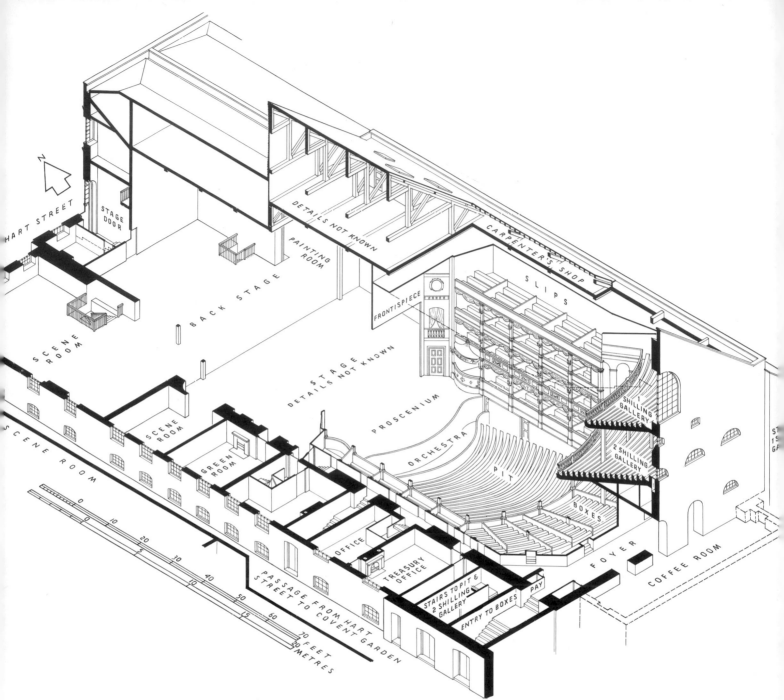

Fig.86. Covent Garden, J. I. Richards, after the alterations of 1782

that of 2 feet.' Although he does not comment on the position of the proscenium doors, he does feel that

'The frontispiece is such a one as no architect would have applied. Were a painted frame to be proposed for a picture, how would a connoisseur exclaim: The scene is the picture, and the frontispiece, or in other words the frame, should contrast the picture, and thereby add to the illusion. The great advance of the stage-floor was made with a view to obviate the great difficulty of hearing in this theatre.'

For the first time the theory is propounded that the performance should be regarded as a picture which needs a frame to complete the illusion, and the painted frame, which previously had sustained the role of hiding from the eyes of the audience the mechanics of the stage, is now regarded as inappropriate to the new role, and must be replaced by a solid, or architectural, frame if the illusion is to be complete.

On the general design of theatres of the 18th century, Saunders says:

'In forming our first theatres, we certainly knew but little of favouring the voice, or if we did, we paid no attention to it, and were as careless with respect to the vision; I am clearly of the opinion we were guided by the form of the stage. Thus the opening gave the width, and height. Sometimes they spread every way like a fan, whose larger end was opposite the stage; and this enabled them to place the galleries without greatly elevating the seats. Attached to the old manner, it was but of late years that the French varied it; and we to this day maintain the old form.'

Major alterations were made to Vanbrugh's Opera House, the Queen's Theatre (known from 1714-1837 as The King's Theatre) in 1778, probably by Robert Adam, when the 'heavy' columns were removed and the theatre made lighter and more elegant, in much the same manner as he had applied to Drury Lane three years earlier. It was further altered in 1782 by Michael Novosielski. A sketch plan of 1782[23] shows Novosielski's proposals for arranging boxes around the pit in a horseshoe 'on the conventional lines of an Italian opera house'.[24] However, the plan of the theatre illustrated by Saunders in his *Treatise* shows 'an oblong . . . with side boxes parallel to one another . . . rounded off at the end opposite the stage'. If this were the case it would have provided better sight lines from the side boxes than were possible with the horseshoe form. Parts of the plan are, however, highly inaccurate (vide the semi-circular stair opening off the east corridor to the auditorium) and the arrangement of the auditorium as shown may be equally unreliable. The horseshoe auditorium is in fact shown on further plans (fig.87), presumably prepared by Novosielski when he replaced this theatre after the fire of 1789 by a larger building designed on very similar lines.

Novosielski increased the width of the auditorium, and consequently of the pit, by building corridors, providing access to the side boxes, outside the walls of the original theatre building. The depth was also increased by the removal of the inner of the two vestibules (fig.71) across the rear of the auditorium, and by reducing the overall depth of the stage from some 64 feet to 50 feet. According to Saunders 'There were three ranges of boxes, 34' (all plans, including Saunders', show 33) 'in each range, besides 18 in a line with the gallery; in all 116 '(?)' . . . allowing the space of two for entrances into the pit'. These entrances were still placed further back in this theatre than was normally the case. 'Those in the first range being on a level with the stage, had their fronts continued in one even line to the central box; but all the ranges above, as also the first gallery, projected in curved

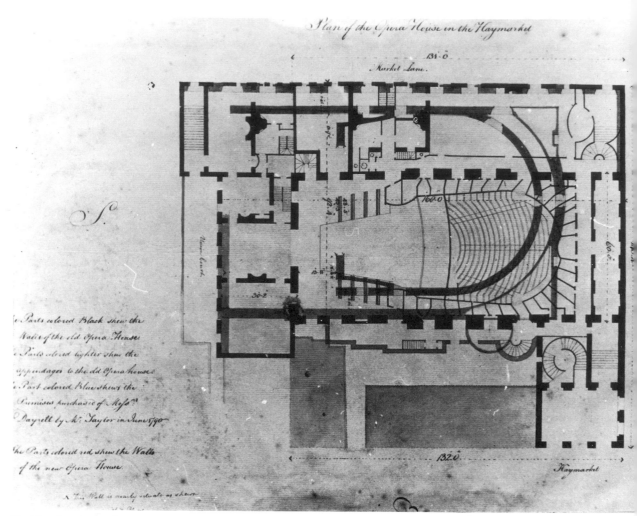

Fig.87. The King's Theatre, Haymarket, M. Novosielski, 1790. Superimposed plans of old and new opera house

lines over the pit. A second gallery was managed in the cove of the ceiling, which was groined for that purpose.' Saunders criticised the acoustics of the theatre, and commented that 'The first gallery was low and inconvenient and very little could be discerned or heard there by those who were situated behind. The second gallery by being next to the ceiling was the best situation in the house for hearing.'

The new theatre was much larger (fig.87), occupying the greater part of the space originally taken up with the long hall, dressing rooms and scene room on the west side of the theatre, and incorporating the space once occupied by the rooms to the south; it was some 92 feet wide by 168 feet long. The stage, 45 feet deep, was separated from the auditorium by a solid wall some 3 feet thick, in which was a 45 feet 5 inches wide stage opening, which does not, however, appear to have reached to the side walls of the theatre. The stage projected some 15 feet into the auditorium with a segmental front, beyond which was a 10 feet wide orchestra pit. The auditorium was arranged with three tiers, each containing 37 boxes surrounding the horseshoe pit, and with two further tiers, each with 26 boxes, flanking a central gallery. In addition there were eight further boxes on either side of the pit at stage level. The corners between the horseshoe box corridors, and the rectangle of the building walls, were occupied by semi-circular niches containing stairs giving access to the box tiers. Both boxes and pit were approached by saloons entered by a stair in the Haymarket extension, which had survived the fire, and although there are no records of the original building, a plan of 1816-18[25] shows a staircase to the gallery built separately in the Haymarket extension.

In 1796, however, the theatre was remodelled, and the proscenium doors with boxes over and flanking Corinthian columns were removed. These were replaced by boxes, and the side boxes were now continued beyond the separating wall on to the stage proper.

'The stage is sixty feet in length, from the wall to the orchestra, and eighty feet in breadth from wall to wall, and forty-six feet across from box to box. From the orchestra to the centre of the front boxes, the pit is sixty-six feet in length and sixty-five feet in breadth, and contains twenty-one benches, besides passage rooms of about three feet wide, which goes (sic) round the seats, and down the centre of the pit to the orchestra. The pit will hold eight hundred persons; price of admission half-a-guinea. In altitude, the internal part of the house fifty-five feet from the floor of the pit to the dome. There are five tiers of boxes, and each box is about seven feet in depth, and four in breadth, and is so constructed as to hold six persons with ease, all of whom command a full view of the stage. Each box has its curtains to enclose it according to the fashion of the Neapolitan theatres, and is furnished with six chairs, but are not raised above each other as the seats of our English Theatres. The boxes hold near nine hundred persons, and price of admission to them is half-a-guinea. The gallery is forty-two feet in depth sixty-two in breadth, and contains seventeen benches, and holds eight hundred persons, price of admission five shillings. The lobbies are about twenty feet square, where women attend to accommodate the company with coffee, tea and fruit.'[26]

Redecoration followed in 1799 and 1807-8, but the continued use of candles was a constant source of dirt and irritation. Chandeliers were suspended on brackets from the fronts of the tiers, but 'The adoption of glass bells or shades would be devoutly wished for. . . . Last night they poured down their wax on the beaux in the most unsparing profusion; and from their situation over the principal avenues of the Pit, have means of annoyance clearly unrivalled by the *noxie* of any of the metropolitan theatres.'[27] In 1815, when the interior was redecorated by Nash and Repton, the opportunity was taken to replace the candles by gas in the form of a splendid lustre hung from the centre of the domed ceiling.

When the season ended on the 1st June, 1792, Covent Garden was closed in order that it might be rebuilt[28] to the designs of Henry Holland. Drury Lane had also been finally condemned,[29] Tate Wilkinson[30] commenting that it had been 'much fritted and patched at very great expense; and, after all, the only way to repair will be to pull it down, and erect a new one.' The 'last performance of the company, on Garrick's stage, was on the 4th June, 1791, when they acted the Country Girl, with No Song, No Supper'.[31] Speaking of the old theatre, Boaden extols the virtues of the earlier fan-shaped auditoria when he says:

'Our present theatres differ materially from that of Garrick. The gallery formed more of his plan, than it does of ours. It came down upon the lower circle of boxes, and its visitors were not seldom exceedingly intelligent persons and passionate admirers of the drama: they sat in a very favourable position for the enjoyment of a play, and seconded the pit in the just distribution of censure and praise. The boxes did not contain anything like the number of persons now nightly visitors to the theatre, but certainly more real fashion. . . . Their private boxes, too, were few . . . upon great occasions seven or eight rows of the pit were laid into the boxes, and then the Old Drury exhibited, two months before it closed, £412 as the total taken at the door for the first benefit of Mrs Siddons, after her return. London, however, was rapidly increasing, and it was conceived that larger theatres were demanded. All the articles of Consumption, too, were upon the rise; among these were the salaries of performers; and the patentees thought that they needed not only more spectators, but greater prices.'[32]

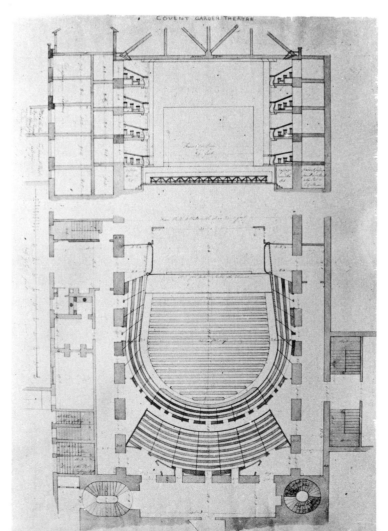

Fig.88. Covent Garden, Henry Holland, plan and section, 1791

So rising costs and greater profits meant larger theatres, and Tate Wilkinson for one looked to France for a lead in well designed theatres, where they 'appear very noble and spacious, and not surrounded by buildings, but good open road for carriages round,'[33] as in the theatre at Bordeaux.[34] Holland had knowledge of the Parisian theatres, plans of a Parisian Opera House having been found in his files.[35] It is not surprising, therefore, to find Holland using the continental horseshoe auditorium for both theatres. A plan and section[36] (fig.88) exist for 'the proposed new Theatre' to be built within the existing shell of Covent Garden, which may well have been further amended before this theatre was built. The general shape of the theatre was, however, in accord with the intentions shown on these drawings, although various alterations had to be made in the first years after its opening. Some of these alterations may be seen in the drawing by Robert Wilkinson of the interior (fig.89) 'as altered previous to the opening on the 15th Sept, 1794' (presumably the date of opening for the current winter season, as the theatre was first opened on the 17th September, 1792), and further alterations were made in 1796, when James Boaden commented: 'The reader has been, no doubt, astonished, with the writer, at the hurry and ignorance, and confidence of architects; the new editions of their works, with corrections and additions, which come out every season',[37] a comment which underlines the problems besetting any attempt to record fully the countless variations which all theatres suffered at the hands of their managements, architects and artists.

Holland's proposed design shows a proscenium stage 15 feet 6 inches deep, flanked by projecting stage boxes for the King and Prince, and proscenium doors once again set at right-angles to the stage front. Holland, unfortunately, provides no information regarding the decorative details of this area, but does indicate a light partition wall separating the auditorium from the main stage area, containing an opening 29 feet wide by 19 feet 7 inches high. An orchestra pit, built over an inverted arch 'to assist the general sound', separated the sloping pit from the stage, with an orchestra partition and nineteen benches set parallel with the straight stage front; a twentieth bench was set against the curved rear wall of the horseshoe pit. Enclosing the pit were 'three rows (or, as they are now called, circles)'[38] each 8 feet 8 inches high, divided into twenty-three boxes on the first circle, and twenty-seven on the second by low partitions, which, unlike those of the previous theatres, were angled towards the centre of the proscenium stage, like those seen in Pozzo's theatre (fig.67). Each circle of boxes was fitted with three rows of benches concentric with the box fronts. 'That sight lines might not be impaired, the two back rows were raised one above the other. All three rows were hinged in such a manner that about a third of each bench could be lifted and swung back in order to allow access to each row'.[39] The lower two circles were carried right round the pit as boxes, the remaining circles over being arranged with ten boxes on either side of the one, and two shilling galleries facing the stage, each fitted with fourteen rows of benches. The retention of galleries facing the stage introduced a typically British feature into the Continental plan with its pit encircled by loges on all levels in the manner illustrated by Pozzo. In the first circle, behind the front boxes with

Fig.89. Covent Garden: the auditorium, 1794

their three rows of benches, and separated from them by partitions and a cross-passage, was a further segment divided into seven boxes each with eight rows of benches. The longitudinal section (fig.90) shows a flat ceiling over the pit area on the underside of the 'present floor of the Carpenter's Shop in the Roof of the House', with a sloping ceiling over the upper gallery. The box fronts were all designed with a bowed front providing good knee room for the occupants of the front benches. This design, however, appears to have undergone some alterations. Descriptions of the theatre at its opening refer to 'three circles of boxes and a spacious gallery',[40] and 'four straight sided horseshoe tiers, the first three entirely given up to boxes, and the fourth to the two-shilling gallery'.[41] The rear boxes facing the stage at first circle level were included and were 'as good places for seeing and hearing as any in the House, though not so good for being seen'.[42] It is not at all clear what arrangement was made at second and third circle levels. Presumably the lower gallery of the

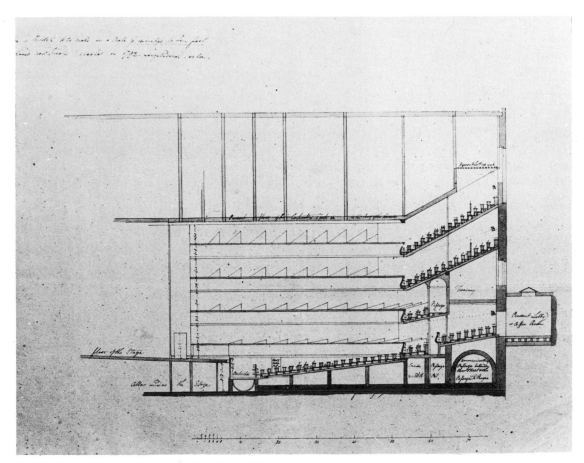

Fig.90. Covent Garden: longitudinal section, 1791

preliminary design had been omitted, but whether it had been replaced by additional offices and foyers, or by additional seating similar to that at first circle level is not clear.

The two-shilling gallery

> 'crowns the whole, and is continued round the Theatre. The seats are considerably elevated, so as to give a complete uninterrupted view of the Stage. Its decorations have been sufficiently attended to: it is neat, airy, and lofty, and has a proper degree of elegance. The ceiling is painted as a sky, the opening to which is surrounded by a Ballustrade supported by enriched frames, which have their bearings on the walls and on the Proscenium. The Proscenium is composed of pilasters and columns of the Corinthian order, fully enriched, having between them the stage doors, over which are the balcony boxes. . . . The Soffit of the entablature forms the sounding board to the proscenium, and the cove is calculated to throw the voice forward.'[43]

The boxes were separated from one another by partitions, low in front and rising behind. Both partitions and ceilings were 'of wainscot, and are not papered for the advantage of sound.'[44] The 'interior of each circle is painted green', according to one account[45] but red according to others.[46] All descriptions agree, however, that the box fronts were decorated in white and gold.

The most important advance made in the design of these boxes, however, was the complete absence of supporting columns, the circles being cantilevered forward some 7 feet from the side walls of the auditorium. This was an obvious advantage in the provision of uninterrupted sight lines, but one for which the average playgoer was as yet unprepared; with the need to give visible evidence of support 'to the people in the pit, those rows of boxes full of company, and having no apparent support, are apt to give an unpleasant sensation.'[47]

Unlike the previous theatres where the passages providing access to the side boxes had been inside the main walls of the theatre building, Holland now followed Novosielski's lead (p.132), and made use of the full 56 feet between the 3 feet thick side walls of the auditorium, by cutting new doors through the walls to passages on either side, 6 feet 6 inches and 7 feet 7 inches wide respectively, connecting with new and enlarged staircases. In addition a large building was erected in Hart Street which provided accommodation for scene-painters, scene-rooms, green room and dressing rooms, and an entrance and saloon for the King.[48] Unfortunately none of the drawings provide information regarding the stage itself, or its furnishings, but there are descriptions which will be noted later (p.153).

The omission of the one-shilling gallery and the consequent demotion of the former two-shilling galleryites led to an outcry on the opening night, 17th September, 1792, which resulted in the management promising to provide a one-shilling gallery. As a temporary measure[49] part of the two-shilling gallery was partitioned off, but subsequently an additional gallery was introduced at a higher level. This can be seen in the Wilkinson view (fig.89) in the top left-hand corner, and is presumably the one referred to in the *Microcosm,* where the galleries are described: 'The first, or two-shilling gallery, is 55 feet wide and 40 feet in depth, contains twelve seats, which are so elevated as to give a complete uninterrupted view of the stage, and holds eight hundred and twenty spectators. The upper gallery is 55 feet wide and 25 feet in depth, contains 7 seats, and holds 361 persons.'[50] Holland had presumably been trying to provide some of the space and air above his gallery suggested as a necessity by Saunders (p.129), but public pressure on this point seems to have defeated any such good intentions. The ceiling was altered in 1794 to permit the occupants of the new gallery to have a better view of the stage, the flat ceiling now ending just in front of the centre of the pit. The proscenium was also altered, when the columns adjoining the curtain were replaced by the pilasters seen in the interior view. Further alterations were carried out in 1796 when 'Seven rows of seats were added to eleven of the centre boxes of the second and third tiers'[51] providing for a further 144 persons.

In 1803 the whole appearance of the interior was changed when the proscenium area was completely redesigned and raised by 10 feet, as may be seen in the Pugin and Rowlandson aquatint in the *Microcosm*.[52] The slips 'instead of carrying the rudeness of the gallery all round the house' were now converted into boxes 'and sixteen private boxes were built, and let at £300 a year each,'[53] apparently on the third tier,[54] an additional bench being provided in the existing boxes.

The theatre was burned down on the night of the 20th September, 1808, at which time the auditorium is reported as holding 3,013 persons: 632 in the pit; 1,200 in the three circles of boxes; 820 in the two-shilling gallery; and 361 in the one-shilling gallery[55] – a considerable increase over Holland's expected capacity of 2,797[56] which was based on an allocation of 1 foot 6 inches each person in the boxes, and 1 foot 2 inches elsewhere in the house. As these dimensions could hardly be 'improved' on, the additional capacity must have been due to the various alterations, but to those should be added the 'standing room' which Holland did not take into account. It is obvious from the various comments and criticisms from those whose view of the stage was blocked, that the admission of such paying customers was a standard practice.

7 The growth of spectacle

Holland's new Drury Lane was opened on the 12th March, 1794,[1] and was now intended to occupy the whole of the approximately 300 feet long by 155 feet wide site enclosed by Bridges Street, Russell Street and Drury Lane, although the main block of the theatre containing stage, dressing rooms and auditorium, measured some 204 feet by 86 feet. On either side of this there was a wing, approximately 20 feet deep by 160 feet long, containing entrance foyers, vestibules and staircases. These wings were intended to be continued around the site with 'a coffee-house, tavern, library, shops of various sorts, and residences for the performers'[2] and the whole island site was to be further enclosed by an open colonnade covering the pavements. The intention was to create a new road – Woburn Street – on the line of the passageways leading to Marquis Court – Vinegar Yard – but this, together with the surrounding buildings, never materialised. This complete architectural composition (fig.91), on the lines of recent French theatres,[3] was intended to increase 'the convenience and safety of the public'[4] although, unlike the French examples, the intended introduction of the surrounding shops and taverns would, to a large extent, have offset the advantages in the restriction of fire spread from or to the theatrical fire-risk offered by an island site. Nevertheless the opportunities provided by the island site for direct escape from the main building in all directions were taken full advantage of. If the question of safety, however, was a matter of prime consideration, it may seem odd that Holland chose to frame the enclosing walls of the main theatre building.

> 'Our readers will recollect, that the immense pile was constructed of timber, and that the frame stood for months, exhibited a very fine carcase of carpenter's work, before the ribs were filled-in with bricks. Timber was then 3 *l* per load; and the architect thought that this wooden core would contribute to the propagation of sound: it did not perhaps succeed in this respect, but it certainly contributed to the conflagration.'[5]

To reduce the fire risk within the building Holland divided the main theatre block into two almost equal halves by a crosswall separating the stage from the auditorium (fig.92).

Fig.91. Drury Lane: Henry Holland's intended design, 1794

This wall was some 2 feet 6 inches thick and contained an opening '43 feet wide and 38 feet high'[6] and such minor doors as were necessary for access between the two parts at stage and cellar levels. From a set of plans[7] and two sections, it would appear that it reached no higher than the top of the 'proscenium opening', or at most to the underside of the roof trusses. The whole of the roof space above both stage and auditorium 'contained, besides the barrel loft, ample room for the scene-painters, and four very large water tanks (fig.93), from which water is distributed over every part of the house for the purpose of instantly extinguishing fire.' (fig.95[BB])[8] The opening in the wall could be closed by a great iron curtain, which was lowered in a groove built into the wall (fig.95[C]). James Boaden writing in 1831 suggested that stage and auditorium 'should certainly be cut off by division-walls to the very roof, reaching from the external walls of the theatre to the frontispiece, and a strong division be also made in the very roof itself, so that the whole roof could never be on fire, nor all of it fall in at the same time',[9] but the important thing was to provide really adequate exits to enable an audience to escape rapidly. He jeers at attempts to control the fire when he calls the iron curtain, the reservoirs and distribution pipes 'tricks to amuse children', but he does not seem to have appreciated that without the iron curtain, or some similar feature, his wall would prove ineffective. Research into methods of fire prevention was being carried out at this time by friends of Holland's, but he rejected their suggestions 'that the theatre be extensively protected by iron plating at a cost of £1,000' and suggested instead 'that effective fire-proofing could be provided by plastering, at a cost of only £600'.[10]

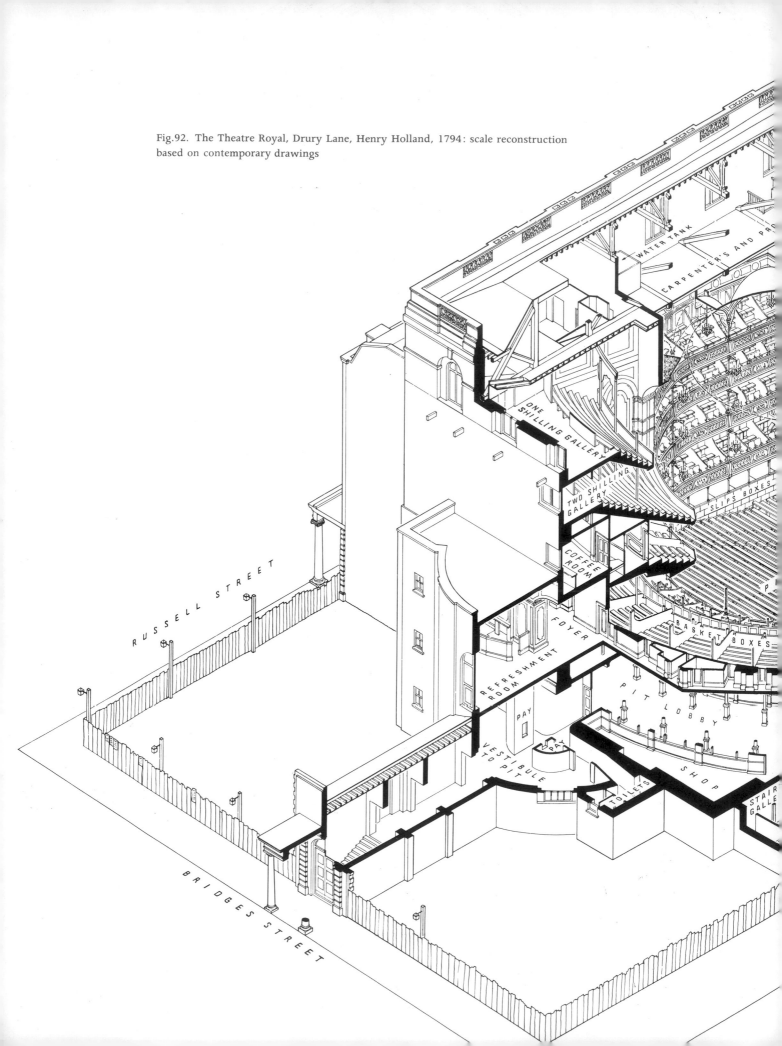

Fig.92. The Theatre Royal, Drury Lane, Henry Holland, 1794: scale reconstruction based on contemporary drawings

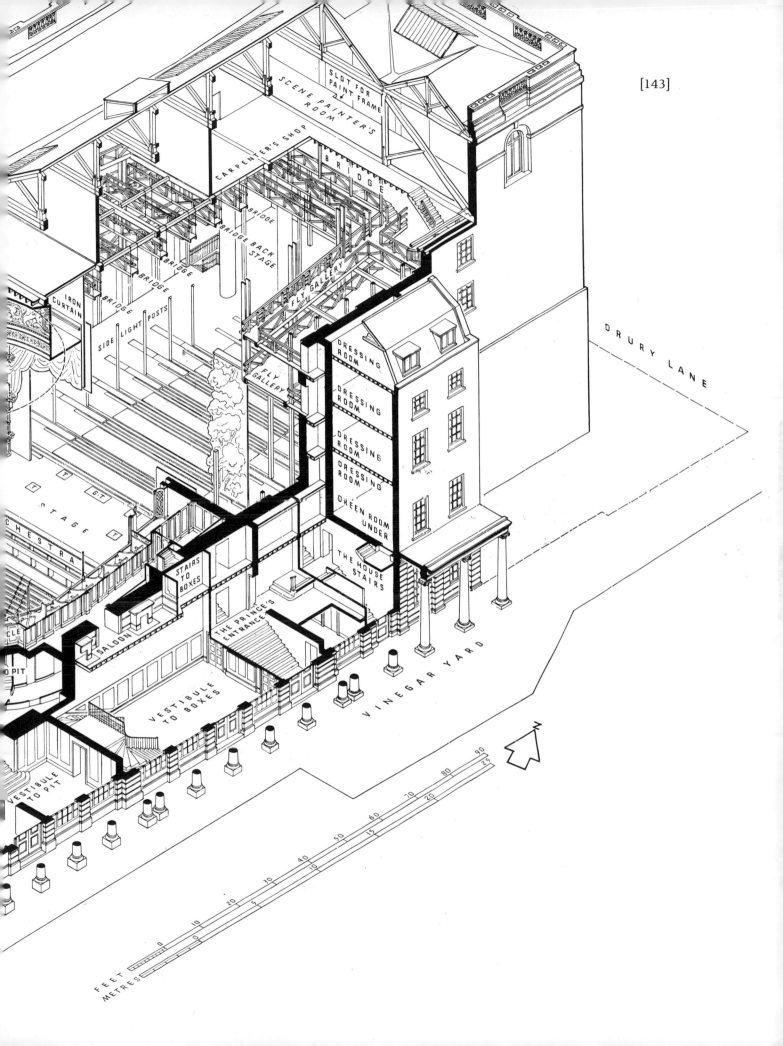

[143]

SLOT FOR PAINT FRAME

SCENE PAINTER'S ROOM

CARPENTER'S SHOP

BRIDGE

BRIDGE

BACK STAGE

BRIDGE

BRIDGE

BRIDGE

FLY GALLERY

IRON CURTAIN

SIDE LIGHT POSTS

FLY GALLERY

DRURY LANE

DRESSING ROOM

DRESSING ROOM

DRESSING ROOM

DRESSING ROOM

GREEN ROOM UNDER

THE HOUSE STAIRS

STAIRS TO BOXES

STAGE

ORCHESTRA

SALOON

THE PRINCE'S ENTRANCE

VESTIBULE TO BOXES

VINEGAR YARD

CLE

PIT

VESTIBULE TO PIT

N

90
80
25
70
20
60
15
50
40
10
30
20
5
10
0

FEET
METRES

Holland repeated the horseshoe form for his auditorium (fig.93), enclosing the pit, equipped with twenty-four (24 on the Soane plan, 25 on the 1806 plan and 26 on the Capon plan) straight backless benches on shallow steps, by tiers of boxes. As first designed, Holland omitted the proscenium doors, and the proscenium stage was flanked on either side by four levels of stage boxes, '8 private boxes on the stage',[11] the whole comprising a proscenium unit with its own flat ceiling, or sounding board, supported on projecting brackets. A contemporary tells us that

> 'The audience part of the theatre is formed nearly on a semicircular plan. It contains a pit, eight boxes on each side the pit, two rows of boxes above them, and two galleries, which command a full niew of every part of the stage. On each side of the galleries are two more rows of boxes, rising to a cove, which is so contrived as to form the cieling (sic) into a complete circle. – The proscenium, or that part of the stage which is contained between the curtain and orchestra, is fitted up with boxes, but without any stage-door, or the usual addition of large columns. – The boxes are furnished with chairs in the front rows, and behind with benches. The trimming and covering are all of blue velvet.
>
> 'The corridors which surround the boxes are spacious, and communicate with each other by means of staircases in the angles of the theatre. At the West end of the theatre there is a very large semi-circular room, opening by an arch to the corridors, and having fire places in it, and bar-rooms, from which the company may be supplied with refreshments.'[12]

We may note from the above description that the proscenium is still considered as a distinct feature with its own 'sound board or cieling . . . painted in compartments,' but that one of the former features of this area, the giant order of columns or pilasters, is here omitted. There were five levels of boxes on either side of the pit, the lowest tier extending only to its centre, with the pit entrances set in the wall at the end of, and at the same level as, these boxes. This tier consisted of 'eight dull and inconvenient slips, also called private, on each side of the pit. It was, at time, difficult to keep the standers in the pit from trespassing on their fronts; and their hats, and, sometimes, great coats, on a wet evening, made the secluded gentry doubtful whether they could enjoy their privilege unmolested.'[13] The pit benches were reached by gangways, some 3 feet wide, alongside the enclosing walls, and it was presumably here that the additional audience was standing.

Alterations to the theatre were carried out in September, 1797,[14] when the pit floor was lowered by about 1 foot, and the entrances moved further round (fig.94), the side gangways being at a lower level, and necessitating the introduction of a central gangway in the rear eighteen benches of the total of twenty-five benches shown in this drawing. Originally, it would seem that diagonal gangways had been provided from the pit entries towards the centre of the stage front, formed by lift-up seats, a feature to be found in many of these theatres (fig.121). This lowering of the pit may have taken into account the inconveniences mentioned above, but the main reason seems to have been the introduction of additional

Fig.93. The auditorium, Drury Lane, 1794: detail of Fig. 92

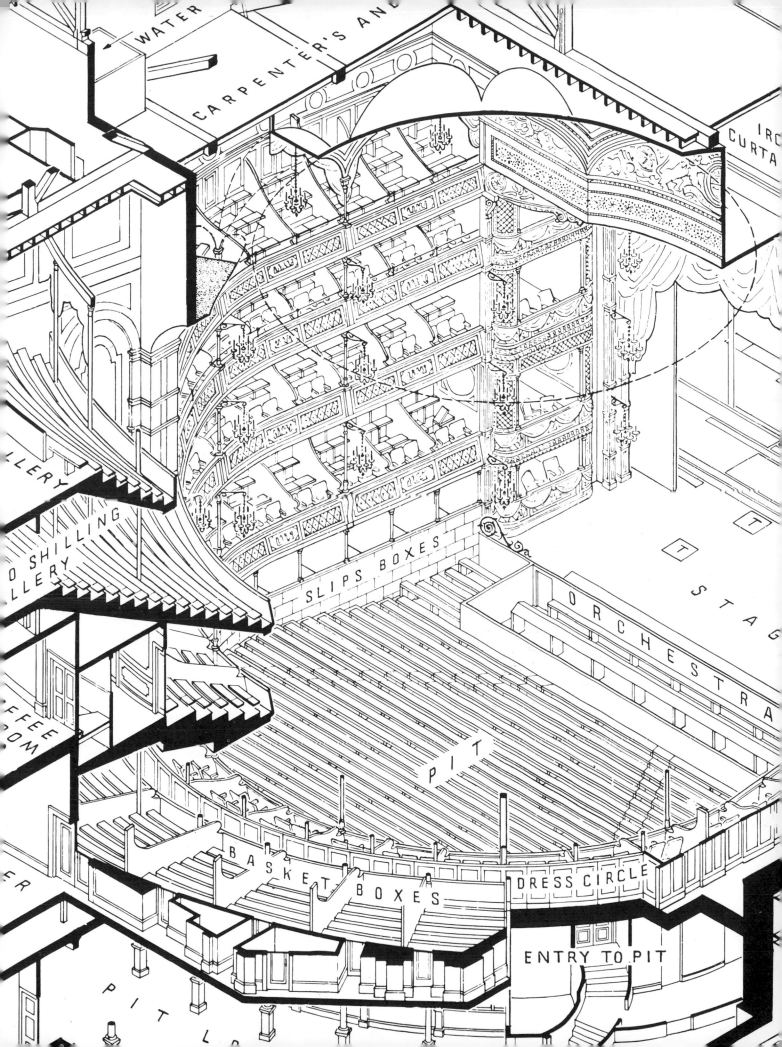

'orchestra boxes', as they are now called, three on each side. The theatre in its original form is seen in the well known watercolour by Edward Dayes[15] and may be contrasted with that prepared by Pugin and Rowlandson[16] which shows these extended boxes, as well as the additions which were probably made at this time to the proscenium area in the form of proscenium doors with boxes above (figs.95,96), set in a cove behind the proscenium wall, resulting in a consequent reduction in the width of the proscenium opening. The orchestra was now extended across the full width of the pit, absorbing the short lengths of seats which had previously flanked the area, thus making it slightly more difficult for the occupants of the pit to climb up on to the stage.

Above these pit boxes was the first, or dress, tier of boxes completely encompassing the pit, the floor of which rose almost to this level. As at Covent Garden these boxes were separated by a cross aisle from a further eleven boxes, containing seven rows of benches and known as 'basket' boxes. All the boxes on all levels were divided by low partitions permitting a view of the stage across them. The second tier of boxes, with three rows of seats at the side, developed into a small amphitheatre with six rows of benches facing the stage, behind which was a foyer across the full width of the boxes and a coffee room behind. The third tier of boxes at the sides flanked the two-shilling gallery facing the stage, with sixteen rows of benches. A one-shilling gallery, with seven benches, was set back with its front above the seventh row of benches in the two-shilling gallery below. A fourth tier at the sides, originally intended as the slips, was actually divided into nine boxes on either side. 'The covings of the upper tier were lofty arches of the pointed order.'[17] Holland's original intention was to cantilever the side boxes from the timber frame of the outer walls, and the partitions between the boxes and adjoining corridors, but he must have taken note of the criticisms levelled at the Covent Garden boxes, and the design as built included light 'candelabra-like' columns at all levels.

Pit entrances on Russell Street and 'Woburn Street', and a later entrance added from Bridges Street, led into a great crescent shaped hall at ground floor level. This room was divided into a nave and aisles by columns, which carried up through the height of the building to support the upper galleries. Spaces opening on to this hall were used as shops. Above this, behind the basket boxes, was a large foyer the full width of the theatre, approached by grand staircases in the Russell and 'Woburn' Street wings, off which opened the large semicircular room mentioned earlier (p.144). 'There are also large saloons on the north and south sides of the Theatre, as also two handsome square Rooms, one of them intended as an Anti-chamber for the use of His Majesty, and the other for the Prince of Wales.'[18] Opening off the pit entrances on either side were stairs leading directly up to the two and one shilling galleries.

The corners of the large foyer (fig.95) were occupied by flights of stairs providing access to the second tier of boxes. Further, very cramped, stairs with winders (fig.95,[A]), set in the thickness of the main walls, connected the stage ends of the pit, and the first and second tiers of boxes.

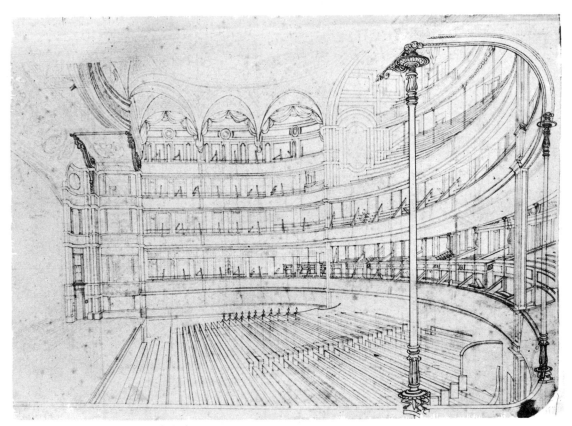

Fig.94. Drury Lane: interior, 1805

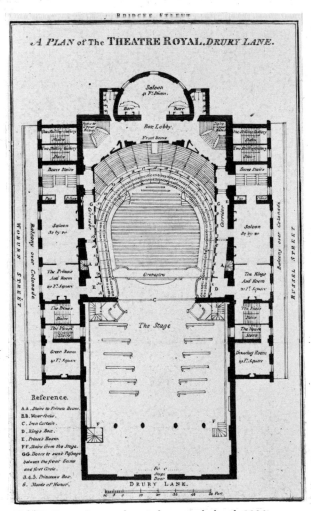

Fig.95. Drury Lane: plan at dress circle level, 1806

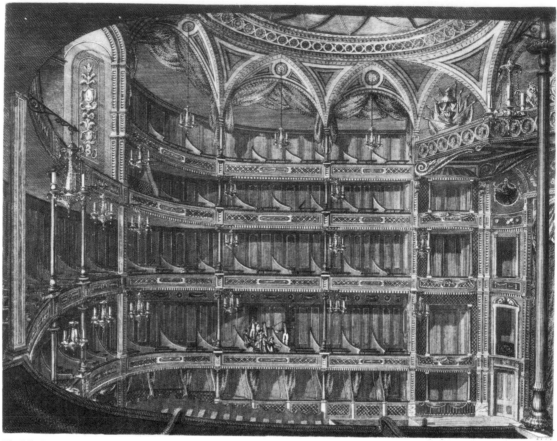

Fig.96. Drury Lane: interior, including proscenium doors, 1820

'The accommodations for the Stage' were

> 'upon a larger scale than in any other Theatre in Europe . . . the painter and Mechanist
> have a large space in which they may exert their abilities, 83 feet wide, 92 feet long,
> and 108 feet high. The scenery may be changed or disposed of either by raising it out
> of sight, or lowering the whole of it, or drawing it off sideways. The Machinery is
> executed upon the newest and most approved principles, contrived to be worked by
> Machinery placed either above or below the stage, thereby preventing the Necessity of
> having a number of Scene Shifters in the Way of the Performances.'[19]

It will be appreciated that this machinery constituted a major design problem calling for a
high degree of technical knowledge, and it is not surprising to find that it is outside the
architect's province. Holland called on Rudolph Cabanel, machinist, 'to prepare plans of and
for the Stage and Machinery'.[20] Holland, however, did inform Cabanel of a number of
decisions that had been made which included the provision of a painted, and adaptable,

frame to reduce the structural proscenium opening to a 35 feet wide by 24 feet 6 inches high opening. In addition he set out

> 'that the first set of wings shall be close to this painted or shifting decoration, that the openings shall be as follows, clear of the lamps, 7'0" – 6'0" – 6'0" – 5'6" – 5'0" – 5'0", that the inclination of the Stage shall be half an inch to the foot, that the floor, traps, placing of the Barrels, working the wings and scenes, shall be according to your model'.[21]

The increased size of the stage necessitated the use of much larger scenery than had been retained from the former theatre.

> 'The present stage required scenery, certainly, thirty-four feet in height, and about forty-two feet in width, so that an entire suite of new scenes was essential on great occasions, though where *display* was not material, the old pierced flats might be run on still, and the large gaps between them and the wings, filled up by any other scenes drawn forward, merely "to keep the wind away".'[22]

Elsewhere the same author describes the scenery as 'about 42 feet wide and 34 feet to the top of the scene'.[23]

Capon's set of plans shows that the stage, as designed by Mr Cabanel, was laid out with bridges, traps and wings. In addition it would appear as though the whole of the stage structure was carried on vertical posts set at approximately 8 feet centres, some 2 feet clear of the main walls. Above the stage there was 'a double range of galleries, called flies, containing machinery, and where the greatest part of the scenery is worked; but which, from the number of blocks, wheels, and ropes which crossed each other in every direction, give it very much the appearance of a ship's deck'.[24] Capon's plans show the first fly gallery at the level of the two-shilling gallery, its inner face following the lines of the diminishing scenic vista. Each gallery was approximately 10 feet wide next to the proscenium wall, and 20 feet wide at the rear. There was a 2 feet wide gap between the galleries and the walls, reflecting the gap at stage level, these openings most probably providing space for the movement of counterweights attached to the various scenic machines. There is no direct evidence as to whether the lower fly gallery was set horizontally, or if it sloped up parallel with the stage floor, as in later examples. In the reconstruction (fig.97) a horizontal gallery has been shown in the same manner, and at the same height, as the gallery indicated on Wyatt's preliminary designs for the succeeding theatre.[25] Wyatt later amended his design (p.177) to accommodate a sloping gallery at a lesser height above the stage, and it may reasonably be assumed that in the early designs he would have repeated the arrangements existing in the previous theatre, but later investigations regarding the desirable sizes of stage and scenes would have led him to reconsider the situation. Further evidence regarding the upper scene grooves in Holland's theatre as being 'all of one Height – five cuts in each groove'[26] also suggests a level fly gallery.

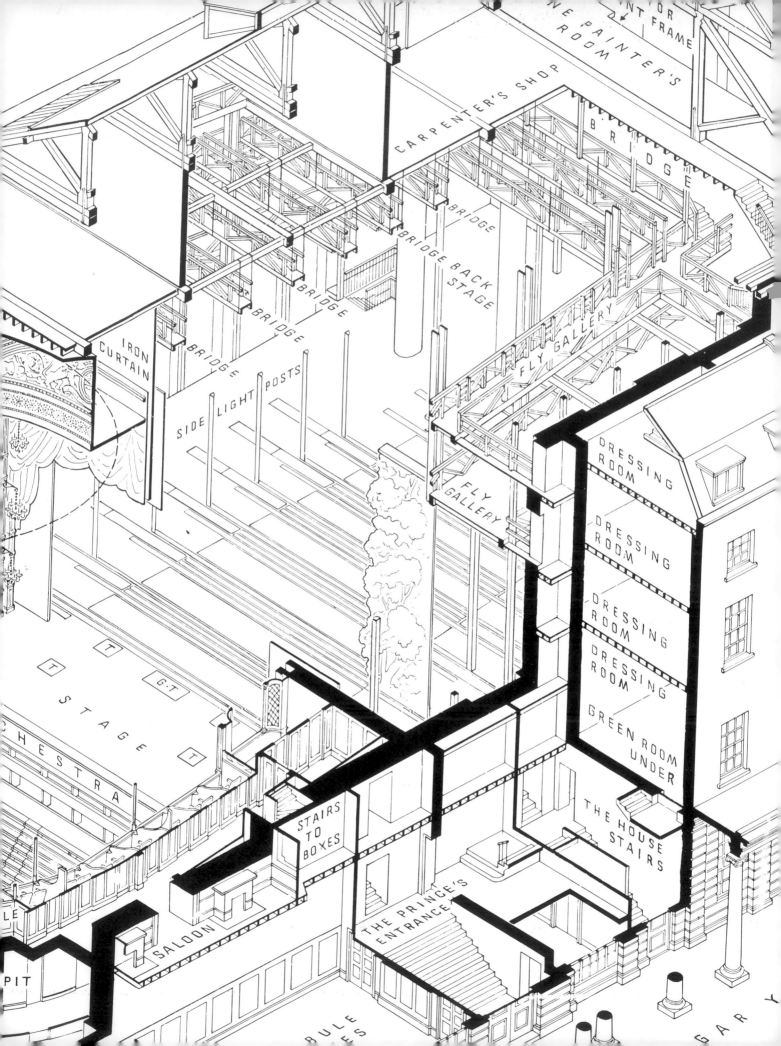

Behind the stage was a scene painter's room, some 22 feet wide, supported on four great piers. Slots in the floor at front and back were most probably designed for use with movable frames on which the scenery could be painted (figs.141,146). At a level with the upper part of the two-shilling gallery were further fly galleries lining with the inner face of the lower galleries, but, in this instance, no more than 4 feet 6 inches wide throughout their length. They were reached by stairs from the rear end of the lower gallery, and by bridges connecting with the stairs in the side wings, which provided access to the dressing and other rooms situated on the upper floors of these side wings. A bridge joined the galleries across the rear of the stage, and they were further linked by a floor above the proscenium ceiling. Further pairs of lines spanning the stage have been interpreted as catwalks providing access to the hanging scenes, several bridges and cross flies being provided by E. G. Saunders, the general carpenter, as part of the stage equipment (see footnote 29).

At roof level the first two bays at the front of the stage were open to the stage below, with side floors matching the lines of the fly galleries beneath, forming what was probably the 'barrel loft'. The rear two bays above the paint shop were also open, the remainder of the roof being subdivided into a number of spaces for use by the carpenters and painters. Spiral stairs led up to a terrace on the roof and to a large turret, designed in the manner of the Tower of the Winds, supporting a 10 feet high statue of Apollo. The turret contained a large ventilator to the auditorium below.[27] Dressing, and other, rooms were provided beneath the backstage area, adjoining the centrally placed stage entrance from Drury Lane. A large trap, 14 feet by 6 feet, in the stage floor gave direct access to the entry lobby beneath, possibly provided in a similar manner to that in the Theatre Royal, Leicester (fig.130). There were further dressing rooms in the side wings, to which, in 1795, were added 'a new Green Room for the actors' and a scene room constructed 'to preserve the scenes in prime order for years'.[28] There was now a 'Common Green Room and a Best Green Room',[29] 'one for the use of chorus-singers, supernumeraries, and figurants; the other for the principal performers'.[30] The latter is presumably that shown on plans as opening off the stage on the 'Woburn Street' side, the former above it at first floor level (fig.95).

In Volume 12 of Rees's *Cyclopaedia*, 1803-19, under the heading DRAMATIC, stage machinery, with traps and other stage apertures similar to those shown by Capon on his plan of Drury Lane stage and included on the reconstruction (fig.97), is described. In several instances various pieces are noted as being 'as used in the late Theatre Royal, Covent Garden,'[31] which provides some of the information which Holland did not include on his drawings (figs.88,90) for that theatre.

> 'The first aperture in the stage immediately behind the orchestra, and in front of the proscenium and curtain, is that for raising and lowering the foot lights, both for the purpose of trimming the lamps, and of darkening the stage when required . . . The next apertures are the side traps, of which any convenient number may be constructed.'

At Drury Lane there were four of these, two in front of the curtain and two behind. The

Fig.97. Drury Lane, 1794: detail of Fig.92

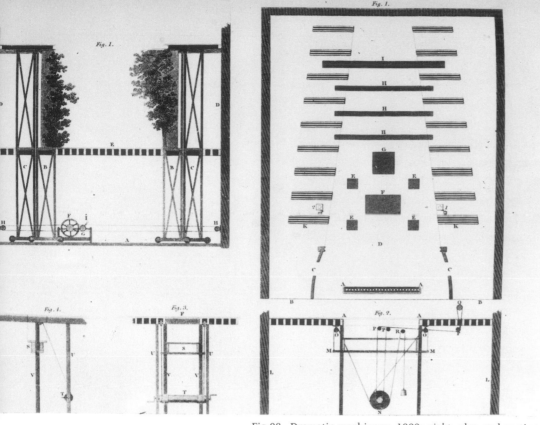

Fig.98. Dramatic machinery, 1800: *right*, plan and section of a typical stage; *left top*, wings and carriages as used at Covent Garden.

Fig.99. 'A startling effect' –
The Grave Trap, after Cruickshank

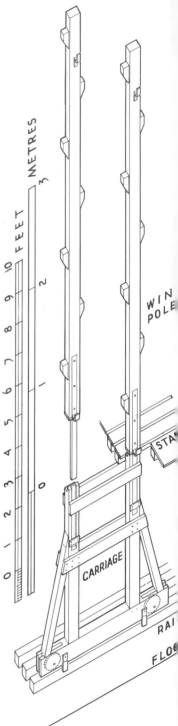

Fig.100. Wing carriage

plan (fig.98) illustrated in the *Cyclopaedia*[32] also has four (E), but here all are behind the curtain. 'In the middle are two larger traps. The first . . . is of oblong form from six to seven feet in length, and from three to four feet in breadth. It is most frequently used for the grave scene in Shakespeare's tragedy of Hamlet' (fig.99). This trap is included at Drury Lane, but the second appears only on the *Cyclopaedia* plan (G), where it is square,

> 'and is chiefly used for the sinking of the cauldron in the tragedy of Macbeth . . . Behind these, in large theatres, where many changes of the scenery are frequently required, there are a number of longitudinal apertures across the stage, which are covered by planks movable upon hinges, so that by throwing them back, the stage may be opened in a moment. The use of these is to allow the flat scenes to sink through the stage, when required. These are called "flaps".'

> 'In the late Theatre Royal of Covent Garden, much of the scenery, not in immediate use, was kept in the cellar under the stage. For the purpose of raising and lowering these scenes with facility, other apertures were made, and closed with square or rectangular pieces of wood, which could be placed or displaced in a few minutes; these were called sliders . . . No machinery whatever is permanently attached to the flaps or sliders, for as these apertures serve generally for the passage of the flat scenes through the stage, the machinery must depend upon the particular effect which it is necessary to produce. The flat scenery is generally raised by a crane, unless a very rapid ascent or descent be required, when it may be done by the application of a counterpoise.'

At a later date such narrow openings were to be equipped with specific machinery (p.212). The *Cyclopaedia* does not describe the wider openings which are shown on the reconstruction (fig.97). These are almost certainly bridges, the nature and use of which will be described in terms of specific examples (p.209ff).

Scenery at this time is described as consisting of

> 'the flat scenes which form the termination of the perspective across the stage, and the side scenes, or wings, which are disposed upon each side of the stage so as to be shifted as often as may be necessary, and to afford opportunities for the actors to come upon the stage, or quit it, at any of the intervals between the respective sets. Besides these, there are scenes which may be occasionally placed and displaced, such as the fronts of cottages, cascades, rocks, bridges, and other appendages, requisite in the representation of particular dramas. These are generally called pieces.'

The backshutters, now known as 'flats', were still in two pieces which met in the middle, and could be drawn off to the sides of the stage. Such flats were, however, being replaced by 'drops, or curtains, where the canvas is furled or unfurled upon a roller, placed either at the top or bottom of the scene'. The side wings were still a standard feature of the scene, and these and the flats could be moved by hand in top and bottom grooves fixed to the stage, and to the underside of the fly galleries. In the case of the flats the upper grooves were 'sometimes constructed; to save room, upon joints, by which they may either be lowered to the horizontal position, or drawn up to the side walls (figs.138a.b.c). In this respect their construction is pretty similar to that of a common draw-bridge. This plan was used in the late Theatre Royal, Covent Garden, where they were called flys.'

Not all such scenes were moved by hand, however, and the scenes at Covent Garden are described and illustrated in the *Cyclopaedia* (fig.98)[33] as being moved by the aid of machinery in the form of carriages or 'frames'. It would appear from the manner in which Holland described the scene changes at Drury Lane (p.148) as being worked by machines which 'prevented the Necessity of having a number of Scene Shifters' normally required if each wing was to be pushed along its grooves by hand 'in the Way of the Performances' at stage level, that he also used this continental method of moving the wings here as well. The mention of upper scene grooves (p.149) might at first sight suggest that it was the manual groove system that was in use here and not the carriages, until it is realised that the wings used were at least 30 feet high, a size that would have made it virtually impossible to slide them without some mechanical help, the upper grooves being invaluable in helping to maintain the wings in a vertical position. As noted above, grooves and carriages were used together at Covent Garden.

The frames to which the wings were attached ran on rails, or 'sleepers', in a basement beneath the stage, and were arranged in pairs, one on either side of the stage.

'Each frame runs upon two small wheels, to diminish the friction, and all passing through longitudinal apertures in the stage, which serve as guides, rise to a sufficient height above the stage to support the wings, which are attached to them in front, so as to be quickly removed, and others substituted.' (fig.100; fig.98 – top left).

All the frames were attached by ropes to a central cylinder, or barrel, running from front to back of the stage. There were two pairs of frames at each wing position, and all were attached to the barrel in such a way that 'when the upper part of the barrel is moved towards the right, the front frames B,B, will move forward upon the stage, and the back frames, C,C, will be withdrawn . . . When the motion of the barrel is reversed; the back frames will advance, and the front ones will recede.' The off-stage wings could then be removed from the frames and be replaced by a new set ready to advance on to the stage when required.

It is possible that similar carriages were used in the original Covent Garden as the inventory included the '12 pr of scene ladders fixt with ropes' already noted (p.118), this item being taken together with the information that when a Mr Chetwood went to Dublin in 1749 he 'alter'd the Stage after the Manner of the Theatres in France and England' and 'worked the wings by means of a barrel underneath'.[34] Scene frames were also in use in Drury Lane cellar in 1714. In addition to the footlights the scene was lit by side lights:

'these are generally placed between the wings, to turn upon a hinge, for the purpose of darkening the stage when necessary . . . The apparatus consists merely of an upright post, to which is attached a piece of tinned iron, forming two sides of a square, and movable upon joints or hinges, and furnished with shelves to receive the lamps or candles . . . Side lights are placed between every set of wings, on both sides of the stage.'[35]

Further barrels were provided in the barrel loft for the movement of the borders and other hanging scenes, and examples of these will be illustrated and discussed later (pp.200,203).

It was originally intended that Drury Lane should hold 3,919, although the final capacity is usually given as 3,611, a figure which varied according to the different changes made during its lifetime. Although these figures constitute a very great change from the 2,000 persons that the second Drury Lane is supposed to have seated in its final form,[36] it represents too a considerable increase in the size of the building (compare figs.83,92), which affected not only the nature of the presentations but also the method of acting, it being now necessary for the actor to make himself heard in the farthest recesses of the theatre, a distance of some 100 feet as compared with 60 feet in Adam's Drury Lane. Boaden records that 'A person in the gallery called out – "We can't hear" ' . . . to which Mr. Kemble replied '(with increased spirit) "I will *raise* my voice, and the GALLERIES shall *hear* me." (Great tumult.)'[37]

> 'Since the stages of Drury Lane and Covent Garden have been so enlarged in their dimensions as to be henceforward theatres for spectators rather than playhouses for hearers, it is hardly to be wondered at if managers and directors encourage those representations, to which their structure is best adapted. The splendor of the scenes, the ingenuity of the machinist and the rich display of dresses, aided by the captivating charms of music, now in a great degree supercede the labours of the poet. There can be nothing very gratifying in watching the movements of an actor's lips, when we cannot hear the words that proceed from them, but when the animating march strikes up, and the stage lays open its recesses to the depth of a hundred feet for the procession to advance, even the most distant spectator can enjoy his shilling's-worth of show . . . On the stage of Old Drury in the days of Garrick the moving brow and penetrating eye of that matchless actor came home to the spectator. As the passions shifted, and were by turns reflected from the mirror of his expressive countenance, nothing was lost; upon the scale of modern Drury many of the finest touches of his act would of necessity fall short. The distant audience might chance to catch the text, but would not see the comment, that was wont so exquisitely to elucidate the poet's meaning, and impress it on the hearer's heart.'[38]

As a result the emphasis was placed on the spectacular, with larger and more imposing scenes by such artists as William Capon and De Loutherbourg.

In spite of the various fire precautions incorporated in the design, Holland's Drury Lane was burnt to the ground on 24th February, 1809, the amount of timber in the structure contributing to the conflagration. As the fire broke out about 11 o'clock at night on a day when there had been no performance, the efficiency of the means of exit from the various parts of the building was happily not put to the test. Various comments and criticisms were published regarding the reservoirs and iron curtain, the latter being reported in one instance[39] as having been removed a few months before the fire, as it had become too rusty to work, and the reservoirs were said to have been empty and forgotten. The latter had certainly been filled five months earlier when Covent Garden burnt down and sparks were carried in the direction of Drury Lane and 'A great number of people mounted the roof, ready, in case of actual fire to open the large cistern of water provided there.'[40] Boaden further reports that

> 'If what White, the fireman belonging to the British, (Insurance company) said was true, he had himself, two days before the accident, inspected the reservoir, and all the plugs and pipes, which opening upon the tiers of boxes, could most certainly have been played, in *time*, upon the running flames, had there been a single *hose* merely on the alert in the theatre.'[41]

He also commented that 'the iron curtain did not of *itself* drop, to stop its accession to the stage'.[42] Whatever the truth of the matter, it would appear that any provisions made for containing or extinguishing a fire depended in the final analysis on the provision and watchfulness of competent watchmen who could put them into operation.

In complete contrast to the enormous scale of Holland's building, the theatre built at Richmond, Yorks, in 1788 (fig.101) is an example of one of the theatres erected in the smaller towns visited by the touring circuit companies which proliferated throughout the country at this time. The Yorkshire circuit was under the control of Samuel Butler, and included Harrogate, Richmond, Kendal, Ripon, Northallerton and Beverley.[43]

The theatre occupies a stone walled building 28 feet wide by an average of 61 feet long, divided almost equally internally between stage and auditorium, the latter overlapping the former by some 5 feet. A rectangular pit was enclosed by boxes, with two rows of benches at the sides, and three facing the stage. These front boxes were backed by a curved wall similar in character to those at Drury Lane (fig.63) and the Theatre Royal, Bristol (fig.76). The front row of benches in the side boxes and the two front rows of the front boxes were divided by low partitions of the same height as the box fronts, each related to one of the small timber Doric columns supporting the side galleries and the main gallery facing the stage, situated above the front boxes. A proscenium door on either side provided access to the front of the stage; these were separated from the side boxes by timber partitions with double doors. Above the proscenium doors are boxes, again separated from the side galleries by boarded partitions, with arched openings to the stage. A flat ceiling over the pit and side boxes ends at the upstage post flanking the proscenium doors, at which point the curtain would have been hung (fig.102). The ceiling slopes gently up above the seven-tiered gallery to provide minimum headroom. A small foyer is fitted between the curved rear wall of the boxes and the oblique outer north wall of the theatre front. An entry door in the north-west corner of the theatre gave access to a landing with a single pay box which all members of

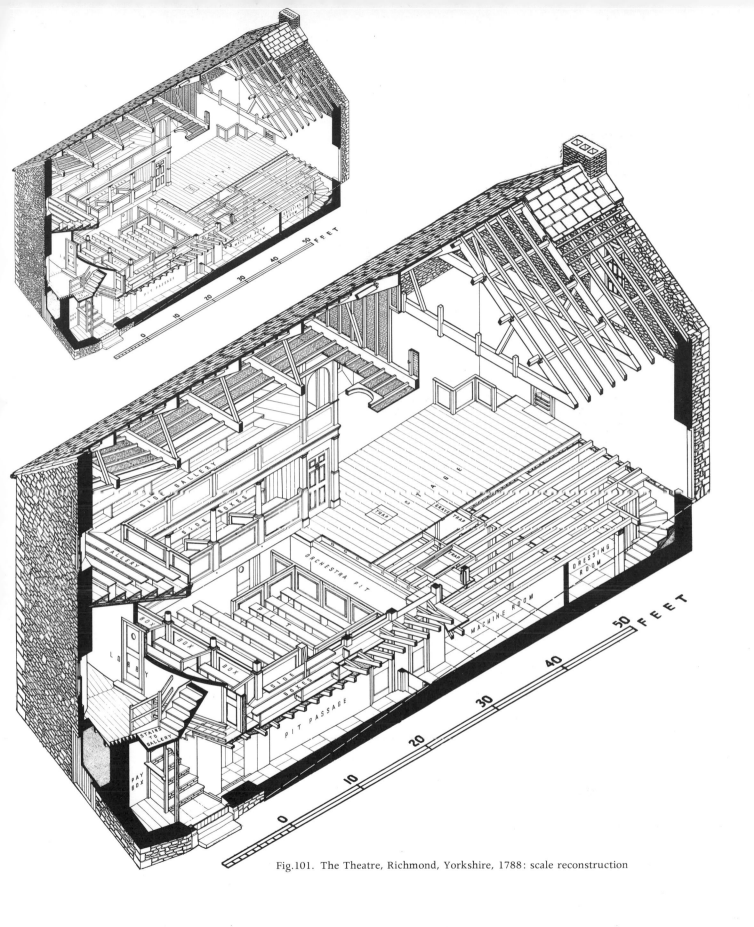

Fig.101. The Theatre, Richmond, Yorkshire, 1788: scale reconstruction

Fig.102. The Theatre, Richmond: interior

the audience had to pass. From here steps led up to the foyer with access doors in the curved wall to the boxes, and a flight of stairs doubled back over the pay box leading to the galleries above; steps also led down from the entrance landing to a passage beneath the side boxes on the western side only of the theatre. It was noted earlier (p.93) that the timber structures of boxes and galleries were normally supported on solid walls of stone or brick, and this had been the case at Richmond, until the theatre fell into disuse and a wine cellar was built beneath the auditorium and stage. This has since been removed, and the pit walls and floor replaced (figs.103a.b,104), the former to marks on the underside of the supporting beams beneath the side boxes, and the latter to dimensions obtained from traces of a similar floor in the remains of the theatre in Loughborough.[44]

At the front of the stage there was a cut for the footlights, similar to that described in Rees's *Cyclopaedia* (p.151), and behind this there were only three other openings in the sloping stage: two square corner traps and one central rectangular grave trap. In the rear wall of the stage there was a fireplace, and marks on the walls clearly indicated the position of two winding stairs leading down in each corner to the understage area which was divided into three rooms. The largest of these occupied the full width of the theatre beneath the front half of the stage, and was used as a machine room where the traps and the mobile footlights could be operated. The remaining under-stage area was divided by a central wall into two dressing rooms, opening off the machine room, and each connecting directly with the stage above by the corner stairs. The pit, pit passage, machine room and dressing rooms were all excavated below ground level as a basement.

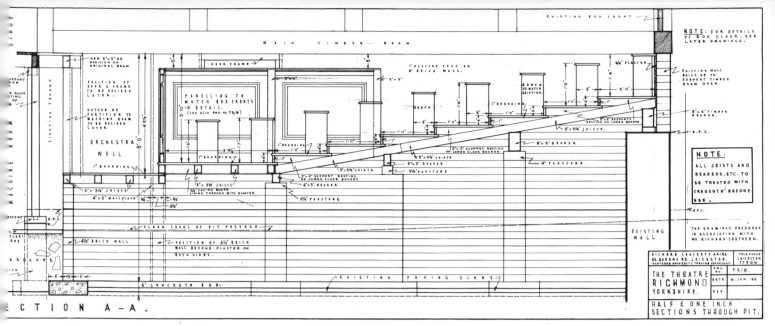

(a) section, with stage *to left*

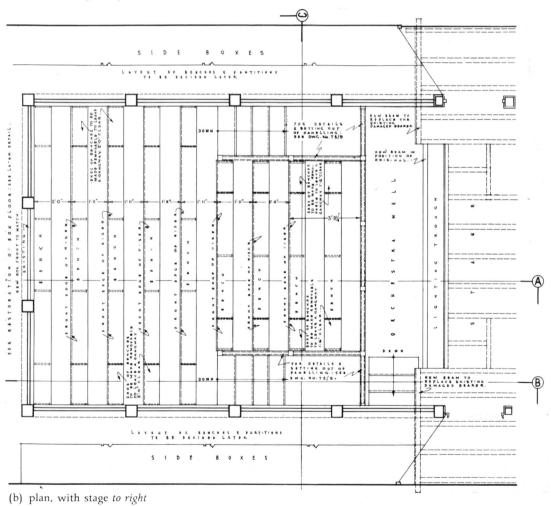

(b) plan, with stage *to right*

Fig.103. The Theatre, Richmond: drawings for restoration of the pit in 1949

Fig.104. The Theatre, Richmond:
interior during restoration in 1949

Examples of similar circuit theatres existed throughout the country, and their size and layout varied very little. Unless they occupied a particularly difficult site they were built as a rectangle between 50 and 60 feet in length and from 25 to 30 feet in width. An entrance vestibule occupied a fairly small area at the auditorium end, and the remainder of the building was almost equally divided between stage and auditorium, the latter normally extending over the vestibule as an upper gallery to the outer wall of the theatre.[45]

In his *Treatise on Theatres* (1790), George Saunders not only described and criticised existing theatres at home and abroad, but also included designs for an ideal theatre, and a similar opera house. These designs were based on what may perhaps be considered today as a somewhat naive approach to acoustics, but which nevertheless took the limits of the human voice as the vital factor in the theatre's dimensions. Saunders was also concerned with the problem of viewing the actor, whom he thought to be more important than the scene, and as a result sight lines were an additional feature to be considered in his designs. He investigated the angles and distances from which an actor could best be viewed:

> 'if we view a person at a greater height than an angle of 45 degrees . . . the features appear distorted and the expressions grimace. To discern well the motions of the features, we cannot be too near the actor: it is with great difficulty we comprehend them, at the distance of 75 feet.'

As a result of experiments he concluded that whereas an oval or horseshoe form of auditorium might satisfy sound requirements, nevertheless these forms were not desirable from the point of view of those spectators placed to the sides of either shape. A circle, he concluded, is the best form with its centre 17 feet 'from the front of the speaker'; hearers seated on this circle 'will equally participate the advantages. In order to make it (the circle) as capacious as possible, and at the same time to reduce the opening of the stage, we will give 3-4ths of the diameter of a circle to the body of the theatre, and 1-8th more for the frontispiece.' The section is likewise conditioned by his experiments, from which he concluded that

'in a given distance we hear worse the higher we are situated; and as such a situation is equally bad for viewing, it will be proper to keep down the ceiling of the theatre as low as may be, agreeably to the necessary accommodation and beauty of the building. It does not however appear that heightening the ceiling will in any wise sensibly affect the voice; it will in all cases be a conductor of sound to the upper range of seats, which leaves us at great liberty in that respect. To me, the proportioned height appears to be 3-4ths of the diameter, or the length from the stage to the front of the opposite boxes. Suppose the diameter . . . to be 60 feet, it will follow that the height should be 45 feet from the level of the stage: which height includes all the visual rays within the angle of 45 degrees. With regard to the size, it would not be advisable to have a greater distance than 60 feet from the stage, on a level with the speaker, or 70 feet to the utmost extent, in either theatre or opera-house.'

Saunders considers that

'the great advance of some stages into the body of the theatre is too absurd, I imagine, ever to be again practised; as the performance is chiefly conducted on that spot where the entrances and exits are made, and short scenes will not admit of the actor's advancing: besides that all the plots, which compose so great a part of dramatic representation, must be among the machinery . . . The actors, instead of being so brought forwards, ought to be thrown back at a certain distance from the spectator's eye, and stand within the scenery of the stage, in order to make a part of that pleasing illusion for which all dramatic exhibitions are calculated.'

He suggests that the front of the stage should be straight and not curved and complains of the dazzling footlights, which he proposes replacing by a French method of illuminating the stage by lights placed 'at the extremity of the boxes, on each side of the stage'. Protection against fire is also considered.

'The whole of the theatre should be surrounded by a thick wall, as well next the stage, as on every other part. Over the opening of the stage an arch may be turned, on which the wall may be continued up quite through the roof, so as to prevent all communication of the timbers. The passages communicating with the boxes should all be arched, and have an easy access to spacious stone staircases, that would in case of fire enable the audience to depart without the least hazard.'

The stage within the auditorium was fast becoming a thing of the past: Saunders' view was that 'the stage and its accompaniments may be regarded as a distinct part of the building;

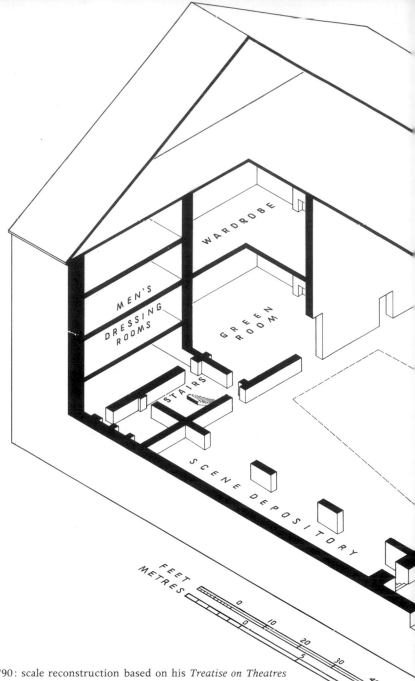

Fig.105. Saunders' Ideal Theatre, 1790: scale reconstruction based on his *Treatise on Theatres*

being for the accommodation of the scenery with all its attendant machinery, actors, dancers, assistants'. In his design for an Ideal Theatre (fig.105) 'The Stage-opening is 38 feet 6 inches wide; the front of the stage floor is preserved straight, which together with the frontispiece projects 7 feet 6 inches before the scene. The actor will consequently have very little advance to make, and will appear (as he certainly should do) among the scenery.'

It has been noted that at both Drury Lane and Covent Garden, following the French practice, the Royal Box was one or other of the side boxes adjoining the proscenium, which the Duke of York called 'the worst box in the theatre for seeing the play!' 'I have often

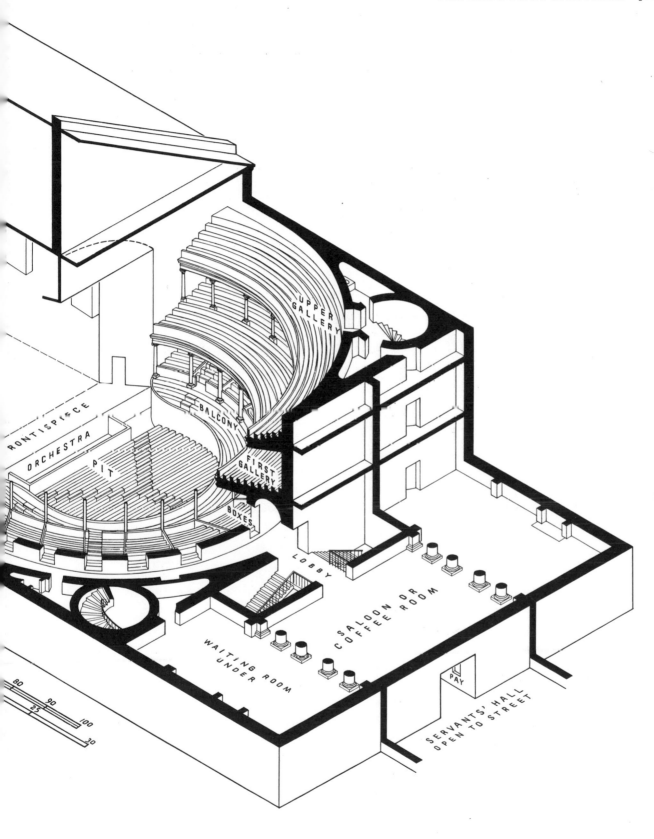

FRONTISPIECE

ORCHESTRA

PIT

BALCONY

FIRST GALLERY

UPPER GALLERY

BOXES

LOBBY

SALOON OR COFFEE ROOM

WAITING ROOM UNDER

PAY

SERVANTS' HALL OPEN TO STREET

80

90

25

100

30

wondered, and so have others, why new stage boxes (placed where the useful stage doors used to be) were frequented; but, in short, there are persons always who would prefer such a box, were it much higher on the stage, so few want really to see the piece attentively.'[46] It can only be presumed that the original position of the Royal Box facing the stage had passed from memory, as Saunders suggests this position as being better than that in use.

> 'A happy opportunity here offers for placing the King's box opposite the stage, which projecting to the front of the balcony, with a small canopy over it, would be within view of nearly all the spectators; being situated at a point which unites the illusion of the scenery with the advantage of hearing: a desirable circumstance, which in this country has never yet been attained.'

At Drury Lane 'on nights when the theatre is honoured with their Majesties' presence, the partitions of the stage-box are taken down, and it is brought forward near two feet; a canopy is erected.'[47]

Saunders also wanted to move the entry doors to the pit from their position near the stage front, where they had been placed from necessity, when the approach passages were beneath the side boxes, and headroom had dictated their connecting with the pit at its lowest level. In his descriptions of 'Old Drury', James Boaden also criticised this position for the pit entrances when he said

> 'It had the common defect of all our theatres, except the Opera House' (fig.71), 'namely, that the pit doors of entrance were close to the orchestra, and, as they did not choose to leave the most valuable part of the house without its complement, and there was no mode of forcing the people who sat at a distance to inconvenience themselves, the door-keepers, by the box-screw, kept *winding* in their late arrivals; and the pressure into the mass close to it, already ill at ease, and dreading a new attack every moment from a rushing current of cold air, which ushered in the stranger, occasioned *fits* among the women, and *fights* among the men, while the *stage* and the *boxes* alike suspended every other amusement, but looking on, till silence was restored.'[48]

Obviously this problem would have existed wherever the entrances were placed, so long as there were no proper gangways and such as there were were blocked by standers: it is interesting to note that in his Ideal Theatre (fig.105) Saunders still illustrates the use of the hinged seat gangways in the body of the pit. With the doors at the front, however, the disturbance was seen by almost all the house, and had the maximum effect.

The convenience and safety of the audience is given considerable thought. 'Each box will have its separate door communicating with an arched corridor, and four doors lead in to the balcony, which together with three large outer doors will render the departure, in case of an alarm, safe, easy and expeditious.' The staircases were to be enclosed by walls and constructed of stone as a further safety precaution, and the main stairs connected both with the theatre and the coffee-room, which was placed at 'a convenient distance, so that the audience may not be disturbed by those who frequent that place'. In addition there was a waiting room adjoining the entrance hall where patrons might await their carriages. He comments that

> 'the long passages which conduct to the different parts of our present theatres are productive of much mischief. The paying-doors, instead of being at the outward end, are always in the contrary situation; thereby giving the best of opportunities for the depredations of pick-pockets, and confining the company in a narrow space without the possibility of relief in case of an accident.'

He provides additional space at either side of the stage, connected by three arched openings, for 'the convenience of shifting the scenes and machinery; and ample room will be left for forming the bodies of choruses, dancers, attendants, &c'. Four storeys of dressing rooms, eight for women and eight for men, connect by stairs with the Green Room at the rear of the stage, above which is the wardrobe, situated 'in the centre of the dressing rooms, and the clothes may be served to the different persons without carrying them about to an inconvenient distance'. Beneath the stage he suggests placing 'the housekeeper's apartments, performers' entrance, carpenter's shop, painter's room, &c, &c'.

8 Picture frames and proscenium walls

The theatre which replaced Holland's Drury Lane was designed by Benjamin Wyatt, the foundation stone being laid on the 29th October, 1811, and the theatre opened on the 10th October, 1812. According to his own description[1] he based the design on four main considerations: '(1) The Size or Capacity of the Theatre, as governed by the width of the Proscenium, or Stage-Opening' and the 'pecuniary return to be made to those whose Property might be embarked in the Concern'. '(2) The Form or Shape of the Theatre, as connected with the primary objects of DISTINCT SOUND and VISION.' '(3) The facility of Ingress and Egress' . . . with particular reference to ease of access and escape in case of accident or alarm. His fourth concern was with the control of nuisances within the theatre – riots, prostitution and similar activities – and the protection of 'the more rational and respectable class of Spectators from those nuisances to which they have long been exposed, by being obliged to pass through Lobbies, Rooms, and Avenues, crowded with the most disreputable Members of the Community, and subject to scenes of the most disgusting indecency'.

Wyatt was conversant with Saunders' *Treatise*, and indeed quotes from it, but he is probably more concerned than Saunders was with the commercial aspects of the theatre. He makes his Proscenium Opening (fig.106) the same width as in the previous theatre, 33 feet, or 5 feet 6 inches narrower than that prescribed by Saunders. The width for Holland's theatre which he worked to was presumably the final width of the proscenium opening after the stage doors and boxes had been added behind the original proscenium opening (fig.95). This he does not only on the basis that 'the working of the Scenes and machinery is rendered either easy and secure, or difficult and uncertain, in proportion to the breadth and height of the Scenes, and the corresponding magnitude and weight of the machinery, by which the Scenes are moved', but also on the financial savings involved in the use of 'a smaller number of *extra* Performers fully occupying the whole Stage, than would be necessary, to prevent its appearing unoccupied and bare, in proportion as the Stage should be extended beyond the limit which I adopted in my Design'. He also bore in mind 'that, for every additional foot given to the width of the Stage-opening . . . a great many additional yards of canvas' must be 'used in every one of the Drop Scenes, and Flats, as they are termed; and the size of the Painting Rooms, Carpenter's Shops, and other Appurtenances to the Stage, as well as the expense of Colours, and of the Painter's time, must be proportionately increased; all of which create charges and difficulties of great magnitude; and consequently, in an indirect way, tend to embarass and deteriorate the Public Performances.' Nevertheless the vastness of Wyatt's stage was criticised by Boaden[2] writing in 1825, who further said that the actor 'was here lost in an immense space, and the scenery which should have borne upon his performance, and given a locality to the character, was a diminutive picture, hung behind him at a distance'.

The predominance of scenic spectacle over the actor at this time is clearly underlined by Wyatt when he calls the auditorium the 'Spectatory', and defines the Proscenium as being a frame to the picture.

> 'With respect to the style and character of the decoration of the Proscenium, I never felt a doubt, in my mind, that they ought to accord with the decoration of the Spectatory; for being before the Curtain, and in view of the Spectators, when the Scene is excluded, the Proscenium must be considered as forming a part of the Spectatory, and not a part of the Scene; – It is unquestionably *not* a part of the Scene; and, if it be not properly and absolutely a part of the Spectatory, it is a line of separation between the two, and is to the Scene what the frame of a Picture is to the Picture itself: namely, a boundary line to confine the eye to the Subject within that line, and prevent it from wandering to other objects. The style of decoration or ornament in the Proscenium will never divert the eye or the mind from the Scene upon the Stage; the mind is not prepared to connect or confuse the two, and it will no more be liable to notice the Proscenium to the injury of the Scene itself, than, in viewing a Picture, it will be liable to be diverted from the contemplation of the Picture itself, by the richness of the Picture-frame.'

This quotation is important in that it plainly sets out the state of mind which, taken together with the attempts to control the spread of fire, resulted in the eventual separation of stage and auditorium, actor and audience, in the pattern known today as the traditional 'picture-frame' theatre.

Wyatt omitted the doors 'which are usually placed on each side of the Proscenium; nothing being more absurd, than an indiscriminate application of such doors to Scenes entirely dissimilar in themselves, and totally incongruous with such features'. In place of the doors were 'two very fine large lamps, with tripods on triangular pedestals, each lamp containing a circle of small burners with lights. As these drew the attention of the audience from the performers', and were always being blown out by the draught from the rise and fall of the curtain

> 'they were afterwards removed, and the stage doors restored. On each side are two stage boxes, forming an acute angle with the stage, and above them are niches with

Fig.106. The Theatre Royal, Drury Lane, Benjamin Wyatt, 1811: scale reconstruction based on contemporary drawings

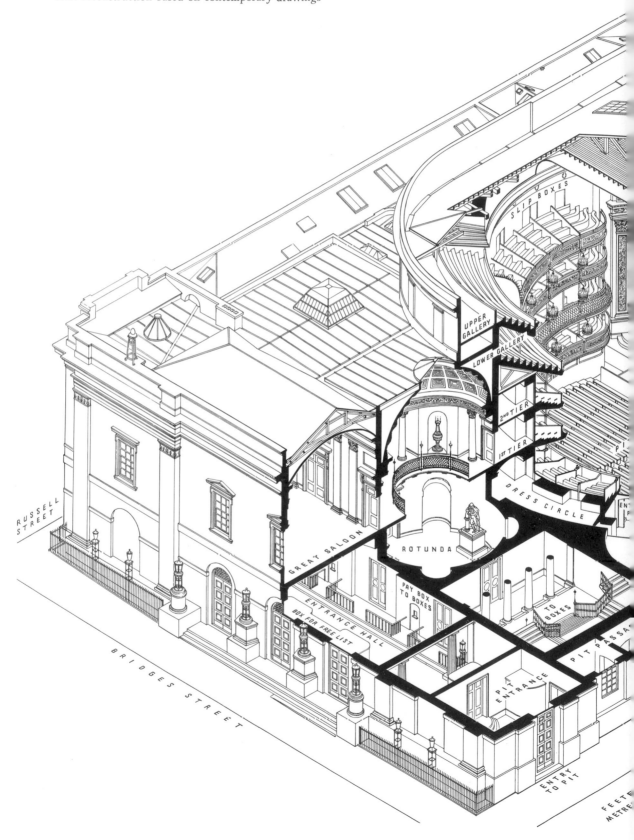

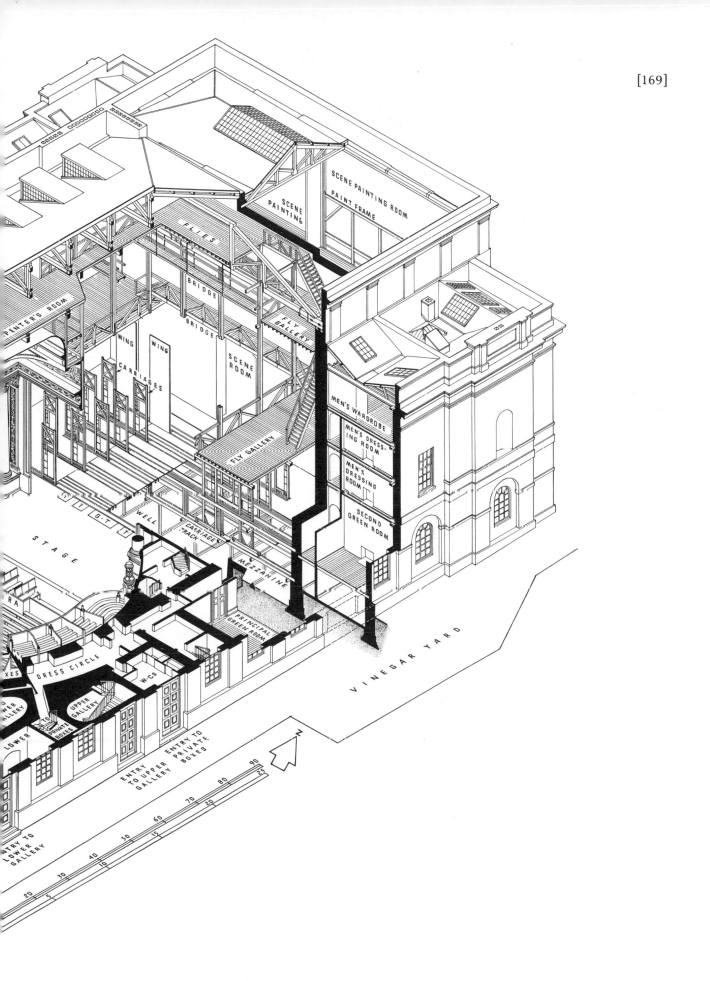

SCENE PAINTING ROOM

PAINT FRAME

SCENE PAINTING

FLIES

BRIDGE

BRIDGE

FLY GALLERY

CARPENTERS ROOM

WING

WING

SCENE ROOM

CARRIAGES

FLY GALLERY

MEN'S WARDROBE

MEN'S DRESS- ING ROOM

MEN'S DRESSING ROOM

SECOND GREEN ROOM

WELL

CARRIAGE RACK

STAGE

MEZZANINE

PRINCIPAL GREEN ROOM

VINEGAR YARD

ORCHESTRA

DRESS CIRCLE

W·C·S

BOXES

LOWER GALLERY

UPPER GALLERY

PRIVATE BOXES

ENTRY TO UPPER GALLERY

ENTRY TO PRIVATE BOXES

ENTRY TO LOWER GALLERY

N

5 10 15 20 25
20 30 40 50 60 70 80 90

statues . . . Between the pedestal lamps and the curtain on each side is a massy Corinthian column of verd antique, with the gilt capital supporting the arch over the stage, in the circle of which are the arms of his majesty. Corresponding with these columns are three pilasters, ornamented with connected rigs entwined with grapes and vine leaves, all richly gilt.'[3]

Writing of this theatre, W. J. Lawrence tells us:

'For the old-fashioned proscenium arch was substituted a gilded picture frame, remote from the footlights, over which the actors were forbidden to step. Grumblings both loud and deep were heard among the players over their various deprivations, and finally old Dowton, pluckier than the rest, broke into open rebellion. ''Don't tell me of frames and pictures!'' he exclaimed, with choler. ''If I can't be heard by the audience in the frame, I'll walk out of it.'' And out of it he came.'[4]

In spite therefore of the architect's theorising on the subject, this move to make the actors a part of the scenic picture was not popular with them, and it must certainly have been something of a trial that with a 'fore-stage' still provided in front of the 'picture-frame', they were not permitted to use it. However, under the circumstances the change was inevitable, and although the proscenium doors and stage persisted in the smaller theatres, by the middle of the 19th century most large theatres had finally done away with the proscenium stage and its doors. When the Haymarket Theatre (figs.107a.b.), built by John Nash in 1820, was altered in 1843, the management proudly advertised:

'During the recess, the theatre has undergone Extensive Alterations, the Proscenium has been entirely remodelled, and the whole of the Interior decorated in a most Costly and Elegant Style. By a curtailment of the useless portion of the Stage in front of the Curtain, and advancing Orchestra and Lights near the Actors and Scenic Effects, the Lessee has been enabled to appropriate the portion so obtained, to form a certain number of Orchestra Stalls, which can be retained for the parties taking them for the whole of the Evening.'[5]

So, having pushed the actor back into the picture, the management made a virtue of the need to move the lights closer to his now remote position, and appropriated the 'useless' area of stage.

Not only was the stage being cut back to provide for extra seating, but the cheaper pit seats were now being replaced by more expensive stalls directly adjoining the stage. Nash had earlier, in 1815, made similar alterations at His Majesty's when he provided eight rows of stalls adjoining the orchestra, with fourteen rows of pit benches behind. The front rows of the gallery were also designated as 'gallery stalls', and priced more highly than the remainder of the gallery seats. The appropriation of this area of the stages by the managements did provide more seats, but it did not take into account the fact that most theatres were still designed for the actors to be seen on the 'fore-stage'; with the actor behind the pro-

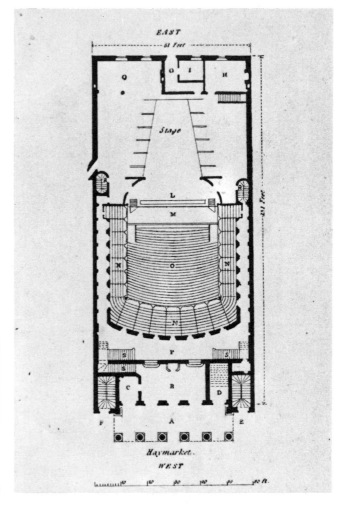

A. Portico.
B. Lobby.
C. Box Office.
D. Entrance to Pit.
E. D° to Upper Gallery.
F. D° to Lower Gallery.
G. Private Entrance.
H. Green Room.
I. Waiting Room.

L. Proscenium.
M. Orchestra.
N. Boxes.
O. Pit.
P. Lobby to Dress Boxes
Q. Scene Room.
R. Stairs to Private Boxes.
S. Stairs to Boxes.

(a) plan

(b) interior, 1825

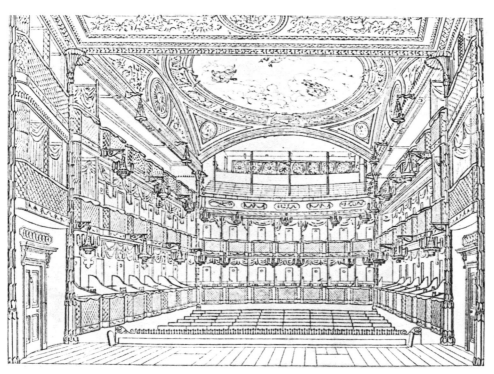

Fig.107. The Haymarket Theatre,
John Nash, 1820

scenium opening, the audience in the side seats of the horseshoe circles were no longer well placed to see him. When the Haymarket was rebuilt in 1880[6] a gilt 'picture-frame' completely encircled the stage opening, and there was no sign of any 'fore-stage'.

This, however, is jumping too far ahead. In deciding on the size and form of his Spectatory, Wyatt was influenced both by his own experiments on sound, which were largely based on those described by Saunders, and by the need to provide a commercially viable theatre capable of accommodating 'Spectators to the amount of not less than £600 (exclusive of Private Boxes) at one time.' He is at pains to point out that here he is referring only to seating accommodation, and not to 'the additional multitude, who, on a crowded night, will fill the Rooms and Lobbies of the Theatre'. 'I was aware,' he writes,

> 'of the existence of a very popular notion, that our Theatres ought to be *very small*; but it appeared to me, that, if that popular notion should be suffered to proceed too far, it would tend, in every way, to deteriorate our Dramatic Performance; by depriving the Proprietors of that Revenue, which is indispensable to defray the heavy expenses of such a Concern, and to leave a reasonable Profit to those whose Property might be embarked in the undertaking.'

His experiments in sound convinced him that a speaker's voice could be heard in the open air 92 feet in front of him, 75 feet on either side, and some 30 feet behind; figures which correspond almost exactly to those quoted by Saunders. On the principle that an actor would have moved around the stage, and would turn his head first this way and then that, he concluded that the distances relative to sound as heard at the sides should be the limits to be considered, and working on this principle he made the overall diameter to the rear of the boxes in the region of 75 feet, with a distance of 53 feet 9 inches from the front of the stage to the rear wall of the boxes facing the stage. Commenting on his design, Wyatt said that

> 'This limitation of the Area of the Theatre, combined with all the principles before stated, I considered as an ample provision for the absorption of Sound resulting from the number of persons, their woollen clothes, and the state of the atmosphere, in a Theatre, and an effectual security for the Sound being distinctly heard in every part of the House: In this calculation I have been compleatly justified, by the practical result, since the Theatre has been open to the Public.'

Boaden, however, did not agree and said 'Nor did the architect quite answer the expectations he had raised from his pamphlet – the structure was *not* admirable for the conveyance of the voice — much of the dialogue came imperfectly even to my ear.'[7]

Wyatt continues:

> 'I have already stated, that the extreme distance from the front line of the Stage to the *back* wall of the Boxes, facing the Stage, according to my plan, is 53 feet 9 inches; in the late Theatre in Drury Lane it was 74 feet, or 20 feet 3 inches more than at present; in

the Old Theatre in Covent Garden (I mean as built about the year 1730), the distance between the front of the Stage, and the back wall of the front Boxes, was 54 feet 6 inches, or 1 foot 3 inches more than in my design. In the Old Opera House, built by Sir John Vanbrugh, in the Haymarket, it was 66 feet, or 12 feet 3 inches more than in my design.' . . .

(These dimensions refer to the theatres in their final form. As originally built Covent Garden was approximately 40 feet, and in Vanbrugh's design, 46 feet.)

Like Saunders, Wyatt points out his objections to the oval or horseshoe forms of auditoria as placing too many spectators in positions where they could not, without discomfort, easily view the scenes. The use of the semi-circle, on the lines of the Greek and Roman theatres, would involve too great a proscenium opening, with consequent enlargement of the scenes and increase in the number of extras involved. The circular form adopted for this design permits better sight-lines from a greater number of seats, not only in plan but in section also. To improve the sight-lines from those boxes nearest the stage, Wyatt carried round the rear wall of the boxes, rather than the front, to form the concave walls of his proscenium, curving back the front of the boxes (fig.106), and with them the box seats, so that the extreme rear seats here had a reasonable view of the scene, which Wyatt claims '(excepting in cases of Spectacle) is seldom extended, in depth, beyond 30 feet from the front line of the Stage'.

This Spectatory

'consisting of three-fourths of a Circle . . . contains, in four different heights, 80 boxes, holding 1,098 persons; with four Boxes (of larger size than the rest) next to the Stage, on each side of the Theatre, capable of containing 188 Spectators in addition to the 1,098 before mentioned; amounting in the aggregate to 1,286 persons. A Pit capable of containing 920 persons, a Two-shilling Gallery for 550 persons, a One Shilling Gallery for 350 persons, exclusive of four Private Boxes in the Proscenium, and 14 in the Basement of the Theatre, immediately under the Dress Boxes.'

Wyatt's plan shows that the pit audience entered from either side of the building, passing through passages, with waiting benches, to pay boxes, and by further passages to either side at the back of the pit. These entrances gave access to gangways around the ends of the pit benches, with steps up to an additional central gangway. There were eighteen benches, with a further short bench on either side of a projection in the centre of the orchestra pit. Writing at a time when the lamps had been replaced by stage doors, and other minor alterations had presumably been made, Oulton described the colour of the interior as being 'gold on green, with the boxes relieved in rich crimson'.[8] The pit at this time contained seventeen rows of seats with four shorter rows. The orchestra was 8 feet wide and extended nearly the whole width of the pit. The auditorium would appear to have been illuminated by candelabras hanging from brackets above each column supporting the box tiers.[9] It is not clear if there was originally a central chandelier forming part of the Apollo's Head mentioned below, but by 1819 mention is made of one, hanging in the centre of the ceiling over the pit, which was lit by gas.[10]

The ceiling was 48 feet above the floor of the pit, which Wyatt claims was 8 feet 6 inches less than that in Holland's theatre. (Holland's theatre was 48 feet at the rear of the pit.) Wyatt contrived to keep all the boxes of equal depth, so that there was

> 'no gloomy recess in *any part* of the Boxes, to favour the riotous or improper proceedings of disorderly persons; everyone is brought in full view of the House, and within the light of the Chandeliers; and, that being the case, many are, no doubt, held in awe of observation, who might otherwise have disturbed the House by noisy and licentious conduct'.

The basket boxes which Holland placed behind his first tier of boxes, and the corridors leading to both, had apparently come to be the main domain of the 'Women of the Town', so that virtuous women who might have occupied the front row of 'Dress Boxes' were deterred from doing so by having to run the gauntlet of those who hung around the prostitutes in the basket boxes, the coffee rooms, and the surrounding passages. In designing his theatre Wyatt did not attempt to debar 'these disreputable Members of the Community', but instead designed the building in such a manner that 'the more rational and respectable spectators' might be enabled to proceed direct to the parts of the theatre designed for them, without running the risk of being subjected to 'scenes of the most disgusting indecency'. It is sometimes thought that Puritan criticisms of the Elizabethan and Restoration playhouse audiences were far-fetched, but the problem seems to have been sufficiently serious for Wyatt to give it equal consideration with the capacity, the shape, and the safety of the theatre, and yet, at the same time, he considered it necessary to provide accommodation for these lower elements, who presumably brought in revenue by their attendance, and by the persons attracted by their charms. 'The presence of the prostitutes undoubtedly influences the sale of the half-price tickets – which they themselves must buy – because many men only attend the theatre in order to meet them.'[11] It would seem that managements turned a blind eye to their activities, and those parts of the theatre from which it was obviously impossible to see the stage provided dark corners for those members of the audience who were less concerned with seeing or hearing the play, than in indulging their appetites in such activities as were possible.

The circles of boxes were reached from the main entrance hall where the servants might wait, and where provision was made near the entry doors for the 'Boxes for the Free Lists', and opposite these, beside the entry ways to the Rotunda and Principal Staircases, were the 'Pay places for the Boxes'. The Dress tier of boxes was approached from the first half-landing of the main stairs, the first tier from the upper landing and rotunda gallery, and the second tier from the final half-landing. Stairs from the ends of the box corridors at this level led to the seven slips boxes on either side of the lower or two-shilling gallery, which was directly approached, by two staircases rising around an open triangular well, from entrances on either side of the theatre, the two-shilling pay boxes being placed at the top of these stairs. The one-shilling gallery originally had two staircases, one on either side, but one of these was appropriated to the special use of the Royal Box, so that this gallery area was left with only one fire escape.

Wyatt protected his theatre against fire by incorporating a system of perforated water pipes, connected to an air-tight reservoir from which the water could be driven by compressed air. Pipes of varying diameter were led to all parts of the theatre, the diameter varying with the degree of fire-risk. From an outside engine-house, water could be directed to any, or all, parts of the house as required.

> 'The Stage is divided into eight different compartments, each of which may be deluged, independently of the rest, by opening particular cocks, or valves, so as to avoid doing more mischief to the scenery, &c, by water, than the extent of the fire may require; though in case of more extended conflagration, the whole may be drowned at once, by opening all the valves . . . The Spectatory is further guarded by a singular contrivance, which is concealed by the Apollo's head, in the centre of the Pit ceiling; it consists of a four-inch pipe, eight feet long, with a rose at each end, and with large holes in its sides, from which the water, rushing with great force, causes this pipe to revolve on its centre . . . and thus, by it's rotary motion, to throw the various streams rushing from it to a great distance in every direction, so as, in a very short time, to wet the whole inside circle of Boxes, Pit, &c.'

Although Wyatt incorporated these devices he omitted the solid wall between stage and auditorium which Holland had introduced in the previous theatre, presumably on the assumption that it had done little good anyway. He did, however, enclose both stage and auditorium within a single shell which rose above the surrounding buildings containing the foyers, stairs and toilets at the front, and two wings of offices and dressing rooms, the women's on one side, the men's on the other, and on the top floors the wardrobes, and tailor's and property maker's workshops. At stage level were the stage manager's rooms, manager's office, music copyist's room and two Green Rooms. Openings between these side wings and the stage were kept to a minimum, but numerous entrances had to be made in the wall surrounding the auditorium as access to the boxes. In an early design,[12] possibly that with which the competition for the work was won, Wyatt provided one door to each box, but this multiplicity of openings was halved in the later designs, when each door provided access to a pair of boxes. At the rear of the stage were two large scene rooms, beneath which were the carpenter's shop and property room. Above were the scene painter's rooms, with slots in the floor 'for the purpose of sliding the scenes up and down, while painting; as well as for conveying the frames to and from the Painting Rooms, before and after being painted'. In spite of providing carpenter's and property rooms in the basement, it would appear that the space in the roof was still used by these personnel.

A design prepared by Wyatt for this building in October, 1811, suggests that he originally

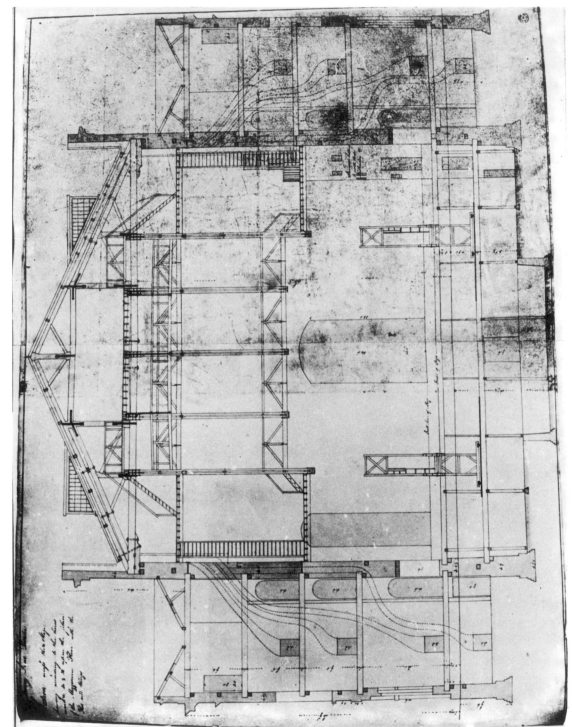

Fig.108. Drury Lane: cross-section through stage by Benjamin Wyatt

accepted Holland's ideas regarding the size of scenery,[13] as his sections of the stage show the fly gallery set at a height of some 30 to 32 feet above the sloping stage. His considerations regarding the size of the proscenium opening (p.168) suggest that he gave considerable thought to this problem, and presumably received help and advice on the subject of the stage structure generally. It is not usual to find architects including scenic details on drawings at this period, but in this instance two detail drawings prepared by Wyatt, to a scale of 1 inch to 4 feet, show constructional details of the stage and upper works (fig.108).[14] He now shows two fly galleries at either side of the stage, the lower, sloping up with the stage, some 25 feet 6 inches above stage level, the upper, set horizontally, at 24 feet higher. Both pairs of galleries are shown as 17 feet wide, and are hung from the roof trusses (fig.109). Two bridges join the galleries at the back of the stage, and three catwalks span the stage at the upper level, providing access to the cloths and borders hanging from the grid at roof truss level. Stairs from the upper fly floors lead by bridges to a floor built in the open part of the queen-post roof truss.

These drawings show that Wyatt was using the continental method of scene movement, in the form of wing carriages running on 18 feet 6 inches long tracks, set at mezzanine level 7 feet 6 inches beneath stage level. The stage cellar was 16 feet deep, with a 5 feet central well into which the bridges and scenes could sink. There are six pairs of carriages on either side of the stage, each with its own set of sloat cuts (p.213) and bridges, but unfortunately there is no indication of any of the smaller traps (p.153) which we might reasonably expect to find in the forward stage area. Wyatt provides only a minimum of information about the stage on his published plans,[15] merely indicating the slots for the chariots, and the position of fly galleries and cross bridges. His longitudinal section[16] shows only the public part of the house, stopping short at the proscenium line.

The main walls of the theatre are shown as 3 feet thick for the greater part of their height, increasing to 3 feet 9 inches in the basement, and are of brick with horizontal timbers set into them. These timbers mostly occur where they act as wall plates to adjoining floors, but a number appear to have no other purpose than to act as binders to the walls. The walls were faced externally with London Stocks, but the main front was stuccoed to resemble stone.

At four o'clock in the morning of 20th September, 1808, Covent Garden was destroyed by fire, to be reopened on the 18th September, 1809,[17] to a new design by Robert Smirke, who obviously did not agree with Wyatt on his views concerning theatre design, as his auditorium had three tiers of boxes arranged in a true horseshoe around the sloping pit, containing twenty rows of benches.[18] Each tier was divided into twenty-six boxes, and was an average 6 feet 6 inches in depth and contained three rows of benches. The first two tiers of boxes were open to the general public and were separated by low partitions, but on the third tier a further continental feature was introduced in the form of private boxes, let out on an annual basis. These were all separated by full-height partitions, and each box had 'a small anti-room about six feet wide', with a fireplace, 'opening outwards into a general saloon, appropriated to the renters; as that below was to the public'.[19]

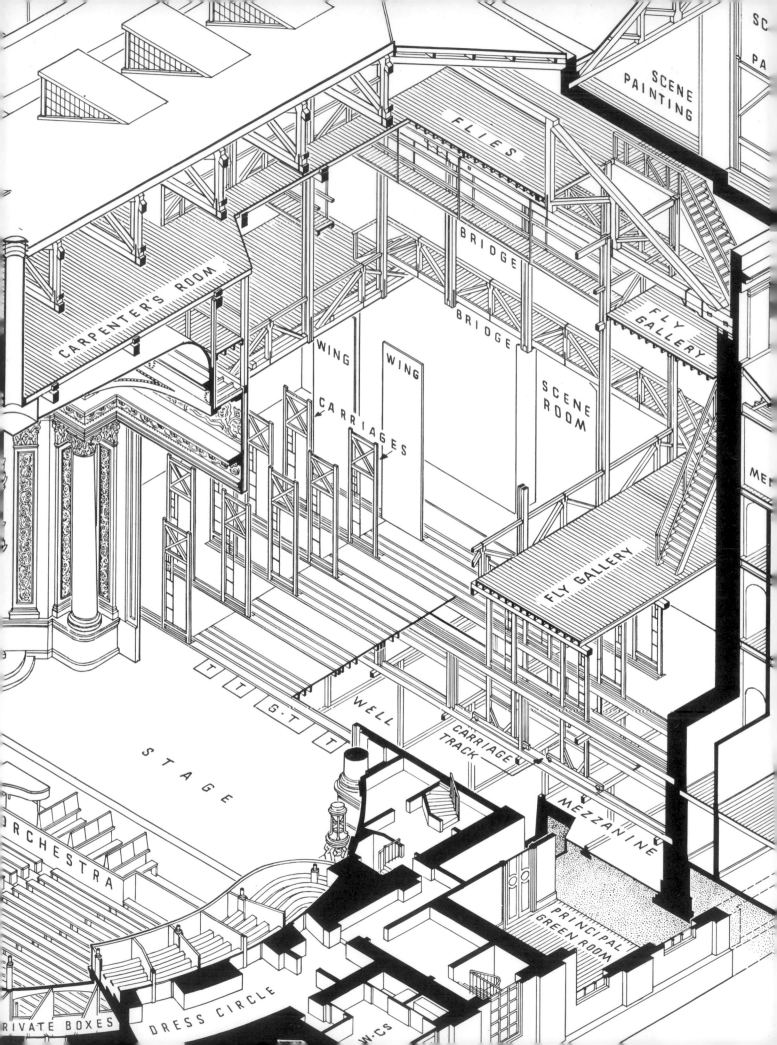

SC
PA

SCENE
PAINTING

F L I E S

BRIDGE

BRIDGE

FLY
GALLERY

CARPENTER'S ROOM

WING

WING

SCENE
ROOM

CARRIAGES

ME

FLY GALLERY

WELL

CARRIAGE
TRACK

MEZZANINE

T T T
G·T T

CARRIAGE
TRACK

STAGE

ORCHESTRA

PRINCIPAL
GREEN ROOM

RIVATE BOXES

DRESS CIRCLE

W·CS

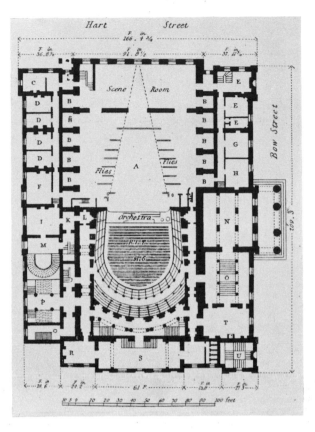

Fig.110. Covent Garden, Sir Robert Smirke, 1809: plan, including basket boxes (for key, see p.331).

'By devoting one entire tier to the nobility and gentry, the proprietors of Covent Garden Theatre could offer to their patrons a box accessible at any time, with an ante-room, when they chose to withdraw for conversation or refreshment; there was, besides, a general saloon for the occasional promenade of the privileged orders, and every arrangement made to render a place of entertainment to them as select and private as their own residences – they quitted their boxes by exclusive staircases, and left the theatre from doors equally devoted to themselves.'[20]

Behind the first – dress – tier of boxes, facing the stage, there were eight basket boxes (fig.110) similar to those in Holland's theatre. A fourth tier had side boxes 'without roof or canopy'[21] flanking the two-shilling gallery, with its ten rows of benches facing the stage. These side boxes were backed by the enclosing wall of the auditorium painted to resemble drapery, above which a series of arched and vaulted openings supported the flat-domed ceiling of the auditorium (fig.111). Into these 'pigeon holes' was cooped the seating for the slips, over the side box corridors, and the one-shilling gallery.

The fronts of the boxes were supported 'by slender reeded pillars, in burnished gold',[22] and the 'house *was* lighted by glass chandeliers in front of each circle – 270 wax candles was the nightly supply, 300 patent lamps lighted the stage and its scenery'.[23]

Fig.109. Drury Lane: detail of Fig. 106

Fig.111. Covent Garden: interior, 1810

The main entrance to the theatre was in Bow Street through a portico in the Grecian manner, leading into a hall off which opened a grand staircase leading up to the level of the dress tier of boxes. Here a foyer, across the rear of the auditorium, gave access to corridors along its sides; the foyer was separated from the auditorium by a curved wall, 5 feet 6 inches thick, through which doorways entered into the eight basket boxes. The side passages were also separated from the auditorium by walls, some 2 feet thick, pierced by doorways to each pair of boxes, and a cross-passage separating the dress boxes from the basket boxes provided access to the former. In the corners of the foyer two semi-circular stairs ascended to the boxes above, including, presumably, the third – private – tier, although, as has previously been noted, this tier had its own private staircase and entrance on the west side of the theatre adjoining the King's private entrance and staircase. There was a Royal Saloon and private ante-room, but it looks as though permanent provision may not have been made for a Royal Box, as we read that 'The King's box is always fitted up on the left of the audience, in the dress circle, and occupies the extent of three or four of the boxes.'[24]

At dress circle level a great saloon opened off the south side of the foyer, at either end of which were rooms for refreshments. Above this was a further saloon, with fireplaces, for the use of the private boxes. Below was the entrance foyer, from Covent Garden, to the pit, which was entered on either side from beneath the dress circle boxes. A staircase in the south-west corner led to the lower gallery, and a further stair in the south-east corner led to this and to the upper gallery. The boxes and their approach corridors were separated from the stage by a solid wall, some 2 feet 3 inches thick, but there seems to have been no attempt to close the 42 feet wide opening in this wall, as Holland had done at Drury Lane; indeed this would hardly have been possible here as Smirke contrived his proscenium stage behind this wall on the main stage. A staircase in the eastern corner of the stage gave direct access to the box passage on that side. The front of the stage lined with the audience side of this cross-wall, and was separated from the pit by a full-width orchestra well. The proscenium stage, 10 feet deep, was flanked by proscenium doors, each with two boxes above, enclosed between two tall pilasters of scagliola, with gilt capitals. The pilasters supported an entablature in line with the fourth tier box fronts, and a flat arch which roofed the proscenium area. From an overall width of 42 feet at the front the proscenium stage was reduced to an opening 38 feet 6 inches wide, and the scene opening was further reduced by 'pilasters, imitative of Sienna marble, which slide backward and forward, in order to widen or contract the stage'.[25] Presumably these were in the form of painted wings, which are shown on a plan of 1st October, 1824,[26] as being 32 feet 6 inches apart, and forming the front of a diminishing vista of six sets of wings, the sloping lines of which are parallel with the straight sides of the box fronts. According to Dibdin these wings were each 21 feet high by 4 feet wide, while 'The height of the flats (or flat scenes), which stand transversely on the stage' was 21 feet, with a total width of 28 feet – 14 feet each half. The scenery as shown on the reconstruction (fig.112) has, however, been based on the plan and section illustrated by Contant[27] in 1859, where the wings are shown arranged in two parallel columns.

A main block, approximately 90 feet wide by 155 feet long, contained three levels of scene rooms, the stage and the auditorium; this rose to a greater height than the side wings on east, west and south, with high parapets masking the main roof, which contained the usual carpenter's rooms and property stores lit by a series of dormer windows set behind arched openings in the parapet walls.

On either side the stage walls were pierced by a series of arched openings forming bays, 12 feet deep, for the storage of scenery, similar to those suggested by Saunders (fig.105). A continuous wall, pierced only at front and back by doors, separated the scene docks from corridors off which opened the dressing rooms, green rooms, and offices. There were two levels of fly galleries, the lower parallel with the sloping stage, and on a level with the main scene painting room, which had slots at front and back through which the scenes might be moved for painting. The upper galleries, some 45 feet above the stage, were horizontal. The flies 'are filled with the machinery used in lowering the curtains, drops, wheels, borders, clouds, &c, &c; and adjoining them is the painting-room, which is furnished with sky-lights, and measures in length seventy-two feet, and in width thirty-two feet'.[28] Dibdin's 1824 plan indicates that there were five corner traps and a central square trap, similar to that described in Rees's *Cyclopaedia* (p.153). The remainder of the stage is shown on Contant's plan and

Fig.112. The Theatre Royal, Covent Garden, Sir R. Smirke: the theatre in 1824, including the alterations made prior to that date: scale reconstruction

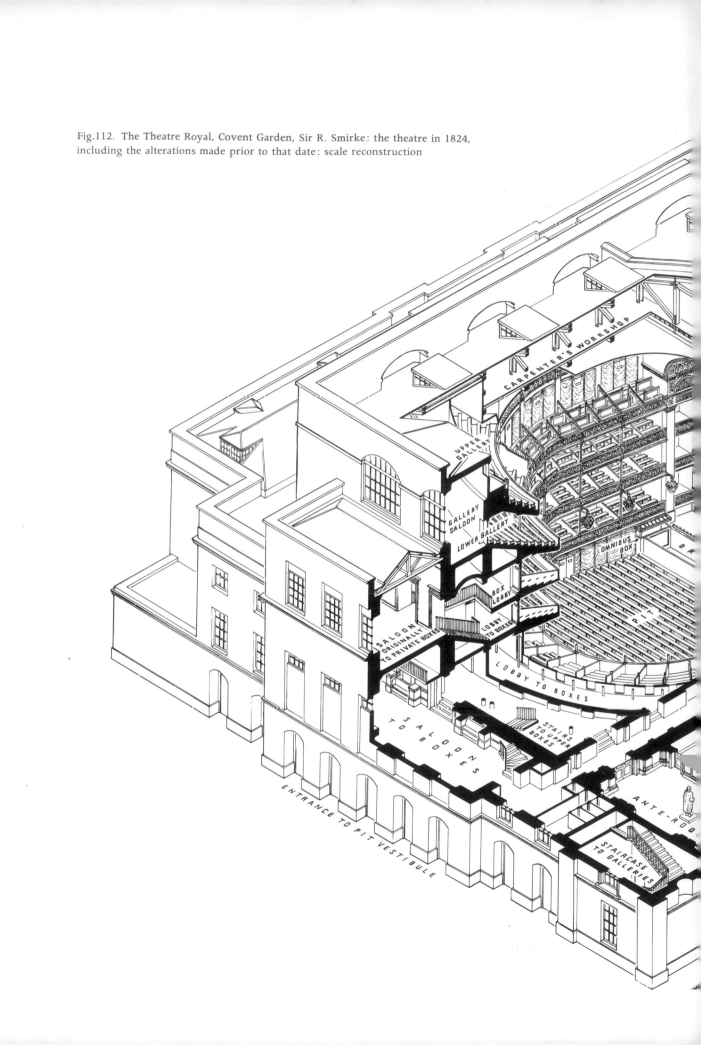

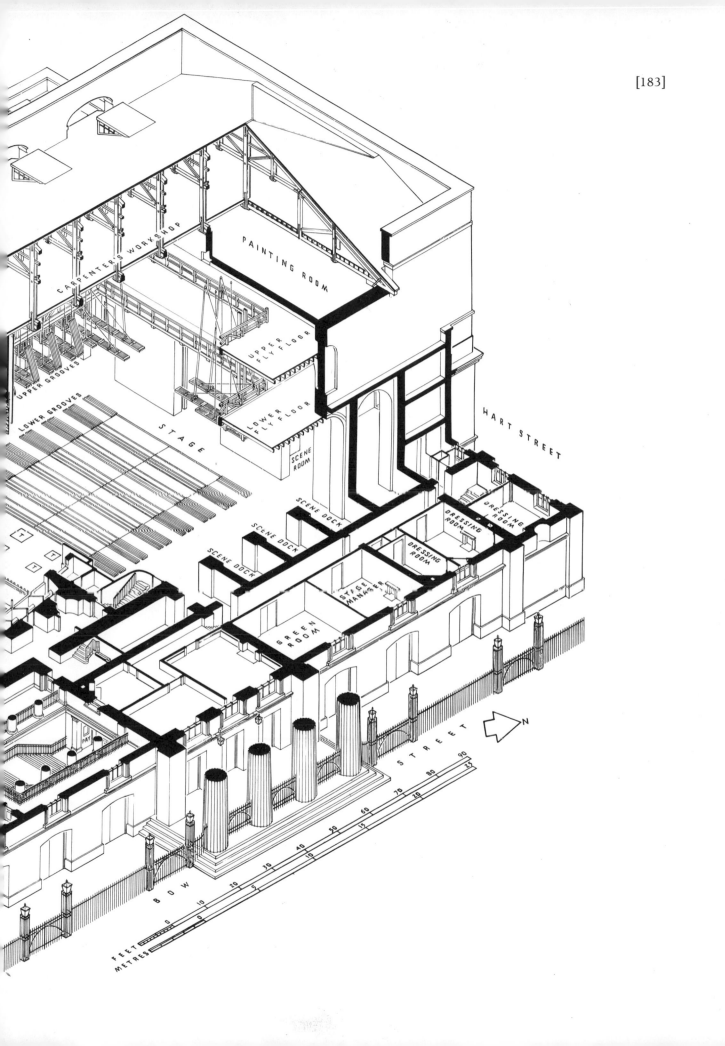

CARPENTER'S WORKSHOP

PAINTING ROOM

UPPER FLY FLOOR

LOWER FLY FLOOR

UPPER GROOVES

LOWER GROOVES

STAGE

SCENE ROOM

HART STREET

SCENE DOCK

SCENE DOCK

SCENE DOCK

DRESSING ROOM

DRESSING ROOM

DRESSING ROOM

STAGE MANAGER

GREEN ROOM

PAY

N

STREET

BOW

90
80
70
60
50
40
30
20
10
0

25
20
15
10
5
0

FEET
METRES

section as being sub-divided into narrow and wide openings similar to those seen at Drury Lane (fig.109), but they also show top and bottom grooves, and so it would look as though the manual movement of wings was in operation in this theatre.

It is not clear if Smirke carried his proscenium wall over the stage opening, but this had certainly been done by May, 1824,[29] when the wall is shown on Dibdin's section as being carried not only through the roof space, but to a height of some 2 feet 6 inches above the roof itself. The stage opening was, however, so large in relation to the total area of the wall, that, without some form of fire-resisting curtain, the wall itself served little purpose save to separate the roof space. It would seem that at some later date, probably during Albano's alterations (p.187), the wall was removed.

'It has been stated that the entire removal of a cross division wall and arch over the Proscenium at some period, probably long subsequent to the original construction of the building, allowed the fire to spread throughout the roof of Sir Robert Smirke's Covent Garden Theatre: Certainly had such a fire proof division across and above the roof remained, a check might have been given to the flames, so that the firemen on duty at the house might possibly have subdued them at the first outbreak.'[30]

Smirke appears to have used binding timbers in his walls similar to those noted in Wyatt's details for the Drury Lane stage (fig.108).

'In all the walls of the original building, bond timbers occurred at distances of nine to twelve courses, – sometimes in pieces of large scantling, at both sides of the wall, bolted through to each other. In some places the timber was burning a week after the date of the fire; and may be, yet. Mr Albano, on the occasion of the important works which he carried out in 1846-7, found at 13 feet from the foundation, a tier of Memel bond timber, – scantling, twelve by six inches, – introduced in the main walls all round. Externally, there was merely the appearance of shrinkage; but on examination, the timber was found to be quite decayed. Not only this, but four other such tiers, – amounting to about 2,000 feet, – as well as the lintels, which had become decayed, were removed.'[31]

To offset the cost of the new building the prices for the pit were raised from 3s.6d. to 4s. and for the boxes from 6s. to 7s. The reaction of the first night audience was immediate – they rioted and continued the O.P., or Old Price, riots for sixty-seven days. During this period their views were expressed on other aspects of the new theatre design, their main dislike being the continental type private boxes on the third tier, with their retiring rooms, and, hardly to be surprised at, the accommodation provided for the one-shilling patrons in the 'pigeon holes'. Agreement was finally reached that the boxes should remain at the new price, but that the pit should revert to 3s.6d. The private boxes in the front of the house should be 'thrown open & restored to the public at the end of the present season'.[32] In the following season there was a renewal of the riots when the audience 'insisted on the strict performance of the original contract, *three* private boxes on each side. The proprietors made the attempt to evade it on the plea that Parliament had, by the act for the rebuilding Drury Lane Theatre, recognised the right to let annual boxes.'[33]

There had been sixteen private boxes in the previous theatre which had been rented on an annual basis, and Holland had proposed including boxes to be rented out on long term leases,[34] when considering the designs for Drury Lane. So it is a little surprising that so much exception was taken to their inclusion here, although it was probably the private rooms behind that were most objected to, as had been the case with those introduced earlier at Drury Lane (p.128).

What is apparent in this theatre is the developing separation of the various areas and classes, each with its own approach ways and amenities. A degree of separation had always been present on a financial basis, even in the Shakespearian playhouses, but it was now extended, as was noted from Wyatt's description of his design problems at Drury Lane, by the growing need to separate the bawdy and rowdy elements from the more respectable members of the audience. Saloons were provided not only for the Royal and private boxes, but also for the dress circle, and the pit now had its own entrance foyer.

As a result of the renewed riots several alterations were made to the building. The semicircular staircases linking the circles of boxes were replaced by wider stairs in straight flights,[35] and the twelve central private boxes were opened to accommodate 120 persons. It was not until two years later that the pigeon holes were removed, those at the side being closed off altogether, and the central five arches were opened up, with columns to support the ceiling, to provide a one-shilling gallery with four rows of benches.[36] Some time prior to the publication of the plan, sections and interior view on which the reconstruction (fig.112) was based,[37] the proscenium was altered, the low arch at fourth tier level being replaced by an elliptical apse springing some 5 feet higher, and rising to the level of the shallow domed ceiling, thereby improving the view of the stage from the upper gallery. The basket boxes were also removed, the front boxes facing the stage being extended in depth, with the addition of two extra rows of benches. The columns which originally marked the back of the front boxes were now inside them, the new rear wall being set on the line of the basket box fronts. The second row of columns, which originally stood on the front row of the basket benches, was now left free-standing in a new foyer occupying the previous basket space. This extra space was needed as a result of the increase in size of the box stairs, and the space taken up by columns required to support the new balcony over. Two flights of stairs were built in the saloon to provide direct access from the upper boxes. Two 'omnibus boxes' had been installed at either end of the orchestra pit, projecting forward from the wall supporting the dress circle of boxes. Omnibus boxes in this position were a special feature normally related to opera or ballet.

In the alterations to the proscenium the stage doors were removed and replaced by boxes, and individually masked footlights now spanned the full width of the stage. When Dibdin described the building in 1826, there were twenty-three rows of benches in the pit, and in

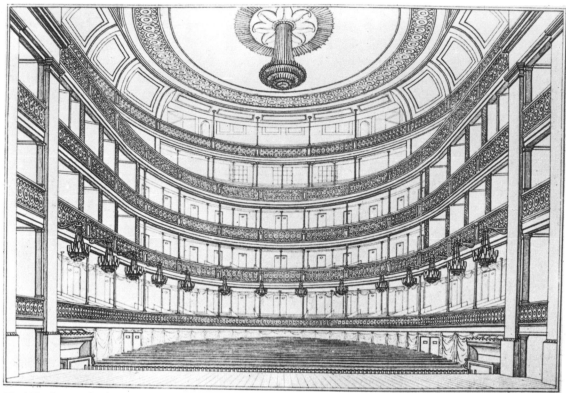

Fig.113. Covent Garden: interior, 1825

spite of the removal of the third tier of private boxes, there were still twenty-six of these, but now spread around the house, with 'three on each side in the proscenium; one on each side even with the orchestra; five on each side of the first circle, and four on each side of the second circle; amounting to thirteen on each side'.[38] Dibdin's section of May, 1824, however, shows all the boxes separated only by low partitions, but his interior view (fig.113) of January, 1825, has four private boxes with full-height partitions on the second circle, and five on the third. From now on, however, the use of the term 'private box' does not necessarily indicate that they were leased on an annual basis; in most instances the term refers to boxes which could be rented by a party for the evening.

Ornamentation on the fronts of the boxes was painted on canvas, the prevailing colour of the house being white, with gold ornament on a light pink ground. The box doors were all of solid mahogany.[39] The back and sides of the pit were decorated to represent dark crimson drapery, as were also the interiors of the boxes. At this stage the capacity of the house is given as 3,000, exclusive of standing room: made up of 1,400 in the boxes, 750 in the pit, 500 in the lower gallery and 350 in the upper.[40]

Gas lighting had been introduced at Drury Lane, as reported on 6th September, 1817, by the *Times*,[41] 'on the sides of the Stage, on which there are 12 perpendicular lines of lamps, each containing 18, and before the proscenium a row of 80.' The *Times* of the following day reported that gas had been introduced at Covent Garden 'on the first wings on either side of the stage'. In the auditorium 'all the former chandeliers are removed, and a great central light descends from the centre of the ceiling, but not so far as to intercept the view of the stage, even from the one shilling gallery'. This was supplemented by five chandeliers bracketed from the fronts of the boxes. By January, 1825, there were fourteen small chandeliers, each with three lights, hanging from the front of the second tier of boxes (fig.113). The introduction of gas to the auditorium made it possible for the lights in this area to be lowered, thus concentrating attention on the brightly lit stage. It is worth remembering that until this time the auditorium had been illuminated throughout the performance. By 1826 the stage was 'principally lighted' by gas.[42]

Opera was established at this theatre in the 1840s, which could account for the introduction of the omnibus boxes, and it was now decided to create 'a new theatre for foreign musical performances'.[43] In 1846 it was proposed that the whole of the auditorium should be stripped down 'from the ceiling to the top of the walls under the pit', presumably those in the area designed for use as stables, 'and including the walls under the galleries and boxes throughout their whole height and to rebuild the latter so as to increase the size of the pit' as well as the distances between the fronts of the boxes, galleries, and the proscenium.[44] This would bring the theatre more nearly in line with the appearance of European opera houses, and at the same time contain more money in the house. The work was carried out under the supervision of Mr Albano. In the auditorium the original four tiers of boxes were now replaced by six, the central portion of the fourth and fifth tiers being 'appropriated as an amphitheatre for the general public, with seven rows of seats in each, extending backward over the corridor below. Above these, in the sixth tier, is the gallery.'[45] A description in *The Builder* of the following week records that the parapet, roof and ceiling of the refreshment room were removed

> 'and a new ceiling and an entirely new building, raised on the old walls, to a height of 32 feet to the ridge. The second amphitheatre and gallery, with two boxes on each side, were taken away, and a new amphitheatre reconstructed at a much greater angle, capable of holding upwards of 600 people, an area about 57 feet by 47 feet. The south wall (supporting the roof of the theatre and carpenter's workshop), was pulled down to the extent of 54 feet in length by 30 feet in height, and 3 feet 6 inches thick. The roof and floor were shored up, and a timber truss, 53 feet span, introduced, into which the timbers of the roof and floor were reframed.'[46]

If these dimensions are applied to the former plan and section[47] it will be found that the amphitheatre mentioned here occupied the whole space above the refreshment room. Two drawings, a set of photographs,[48] and two water colours by J. W. Archer[49] confirm that the walls of the refreshment room were carried up to the same level as the upper walls of the main theatre block, and were treated with similar openings to those already noted in the original design (fig.114). At fourth and fifth floor levels there is a setback beyond the

Fig.114. Covent Garden after the fire of 1856

rear wall of the boxes permitting space for the amphitheatre, above which is a further setback to the new rear wall accommodating the gallery.

The shape of the pit was still a horseshoe, but now extended so that the front of the centre box on the grand tier was '18 feet 9 inches further from the curtain'.[50] The stage projected 9 feet into the auditorium, and the distance from stage front to the centre box was 59 feet. Each tier of boxes was stepped back from the one below, so that the top tier was 2 feet 3 inches further from the stage than the dress circle. There was a maximum width to the auditorium of 62 feet (the width between auditorium walls on the earlier plans is shown as 64 feet). The proscenium opening was 46 feet wide, flanked by Corinthian columns 25 feet 10 inches high. The front of the stage was slightly curved, as was also the 12 feet 6 inches wide orchestra pit containing space for eighty-five musicians. As had earlier been done at the Haymarket and His Majesty's theatres (p.170), the opportunity was now taken to increase the prices in the pit by designating half the seats as 'pit stalls', both these and the pit seatings being arranged on the same curve as the stage front, as were also the seats in the amphitheatres.

Albano used the same shape of box front as Holland had done in his design for Covent Garden, the boxes themselves being lined with wood to assist the acoustics. The total accommodation of the house is now given as 'eight proscenium boxes, thirty in the pit tier'

Fig.115. The auditorium of the Royal Italian Opera House, Covent Garden, B. Albano, 1847

arranged on a level with the earlier omnibus boxes,

> 'thirty-four in the grand tier, thirty-four in the third tier, twenty-eight in the fourth tier, twenty-eight in the fifth tier and twenty-eight in the sixth tier, or 190 in all. Allowing six persons to a box, these will seat commodiously . . . 1,140. The stalls hold 256. The pit, 263. The amphitheatres 148 each, 296. The gallery, 300. Making in the whole . . . 2,255.'[51]

The auditorium (fig.115) was lit by a large central chandelier which 'would of itself light the house sufficiently; there are, however, in addition, branches for wax candles, projecting from the grand tier and second tier',[52] which suggests that Albano was not placing all his faith in the gas light. Stoves under the pit stalls heated air which was conducted by flues built in the walls all over the house, and 'every gas-lamp in the corridors has a ventilating-pipe above it'.[53] Fire precautions in the form of cocks and hosepipes on each tier, fed by cisterns in the upper part of the theatre, were now becoming standard fittings. It still seems to be generally accepted that, in the case of fire, the stage and auditorium would of necessity burn, and fire precautions were mainly concentrated on the protection of escape stairs and corridors. To this end two new stone staircases were 'formed from the level of the corridor behind the ground or pit tier of boxes, to the height of the highest boxes'.[54] The floor of the pit tier corridor was also fireproofed, being supported on brick and cement arches built between the new foundation walls and the existing outer walls of the theatre.

Excavations had been carried down 22 feet below the level of the pit corridor to provide solid foundations for these stone staircases, and the iron columns supporting the front and rear of the box tiers. Each column supported the next above, and the timber joists of the box floors, and was tied back to the surrounding walls by iron ties. The top column of each set was framed up to the existing roof timbers. The new ceiling was formed from timbers partly cantilevered over the columns, and partly hung from the roof timbers. The ceiling was parabolic in section, and elliptical on plan, and was formed from shaped timber ribs covered on the underside by $\frac{1}{2}$ inch planks, from 2 to 3 inches wide. Canvas was glued to the upper side of these boards, and the underside was covered with paper on which the decorations had previously been painted, the whole resulting in a form of construction which could hardly be termed fire-proof.

The open loggia entry to the pit was now enclosed to form a crush-room, which was entered from a new vestibule built in place of the earlier gallery stairs, and the double stairs in the first floor saloon were also removed. On the 6th April, 1847, the theatre was re-opened as the Royal Italian Opera House.

It would appear that most of the alterations at this time related to the front of house, as there is no mention of the stage itself, although a new stage entrance and stage staircase, together with a musicians' room beneath the front of the stage, were all added. Further information may, however, be gathered about the present stage area from evidence given at the inquest on the fire of the 5th March, 1856, when the theatre was totally destroyed. It was then stated that it was possible to stand on the stage near the proscenium and see 'a light through the holes in the floor of the shop above'.

'It should be understood by those not familiar with the plan of theatres, that the carpenters' shop is a room in the roof, floored on the tie-beams, and that it extends over the whole building, – excepting that one small portion of the stage end is parted off, forming the painting-room. The access to the shop is by stairs from the upper 'flies', – the 'flies' being galleries used in working the scenery. The floor of the shop is necessarily ceiled under, in the portion of the house in front of the curtain, – boarding being adopted in the case of the Covent-garden Theatre, – whilst over the stage, the flooring is exposed, and is cut through in many places for the passage of ropes and other purposes.

Over the chandelier there is an aperture, with a shaft above for ventilation, and through the aperture the chandelier is lighted by a rod, with a long wire at the end, on which a piece of wool soaked in spirits of wine can be fixed.

'It had been the practice at Covent-garden – when the 800 burners of the chandelier were lighted, – to extinguish the wool, by plunging it into the spirit, which was contained in a vessel that the gasman carried with him; and the rod was left hanging down, or resting in the basin of the chandelier. – that is to say, below the ceiling of the house.'[55]

Gas fittings had been introduced into the carpenter's shop in preparation for work on the previous Christmas pantomime, and there was evidence regarding reported leaks of gas, a problem which was to be always present in the use of this medium.

In 1883, Walter Emden[56] suggested that the use of gas perhaps provided an even greater source of fires than had the earlier candlelight, in that there were 'such a number of joints left ready for connection to floats and battens for lighting up the scenery, that there is always of necessity a considerable escape', providing the additional hazard of a possible explosion. Gas was used to light the scenery in the form of battens consisting

'of a row of gas burners on a strong length of iron piping attached to an iron curved back which serves as a reflector, and protected in front by wire netting on light metal ribs. The length of the batten is generally the same as the width of the cloths, and there is generally one batten to every set of sliders and bridges on the stage level.'[57]

These battens were attached by flexible rubber or leather tubes to outlets on the fly galleries, so that they might be raised or lowered with the scenery.

Vertical battens replaced the earlier lighting units (pp.118,154) behind each set of wings, but as the gas could itself be turned up or down for lighting effects it was no longer necessary for this unit to be hinged. E. O. Sachs describes these as obtaining their supply 'from pipes through the stage floor and having water joints to prevent the escape of gas, so that when the pipes are disconnected and the "lengths" removed to some other part of the stage for scenic effect, the gas is automatically shut off and escape prevented'. Similar units were fixed to the back of the proscenium opening. The footlights were either attached to the front of the stage, or sunk into it so that the necessary reflectors did not obstruct the view of the audience. ' "Groundrows" are lengths which are placed upon the stage floor to illuminate the bottom of the scenery, and "gas lengths" are often hung at the back of the scene.'[58] Different colour effects could be achieved by drawing a medium, made up of tammy or silk of red, yellow, and blue, sewn together, across a wire guard so arranged as to keep the medium away from the gas flames.[59]

In 1836 it was announced at the Theatre Royal, Norwich, 'That the Theatre would reopen after complete redecoration', and that

'in compliance with the public wish, the manager introduces upon a most complete and splendid scale the "Gas". We can hardly realise that all the brilliant achievements of the local stage up to this date had been carried out, with all their boasted scenic effects, only under the dispiriting and gloomy surroundings of the tallow candles, or the scarcely more brilliant oil lamps of that day. When we see in the prompt copies of the old plays the instruction given "lamps down" or "lamps up" we scarcely believe that the result was not gained as now by the touch of a button or the turning of a tap, which in a second gives the desired change, but by the concerted action of many people at different points, who lowered their respective illuminants as best they could, and the stage was very gradually lightened or darkened as the scene demanded, and the effluvia of the smouldering wick must have been at times painfully obnoxious in the house, especially in the stage boxes, which were in such unpleasant proximity to the wings and the footlights.'[60]

Fig.116. Drury Lane, S. Beazley, 1822–3: scale reconstruction

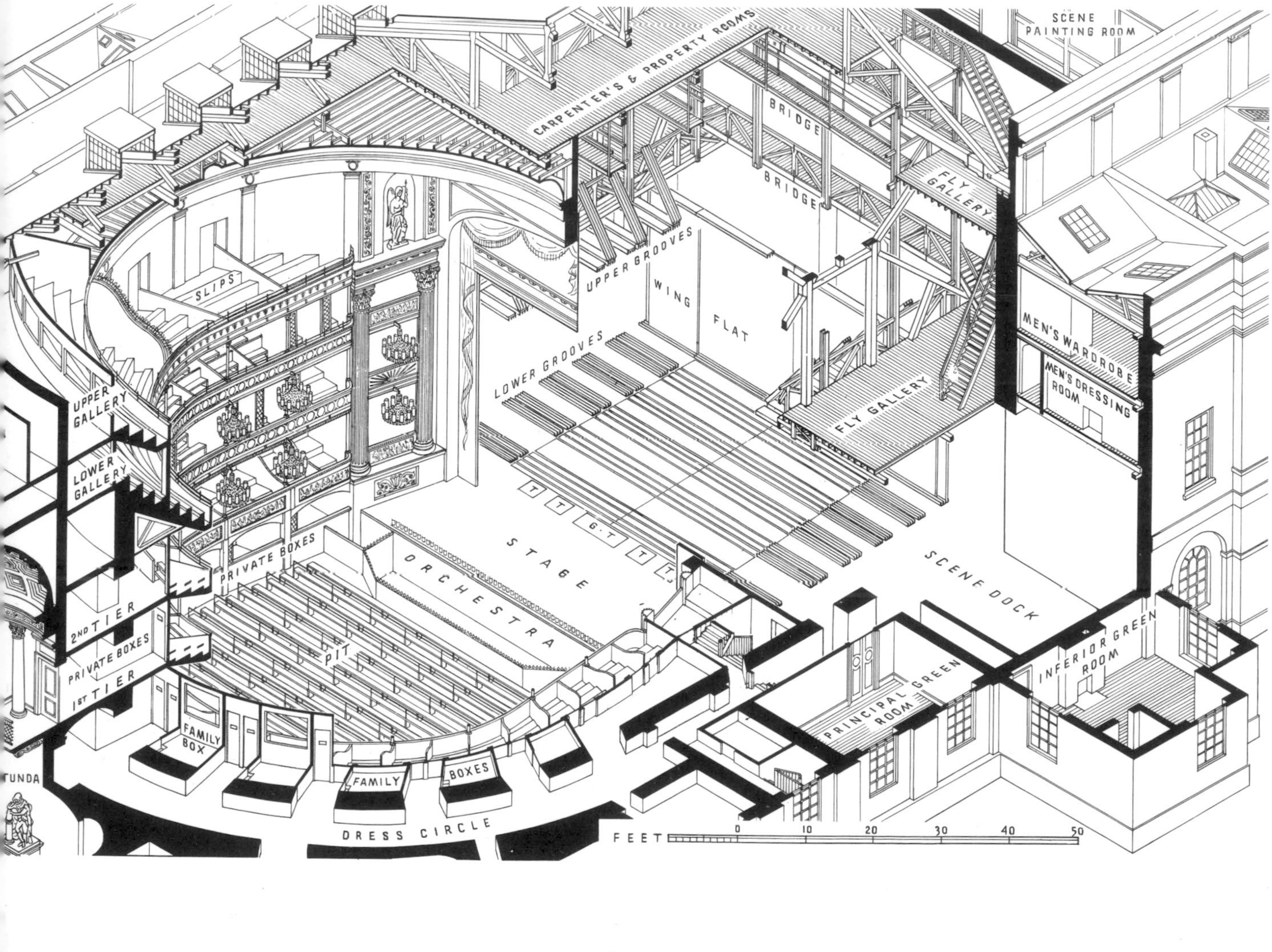

When Drury Lane re-opened for the season in September, 1818, the proscenium had undergone considerable alteration; among other improvements, stage doors were re-introduced. The auditorium was, however, completely remodelled prior to the 1822-3 season from designs by Mr S. Beazley. Wyatt's circular auditorium was adapted to the horseshoe form with, according to a contemporary description, the box fronts on a 51 feet 6 inches diameter circle in place of Wyatt's 58 feet, and the distance from the stage front to the dress boxes was now 48 feet.[61]

There were now twenty-one benches in the pit, covered with crimson cloth, and with a 'rail-work' back to every alternate row. Enclosing the pit there were three private boxes on either side, and adjoining these two larger public boxes without seats. A pit lobby ran across the rear five bays, with entrances to the pit at either end as in Wyatt's design. The dress circle, above, included 'Twenty-six boxes, each furnished with nine chairs; and behind, and looking over them, are ten private or family boxes, let nightly, with six chairs each.'[62] These occupy more or less the position of Wyatt's boxes, with the new dress circle in front, and were neatly fitted between the existing doors in the auditorium wall.

'The next, or first circle, contains fourteen public boxes, (six private ones, let nightly, behind them), and four private boxes at each extreme. The second tier, or upper circle, contains twenty-two double boxes, there being a row of boxes going round the circle, which is separated from the front-row by a partition about three feet high, and at each extreme are two private boxes. In the slips there are three larger boxes, which are parallel to the lower gallery.'[63]

There were, in addition, three private boxes between the columns of the proscenium (fig.117). These columns were of wood, the flutings being apertures 'through which the performances can be seen from the private boxes'.[64] The Royal Box was at dress circle level on the left of the auditorium. The proscenium doors had once again been done away with, and their place was taken by two private boxes with openings just above stage level, normally masked by a removable pierced ornamental panel. In this instance there was no separate ceiling to the proscenium area, except for the segmental areas created by the circular ceiling of the main dome (fig.118).

The house held some 3,060 persons, with 1,230 in the boxes, 130 in the slips, 550 in the lower gallery, 350 in the upper gallery and 800 in the pit. The tiers of boxes were supported on fourteen slender, reeded, iron shafts, and brackets on the first and second tiers supported twenty-eight cut-glass lustres, each of four lights with bell glasses inverted over the gas burners. A further large lustre hung from the centre of the ceiling. Brass guard rails were continued around the fronts of the upper and lower galleries, and the upper circle boxes.

Few changes, if any, seem to have been made in the front of house apart from the auditorium, but a number were made to the stage. The proscenium stage was now 12 feet 9 inches deep, and the proscenium opening, increased to 40 feet in width, was reduced to some 34 feet by painted wings. It would appear that Wyatt's wing chariots had been replaced

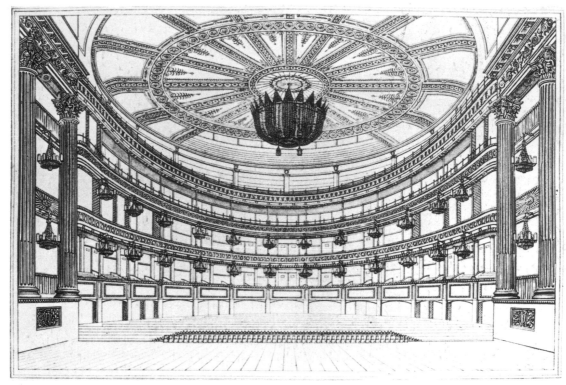

Fig.117. Drury Lane: interior, 1825

by lower grooves, but just when this change took place is not clear. The grooves are shown on Dibdin's plan of the theatre dated January 1825,[65] and the upper grooves are shown on Contant's section.[66] From this it would appear that the under-stage structure had not been changed, as he shows the same arrangement of sloat cuts, bridges and carriage tracks as appeared on Wyatt's detail sections (p.177), while at the same time he repeats the lower grooves on his plan.[67] Dibdin writing in 1826 of these changes notes a deficiency in the depth of the cellar beneath the mezzanine floor 'which occasionally prevents the machinery, in pantomimes, from being worked so readily as the business requires'.[68]

At this time, or possibly earlier, the stage wall was broken through and a scene dock formed in the space originally occupied by the second Green Room, two smaller docks being similarly formed on the opposite side of the stage. A new Green Room was built on the outside of the building, and there were stables for twenty horses somewhere on the same side outside the walls.

The stage was now lit by gas (fig.119), 'the pipes being arranged below the flooring, and having their extremities partially inserted in grooves, so as to admit of their being moved in accordance with the play of the machinery'.[69] It would appear from the published section[70] that the fly galleries had been strengthened by the introduction of a large truss spanning between the two levels of fly floors. It was probably removed in the alterations of 1901

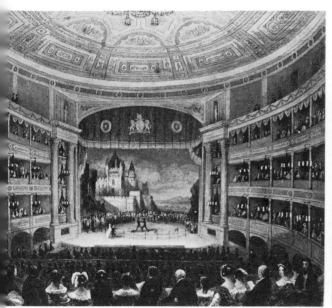
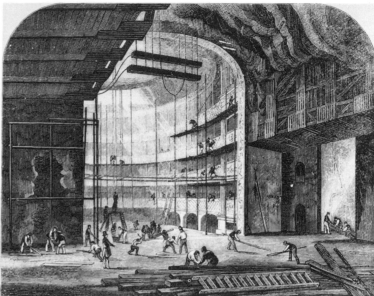

Fig.118. Drury Lane: interior, 1842   Fig.119. The stage of Drury Lane during alterations

(p.286), as it is not to be seen on the drawings prepared in 1902.[71] A scene room had been built outside the building in the north-east corner of the site adjoining Russell Street and Drury Lane, with property workshops above. Carpenter's shops, property rooms and store rooms still occupied the whole of the roof space over both stage and auditorium, no attempt having yet been made to divide this space with a wall, as was done at Covent Garden (fig.112).

In 1858, a Mr M. Nelson, speaking on the Inspection of Theatres, said of Drury Lane:

> 'There is no theatre or opera in the metropolis where so large a space is allotted for staircases, corridors, and entrances. They are all under a separate roof, and divided from the several tiers of boxes, pit, &c, by a thick wall. The result is that in a few minutes an audience, however large, is enabled to leave the theatre, and to enter these spacious fireproof corridors and staircases, where they are secure from any danger in case of accident.'[72]

The Builder, commenting on this speech, pointed out, however, 'that the entrances on the Vinegar-yard side of the house were, till quite recently, closed, and had remained so during many years, unless with very slight intervals of exception'. It would appear that Wyatt's original duplication of entrances, with pay-desks on either side of the theatre, was proving too expensive, or rather the management was saving the expense of check-takers.

The escape stairs, with their open wells, were also criticised, together with the lack of barriers for controlling the crowds massing to buy tickets (fig.120). The present system 'is to admit a vast crowd into a covered space, and then to let them undergo the process of wedging up to the aperture, at the pay-box,' wide enough for the admission of one person, during which they cannot be under control, and on stairs, are, as the accidents have shown, in a state of constant danger from some panic'.

It would also appear that additional gas lights had been introduced as

'each gas light in the pit, under the boxes, with the flame wholly undefended, projects from the wall, at 5 feet from the floor, or about the height of a lady's bonnet; whilst during the attractions of the pantomime, the pit has been so densely crowded, up to the walls, that there has been little room to move, and some slight difficulty occasionally in keeping from contact with the light'.[73]

Fig.120. The Gallery – powerful attraction of talent!

Fig.121. The Benefit Night – a Beggarly Account of Empty Boxes

9 The stage as a machine

During the first quarter of the 19th century the relationship between the pit and the surrounding boxes began to change. A drawing of 'The Benefit Night' (fig.121)[1] shows an arrangement similar to that seen earlier at Richmond (fig.101), with one tier of boxes enclosing a rectangular pit, a gallery, and side galleries. Here the stage is flanked by a proscenium door, with a curtained window above, and although the boxes still enclose the stepped pit they are raised some 3 feet or more above stage level, and the lower part of the pit has been extended beneath them. Mention has already been made of the hinged sections of seating (pp.135,144) which filled the gangways, and examples of these may be seen in the second box from the stage. At the front of the stage the footlights, and the rectangular space through which they may sink, are shown, similar to those mentioned at Richmond (p.158). The front curtain appears to be raised on the festoon principle, and behind the actors are two side wings, with an indication of the upper grooves supporting the front wing. Above is a horizontal border, and upstage of this what was probably a roller drop depicting a street scene.

Not all the provincial theatres, however, were on such a small scale as this drawing suggests, and an example of a larger provincial building was the Theatre Royal, Plymouth. This was designed by John Foulston in 1811 to form part of a very much larger complex incorporating, in addition to the theatre, an assembly room, tea and coffee rooms and a hotel, together with its own answer to the parking problem in the form of a large stable yard, and surrounding stables. The form of the theatre follows closely on the lines suggested by Saunders (fig.105), the auditorium being designed as the greater part of a circle in a similar manner to that adopted by Wyatt at Drury Lane (fig.106). The proscenium stage, some 10 feet in depth, was flanked by a proscenium door on either side, but with decorative panels above in place of the balconies or windows. It had an arched ceiling sloping up towards the saucer dome above the pit, which was carried on a series of shallow arches at gallery level.

Two levels of boxes separated by low partitions, seating 512, surrounded the pit and were entered at the back beneath the large central box of the Dress circle, which had thirteen rows of

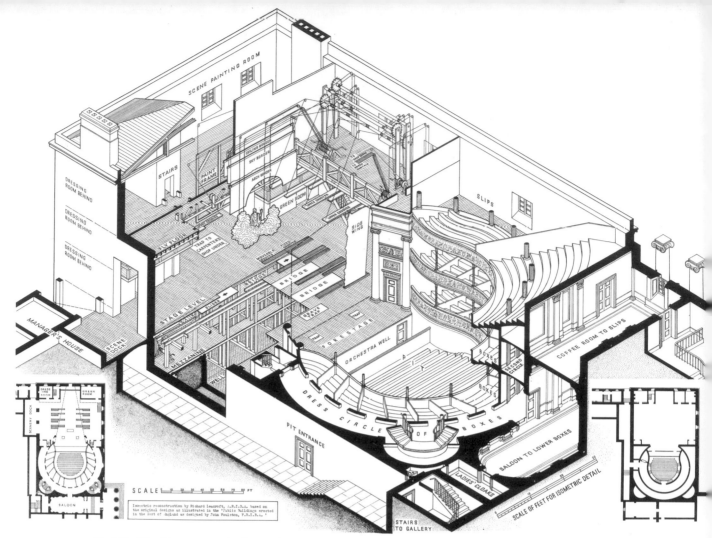

Fig.122. The Theatre Royal, Plymouth, John Foulston, 1811: scale reconstruction

benches seating 200. An orchestra pit, with two doors beneath the stage front, extended the full width between the box fronts. Each box had its own door leading from a surrounding passage, to which access was provided in the now conventional manner by stairs set in the corners of the rectangular building. A large gallery faced the stage with twelve steps for seating, the front four being continued round over the side boxes to form the slips, the whole seating 480. Behind the slips was an open space connecting, beneath the upper part of the gallery, with a coffee room for the occupants of both areas. An external passage along the side of the theatre led to the pit and to the single gallery staircase (fig.122).

As a precaution against fire Foulston introduced a notable advance in theatre design in this building, in that he made all the framing of the auditorium walls, floors and box fronts, together with all the roof members, of cast and wrought iron, and thus became one of the pioneer users of this material on such a scale. His precautions were, however, in vain as the theatre burnt down on the evening of the 5th January, 1863, and was completely destroyed by a further fire on the night of the 13th June, 1878, when 'the old iron roof which collapsed was in so precarious a state that it could well have collapsed on a full house'.[2]

Alterations and decorations had been completed in 1861, the designs for which included some drastic amendments to both stage and auditorium. The stage had been lowered by 4 feet 6 inches, which necessitated dropping the pit, and the opportunity was taken to bring the auditorium into line with the new movement indicated above by extending the pit beneath the dress circle. Stalls and pit-stalls were now provided catering for double the number of persons seated in the old pit. The gallery was also enlarged by 'the opening up and seating of the space at its rear. An entirely new staircase to the gallery leads from the old entrance, while the entrance to the pit is now separate and at the front of the theatre.'[3] One advantage deriving from the sinking of the pit beneath the dress circle was that the persons who used to climb from the cheaper pit seats into the more expensive boxes were no longer able to do so. The dress circle boxes were now furnished with chairs, and the upper circle seats were provided with arms.

Foulston published illustrations of his designs for this theatre,[4] and from these it has been possible to prepare a reconstruction (fig.122). From the examples of stages already illustrated it will be appreciated that much of the scenic machinery not only controlled the design of the stage in plan and section, but formed an integral part of the structure of the building. In this example Foulston provides much information regarding the stage area, and from this it is possible to show in greater detail some of the features which so far it has only been possible to describe. On the sloping stage are shown four pairs of lower grooves: the shorter grooves supporting the side wings, one of which is seen here, and the longer grooves permitting the movement of the two parts of a flat (fig.123). The arrangement of the grooves

Fig.123. The stage of the Theatre Royal, Plymouth: detail of Fig.122

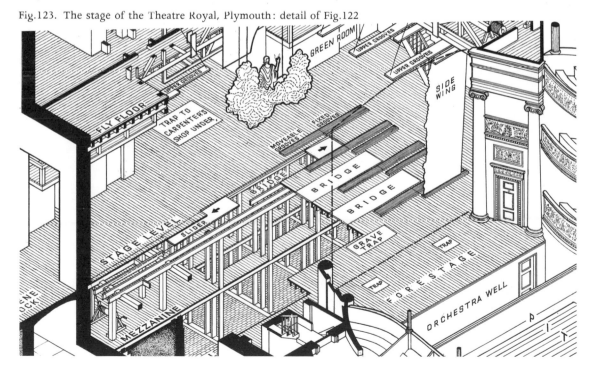

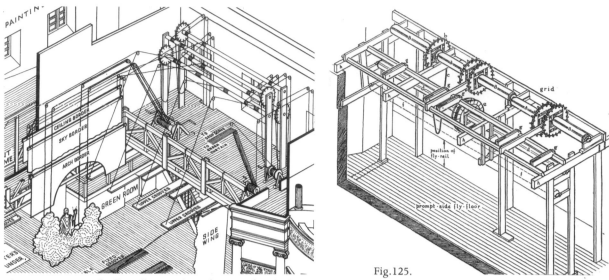

Fig.124. Prompt side fly gallery and machinery: detail of Fig.122

Fig.125.
The Theatre Royal, Bath: barrels on fly gallery

permits the use of flats in any set of grooves, making possible a variety of depths of scene; and the front grooves provide for such scenes as a street or corridor. The longer sections of the grooves were removable when not required for a particular production. Supporting the tops of the wings are the upper grooves: these reflected the pattern below, the 'flat' grooves being hinged in the manner described in Rees's *Cyclopaedia* (p.153), so that they could be drawn up out of sight when not required.

Each set of wings and flats had a corresponding set of borders (fig.124), which are here indicated in the forms most generally used: an arched border for use with high scenes, a sky or cloud border, and a border painted for use as a ceiling. If a scene changed from an exterior to an interior, then all the exterior wings would be drawn off to reveal the interior wings, and the sky borders would be raised to reveal the ceiling borders behind. It was necessary that all the pieces of scenery should be moved at the same time, and to make this possible each set of borders was attached by lines, which passed over pulleys fastened to the under-side of a floor supported on the roof trusses, to a barrel carried on vertical timber posts set between fly floor and roof. Each barrel was turned by pulling on a rope attached to a large wheel, the turning barrel then winding up all the ropes attached to one set of borders, and at the same time unwinding further lines which passed over pulleys to counterweights running next to the side walls of the theatre. Three of these barrels were attached to borders, the fourth being connected to the hinged grooves so that these too could be lifted or lowered together.

Sachs, describing the method used to operate the barrels, drums and shafts, tells us:

> 'the working line is again wound up or down from the windlass in the "flies", and when the windlass is released, the counter-weight descends, causing the shaft to revolve and the scenery to ascend; whilst when the scenery has to be lowered, the windlass

is worked, and the counter-weights wound up. Sometimes a machinist prefers to arrange his counter-weights to practically balance with his scenery, in which case the working of the windlass up and down requires but slight manual effort. Sometimes the counter-weights are, however, arranged so as to be heavier than the object to be raised, and the rope is mounted upon the drum, the working line being on the shaft as the only "brake".'[5]

Speaking of the traditional German stage, Sachs said:

'All the ropes can be brought on to one shaft, and taken by one single working line on to a windlass, so that one single action can simultaneously move the whole scene with all its component parts of several wings on both sides, borders and backcloths, and the entire scene be moved with an evenness which would be impossible if there was not a system of coupling the parts together. The adjustment of the ropes to carry out this single action of movement is, of course, no easy matter. As in England, every pair of "wings" has its "sky border" but the unsightliness of the joint between the "sky border" and the wings has caused the German stage mechanic to frequently use a continuous piece of canvas, consisting of wings and border all in one, in fact a backcloth with its centre cut out in profile.'[6]

At Plymouth, however, the side wings had to be moved individually by hand, whereas at Drury Lane and Covent Garden, with the use of the carriages (p.154) the entire scene could be moved mechanically and simultaneously.

Foulston shows two further winches adjoining the rear of the proscenium opening. These raised and lowered a painted drop scene directly behind the opening, and a green curtain, both being attached to counterweights. Sachs tells us that front curtains were still operated in a similar manner to those seen in the Restoration and Georgian playhouses. He describes them as being 'drawn right and left and gathered in folds', and 'worked from the "flies" over a drum in the gridiron, the arrangement of the ropes only being different, and their number sometimes greater to allow for the "gathering" to be done neatly'. In addition to this curtain there was often an 'act drop' which 'is worked from the "flies" in the same way as the back cloth, over a windlass and round a drum in the gridiron. The so-called "tumbler" on which the canvas or baize is mounted to prevent draughts blowing it through the proscenium opening, adds to its weight.'[7] The use of cloud machines for the ascents and descents of deities was apparently still a feature of stage productions, as Foulston indicates an actor precariously perched on a plank, masked by clouds and hung by pairs of lines from pulleys attached to the upper floor. The cloud machine was operated by a winch at the rear of the fly floor.

There was a vista area at the rear of the main stage similar to that at Drury Lane (fig.63). This area Sachs describes as the 'back stage'. It was

'usually only of the width of the proscenium opening, and has no movable portions in its floor, no "gridiron", no "flies" over, and no "cellar" or "mezzanine" below. It is practically only a piece taken out of the back portion of the building, and may have dressing rooms on either side, and perhaps some other adjunct of the theatre above it. Yet this floor space is most useful for distant scenes, and when not actually used for "setting" upon, it affords space for moving portions of scenes as they are "struck".'[8]

Here it is flanked at stage level by a Green Room on one side and a dressing room and stairs on the other. A second floor of dressing rooms fitted above these, within the height to the fly floors, and there were two further floors of dressing rooms beneath at mezzanine and well levels. Below the vista area was the carpenter's shop, connected to the stage by a large trap, and across the rear stage and dressing rooms at fly floor level was the scene painter's room and a scene store. A slot in the floor of the painter's room next to the wall separating it from the stage permitted the passage of a large paint frame, which could be lowered to stage level to enable the scenes to be fixed to it, and then be raised to the room above for painting. The arrangement of this paint frame in its position on the central axis of the stage is reminiscent of the vertically moving scene which Wilkinson described as being used in an earlier Plymouth theatre in 1764:

'the flat scenes I remember moved on a principle I never saw either before or since; they pushed up and down in a groove in one straight frame like a window-sash, which must be a good plan, as they, so worked, must always be steady, and the canvas not wrinkled as when on rollers:– One inconvenience must attend it – a great height in the building is required.'[9]

In the 1861 alterations the stage was reconstructed, when

'Cumbrous, "old school" appliances have been replaced by an entirely new set of machinery of simpler construction and operation, and affording more elaborate stage appliances . . . The whole stage is movable but so constructed that it possesses the security of a solid floor. It can be immediately transformed in twenty distinct ways or altogether removed then replaced, even while the audience is admiring the drop scene. All is made possible by far-reaching changes wrought in "the cellar" . . . Above the stage a similar revolution has occurred amongst the rollers and levers for raising and lowering scenery.'

It would appear that these had been replaced by individual sets of lines for each cloth and border, such as may be seen on the drawing of the Theatre Royal stage at Leicester (fig.159), for we read that 'Hitherto it has been impossible to separate one portion of scenery from another to secure immediate safety in case of fire. But now, a burning drop can be detached from the rest and the fire extinguished. This is the main feature of the alterations above the stage.'[10]

Until recently actual examples of the sort of barrels noted above could be seen on the prompt-side fly floor of the Theatre Royal, Bath, built by C. J. Phipps in 1863.[11] There were originally two long barrels (fig.125d.f.) running the full length of the fly gallery, but when this machinery was surveyed in 1954 one was missing. These long barrels were each operated by a large wheel (figs.125e,126a.) around which a cable or wire passed to a winch situated on the fly gallery. While these two barrels were presumably used to operate the sets of borders, there were also five shorter barrels (a) for use with individual pieces of scenery. Each had a timber driving wheel (b) (fig.126b) fitted with metal spikes curving gently outward, over which a continuous rope was hung. When the rope was pulled in either direction it was dragged down between the teeth, and was then held with sufficient tenacity to cause the wheel to turn. The item of scenery was moved by a line attached to the drum (a), and was counterweighted by a further line attached to the same drum, and carried back over a pulley block (g) to a weight. The actual date of the machinery is difficult to assess; it is, however, possible that it dates from the rebuilding of 1863.

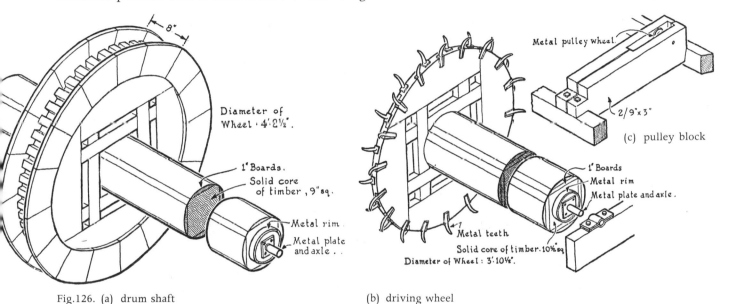

Fig.126. (a) drum shaft   (b) driving wheel

In 1947 the Theatre Royal, Leicester, had much of its under-stage machinery still in position, and it was possible to measure and record the information illustrated here (figs. 130,152). This theatre, opened on Monday, 12th September, 1836, as the New Theatre, was designed by Mr William Parsons, with the main frontage in the 'manner of the Grecian Ionic School'.[12] The auditorium was designed, as were many similar provincial theatres, with the circles arranged in the now familiar horseshoe shape, and with a pit fitted with benches which were 'fixed differently to any before seen in this town, every second one having a rail at the back'[13], and seating 450 persons. It is not clear if the pit extended the full width of the house at this date, as it did after the alterations of 1873, when a new floor was laid,[14] nor is it known if the original floor was stepped or if it sloped gently up from the front as

Fig.127. Drury Lane:
drum and shaft on the grid

did the new floor. Above the pit, the dress circle was divided into boxes, with further boxes on the tier above, which it was later found necessary to separate from the gallery.[15] The boxes accommodated a total of 350 persons, and a further 450 to 500 could be accommodated in the gallery. Little is known of the original appearance of the interior, apart from descriptions of the decorations and the use of 'a magnificent chandelier'[16] which hung from the centre of the flat ceiling.[17]

By 1873 it was found necessary 'to re-model the interior of the theatre',[18] and the work was commenced in the Spring. The alterations were of a very thorough nature, although the main structure of the building appears to have remained basically the same, and it is the house at this stage that is shown on the reconstruction (fig.128), which is itself based on drawings prepared in May, 1888, by James Barradale, when further alterations were in progress.

'Entering the building we found a new office and other rooms have been provided on the ground floor, to be used as a box-office, and on mounting the stairs, which have been considerably widened, we enter a spacious hall leading to the dress circle . . . On the right hand side is provided a spacious refreshment saloon, got up with elaborate paper, and a richly ornamented counter . . . Adjoining this, with a separate entrance, there is a large and comfortable saloon. Instead of one entrance to the dress circle as formerly, there are now two, and the alteration which has been effected here is striking. The walls are papered with light green and gold, and by placing a balcony in front of the old dress boxes, provision has been made for two additional rows of seats. The dress circle has movable seats . . . The old stage boxes have been entirely removed, and a concave wall placed instead of the abutting obstruction which in byegone days has effectually hidden the stage from those whose lot it fell to sit in the side boxes near the stage. The "Gallery proper" has been enlarged (fig.129), and is now one of the most perfect in the kingdom. By a rearrangement of the ceiling each one of the gallery visitors will be enabled to have a view of the stage, a thing which was not always attainable in the old house. In the pit the manner of egress and ingress has been much improved, two doors having been provided in the place of the old one . . . An entirely new boarded floor has been laid, and seats with backs provided, with separations between every two seats to prevent overcrowding. In front of the orchestra "stalls" have been provided, an entrance to which is obtained by a private staircase from the box office.'[19]

Here we have further evidence (p.170) of the moves by managements to obtain more returns from the customers by the reduction in the number of the pit seatings, and their replacement by more expensive, and more comfortable, stalls. We see also a suggestion of the social problems, and the architectural complications which such moves would involve, in the brief mention of the private stair from the box entrance. The occupants of the stalls must not be made to mix with the pitites, and must therefore ascend to the dress circle, traverse the box passage at that level, and descend the stair provided in the corner adjoining the proscenium wall. The pit had a separate entrance and a foyer beneath that to the dress circle, off which opened a small saloon. The occupants of the gallery, however, had no refreshment room until one was built over the circle saloon in 1891.[20] It is also of interest that the divisions to the pit seatings, intended by the architect to prevent overcrowding, were soon removed at the request of the owners[21] as 'the frequenters of the Theatre find

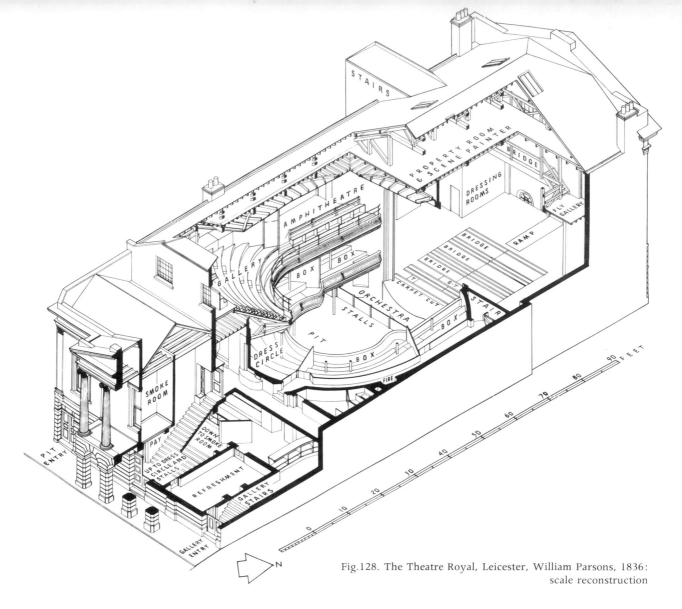

Fig.128. The Theatre Royal, Leicester, William Parsons, 1836:
scale reconstruction

Iron bars inconvenient', presumably because the management were crowding in more than
had been intended.

Although the original stage boxes were removed, the dress circle was still divided into
boxes, as a price list for the opening night confirms with mention of 'Private boxes, at one
and two guineas: centre boxes at 2/6 and side boxes at 2/-.' In 1883 there were '4 rows of
chairs in the centre box',[22] and in 1897 mention was made of two private boxes on either
side and passages round the boxes. A request for permission to install 'four new private
boxes' was made and approved in 1881.[23] Traces of full height partitions were noted on the
underside of the circle ceiling at the time of the theatre's demolition, and it is this evidence
that is included on the reconstruction (fig.128). It is highly likely that these last mentioned
private boxes constituted a further subdivision of the two boxes shown here on either side
of the proscenium opening, as there is mention in 1908[24] of the removal of 'the partition
to the first private box on each side of the Theatre, the stage box on each side to be left
intact as they are now'. The last of these boxes was removed in 1913.[25]

It was probably during these alterations that the upper boxes were removed to leave open 'slips' on either side entered from beneath the gallery proper. These areas, and the front tier of the gallery seating, probably formed the 'amphitheatre stalls' priced at 1s.6d., and separated from the remainder of the padded stepped seats of the 6d. gallery by a low partition. The old chandelier was now replaced by a new sunlight, described as 'a gorgeous piece of mechanism, giving forth the light of 190 gas jets in nineteen clusters'.[26] As at Richmond (p.158), the building was originally heated by coal fires, here placed in the pit and box corridors. These were presumably blocked up when an 'efficient hot water apparatus'[27] was installed in 1918, but were noted in the positions indicated during the demolition of the theatre.

When the theatre was first built the stage and stage machinery were constructed by a Mr Evans of the London Theatres.[28] It was reported to be 48 feet deep by 25 feet wide at the proscenium, the actual measurement from the face of the curved wall at the front of the stage to the rear wall of the theatre being 45 feet. The stage was separated from the auditorium by a brick wall, with a four-centred arched proscenium opening, which later measured 21 feet 6 inches wide by 25 feet 6 inches high. There were never any proscenium doors, with their windows or boxes over, but, as suggested above, the stage did curve forward into the auditorium to a maximum distance of 4 feet 6 inches in front of the 'picture frame' surrounding the opening.

During the alterations of 1873 it is claimed that the stage and scenery were entirely new,[29] the stage machinists being Mr Roberts of Nottingham and Mr Goodger of the Surrey Theatre, London. How much of the stage machinery was actually altered is not clear as there is little information regarding the stage as originally built. In 1853 there was mention of 'the large trap in the Centre (used for raising Pianofortes, etc.) cut through the Middle and a beam placed under it. These alterations made for the convenience of the Ghost in the Corsican

Fig.129. The Theatre Royal, Leicester: the gallery after the alterations of 1888

Brothers, render the trap entirely useless for its original purposes and injures the stability of the Stage.'[30] In 1865 there was mention of the flies, in which it was required that a hand-worked, small fire engine should be kept.[31] If the stage was in fact rebuilt then the remains of the stage machinery, as surveyed in 1947 (fig.130), would probably date from 1873, but it is highly unlikely that all the machinery would have been replaced at this date, and much may well have dated from 1836.

Directly behind the proscenium opening was a narrow cut in the stage, with a hinged flap at stage level. This was the 'carpet cut' which extended the full width of the proscenium opening. Adjoining it were two corner traps, one of which can now be seen in greater detail. In the drawing the platform is shown partly raised through the mezzanine floor beneath the corner trap at stage level. In his article describing the English Wooden Stage, Sachs said:

> 'The "trap" itself is a small wooden platform framed together, and made to rise up and down in grooves between four corner upright posts. The "trap" (fig.131), and the weight put upon it, is made to rise and fall with ease by means of the counterweights which are attached to ropes running over pulleys, and attached to the "trap" . . . The "corner" traps . . . are square on plan, and, like the grave traps, worked by counterweights, but travel between two uprights instead of four.'[32]

Fig.130. The Theatre Royal, Leicester: stage and machinery

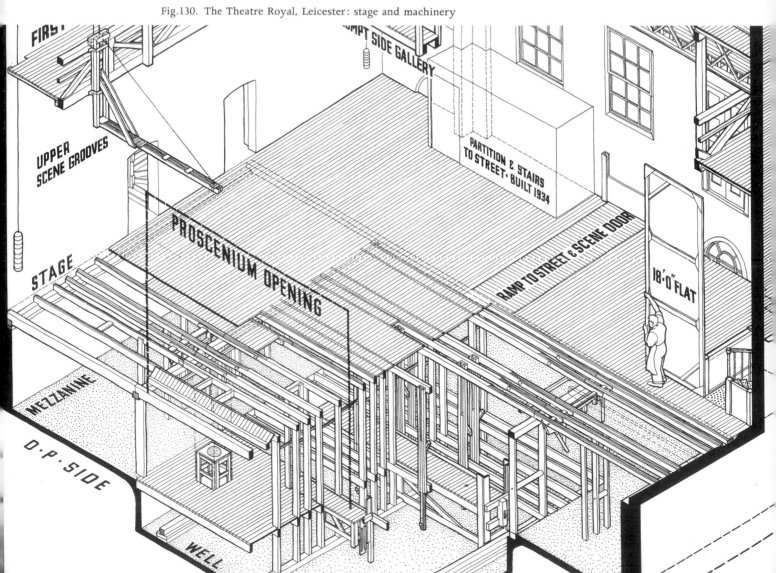

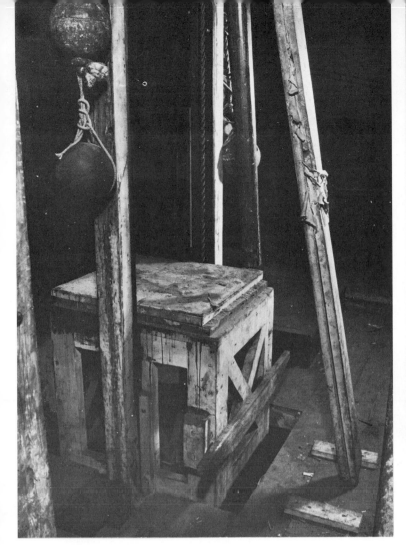

Fig.131. The Theatre Royal, Bristol: a corner trap

Fig.132. The Theatre Royal, Bristol: bridge at mezzanine level

The two uprights, mentioned by Sachs, were missing when the survey was made, and so have not been included in the reconstruction.

It will be noted that the stage joists run across the stage from side to side, and their spacing varies from front to back of the stage. The first two spaces next to the corner traps are both approximately 1 foot in width, and the next space 2 feet wide. Centrally placed here was a rectangular grave trap, 7 feet long, which Sachs described above as working on the same principle as the corner traps. The framework of the grave trap itself can be seen in its lowest position, with the top level with the mezzanine floor, and its sub-structure sunk into the well. The next 15 feet 6 inches of stage was subdivided into three wide spaces from 2 feet 6 inches to 3 feet wide, and six narrower spaces each 1 foot wide. Like the bridges at Plymouth (fig.123), all these spaces had their own separate section of stage made in two movable parts, each 12 feet long. These were also constructed so that they could be dropped at their off-stage ends, and drawn off under the fixed side stages, here some 13 feet 6 inches in width.

'The "cuts" generally correspond in length to the width of the proscenium opening, and assuming the latter to be 30 feet wide, each "slider" would be 15 feet long. In

Fig.133. Her Majesty's, Haymarket: the stage cellar

order to draw off the "sliders" a space equal to 15 feet will be required on each side of the proscenium opening, and the *minimum* width of stage from wall to wall should therefore be 60 feet, or twice the width of the proscenium opening. Where the space is limited, the "sliders" may be worked on the revolving-shutter principle, but this arrangement cannot be recommended.'[33]

The sliders were held in position, flush with the stage, by a timber paddle (fig.134a), which raised a pair of $3\frac{1}{2}$ inches by $\frac{3}{4}$ inch battens joined at the off-stage end, and bolted at the opposite ends to the supporting joists, so that they were free to swivel. Each stage joist had a $5\frac{1}{2}$ inches by 1 inch board fixed to each side, sloping downwards away from the centre of the stage, and acting as a track on which the slider could run. When the paddle was moved out of its vertical position (fig.134b) the hinged battens dropped and lowered the sliders on to the tracks, after which they could be drawn off-stage by lines attached to a winch at mezzanine level, leaving an opening 24 feet wide in the centre of the stage. The wider openings were controlled by a different form of lever (fig.137[5]), but otherwise the process involved was the same. Beneath each of the three wide openings was a 24 feet long 'bridge' (fig.132), which could be raised to stage level in a similar manner to the traps, with a counterweighted system operated by a timber wheel and short barrel (fig.133) beneath the bridge and an independent winch (fig.136). 'The rope passes from the "bridge" on to the "shaft" which is made to revolve by another rope being taken off the "drum" on to the

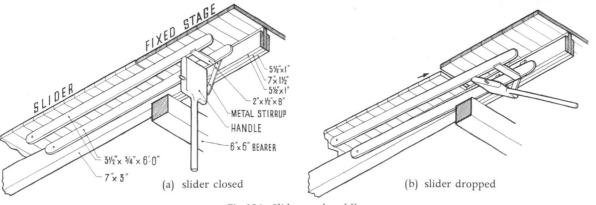

(a) slider closed

5½"×1"
7"×1½"
5½"×1"
2"×½"×8"
METAL STIRRUP
HANDLE
6"×6" BEARER

SLIDER
FIXED STAGE
3½"×¾"×6'0"
7"×3"

(b) slider dropped

Fig.134. Sliders and paddles

Fig.135. The Theatre Royal, Bristol: *centre,* two sloat-cut paddles; *beyond,* a bridge paddle with handle missing

Fig.136. Mezzanine floor at Her Majesty's, Haymarket: *left,* a bridge with double-handled paddle; *centre,* bridge and double-handled paddle; *foreground,* motivating winches

windlass in the "mezzanine", in the same way as the "drums" and "shafts" are employed on the "gridiron" level for raising and lowering the "cloths", whilst they are actually worked from the flies.'[34] One of the bridges is shown (fig.130) in its lowest position.

The narrow widths resembled the 'flaps' and 'sliders' described in Rees's *Cyclopaedia,* in that they were used for raising and lowering single pieces of scenery, which could be the full height of the flats and wings, but were more normally horizontal 'ground-rows'. Unlike the earlier openings (p.153) which had 'no machinery . . . permanently attached', these cuts were each fitted with a pair of 'sloats' for raising and lowering the scenes (fig.137a.b.). Each sloat consisted of a T-shaped batten, with a metal bracket at the bottom into which the scene could be dropped, which rose and fell in a channel made up of further battens. Two of these sloats were fixed to the up-stage joist of each narrow opening or 'sloat cut'. When

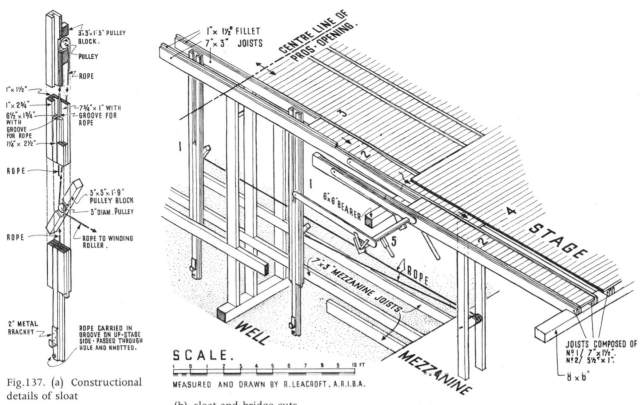

Fig.137. (a) Constructional details of sloat

SCALE.

MEASURED AND DRAWN BY R. LEACROFT. A.R.I.B.A.

(b) sloat and bridge cuts
1. sloats, 2. sloat sliders, 3. bridge sloat, 4. fixed side stage, 5. paddle

the sloat cut sliders were open, a drum was turned which simultaneously operated two lines passing over pulleys, built into the sloats, and thus raised both sloat and scenery up to and above stage level. To provide rigidity in the stage as a whole, especially when it might be subjected to such movement as would result from dancing or similar activities, the stage joists, in the central area, were fastened to each other by metal hooks and eyes to keep them firmly spaced. These could be unhooked in the openings in use, to permit the passage of a scene.

Grooves, like those at Plymouth (fig.123), would have been fixed to the permanent side stages, with the removable grooves being laid in place when required to take the movement of the flats. These would have had to be laid on a slider, which would then have been out of use for that particular part of the production. None of these bottom grooves remained to be measured, but one pair of upper grooves was still fixed in the position indicated on the drawing (fig.130). In the detail (fig.138a) it may be seen that the groove was divided into three 'cuts', each of which could be used to support either a side wing or one half of a back-scene, as required. If side wings only were to be used then the hinged extension piece could be pulled up and folded back (fig.138b), but when provision was to be made for a flat then

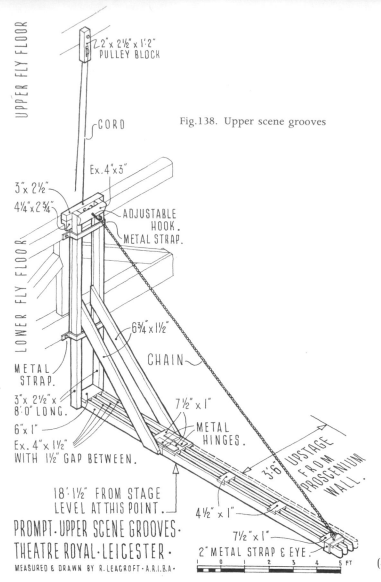

UPPER FLY FLOOR

2.2" x 2½" x 1'.2"
PULLEY BLOCK

CORD

Fig.138. Upper scene grooves

Ex.4"x3"

3" x 2½"
4¼" x 2¾"

ADJUSTABLE
HOOK.
METAL STRAP.

LOWER FLY FLOOR

6¾" x 1½"

CHAIN

METAL
STRAP.

3" x 2½" x
8'.0" LONG.

7½" x 1"

METAL
HINGES.

6" x 1"
Ex. 4" x 1½"
WITH 1½" GAP BETWEEN.

18'.1½" FROM STAGE
LEVEL AT THIS POINT.

3'.6" UPSTAGE FROM PROSCENIUM WALL.

PROMPT·UPPER SCENE GROOVES·
THEATRE ROYAL·LEICESTER·

4½" x 1"

7½" x 1"

2" METAL STRAP & EYE.

MEASURED & DRAWN BY R.LEACROFT·A.R.I.B.A·

1 0 1 2 3 4 5 FT

(a) constructional details

(b) grooves with extension piece raised

(c) grooves with extension piece lowered

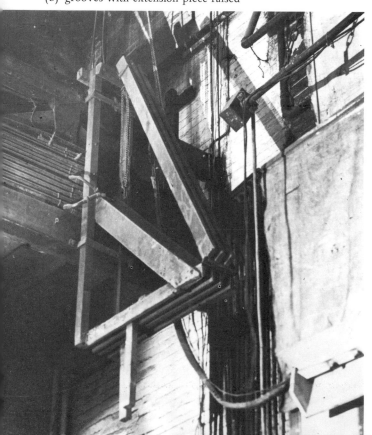

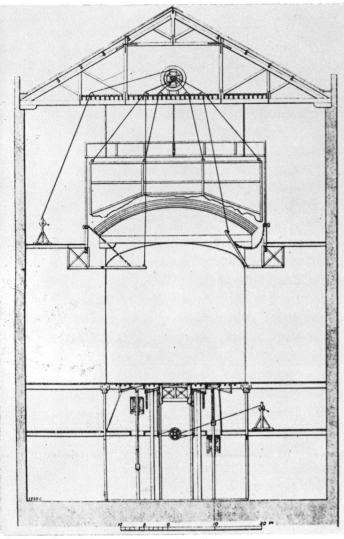

(a) section across stage

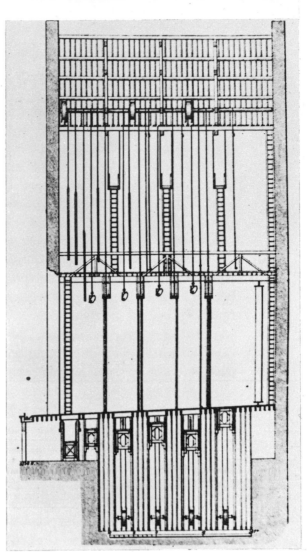

(b) section on centre line of stage

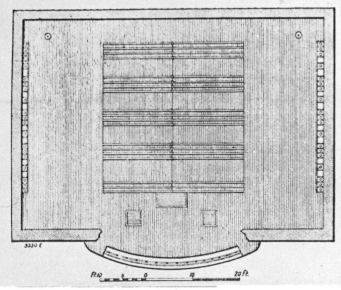

(c) plan at stage level

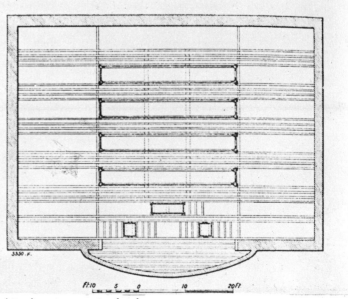

(d) plan at mezzanine level

Fig.139. E. O. Sachs' English wooden stage

the arm could be lowered (fig.138c). Originally all the grooves on each side would have been fixed to such barrels as were noted at Plymouth and Bath (figs.124-5), so that they could all be raised or lowered at the same time, but later it seems as though the use of individual grooves, or pairs to support special pieces of scenery, may have resulted in their independent operation. In this particular instance it is probable that the hinged arms were already falling into disuse when installed, as the flats were by now being gradually replaced by roller drops or cloths, which, as they did not require lower groove extension pieces to be laid, would not have interfered with the working of the sloats.

In 1896 Sachs described a typical wooden stage for an English provincial theatre[35] as having a proscenium opening varying between 28 feet and 30 feet in width, with a corresponding height. This resulted in a total stage width of 65 feet between walls, with a depth which he suggests should be a minimum of 30 feet up to 80 feet. The height from the sloping stage to the gridiron he suggests as 60 feet, or twice the height of the proscenium opening, with a depth of 30 feet for the well beneath the stage; he admits, however, that this is seldom possible to achieve as it involves problems of drainage, especially if the 'area', which he calls the stalls and pit, is much below ground level.

Sachs' plans and sections (figs.139a.b.c.d.) show at the upper levels what he terms the 'rigging loft' or 'gridiron', consisting of 'an open wooden floor laid upon the tie-beams of the principals of the roof trusses'. A considerable weight has to be supported by the gridiron, as from it depend all the 'cloths, borders, and gas battens . . . and everything that is raised upward from the stage'. He shows these items of scenery attached to four lines which pass over pulley blocks, set on the gridiron, to a series of barrels on the central axis of the stage, the barrels in turn being operated by winches placed on the prompt-side fly-gallery, and attached to counterweights boxed in against the side wall of the stage. A variation on this arrangement is shown by Contant[36] when he illustrates an English stage, and here the barrels are indicated as being set in a similar position to that noted at Bath (fig.125), above the fly gallery but beneath the level of the roof trusses and gridiron.

Sachs describes the flies as being connected across the rear of the stage by a bridge, which he mentions is often used by the scene painter (figs.140-1), and by further bridges – catwalks – which permit quick access from one gallery to another, as well as allowing the riggers to reach the cloths hanging above the stage in case they need freeing or adjusting. The sloping stage is described as being set to a rake of '$\frac{1}{2}$ inch to every foot from front to back' and as being necessary to improve the sight lines from 'the lowest seat in the area'. Beneath the stage he describes the mezzanine and well, and says that at the bottom of the latter 'are placed the ''drums'' and ''shafts'' used for lifting the bridges' (fig.133).

The need for a central control point from which the movement of scenes and machines may be co-ordinated is also discussed.

'As regards the facilities for the stage manager on the old wooden stage, I have generally found a simple case known as the ''call-board'' on the ''prompt'' side near the gas-plate. From the ''call-board'' there is generally an extensive system of speaking tubes

Fig.140. The Theatre Royal, Leicester: *upper right,* scene painter's bridge; *centre,* catwalks across stage; *bottom left,* proscenium opening and upper scene grooves

Fig.141. The Theatre Royal, Leicester: scene painting bridge

Fig.142. The Theatre Royal,
Leicester: backstage

and bells, which enable the stage manager to give directions to different parts of the house without having to leave his seat at the ''prompt'' side of the stage. From here he ''rings up and down'' the curtain, he instructs the stage carpenters ''in the flies'' or ''on the mezzanine'', he orders the shifting of a scene, the lowering or turning up of the lights, and gives all other instructions which are necessary to effectually conduct the ''stage business''. He also from this point has to communicate with the orchestra, with the manager in the front of the house, and with the artistes in their greenroom or dressing-rooms. Flash signalling, telephones, &c, belong to the more modern types of stage mechanism.'[37]

From these descriptions it may be realised that these stages were no simple platforms, but were in themselves intricate pieces of scenic machinery, permitting the changing of scenes, which took place with the curtain up, before the eyes of the audience. At a signal from the stage manager all the wings of the chamber scene could be drawn off to either side to reveal a new set of wood wings already in position. The flats too could part in the middle and move to either side, whilst at the same time the chamber or ceiling borders would rise to reveal the wood borders, or perhaps a sky set, again already in position behind. While this was happening, some bridge and sloat sliders would open, and a set of ground-rows would appear through the stage, behind one of which a bevy of fairies, or similar characters, could slowly make their appearance, while at the same time another character might have been descending from the heavens in a cloud machine. Such a scene is shown in operation in the reconstructed view of the Leicester stage (fig.142). Here two carpenters, in their paper hats, may be seen drawing on a pair of flats in the top and bottom grooves, while some fairies and a ground-row appear through the opened stage. The extension arms of the remaining grooves are drawn up, and profiled side wings are seen supported in the fixed sections. Attached to the rear of the wings, and hidden behind the front border, are the gas lighting battens and lengths, this method of illumination having been introduced at the Theatre Royal by 1865, when it is specifically mentioned in the 'Precautions against Fire' required by the authorities at that time.[38]

10 The growth of controls

On the 15th May, 1858, Covent Garden was reopened to the designs of E. M. Barry, who was

> 'determined to carry out a system of fireproof construction wherever practicable, and though perhaps it is hardly possible at present to render a theatre actually fireproof, the new building was intended to be an advance in that direction. The Building Act most properly requires all corridors and staircases in such structures to be of incombustible materials, and these requirements had of course to be observed. In addition, as it had been noticed in previous cases of fire that the roof served as an easy means of connection between the stage and the auditory, it was sought to avoid this source of danger by making the roof and its covering entirely fireproof, and it was decided to use wood as little as possible in the construction of the interior. Regarding the danger of staircases with open well-holes in public places', in this instance 'all staircases used by the public were arranged to consist of solid stone steps, built into a wall at each end.'[1]

Although Barry considered both the circle and the ellipse as shapes for the auditorium, he eventually decided on the horseshoe form which, in spite of its disadvantages, he considered to be a good acoustic form, and he cited the success of Her Majesty's Theatre in this respect. It must be remembered that Covent Garden was now primarily intended for use as an Italian opera house, but to complicate the situation a winter season would still consist of pantomimes and similar fare. 'The requirements of a London theatre for the Italian opera are very peculiar, and differ in many ways from those of ordinary play-houses. As regards the latter, the great desideratum is of course that all the visitors may see and hear to the greatest possible advantage.'[2] The audience for the opera is much more socially conscious than the normal play-going audience, and is prepared to accept side boxes where they may be seen, even though they themselves may not be able to see the production to the best advantage. With the royal box in the grand tier, this level 'is the great resort of fashion, and any seat at this level will sell . . . it is obviously a great desideratum to obtain as many boxes as possible at this level, where it is found that even side boxes (in spite of drawbacks of position) are always eagerly sought for'.[3]

For State occasions the royal box was fitted up in its original position, directly facing the stage in the grand tier. It was adapted from two ordinary boxes on this level, and on the tier above when required. Special permission was obtained from the Queen to place the royal entrance and retiring room on the right-hand side of the auditorium, opposite to the generally accepted position, as it was easier to obtain an approach from Hart Street on this side. A plan of 1882,[4] moreover, shows Her Majesty's Private Box adjoining that of the Duke of Bedford's, itself immediately adjacent to the proscenium opening on the right-hand side of the auditorium. The main entrance to the box tiers was from a covered carriage way leading into the Grand Entrance Hall, from which the Grand Staircase led up to a Saloon or Crush Room. A door in the centre of the long side of this room led to the corridor around the boxes, with access stairs to the upper box tiers in the left-hand rear corner, between the curved wall enclosing the rear of the auditorium and the rectangular walls of the house proper (fig.143). A further flight of winding stairs connected all the box corridors at the left-hand end adjoining the proscenium wall. Two enclosed staircases on the Hart Street frontage led to the front and rear of the gallery, subdivided into the amphitheatre stalls at the front and the amphitheatre, on a slightly higher level, behind. As contrasted with Wyatt's Drury Lane, Barry does not seem to have provided as adequate a system of approach and escape stairs, only the pit and pit stalls being provided with direct approaches to the streets on either side. On the opening night, one of the amphitheatre stairs was appropriated to the use of the boxes, so that only the one stair was available to the amphitheatre, and this was 'blocked with people, in slow and toilsome ascent',[5] a pattern which was repeated at the conclusion of the performance. The intention was that the occupants of the amphitheatre stalls, which were bookable, would arrive later than the unreserved amphitheatre, but what appears to have been overlooked was that they would all leave together, and the additional exit should therefore have been available from the gallery. By the following year two additional exits into the Floral Hall, on the side opposite to Hart Street, had been made at pit level, together with an external iron stairway from the principal tier of boxes. Alterations were also made to the amphitheatre exits, and a canopy erected along the Hart Street façade to protect those waiting for entry to the unreserved pit and amphitheatre.[6]

The pit was divided by a partition into two portions, the largest of which contained eleven rows of pit stalls. These were described in an advertisement, which claimed that 'Each person will have a separate armchair, occupying a space of 2 feet.'[7] A view of the interior (fig.144), however, shows that these were no more than benches provided with backs and arm-rests, the rows being spaced at 1 foot 8 inches. This area was reached from the corridor surrounding a pit tier of boxes by descending steps on either side, and doors in the wall surrounding the pit. Beyond the partition there were eight rows of pit seats (a description of the building prior to opening mentions ten rows).[8] These differed from the stalls only in size, with a width of 1 foot 8 inches per seat, and a distance of 1 foot 2 inches between rows. These seats were reached by a doorway at the centre rear from a wide corridor surrounding the pit itself. Steps inside the area led up from this level to gangways surrounding the seats. Three tiers

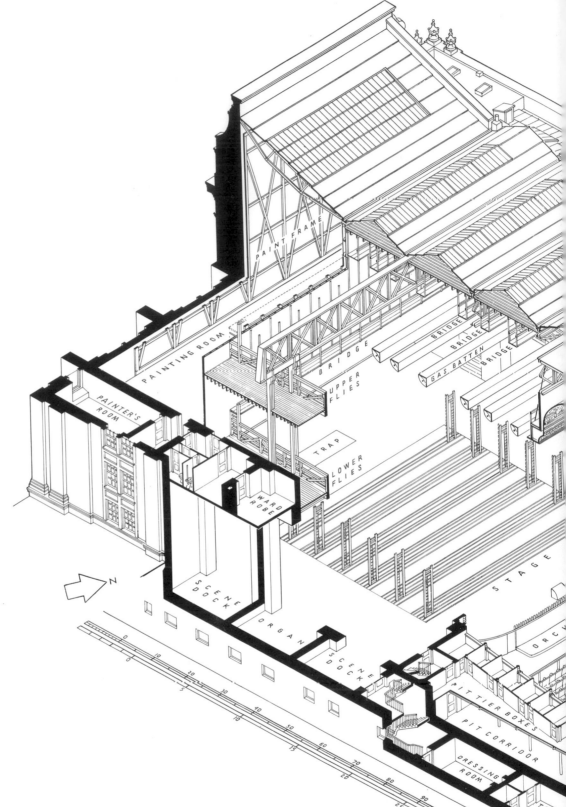

Fig.143. Royal Italian Opera House, Covent Garden, E. M. Barry, 1858: scale reconstruction based on contemporary drawings and L.C.C. survey drawings dated 1882

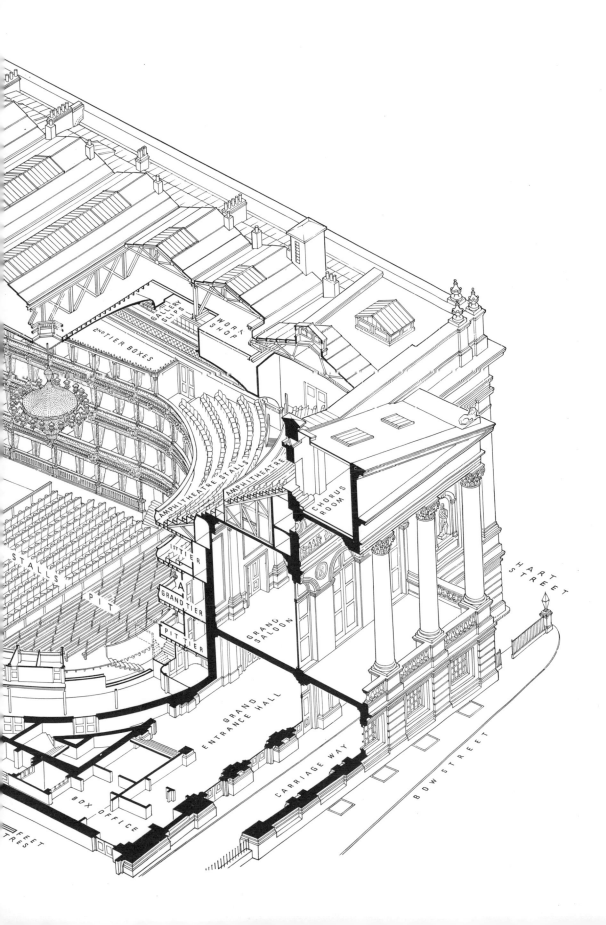

GALLERY SLIPS

2ND TIER BOXES

WORK SHOP

AMPHITHEATRE STALLS

AMPHITHEATRE

CHORUS ROOM

STALLS

PIT

1ST TIER

A

GRAND TIER

PIT TIER

GRAND SALOON

GRAND ENTRANCE HALL

HART STREET

BOX OFFICE

CARRIAGE WAY

BOW STREET

FEET METRES

Fig.144. Covent Garden: interior, 1858

of boxes known as pit, grand and upper tiers, enclosed the pit. On each tier the boxes were separated by full-height partitions of $1\frac{1}{2}$ inch wood framing and canvas, papered. The boxes were so designed that there were no columns at the front to obstruct the view. Columns were placed, however, approximately 6 feet 6 inches from the box fronts, and wrought iron girders, built at their ends into the surrounding masonry walls, were cantilevered through a box-like opening in the columns to support the boxes; each column supported the one above from the pit floor to the top tier. The boxes were originally intended to be only 5 feet 6 inches in depth, with an 8 feet wide corridor surrounding them, but as built they were extended to include the columns in their depth. The surrounding corridors were floored with 3 inch thick York slabs, themselves supported on rolled-iron joists connected between the cantilevers.

Above the three tiers of boxes, the seven rows of amphitheatre stalls, iron-framed, and with well-padded arms, backs and seats, occupied the semi-circular end of the auditorium, and were flanked by eight upper boxes on either side, reached by staircases from the box corridors below. Above, at the rear of the amphitheatre and some 3 feet higher, was the gallery with nine rows of seats, set within a great elliptical arch directly facing the stage. At right angles to this two further arches enclosed a slips or side gallery on either side, with two rows of benches behind an open railing. All three areas were approached by the amphi-theatre staircase, the left-hand slips only being reached by a long passageway beneath the rear of the gallery. Separate refreshment rooms and lavatories were provided for both amphitheatre and amphitheatre stalls.

Vanbrugh's theatre (p.103) had been used for masquerades, and it was an accepted pattern that theatres could be used for other purposes. Covent Garden had been used for masked balls, public dinners and similar functions, and on these occasions the pit had been floored over level with the stage. To make the adaptation of the building easier on such occasions the pit floor was designed to be adjustable. It was supported on a series of trussed timber beams, 2 feet 3 inches in depth, supported in turn on cast-iron columns with split heads into which the beams could be lowered, thus enabling the floor to be raised to the level of the stage, or lowered some feet below it. When the stage was built it was fixed 9 inches too high, so that the occupants of the front row of the stalls had a poor view of the performers. The problem was solved by fixing the front of the pit 9 inches higher than had originally been intended. This, however, reduced the rake of the floor, and as a result the view from all the seats in this area suffered accordingly.[9]

As the theatre was designed to be used for the double purpose of Italian opera and a winter season of pantomime, it was necessary to increase the capacity of the auditorium for the latter purpose, and adapt the seating to conform more closely to that of a playhouse. Arrangements were therefore made for the easy removal of all box partitions and backs

'so that a portion or the whole of the corridor may be taken into the boxes, if required, to form an extended dress-circle. On the pit tier, the boxes, with the floors, fronts, sides and backs, can be entirely taken away, giving facilities thereby for forming a very capacious pit, extending under the dress circle to the semi-circular wall at the back of the corridors.'[10]

When arranged for the opera season, the house was intended to hold some 1,897 persons. There were 274 reserved seats in the pit stalls, in addition to which allowance was made for twenty extra chairs at the ends of the alleys. The pit contained 193 unreserved separate seats at 10s.6d. The pit tier was divided into thirty-four boxes, and the grand tier into thirty-three, together with the boxes for Her Majesty and the Duke of Bedford. On the upper tier there were thirty-six boxes, with a further sixteen on a level with the amphitheatre stalls. All these boxes held four persons each, with the exception of Her Majesty's and the Duke's, which held eight and six respectively. In the amphitheatre stalls there were 320 reserved seats which were priced at 10s.6d. for the front row, 7s.6d. for the second and 5s. for the back row. In the main portion of the gallery were 380 unreserved seats, and a further 220 in the side galleries; both areas were priced at 2s.6d. In the winter season it was hoped to add 600 persons for the increased numbers in the pit and boxes resulting from the removal of the divisions, and to crowd an extra 200 into the galleries, making a total of some 2,697.[11]

Although Barry went to considerable lengths to avoid the use of combustible materials, particularly in the roof space, no attempt was made to separate the stage and auditorium, and as late as 1867, M. G. Davioud, a French architect engaged on a survey of London theatres,

Fig.145. Covent Garden:
detail of the proscenium frame

was to criticise this aspect of the theatre when he commented that

> 'the wall which separates the stage from the body of the house and which receives the curtain, is built of light masonry, and partly wood, and that it does not rise above the *voûte de la salle*; so that should fire break out in the upper part of the stage machinery or scenes, it would spread with the greatest rapidity over the whole edifice . . . In Paris the same wall would have been built of strong masonry and carried up to the roof of the house so as to effectually cut the building into two parts, and the opening on to the stage would be furnished with an iron blind which would descend every evening after the performance and close it' . . . By comparison with the requirements of the Préfet of the Parisian police the English laws regarding safety of the public seem slight . . . 'The particular mode of construction for the interior and the stage is left an open question, no apparatus in case of fire is fixed upon, heating and ventilation are not obligatory, workshops are not interdicted, neither are there any stringent regulations relating to the comfortable seating of the public, obligatory items which materially encumber the constructors of Parisian theatres, and upon which an ordinance of the Préfet, dated 1st July, 1864, insists more stringently than before.'[12]

The main side walls of the theatre were built on a cellular principle with two walls approximately 10 feet apart. Cross walls, spaced at 20 feet intervals, bound these together for their full height. This arrangement continued for the full length of the building with the exception of the space occupied by the crush room and main staircase, which together filled the entire width of the building at the front. The opportunity was taken to contain eight floors of stairs, offices, and dressing rooms within the cells created. On either side of the stage two of the three cells flanking it to the height of the first fly gallery were used as scene docks. The central space on the O.P. side was filled with an organ, while the down-stage bay on the prompt side was used as a retiring room for the occupants of the Duke of Bedford's box.

The proscenium opening was 50 feet wide, and was treated as a simple gilt frame to the spectacle (fig.145): 'the proscenium columns are arranged to slide on wheels, so as to expand or contract the opening when desired'.[13] The actual opening in use for the scenes was therefore 4 or 5 feet less than the fixed opening. The stage projected some 9 feet in a flat ellipse into the auditorium, this being retained as the area 'from which the principal artistes commonly sing'[14] and over this advanced area of stage a parabolic curved reflector was placed. The orchestra occupied a further 10 feet width beyond the furthest advance of the stage.

The gradual change from the standard wing and shutter arrangement of scenery to one employing numerous set pieces, either in the form of heavily-built stairs and rostra or of cut-out pieces, resulted in some changes in the stage mechanism.

> 'The grooves so commonly used for the support of the scenes are entirely done away with, it being considered that their undoubted convenience is more than counterbalanced by their attendant disadvantages, and more particularly by the obstacles they afford to the formation of a grand open scene embracing the whole extent of the stage.'

The flats were now replaced by back-scenes composed

> 'of single sheets of canvas, lowered from the top, and secured to rollers resting ultimately upon the main beams of the roof. The side scenes and set pieces are fixed to the wing ladders behind which the side gas-lights for lighting the stage are placed. The wing ladders being unattached to anything above, the artist is enabled to place large set-pieces, such as trees, rocks, houses, &c, against them and still preserve the total height of the stage, while they are so constructed that they may be moved completely across the stage. The upper pieces of scenery, known technically as borders, are of somewhat novel construction, owing to the great size of the stage . . . they are made . . . in three pieces – a centre and two wings; the latter being so arranged as to slide forward and back, so as to form an arch of any required diameter.'[15]

The stage itself was constructed on a pattern similar to that seen in detail in the drawings of the Theatre Royal, Leicester (fig.130). The side stages were fixed, while the central area behind the proscenium opening was made movable with a series of 'twenty-seven [this number seems to have included the wing ladder slides] small slides for scenery through which it can descend bodily, and five wide slides for larger matters'.[16] These latter were, presumably, the normal bridges. As the grooves had been dispensed with, it is not surprising to find a return to the wing carriages in the form of five pairs of 'wing ladders' which moved in similar narrow slides, 'running on a rail fixed to the uprights below the level of the stage'.[17] The openings were separated by joists grooved on either side to carry the moving sliders, which were 'formed of $1\frac{1}{4}$ battens by $3\frac{1}{4}$ wide, in very short pieces running from front to back (in between oak slips which run from side to side) and framed so as to slide under the floor at the sides which is fixed'.[18] In addition to these openings there were four corner traps and a grave trap; but their positions on the stage are not indicated on any of the drawings at this date. The stage sloped up at a rise of half-an-inch to a foot for some 60 feet, after which the rear bay was flat. A trap 20 feet long by 6 feet wide was near the centre of this area, directly below a similar trap in the floor of the painting room above. This latter occupied the full width of the rear stage and was 30 feet wide, on a level with the upper end of the lower fly galleries, which were 8 feet wide and sloped up with the line of the stage at a height of 28 feet. Upper fly galleries of the same width, but level, were placed some 23 feet higher still at the proscenium end. Ladders from these led up a further 8 feet to six bridges spanning the stage 6 feet below the grid floor. Beneath each of these: 'The gas battens to light the upper part of the scenes, six in number, are 71 feet long, supplied by flexible pipes, so that they can be raised or lowered according to circumstances. These have metal guards to receive gauze covering, so as to provide blue or red light.'[19]

The painting room, carried on an iron girder spanning the stage, was lit by a continuous roof light, and had slots in the floor at front and rear through which the paint-frames could be lowered (fig.146); a slot at the rear of the stage permitted the paint-frame on the rear wall (fig.183) to be lowered into the basement. This main frame was 47 feet high and 71 feet wide. 'Under the floor of the painting room are fixed the contrivances for simulating the noise of thunder, rain, and the like, and the great bell, whose mournful notes have sounded the knell of so many a disconsolate tenor.'[20]

The basement was 24 feet 6 inches below the rear stage, with a mezzanine floor 8 feet below stage level. The arrangement of mezzanine and wing ladders was criticised by C. J. Phipps when he said of the wings:

'On the Continent they often run on small tramways on the mezzanine fixed to the wing or gas ladders; and, at Covent Garden, the same principle has been imperfectly carried out, as there the wing works on tramways placed a few feet below the stage floor, completely cutting the mezzanine in two, and compelling persons to bend their backs in walking.'[21]

The stage joists were carried on a multitude of timber uprights

'some of which are 9 inches by 3 inches, others 8 inches by 6 inches, and some $4\frac{1}{2}$ inches by 3 inches. These uprights rest upon what are termed oak sleepers 9 inches by 4 inches, the whole being sustained by pillars, – the lower portions of which are of concrete, and the upper, 18 inches square, of sound brickwork set in cement.'[22]

The new building, at right angles to all the previous theatres, occupied a comparatively

Fig.146. Covent Garden: scene painting room   Fig.147. Covent Garden: the roof space over the auditorium

small area of the existing site, part being allocated to the Floral Hall, a building of iron and glass. Barry therefore considered it important to make as much use of the roof space as possible for the carpenter's and other shops which it was customary to place in this position. Normally a limited space with good headroom was obtained by the use of queen-post trusses, but 'it soon appeared that a system of beams passing from wall to wall, with small roofs between, offered peculiar advantages as regards space, when compared with the limited area allowed by the queen-post truss arrangement'.[23] These framed beams were 96 feet long and 9 feet deep, and were placed in line with the cross walls at intervals of 20 feet. Four bays of the roof over the auditorium (fig.147) were floored in level with the lower flange of the girders to form the workshops. Each bay was spanned by a low pitched roof of iron, glass and slate, producing a continuous roof over the stage and auditorium of the ridge and furrow pattern. A single pitched roof of some 36 feet span covered the gallery, and there was a lean-to roof, with its highest end above the main paint-frame, to give the greatest possible travel for this unit, over the paint room (fig.146). To enable large pieces of scenery to be lowered from the carpenter's shop to the stage, the girder at this position above the pro-scenium opening was dropped so that its top supported the shop floor. The roof was here supported on two stancheons set 40 feet apart on top of this girder, thus providing large openings through which the scenery could be lowered. The open grid-iron ceiling to the stage was carried on the tops of the main girders, thus providing a maximum height of approximately 70 feet for the scenes above the stage.

The building was heated by hot air rising from hot water pipes below the pit, the water being heated by a boiler beneath the Grand Staircase:

> 'an air-grating round the pit, allows the hot air to escape into the house. The principle exit for the heated and vitiated air is through the aperture, 10 feet wide, over the chandelier; above which there are openings into the external atmosphere. There are air-valves to the boxes over the doors, and a number of small holes are drilled in the risers of the gallery seats, giving a passage for the air from the halls and corridors to the chandelier, but not in sufficient quantities at any one place to create a draught. There are also air-flues in the corridors and in the crush-room, to carry off the products of combustion from the numerous gas-lights; and there are outlets into the roof from the side galleries. None but these simple expedients for ventilation are adopted, experience having, I think, shown that most elaborate systems of ventilation are liable to failures, more or less complete, in proportion to their greater or less elaboration.'[24]

This was a point of view which M. Davioud considered to be 'voluntarily neglected'.[25]

Although Barry did not consider a fire-curtain of any value, he put all his faith in a copious supply of water. A large cistern, divided into two unequal parts, was placed over the north-west stage stairs. The closets, sinks and taps were supplied from the smaller, while the larger provided a high-pressure supply of water to twenty-five fire-cocks.

In 1878 the Metropolis Management and Building Acts Amendment Act gave the Metropolitan Board of Works powers over the construction of theatres, with particular regard to fireproofing and the provision of adequate exits. The effects of this Act were seen at Covent Garden in 1882. Until this date the theatre appears to have remained much the same, as may be seen from a set of survey drawings prepared at that date.[26] The Building Act Committee then required alterations to be made in accordance with the Act to bring the theatre into line with the new fireproofing regulations. The main requirement was the installation of a proper proscenium wall to divide the stage from the auditorium: this was to be carried through from foundations to the underside of the stage, and to a height of 3 feet above the roof. Any openings in this wall, or in the side walls of the stage, and between dressing room areas and staircases, should all be closed by wrought-iron doors in wrought-iron frames, and arranged to close automatically. The floors of the workshops in the roof over the auditorium were to be re-formed of fire-resisting materials, or 'covered with Drake's concrete slabs'.[27] An additional staircase providing an escape from the gallery and amphitheatre was required, and overlays on the survey drawings show that this was formed on the left-hand side of the auditorium, with an exit on the main front, adjoining the Floral Hall, in Bow Street. A further overlay on the Grand Tier plan shows that a double flight of stairs, still remaining, was built in the Grand Saloon to provide a direct approach from the upper tier of boxes to this saloon.

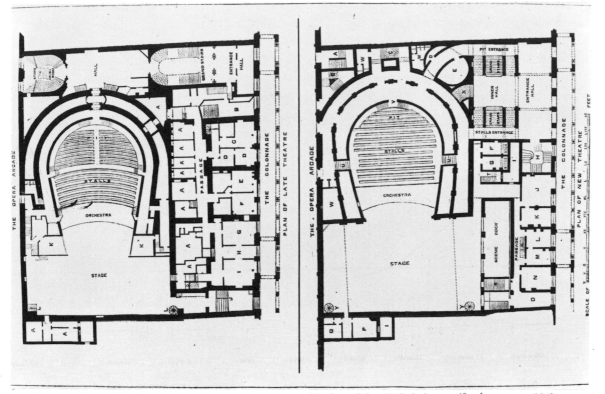

(a) plan of the 1790 theatre   (b) plan of the 1868–9 theatre (for key, see p.334)

Fig.148. Her Majesty's Theatre, Haymarket

Fig.149. Theatre Royal, Leicester: auditorium

The survey also shows that an extra building had been erected behind the theatre on the Hart Street frontage providing storage for properties and wardrobes for men and women.

In 1868-9, Her Majesty's Theatre was rebuilt, after a fire of 6th December, 1867, by Charles Lee on the lines of Barry's Covent Garden.[28] The plan varied little in its general form from the previous building, but by moving the auditorium back to occupy part of the previous hall (fig.148a.b.), it was possible to increase the depth of the stage by approximately 20 feet. Entrances and exits were improved so that there were at least two 'staircases or passages of communication'[29] to each part of the house. There were now four and a half tiers of boxes which had all been increased in height, and three saloons exclusively for ladies. The space over the auditorium was no longer used as a carpenter's shop or painting rooms, these latter now being 'placed next the Haymarket, on the east side of the stage', the carpenter's shop and property stores being provided for in the basement. The stage was separated from the auditorium by a thick wall continued upward through the roof. 'The floors of all the saloons, dressing rooms, passages and landings will be formed of Dennett's cement arches, and all the staircases will be of stone, enclosed with brick walls.' There were three levels of fly floors, the lowest of which sloped with the stage, and the topmost was joined across the stage by four bridges. The roof appears to have been supported on low lattice girders.

From this description it may be gathered that considerable advances were now being made in theatre design with regard to the safety of the occupants of the building, but there were nevertheless many points of design to which exception was taken. In discussing such theatres as the rebuilt Theatres Royal at Plymouth and Leicester (fig.149), the tendency to spread the pit beneath the raised first circle was discussed and some advantages of this arrangement were noted (p.199), an arrangement which was also incorporated at Covent Garden as a means of providing additional seating for the winter season. The theatre architect, C. J. Phipps, comments on this 'objectionable practice'. He considered the pit to be the best part of the house which 'should be throughout at the highest price, forming, in fact, a continuation of the first circle. The extending it is destruction to the design, and apt to cause great defects in the sound, to say nothing of the intolerable atmosphere which a crowded pit is sure to produce.'[30] None of these factors seem to have real validity, but he is on surer ground when he points out that by raising the circle, the problems of sight lines are increased, particularly from the rear seats. At the same time the whole height of the auditorium is raised unnecessarily, creating a very much greater volume, and increasing the slopes of the upper galleries to permit a full view of the stage.

Other writers agreed with Phipps regarding the importance of the pit and gallery, which are described in 1875 as being 'without doubt the money-making portions of the house, and therefore, should receive the very careful attention of the architect'.[31] Obviously it was worth increasing the capacity of this area, and the enlarged pit slowly became standard practice. In 1876 we read of 'Alterations to the Theatre Royal, Birmingham in Sept. 1876', during which 'the pit was lowered by 4 feet so that it could be extended under the lower circle, to provide extra accommodation in this area, amounting to a total of between 500 and 600 persons. In lowering the pit it was necessary to lower the stage to a corresponding degree.'[32]

Another writer of the time comments adversely on the architect's problems brought about by the management's desire to provide seats for as many people as can be crammed into them, resulting in the need to pile up 'tier on tier of boxes to the very ceiling, not a little preposterously, it being impossible for those who are accommodated with places by being pitchforked into what is literally a loft, to obtain more than a very unsatisfactory bird's-eye view of the stage'.[33] Writing in 1862, A. W. of *The Builder*[34] made various suggestions regarding the internal arrangements of theatres, but what is surprising is that so many of the suggestions put forward from time to time were already in operation in this country. He suggests, for example, that each tier should have a separate staircase, the principle of drawing people on to one staircase being a bad feature, but this idea had already been put into effect, indeed duplicated, at Drury Lane. Semper's theatre at Dresden (1837-40), with its external expression of the internal volume, seems to have caught the fancy of various writers, including A.W., who suggests that 'the external form of house should be the same as the internal', without apparently realising that exactly this arrangement (fig. 106) is to be found in Wyatt's Drury Lane. Phipps repeats A.W.'s first comment when he speaks of 'ample entrance for each class of spectators, as widely separated as possible, so that a crowd of persons shall not mingle, or jostle each other'.[35] He requires wide and direct stairs for safety, and retiring rooms and conveniences for comfort.

Phipps suggests that the walls separating corridors and auditory should be of brick or stone, which one would assume he was suggesting for fire-resisting reasons, but surprisingly his reason is

> 'to keep back the sound of persons walking or talking in them; whilst the inside lining of these walls should be in thin strips of wood, which is a good conductor of sound. All the doors from the lobbies should shut flush with the inside of the auditory, so that no breaks in the wall may impede the sound, notwithstanding a manager's supposition so often urged that several persons can stand in the recess of a door; and all doors should open externally throughout the building, to facilitate exit in case of panic.'[36]

It is interesting to note the extent to which standing spectators are permitted, and Phipps does not appear to condemn a practice which would seem to block both gangways and exits. Reasons for moving the pit entrances from near the stage to the rear of the pit were noted earlier (p.164), but now that many entrances were placed in this position, Phipps suggests the former as the best position. He claims that as such doors are often left open sounds from outside can more easily drown the actor's voice, weakened by the distance to the rear of the pit.

A letter-writer of 1857[37] criticised the side boxes, particularly those adjoining the stage, and pointed out that spectators here have too close a view of the stage, particularly of the activities in the off-stage areas which their oblique position enabled them to view between the scenic wings. Criticisms were also levelled, once again, at the footlights.

> 'What occupant of the pit or stall has not often felt annoyed that he could only see the heads of the actors (when half-way down the stage) over or between these unsightly obstacles, which, though sometimes 18 inches high, barely shelter his eye from the flaring, smoky glare of the gas Argands, and which form a harsh foreground which would mar the effect of the best pictorial group or stage scene ever produced.'[38]

The writer recognises the need for footlights, although he suggests the possibility of using reflectors from above, which he claims have been used with success, but asks 'why not have a thin, close, continuous, and bright line of jets an inch apart, and shaded from the audience by one shallow rim running in an unbroken line along the whole front, and which need not be more than four or five inches above the level of the stage?' This suggestion was soon to replace the individual masks of earlier candle and oil days.

These considerations point to a need for all the spectators to view the scene, but at the same time it is undesirable that their illusions of realism should be dissipated by seeing aspects of the stage workings which should be hidden.

> ' "Spectacle", as a branch of dramatic art, – and such *spectacle* as is designed on the supposition that each person in the house has an equally good view, – impracticable as that supposition actually is, – is becoming more and more predominant; that even out of the field of pantomimes and extravaganzas, the same requirement of a view of the business of the scene, should be better recognised than it is.'[39]

Writing on theatre design in 1883, an architect, W. Emden, considered that the best form of auditorium for good acoustics was the old-fashioned horseshoe. 'If desired, some extra accommodation may be acquired to the dress-circle if a row of seats be thrown forward as a balcony to the general lines of the circles of the house' (fig.149), as was done at Leicester and at Drury Lane, (pp.205,286)

> 'but every extension over the pit tends to destroy the sound in it. At the sides of the circle, where it joins the proscenium front, it is usual to place private boxes, and this is not only, perhaps, the best position for them, but it is the natural one, inasmuch as it would be impossible in this portion of the theatre to place rows of seats, as only the front row would have a good view, and a large portion of the others would be unable to see at all.'[40]

Sight lines from the rear seats of the dress circle to the proscenium decide the position where circle and private boxes meet.

Emden gives 30 feet as the width for a proscenium opening, and suggests that the heights of circles should be no more than absolutely necessary, otherwise the theatre becomes too high, and the gallery may be too steep. In the circles it should be possible for each member of the audience to see over the head of the person in front. The stage should be some 4 feet

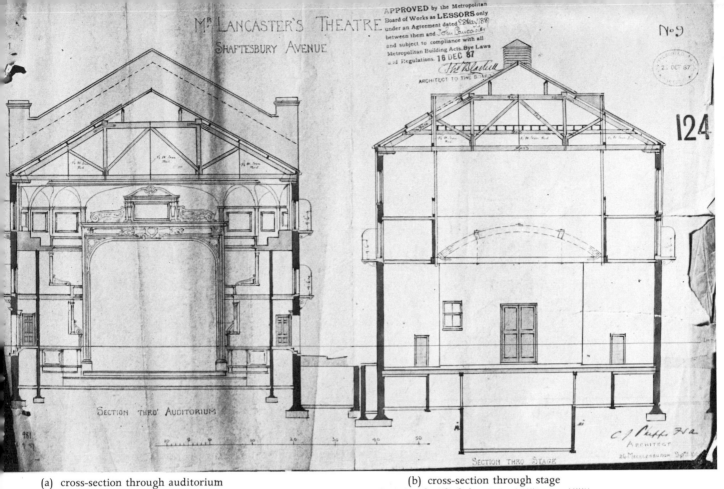

(a) cross-section through auditorium

(b) cross-section through stage

(c) plan at upper circle level

Fig.130. Mr Lancaster's Theatre, The Shaftsbury, E. J. Phipps, 1887

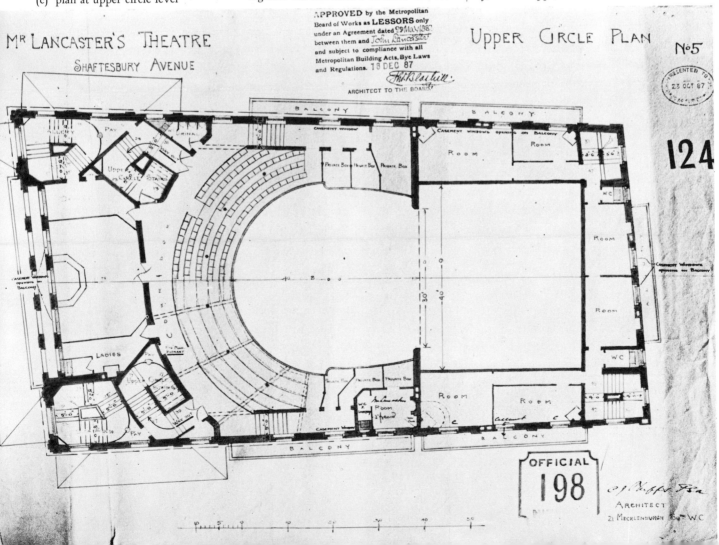

6 inches above the pit floor, and be laid, like the floor of the pit, on a rake. It should also project a few feet into the auditorium 'so that when singing or speaking the actor may be more into the body of the house, and his voice thus better heard, and not so immediately affected by the great space in the height behind the scenes'.

He criticises the placing of dressing rooms in the flies, such as was done at the Shaftesbury Theatre (fig.150), and at Daly's (fig.167), and advises that they 'should be constructed in a building separate from the stage, communicating with it by a single opening only'. Where possible the dressing rooms should connect with the prompt side of the stage, where the actors are under the control of the stage manager. Good examples of this arrangement are quoted by Woodrow as being Emden's 'new theatre in St. Martin's Lane' and the Garrick.[41] Emden suggests that if the proscenium wall is set at an angle to the side walls of the theatre, the resultant space may be used to provide stairs to the under-stage areas, an arrangement which may be seen (fig.128) in the Theatre Royal, Leicester, where the stairs also connect with the upper levels of the auditorium and the fly galleries, by means of pass doors which must now be of iron.

In addition to considering the comfort of the audience by the provision of toilet facilities for all sections of the auditorium, he also suggests that the back-stage staff be provided with the following accommodation: 'house-keeper's room, hall-porter's room, ballet and supers'-rooms, band-room, store-rooms for properties, carpenter's shop, . . . artist's room, . . . and a bridge for him to paint the scenery from; scene-dock, for stowing scenery in; and lavatories'.

The development of touring companies, complete with their own scenery, and the increasing tendency for scenery to be prepared by artists in their own studios away from the theatre, is reflected in Emden's requirement of 'a long narrow door or opening through the outer wall of the theatre, enclosing the stage, into the street, through which to bring in or take-out scenery' such as may be seen in his theatre in St Martin's Lane (fig.164). The painting bridge which he describes is again similar to that at Leicester (figs.141,152), supported on a girder running between the two fly floors.

> 'Against the back wall is a frame on which the scene to be painted is fixed, and which can be raised or lowered, so that the artist on the bridge can get at any portion of the scene on which he is engaged. There should be a small room in the "flies" cut off from them for the private use of the artist, in which his colours, sketches, &c, may be kept in safety.'

Joseph Harker describing the painting room at the Globe tells us that it was

> 'a miserable little cubicle of a place at the back of the stage, with the gas-battens just under the floor. There was literally no room in which to swing the proverbial cat, and the heat when the gas was going was tropical – quite in accord, that is, with the language of my fellow-painters, whose fluency at such times was astonishing.'[42]

The whole problem of ventilating theatres was dealt with at some length by Mr Emden. Reference has already been made to the need for ventilators in the auditorium ceiling, provided in attempts to draw off the foul air from the over-crowded house. When the New Theatre in Bath was reconstructed in 1775, it was recorded that

'One of the great drawbacks of the house previously had been the difficulty to keep it cool; the heat was a constant source of complaint, (The curtain had to be drawn up between the play and the farce on account of the intolerable heat if it were allowed to remain down), and this was now relieved by providing a suitable ventilator at the top of the building, which, an old playgoer wrote, supplied a quantity of fresh air, equally diffused over the whole house, and prevented . . . its rushing in streams or currants (sic) which are so apt to give colds.'[43]

The widespread use of gas for lighting both stage and auditorium had greatly aggravated a problem which had already existed with the earlier candlelight. 'The heat from the people's bodies, and breathing, added to the ill-effects on the atmosphere by the burning of large quantities of gas, make it impossible under the present circumstances, where gas is used, to accomplish ventilation with any degree of perfection.'[44] However, the very heat could be used to help draw off the vitiated air, if provision was made in the form of ducts in the circle ceilings, and particularly by leaving space above the large gas 'sunlight' that now replaced the earlier central chandelier. The hot air thus drawn off into the roof space, could then be discharged into the open air by a large ventilator set in the roof, preferably directly above the 'sunlight', as was done at Covent Garden. The hot air, once drawn off, had to be replaced by fresh, which, it is suggested, could have been drawn in from the exterior by shafts set above the heads of the audience at each auditorium level, in place of the earlier habit of merely leaving doors open. It would seem from Emden's comments that many theatres were still not ventilated above the stage:

'as a rule, there is very little, if any, ventilation provided over the stage, and, after a time, the heated air having filled the space over the stage, and, having no exit, finds its way into the auditorium; therefore, to prevent this, there should be ventilation through the roof over the stage, besides that over the auditorium, and also some small direct openings for the admission of fresh air.'[45]

'It is now a requirement of the rules of the Board of Works, that there shall be at least two exits from every part of the house;' . . . and that fire-resisting materials should be used for all exit passages, staircases, lobbies, corridors, and landings . . . 'and every staircase for the use of the audience shall be separate and enclosed by brick walls.'

Winders were no longer permitted on staircases, and all openings in the proscenium wall 'shall be closed by an iron door',[46] and be of a specified size. Greater safety could be achieved not just by duplication of exits for all parts of the house, but by their symmetrical placing on either side in easily recognisable and expected positions. Both pit and gallery should have their own exits direct to the street, not communicating with other parts of the house. The width of passages and stairs was now controlled at a minimum 4 feet 6 inches for up to 400 persons, an increase of 6 inches width being allowed for every additional 100 persons up to a maximum of 9 feet. Emden considered, however, that the gallery stairs should not be less than 6 feet in width whatever the number accommodated, stairs being in short flights with half-landings. In addition to the separation of stage and auditorium by a wall passing through the roof he tells us that 'it is necessary for the scene-dock, property-rooms, carpenter's shops, and store-rooms to be closed off from the rest of the buildings by brick and fireproof construction', and the need for easy access to the flies is stressed.[47]

While suggesting that the fixed sides of the stage could be constructed of iron and concrete, he apparently accepts as inevitable the need to make all the moving parts of the stage, the traps and bridges, of timber, which he suggests could be coated with asbestos paint, such timbers as may be necessary in the auditorium being similarly treated. The high percentage of timber used in the stage machinery, together with that used in the scenes, and the quantities of rope and canvas, make a stage risk which Mr Emden accepts as inevitable, and which therefore leads him to concentrate on the means to restrict a stage fire to that area and keep it from gaining access to the auditorium. He is unhappy as to the value of an iron curtain as a covering to the proscenium opening as he feels it to be both cumbersome and 'liable to get out of order'. He mentions the use in France of an 'iron wire gauze curtain',[48] but feels that an asbestos curtain would probably be effective in restricting the fire long enough to enable the audience to make good their escape.

11 Stage reforms and safety theatres

During the 1860s a new interest in social plays led to a breakaway from the stock characters and somewhat unreal situations of the melodramas, which had become accepted as standard while the public were mainly attracted by the spectacular scenic devices which the theatres offered. The greater realism introduced into such plays as Thomas Robertson's *Caste*, for example, affected the settings, which were now required to portray more accurately the homes of the characters involved. There was, too, a general dissatisfaction with the wing, border, and flat settings, and complaints became frequent concerning their limitations. Actors were criticised for making their entries between the wings in positions where no door was painted; patrons objected to seeing the stage carpenters, in their paper hats, leading on the flats so that they should not jam in the grooves, and leaving dirty marks where they grasped the edges of the scenery. The occupants of the stage boxes, as we have noted, objected to being able to see beyond the boundaries of the scene into the wings, where actors and stage-hands could be observed awaiting their cue or enjoying a drink. Objections were also raised to the joints which could always be clearly seen where each pair of flats met. Certainly if one was looking for realism, then the wing and flat system was not the answer, and other ideas had to be sought.

Some realism began to creep into the normal wing and border scene with the use of individual set pieces, and such features as the practical stair and counters seen in a set design for *The Minister and the Mercer*, produced at Drury Lane in February, 1834.[1] The introduction into this country of the boxed-in setting is attributed to Madam Vestris, while she was managing the Olympic Theatre in London,[2] where she is said to have arranged the scene for her production of *The Conquering Game* in November, 1832, with side walls containing practical doors. This was not, however, a complete box-set, which today would have a horizontal canvas ceiling, as here the ceiling was represented by the normal borders, so that the overhead gas lighting battens could be used. A further innovation was to construct the stage of the Lyceum Theatre in the French fashion, with the stage floor made in removable sections[3] some 'six feet long by four or five feet wide', any or all of which could be readily removed, to permit furnishings and properties to be raised into position on the stage as and where required, instead of being carried on by liveried footmen, as was the normal practice when the scenes were changed in full view of the audience. The sides of the box-set could be made up of a pair of side flats, to which were added raking cills, to fit them to the slope of the stage.

These arrangements of scenery permitted the settings to resemble real rooms, and as this realism developed, so the scenery had to be arranged at varying angles and positions, with the result that the old grooves, bridges, and sloats gradually became obsolete. Nevertheless J. G. Buckle, writing in 1888,[4] described the stage floor as being 'constructed with a number of "cuts", or narrow openings parallel with the curtain'. And, in 1896, Sachs was still able to say 'In all countries the first principle for setting scenery is a series of side scenes, or "wings", with a backcloth, and however complicated a scene may become, it is always built upon this one idea, which is obviously the simplest, if the least effective, way of filling the proscenium opening with a stage picture.'[5] On the English stage, in addition to these standard wings, borders and backcloths, use was made of 'flats', which are now described as being made of canvas stretched over a wooden frame. Unlike the earlier flats, however, these were used for making such scenes as the three sides of a room.

Additional features were also found, such as

'The heavy "rostrums" which are employed to obtain platforms of higher levels than the stage floor, because no part of the stage floor can be raised above its own level, are most cumbersome to move, and take up a lot of room in the side stage or scene dock. They are, however, frequently most cleverly put together, made in parts with folding trestles, and run on wheels, but the putting together and taking apart all wastes time, and creates long waits for the audience'[6] (fig.151).

These additional scenic features were all part of the movement towards a greater simulation of nature, which Sachs commented on as

'a Movement known by the name of "stage reform" . . . In England, the primary object of stage reform, *i.e.* the possible imitation of nature in the *mise-en-scène* of our opera and drama, has certainly found favour. This is, however, practically only due to the public having associated the movement with the encouragement of that crude realism which has of late met with such general appreciation in all branches of arts and letters. There has been no outcry against the non-descript mounting of a play, and the realism of a spectacle has been generally more appreciated by audiences than its merits as a work of art. Stage reform in this country is still associated with the sensational shipwreck, the *bonâ-fide* race, or other realistic items of a programme, and its popularity is practically due to the successful rendering of such scenes.'[7]

Sachs points out that reform is difficult in England where the purse-strings of productions are controlled by speculative enterprise, in comparison with the continent where funds were

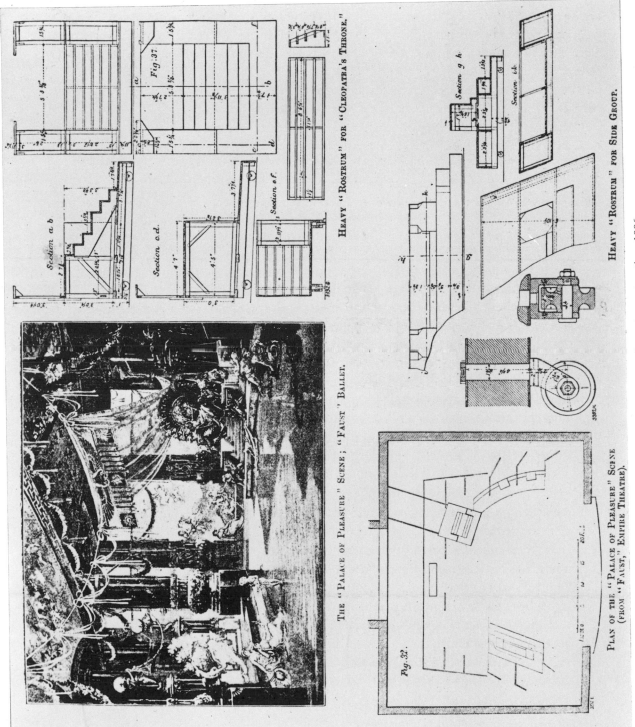

HEAVY "ROSTRUM" FOR "CLEOPATRA'S THRONE."

Fig. 37.

Section a b.

Section o d.

Section o f.

THE "PALACE OF PLEASURE" SCENE; "FAUST" BALLET.

HEAVY "ROSTRUM" FOR SIDE GROUP.

Section g h.

Section i k.

PLAN OF THE "PALACE OF PLEASURE" SCENE
(FROM "FAUST," EMPIRE THEATRE).

Fig. 32.

Fig. 151. Typical stage setting and scenic construction, 1896

available for experiment. He notes that the main centre of experimentation was in the private theatre of a Professor Herkomer at Bushey. He further comments on the absence of extreme reforms on the English stage, noting that these are mainly confined to the introduction of electricity in place of gas, and 'some miniature mechanical appliances to facilitate what is termed a "quick change".' He observes that one of the main reasons for this may be due to our preference for 'long runs', as compared with the pattern of a continually changing playbill, which is the normal repertoire of the continental houses.

The construction of the English stage was carried out by ordinary stage carpenters 'whose position in the theatre is likewise no better than that of a foreman of any ordinary work. Abroad, even for the wood stage, the commissions are held by educated and fully qualified engineers, whose position and influence is important.' He feels that the whole scenic production should be under the control of one master mind, and quotes Professor Herkomer, who pleaded

'that the "make-up" (as it were) of the background should be held of equal importance with the actor's personal "make-up", . . . if we accept a rose-bush cut out of thin boards, the edges of which we can hold between our Thumb and first finger, or a street scene painted on canvas and hung across the stage upon which the shadows of the passing actors are thrown by the footlights – a sheet that is moved like a sail by every draught of the stage – we ought, in all truth, to accept an actor whose wig has been so badly put on that his own black hair shows underneath the artificial bald head.

'When our audiences begin to howl down a ridiculous stage moon, we shall soon learn to mend that luminary. It is quite safe at present to let our moon rise perpendicularly "up" the sky very quickly until your mechanism is exhausted, and then let it stop. Further, it is quite an accepted arrangement that the moment this red rising moon appears over the horizon, it shall send rays of blue light from the opposite direction from which it came. It is safe to let down a "wobbly" sheet of canvas, also close to the footlights, with a scene painted thereon, and, perhaps, a sinking ship in the distance, to which an actor may have to refer in his speech. It is safe to have layers of canvas hanging from the "sky", like so much washing on a line; and certainly nobody has ever questioned the prerogative of the "firmament" to come together at right angles in the corners . . . But our old stage methods prevent the realising of such an aim, and the impression of an audience that they are only witnessing a play is often far too palpable. Why have the horizon cut horizontally by a crease, showing where the cloth has to be canked? Why let our beautifully-painted panoramic scenes jerk along according to the jerky manner in which the scene-shifter handles his drums? The panoramic scenes may cost £1,000, and yet the simplest mechanical contrivance to ensure their smooth working is grudged and the effect entirely spoilt.'[8]

In the interests of realism it was also considered important that the frame should fit the picture, and Sachs criticises the usual tall proscenium opening which has to be masked down on the inside with a false 'inner frame'. Professor Herkomer put forward the suggestion of an adaptable proscenium, which could reduce or expand to match a particular scene. So the move towards naturalism was already bringing with it new problems. Previously the conventions had permitted the use of the proscenium doors for entries and exits, or the spaces between the side wings could serve the same purpose, and while the scenes remained a part of the illusionistic conventions, they could happily change in full view of the audience, and their movement in itself provided a part of the theatrical pattern. As theatrical productions moved towards the presentation of 'real people' in a 'real place', the disintegration of the scene before the eyes of the audience broke through the illusion of reality, the magical quality of such a change finally remaining only in the transformation scene of the panto-mime. Even when the scenery had moved in full view of the audience, it had always been possible to set certain scenes consisting of set-pieces, or platforms and rostrums, out of sight of the audience, in an extension of the manner in which it had been possible to change the 'scenes of relieve' behind the backshutters of Inigo Jones's masks. Such methods for providing continuity of production were now made possible by the use of a front 'act-drop', which could be lowered to conceal the change of scene behind.

As scenes became more realistic, however, they also became more complicated to set and furnish, with the result that scene-changes were inconveniently long, and ways and means had to be found of overcoming these new problems. Buckle tells us that

> 'Various arrangements of mechanical stages have been suggested and partially adopted in American and Continental theatres, but any contrivances that increase the number and complexity of the working parts of a stage cannot be recommended. An enormous revolving turntable on the stage – a peculiar characteristic of Japanese theatres – enables one scene to be prepared in the rear whilst the performance is going on in front. This arrangement, although apparently simple, would, no doubt, lead to complication and trouble in working the "slider" and "bridges", &c, and for other reasons could seldom be used with effect. Mechanical changes of scene may be desirable in order to avoid "waits", but when carried out in view of the audience are generally clumsy, *always* inartistic. They tend to destroy the pleasing illusion of the play by the introduction of unnatural contrivances that are best hidden from the audience by "change curtains".'[9]

Although there was a strong need for a reform of stage mechanism to permit more rapid changes of naturalistic scenery, such reforms were unlikely to be initiated in the English theatre, particularly when new thought was so strongly inhibited by the status quo, as is suggested by Buckle's comments quoted above. As a result Buckle's description of a typical stage of 1888 differs little from previous examples, although he begins by telling us that 'large stages are not advocated, small stages being more desirable for comedies, farces, and comic opera, as the audience are better able to see the facial expressions and grasp the finer points of the acting'.

In dealing with the height of a stage, however, he now required that it be

'twice that of the proscenium opening. Assuming the proscenium to be 30 feet high, the height of the "gridiron" should be about 60 feet from the stage floor. In actual practice it will not be found necessary to adhere implicitly to this rule, for, as already pointed out, the use of proscenium "wings" and "borders" considerably reduce the structural opening in height, say 6 or 7 ft., which permits a corresponding reduction in the height of the "cloths". The height of the "cloths" in an ordinary theatre, having a proscenium 32 ft. high by 30 ft. wide, would be about 28 ft., whilst the width of the "cloths" would be governed absolutely by the distance between the "fly-galleries". The "cloths" are invariably wider than the proscenium opening, and this varies from 5 ft. to 10 ft. in ordinary-sized theatres, and 20 ft. in larger theatres, such as Covent Garden or Her Majesty's, London . . . It should be possible in a well-constructed stage to draw up the "cloths" without rolling or folding. The use of "tumblers" when the "cloths" are folded – consequent on want of height in the stage –, demands extra ropes and additional hands to manipulate them, whilst the cloths occupy three times more room than would be the case were they hanging down straight without folds. When the cloths are folded less scenery can be slung, hence crowding, confusion, and increased risk of fire.'[10]

The fly galleries should not be less than 20 feet above the stage, and preferably between 28 and 30 feet, 'when they are less liable to be seen from the auditorium'. Buckle comments that

'The "grooves" fixed to the underside of the fly galleries in the older theatres, and used for steadying the "flats" and "wings", are now almost entirely dispensed with in modern theatres, as they necessitate all the scenes being set parallel with the proscenium. "Grooves" are still used in a modified form, but are attached to the lower rail of the "fly-truss", and turn on a pivot, by which means wings, &c, may be set at any desired angle. Another arrangement is to fix iron sockets to the upper and lower plates of the "fly-truss", in which a long wood bar, about 3 in. square, works up and down, being fixed in any position by means of an iron pin fitting into a series of holes, specially drilled. At the lower end of this bar is attached a contrivance very similar to an enlarged garden rake. This works upon a pivot and between the teeth the upper edge of the "wing" or "flat" is secured.

'These survivals of antiquated methods are entirely dispensed with in the more recent theatres, when the scenery is strapped together by cleats and cords, and secured to the floor of the stage by means of iron rods or braces, hooked to eyes attached to the framework of the scenery, whilst the other end is secured to the floor with "stage screws".'[11]

Buckle states that a second tier of fly galleries may be required in some theatres, and sometimes even a third or fourth. Now that there was no longer a carpenter's shop over the stage, the floor at this point could be in the form of a gridiron, the joists of which were

'covered with battens 3 in. by $1\frac{1}{4}$ in., laid about three inches apart, or six inches from centre to centre. In the interspaces are fixed the blocks and wheels through which the ropes run that suspend the "cloths", the ends of the ropes being secured to the "cleats" attached to the fly-rails.'

He suggests, however, that 'the substitution of iron for wood in the construction of the gridiron, and, indeed, every part of the stage fittings, as far as practicable, would contribute to increased stability and safety'.

He claims that in some continental and American theatres 'the stage is level, but the slight inclination given the stage floor in English theatres possesses many advantages to recommend it. The floor should rise from the footlights towards the back wall of the stage, the rake varying from 1 in 18 to 1 in 24. The latter is most usually adopted.' He discussed the need for a mezzanine floor and a cellar, the former being 6 feet high, and the latter 7 to 10 feet. There should be scene docks at the sides, rather than at the rear of the stage, so that the scenes may be 'run into them direct', features which were earlier suggested by Saunders, and were already to be found at both Covent Garden and Drury Lane. One dimension of the docks should equal half the width of the proscenium, a dimension presumably based on the width of one half of a pair of flats which would have needed this space. If this is so then he was basing his suggestions on scenic elements which were already being superseded. He says, however, that it 'is not desirable to have more scenery on the stage than is requisite for immediate use, SCENE STORES should be arranged for the storage of scenery not in use'.[12]

Eight years later the American, W. H. Birkmire, also mentions the slides, bridges and traps as being essential features of the stage floor, but he seems to have little understanding of these elements, and indeed suggests that 'before the architect can successfully design this portion of the theatre with all its structural requirements the aid of these mechanics (stage carpenters and machinists) is required'.[13] His diagram of the stage floor shows one innovation, however, and that is the replacement of the timber stage joists by iron or steel beams. His flies are constructed of iron or steel beams supporting terracotta arches, and covered with a cement floor. Both Buckle and Birkmire suggest supporting the fly galleries on deep trusses which form the gallery handrail. Both authors also require the complete separation of stage and auditorium by a brick wall, which must extend through and above the roof. Buckle felt that there should be no other openings in the wall besides the proscenium opening, but he quotes the Chief of the Metropolitan Fire Brigade as advocating 'openings in the proscenium wall at each tier level, fitted with double iron doors.'[14]

The proscenium opening must be capable of being closed by 'a fire-resisting and smoke-proof curtain or shutter'; he tells us that many forms of curtain have been proposed 'from water to solid iron', and suggests the use of a double thickness of baize saturated by a perforated pipe at the top. Asbestos curtains are also mentioned, and he describes the curtains in use at the Lyceum Theatre, Edinburgh, and at the Prince of Wales's Theatre, London.

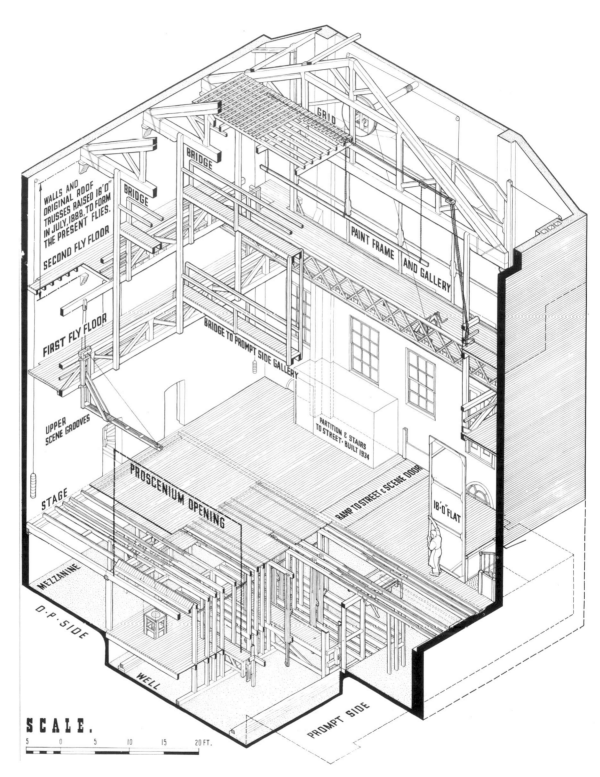

Fig.152. The Theatre Royal, Leicester: stage and stage machinery after alterations of 1888: scale reconstruction

These measured approximately 32 feet 6 inches by 26 feet 6 inches, and were made of two screens of $\frac{1}{8}$ inch wrought-iron plates, with a 6 inches air space between. The curtains were raised and lowered by the use of hydraulic rams. By 1896 Sachs notes that the London County Council were in a position to require the installation of a fire curtain in new buildings, but were 'without powers to enforce its constant use'.[15]

Practical evidence of these various ideas in operation may be seen in the alterations made to the Theatre Royal, Leicester, in 1888. When first built, the roof over the theatre (fig.154a) was at one continuous level over both auditorium and stage, the roof space being occupied by the property room and the scene painter, but further alterations were now made to the stage under the supervision of Mr Barradale, which permitted the use of the new methods of changing the scenery. The Directors' Annual Report for 1889 announced that 'The roof and walls' of the stage 'have been raised an additional 16' in height, which enables the scenes to "hang" without being rolled up or folded, which not only prevents damage to the scenes by creasing, but also allows twice the number of scenes to be used'.[16] The roof trusses were raised to provide the extra height, the brick and stone corbels which originally supported them being left in position (fig.152). The extra height permitted the insertion of an additional fly gallery on either side, both levels of galleries being connected across the stage by catwalks providing access to the hanging scenery (figs.140,153). At mid-height between these fly galleries, across the rear of the stage, was the painter's gallery. The roof space over the auditorium was now blocked off when the proscenium wall was carried up solidly to form the front of the new 'fly tower' (fig.154b), only a small access hole being left for maintenance purposes. This was in accordance with the requirements of the authorities, who, in 1887 had stipulated that 'The scenery and property room in the roof over the auditorium is exceedingly dangerous and should be abolished, and the opening in the proscenium wall 24 ft in width should be built up, and the wall carried through the roof.'[17] Many improvements with regard to the safety of the occupants were now required, including the widening and straightening of passages and staircases, the provision of 'iron doors . . . on each floor to the staircases next the stage', and the introduction of 'A drop curtain of asbestos or some other un-inflammable material.'

A dressing room and scene dock, which earlier occupied the rear 13 feet of the stage, were removed, permitting the stage entrance to be 'so enlarged and improved that the whole of the scenery can now pass through, and be placed direct from the street on to the Stage.'[18] This was accomplished by the insertion of a hinged section of stage which let down to form a ramp to street level. The clearing of this area also permitted the insertion of a paint-frame against the rear wall (figs.141,152), which could be lowered to stage level so that scenes might be fixed to it, after which it could be raised progressively past the paint gallery and so permit the scene painter to reach all parts of the cloths and flats. The frame was raised and lowered by means of a timber drum and wheel, worked by a windlass attached to the gallery floor, and counterbalanced by weights.

A timber gridiron now formed a 'ceiling' over the stage, on which were placed the sets

Fig.153. The Theatre Royal,
Leicester: upper fly gallery

of pulley blocks needed for raising and lowering the scenes. Sets of four pulleys were fixed at intervals of approximately 1 foot 6 inches from the front of the stage to the front edge of the paint gallery. Each set of pulleys consisted of a single pulley placed centrally above the stage, with a further single pulley placed some 12 feet 6 inches to either side (fig.159). Above the rail of the prompt-side fly gallery was placed a headblock, containing three pulleys. Three lines were led over these, and down to stage level, one over each of the single pulleys, and at their opposite end the lines were taken down to a cleat attached to the fly-rail of the top gallery (figs.153,171), to which they were tied off. These three lines, short – centre – long, could then be tied off to the top batten of a piece of scenery, and the whole hauled manually up into the flies by fly-men working on the top gallery. When raised to the correct height, the lines would be tied off to the cleat, and, where there was a second gallery below, as here, the surplus rope coiled up neatly on this gallery.

It is not only in the stage area that changes were now being made; the use of new materials,

Fig.154. The Theatre Royal, Leicester: showing
(a) continuous roof over the whole building prior to 1888

(b) fly tower raised above stage in 1888

and new constructional methods, was permitting alterations to be made in the form and arrangement of auditoria. In 1891, Rupert D'Oyly Carte opened his New English Opera House in Cambridge Circus, which still remains today as the Palace Theatre of Varieties. It was designed by D'Oyly Carte and the builder G. H. Holloway, with elevations by T. E. Collcutt, and advice on the general disposition of the auditorium from J. G. Buckle. The use of the cantilever system on a much larger scale than had previously been employed enabled large column-free tiers of seats, from seven to nine rows in depth, to be introduced directly facing the stage. Sachs[19] mentions the Alhambra Variety Theatre, built in 1883, as being one of the first theatres to make use of this principle, but in fact the arrangement at the Alhambra was little different to that already noted at Covent Garden (p.224), with no more than four rows of seats in advance of the columns. Of the New English Opera House Sachs notes: 'It will be seen that the principal feature of the planning is the arrangement of the Auditorium, with its excellent disposition of seats and tiers. The latter call for special attention on account of the elaborate cantilever work, which is unparalleled in any other theatre in Europe.'[20]

The new relationship of the pit to the auditorium has been accepted here, and, with the exception of the space occupied by a large orchestra accommodating 63 musicians, it now extends over the whole of the auditorium floor (fig.155), with the upper level of its sloping floor on a line with the street. The area is divided, as we would now expect, between orchestra stalls and a railed-off pit. The problems besetting the preparation of any theatre reconstruction are well illustrated by this theatre, where numerous variations and alterations were made to the design, both in preparation, and subsequent to the completion of the work. The plans dated 16th November, 1888,[21] as originally approved by the Metropolitan Board of Works on the 4th March, 1889, show 8 rows of stalls and 14 rows of pit benches, with a

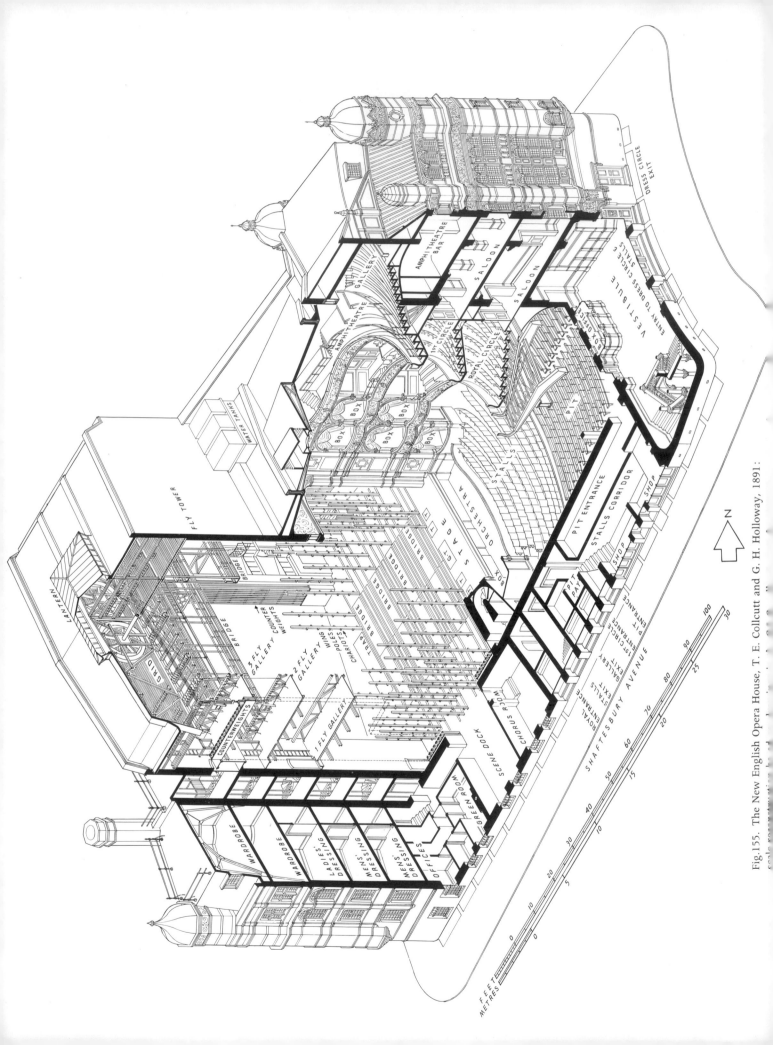

FEET
METRES

0   10   20   30   40   50   60   70   80   90   100
0   5   10   15   20   25   30

N

Fig.155. The New English Opera House, T. E. Collcutt and G. H. Holloway, 1891:

LANTERN
WATER TANKS
FLY TOWER
GRID
BRIDGE
BRIDGE
BRIDGE
COUNTERWEIGHTS
3 FLY GALLERY COUNTER WEIGHTS
2 FLY GALLERY
WING POLES
CHARIOTS
1 FLY GALLERY
TRAP BRIDGE
WARDROBE
WARDROBE
LADIES' DRESSING
MEN'S DRESSING
MEN'S DRESSING
OFFICES
GREEN ROOM
CHORUS ROOM
SCENE DOCK
STAGE
BRIDGE
ORCHESTRA
BOX
BOX
BOX
BOX
BOX
BOX
BOX
AMPHITHEATRE GALLERY
AMPHITHEATRE GALLERY
AMPHITHEATRE BAR
SALOON
SALOON
UPPER CIRCLE
ROYAL CIRCLE
STALLS
STALLS
PIT
DRESS CIRCLE STALLS
ENTRY TO DRESS CIRCLE
VESTIBULE
BOX OFFICE
PIT ENTRANCE
STALLS CORRIDOR
SHOP
SHOP
SHOP
PIT PAY
1ST CIRCLE ENTRANCE
PIT ENTRANCE
GALLERY EXIT
STALLS EXIT
ROYAL ENTRANCE
SHAFTESBURY AVENUE
DRESS CIRCLE EXIT

central gangway 3 feet wide in the latter. Plans, submitted to the Theatre Department on the 4th June, 1890,[22] show the same number of stalls, but 16 rows of pit benches, and omit the central gangway. Plans published in the *Building News* of the 6th February, 1891, show only 6 rows of stalls and 16 rows of pit benches, with the central gangway replaced. A brochure published at the opening of the theatre[23] mentions '270 in ten rows of Orchestra Stalls. 500 in 12 rows in the Pit.' A report of the 7th January, 1893,[24] claims that 'two additional rows of stalls have been added over and above those shown on the plan, but as the gangway at the back is of the same width (i.e. 7′ 6″) this appears immaterial especially as a centre gangway has been formed'. By the 25th June, 1890, however, a further report[25] stated:

> '(20) Two additional rows of seats were proposed to be placed in the pit, the backs of the seats were omitted and the seats placed closer together, and the back and side gangways remaining the same. This would give accommodation for 60 more persons in the pit. The centre gangway was omitted. This alteration should be thought (sic) be resisted. Not more than 14 rows of seats should be permitted in the pit. A gangway 3 feet wide should be provided in the centre and the single step at the ends of the last row of seats should be abolished.'

The central gangway was included, but became the source of much argument in the form of numerous letters between D'Oyly Carte and the authorities. After many variations had been suggested the pit was entered at the back from Shaftesbury Avenue, with exits at front and rear on the opposite side direct to Romilly Street. We now see further evidence of the problems created in auditoria design by the need to make separate provision for the various classes of audience. To avoid mixing with the occupants of the pit, the occupants of the stalls must descend the Grand Staircase to a passage at basement level, ascending once again to enter the auditorium on the left-hand side. An escape direct to Shaftesbury Avenue was placed immediately adjacent to this entrance, with a further escape on the opposite side of the theatre. Two private boxes adjoined the deep reveals, flanking the proscenium opening (fig.156), which contained stairs to serve the boxes on this level, and the two on either side at first and second tier levels. All these were approached by way of the Grand Stairs and corridors flanking the first and second tiers.

These tiers, consisting of nine and seven rows of seats respectively, and known as the Royal, or Dress, and First Circles, were arranged, with the exception of the front rows, which conformed nearly to a semi-circle, in shallow arcs directly facing the stage. Above was an amphitheatre and a gallery, the former with four rows of seats arranged on a semi-circle, the latter with ten (eleven in the brochure) arranged on an arc facing the stage.[26] In 1908 the whole of this upper area was redesigned to accommodate thirteen rows of seats directly facing the stage, the front rows arranged to an ogee-shape, with a single row of badly placed seats as slips on either side of the house, behind which was standing room with convenient leaning rails. The house originally had seating for nearly 2,000, with an increase of 300 allowed for standing.

Sachs' only reservation regarding the building concerned this upper area. 'The sighting and hearing are perfect, and if there be anything to complain of, it is that the uppermost tier has been continued so as to form a deep "well" or chute which, to my mind, is a disgrace to a modern theatre that claims to provide for the comfort of its audience.'[27] Sachs, however, illustrated the original designs prepared in 1888 in his work, and it is not clear if he is criticising these or the actual building as completed. The final design was certainly a great deal better in this respect than that which he published. In spite of the advantages of the column-free sight-lines, even Sachs has not yet got used to the appearance of apparently unsupported tiers, and comments unfavourably on this feature of the design.

In some respects auditorium design was moving back towards the arrangement devised by Wren for his Drury Lane, where the majority of seats directly faced the stage in a series of shallow arcs. This design, being conceived in terms of a wooden structure, was encumbered with columns supporting the fronts of the tiers, but the use of steel and concrete enabled seats to be placed in the same advantageous positions without the need for columns and on a far larger scale than had previously been possible. At the same time the fire-risk was reduced to the point at which it might be said of the Royal English Opera House: 'So entirely fireproof is the structure, that there is absolutely no woodwork in the building save that required by the stage carpenter, and the building will require no fire insurance, as it is impossible for it to burn.'[28]

In a series of articles on theatre design Woodrow described the old system of supporting the tiers of an auditorium. In this it was customary

> 'to support raking wooden girders by walls and columns, and to build up the steppings, or platforms, for the seats on wooden bearers, finishing with a wooden floor. . . . The boards were so placed that after a time the joints gaped open, assisted by the great heat of the imperfectly ventilated house; then dust, dirt, and refuse from the sweeper's broom, found a way through the open joints into the cavity below; this collected year after year, adding constantly to the inflammability and danger of the house.'[29]

He quotes at length from a paper read by Mr Emden to the Society of Architects in 1888, in which he described the system of construction he adopted.

> 'I erect a skeleton of iron, avoiding columns as far as possible, unless in the shape of stanchions in the walls, each circle of steps and piers forming a perfect bridge between the two stringers, which are large, narrow, but deep, girders at each side of the auditorium. The roof and dome being formed in a similar manner. I cover the whole of the ironwork with concrete made of coke breeze and Portland cement, mixed from 3 to 4 to 1. On this I put a topping of Portland cement and ground slag of iron, which makes an extremely hard and durable concrete, which fire will not burst even when water is poured on it while hot. The coke breeze concrete under being a very slow conductor of heat, it is almost impossible for the iron to be heated from above. Underneath this

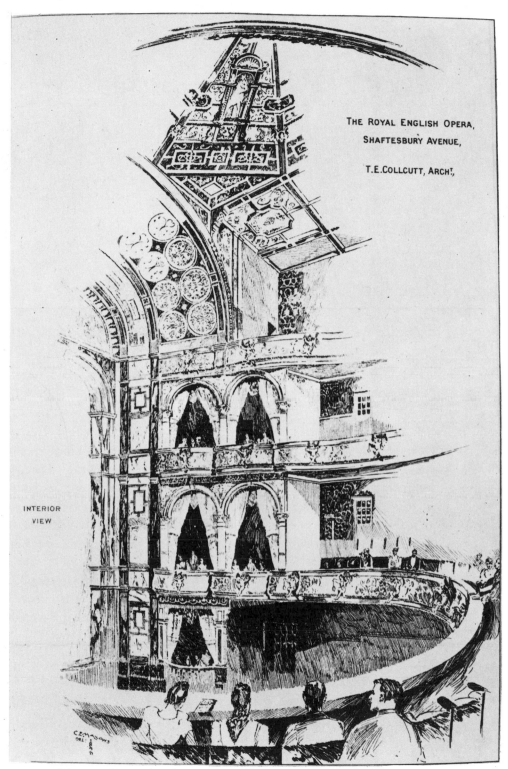

Fig.156. The New English Opera House: interior

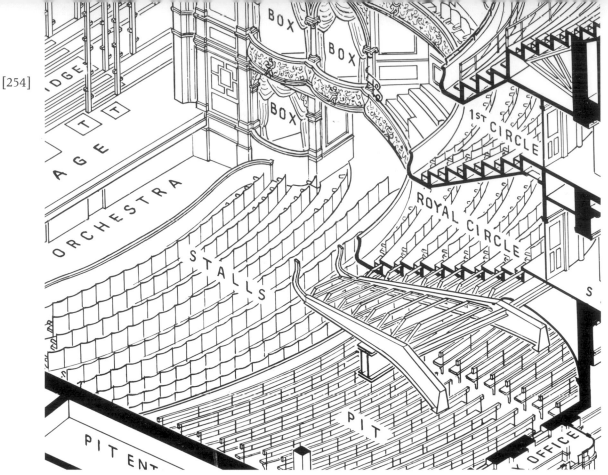

[254]

Fig.157. The New English Opera House: construction of the cantilevered circles: detail of Fig.155

ironwork, leaving plenty of air space, I fix wire netting, on which I put heavy coats of plaster, forming, by pushing through the mesh as much coarse plaster as possible, a thoroughly fireproof pugging in all cases where necessity in the construction brings the plaster near the ironwork. I use the wire netting so as to give as much thickness of plaster as possible below the iron, the wire netting being used for the most part in continuous rolls. The ornamental part is made of fibrous plaster backed, where in the box fronts, or where exposed by the plaster, on wire. The partitions are made of plaster on wire, or of small hollow firebricks made to interlock . . . Except for the mere doors and windows, I use no wood, and what I do use is coated with fireproof paint before decoration. Thus, except for the curtains – that is to say, the silk, plush, or woollen stuffs used in upholstery – there is nothing to burn, and these materials even are well known rather to smoulder than flare up.'[30]

In the Royal English Opera House the dress, or Royal, circle was supported on a series of steel cantilevers tied at their outer ends into the main walls at the rear of the auditorium (fig.157), those of the gallery being held down at this point by a box girder. They are supported at approximately half their span by 'a deep box steel girder (which) runs transversely across the theatre from side wall to side wall, the main bearing being taken by huge stanchions at either end about 6 ft. from the side walls. Other girders, it will be seen, branch off from this main girder at an angle' supporting the cantilevers which carry the curved sides of the tiers. The stepped floors to the tiers are of concrete on angle-irons supported on firebrick walls forming the face of the steps, which in turn are carried on metal bearers spanning between, and bracing, the cantilevers.

Like the Duke of York's Theatre (fig.164), the roof over the auditorium was of steel and concrete in a single skin, so that 'there is no intervening space between the ceiling and the roof wherein to form rooms and stores',[31] a practice which Woodrow now states as being forbidden in all countries. The stage and auditorium are enclosed by solid walls separating them from the foyers, stairs, dressing rooms, ballet room, offices and wardrobes, and are further separated from each other by a wall which rises with the stage some 39 feet above the auditorium roof. This wall is pierced only by the proscenium opening which is a square of 34 feet. Strangely, no attempt appears to have been made to close this opening, and it is not until March, 1903, that we find mention that 'steps are being taken to comply with the requirement for the provision of fire-resisting screen and sprinkler', and we learn that '(1) The proscenium wall should be made good to the underside of the stage flooring and the portion of the stage floor between the back of the proscenium wall and the back of the curtain to be made fire-resisting. (2) The curtain should be provided with an arrangement for pouring water on its surface.'[32] A design for this fire-proof curtain was submitted in April, 1903 for approval on the 5th May, 1903.[33]

The various levels of dressing rooms and stage are connected by a lift built in the well of a stair, the whole separated from the stage by enclosing walls. The stage itself, some 49 feet deep on the centre line by some 68 feet wide and with a height of 71 feet to the gridiron at the proscenium wall, was described by Sachs as being 'practically the only stage in the Metropolis where the ante-diluvian methods of the stage carpenter have been improved upon'.[34] But, as with the drawings which he illustrates, he is speaking more of intentions than completed fact. Woodrow is nearer the mark when he tells us that

'When the Royal English Opera was first started, I remember hearing of the great improvements that were to be made in stage machinery, and that nearly everything but the boards of the stage was to be in iron. True, there are some minor improvements in the details, but the broad principles on which this stage is built is the same as used generations ago.'[35]

Sachs was to record that although the original intention as expressed in the drawings first submitted to the authorities for approval was to build the stage entirely in iron, a modified form using a certain amount of wood was built. This is confirmed by a report of the L.C.C. Theatres and Music Halls Committee of the 25th June, 1890, which states: '(9) The stage machinery is shown entirely of wood on revised drawing. In the specifications accompanying the drawing approved by the late Metropolitan Board of Works, it is provided that . . . ''the slider frames be of iron joists supported only at the ends, and sufficiently trussed''.'[36]

At first sight the arrangement used would seem to continue the standard practice of the earlier wood stages. Nevertheless, the use of iron, wire and counterweights enabled the various scenic items to be

> 'moved with greater facility and precision, and the unevenness in the movement of scenery avoided. The cloth can be raised and lowered without the jerks in the movement so often seen when the primitive methods of manipulating are used. Economy in labour and therefore a saving in the weekly outlay of the theatre treasury is also obtained, because less manual force is required to work a stage fitted on the lines laid down by Mr. Dando than is needed for a wooden stage, where his improvements have not been adopted. By the use of wire ropes and pulleys . . . and by a prodigious arrangement of counterweights, scenes can be manipulated with great facility and steadiness, and, if desired, the whole of the back scenes, together with the set scenes, can be moved simultaneously, giving a desirable effect by raising or lowering the whole of a scene in one even and unbroken movement.'[37]

The features which remained the same as in the earlier stage fittings were the sliders, or sloat cuts, for raising and lowering the 'rise and sink' scenery, but these were now operated by wire in place of the earlier ropes, over a series of drums placed in the well, which could, if required, be linked together with special coupling-bars, so that all the scenic units could be raised or lowered simultaneously. The foremost of the cuts

> 'is a novelty in stage construction; it is known as the carpet cut, (p.208) . . . The use of this cut is to enable the stage cloth or carpet upon the stage to be removed without any of the stage hands or flunkeys appearing before the audience and rolling up the carpet in their sight . . . The carpet is dragged through the cut . . . to the mezzanine below, where it is wound up on a roller.'[38]

A number of similar 'first time' claims are made for the equipment used in this theatre, but these, like the carpet cut, have already been noted in other, and earlier, theatres. Four bridges were provided, and a grave trap and four corner traps were placed just behind the proscenium. There was also a further trap in the rear stage area through which scenery could be passed to stores in the three mezzanine levels. These three levels, together with the well, were some 27 feet in depth, a considerably greater dimension than any previously noted. Indeed the depth involved beneath street level gave the builder great problems, notably of waterproofing, which were only solved after the application of 'successive linings of concrete and asphalte'.[39]

The earlier wings were now replaced by set-pieces and the units making up the walls of box sets were held 'upright by means of a brace fastened to the wooden frame holding the canvas, and the stage floor by means of gimlets.[40] This was a method which Sachs criticises as being 'exceedingly destructive to the boards of the stage floor, "worm-eating" them, so to speak, with numerous holes. This method goes by the name of "bracing" or "gimleting", and is still in extreme use in all English Theatres but the Palace.'

Fig.158. The New English Opera House: stage and stage machinery: detail of Fig.155

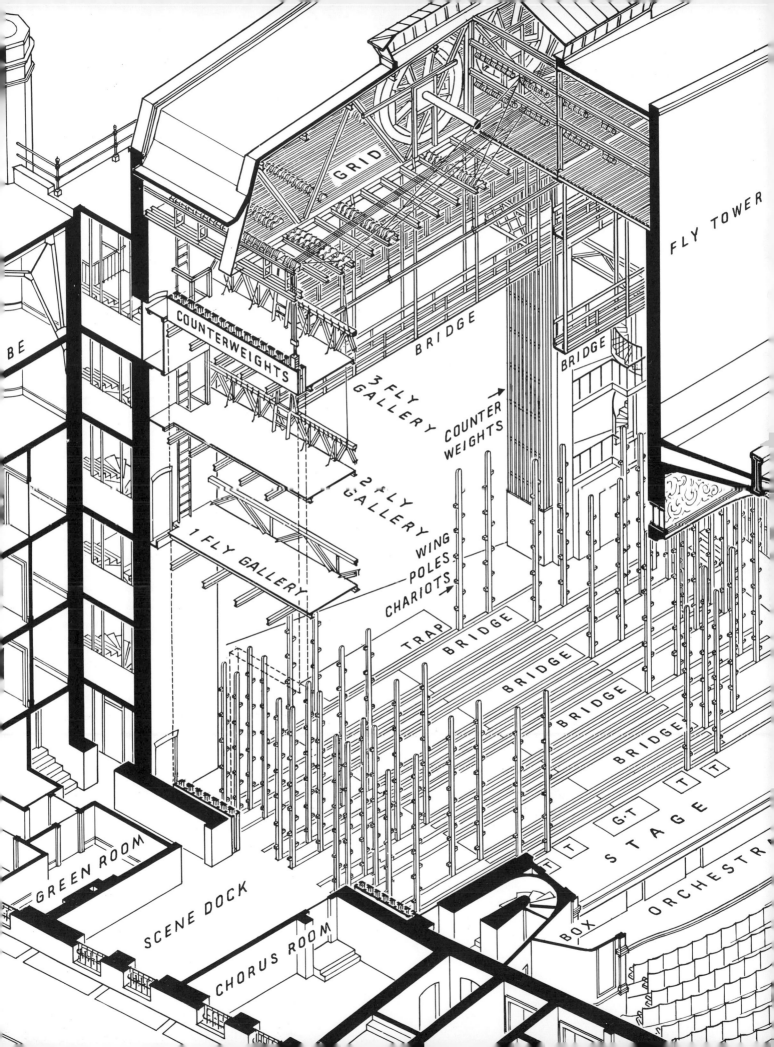

GRID

FLY TOWER

BE

COUNTERWEIGHTS

BRIDGE

BRIDGE

3 FLY GALLERY

COUNTER WEIGHTS

2 FLY GALLERY

1 FLY GALLERY

WING POLES CHARIOTS

TRAP

BRIDGE

BRIDGE

BRIDGE

BRIDGE

BRIDGE

S T A G E

G.T

T

T

T

GREEN ROOM

SCENE DOCK

CHORUS ROOM

BOX

ORCHESTRA

At the Royal English Opera Mr Dando again introduced 'for the first time in England', the continental 'chariot and pole' (fig.158), but here, as at Barry's Covent Garden, they were designed to support, not just the wings at either side of the stage, but individual set-pieces at any position across the width of the stage. To this end continuous slots were constructed right across the stage, along which the pole could move, the slots being filled in before and behind the pole with small wooden blocks which were free to run ahead of the movement of the pole, thus effectively filling the opening and providing a continuous floor surface safe for actors or dancers to perform on. Presumably this arrangement may well have been introduced to improve on that at Covent Garden, where no such provision is mentioned. The foremost chariot groove, however, was arranged in two parts, projecting only some seven feet within the proscenium width on either side, and operated in the same manner as its continental and English predecessors, namely, to carry the side wings, in this instance the curtain wings, which acted as an inner – flexible – proscenium opening.

Although much of the construction beneath the stage was of oak, particularly in those areas where there was movement, the 'top machinery is entirely of iron'. Iron trusses carried the roof and supported an open iron grid on their bottom flange. Beneath are three levels of fly galleries on either side, each 7 feet 6 inches wide, also of iron, the upper two being connected across the stage by two tiers of hanging iron bridges. 'A special feature in the design of the stage machinery of the Royal English Opera House is the abolition of the heavy and cumbersome drums' (two, however, are still to be seen on the grid) 'used in all other English stages, and the substitution of the pulleys and counterweights; the wooden wind-lasses are abolished, and iron crabs are used instead.'[41]

Each cloth was now hung on a set of four wire lines carried over pulleys on the grid floor to a master pulley set higher on cross beams between the roof trusses (figs.158,160-1), and from there to a pulley on the side wall from which it descended to a counterweight travelling the full height of the stage in a special shaft: where a sufficient height was not available over the entrance to the scene dock, a counterweight with a double-purchase pulley was used. These shafts, which could well have been constructed in metal, were in fact built up of timber; some examples can still be seen, although the original flying system has since been replaced (fig.162). The counterweights could be loaded from any of the three galleries, to balance the weight of the scenic item attached to the batten. When this was done both scene and counterweight could be easily moved by one man pulling on a further line which was attached to the centre of the batten, and after passing over pulleys above the grid descended to be attached to iron cleats on the lower fly rail.

The normal hand-operated rope system (p.248) consisted of a minimum of three lines – long, centre and short – (fig.159), all naturally of different lengths, which could be pulled on as a group, or individually, to raise or lower or adjust the level of the hanging cloth to such advice as 'up a bit on the long' or 'let out your centre slightly'. Under the new system each wire connecting the batten to the counterweight was of a predetermined length, so that each batten was set in advance to hang level, and could not be altered by the fly-man,

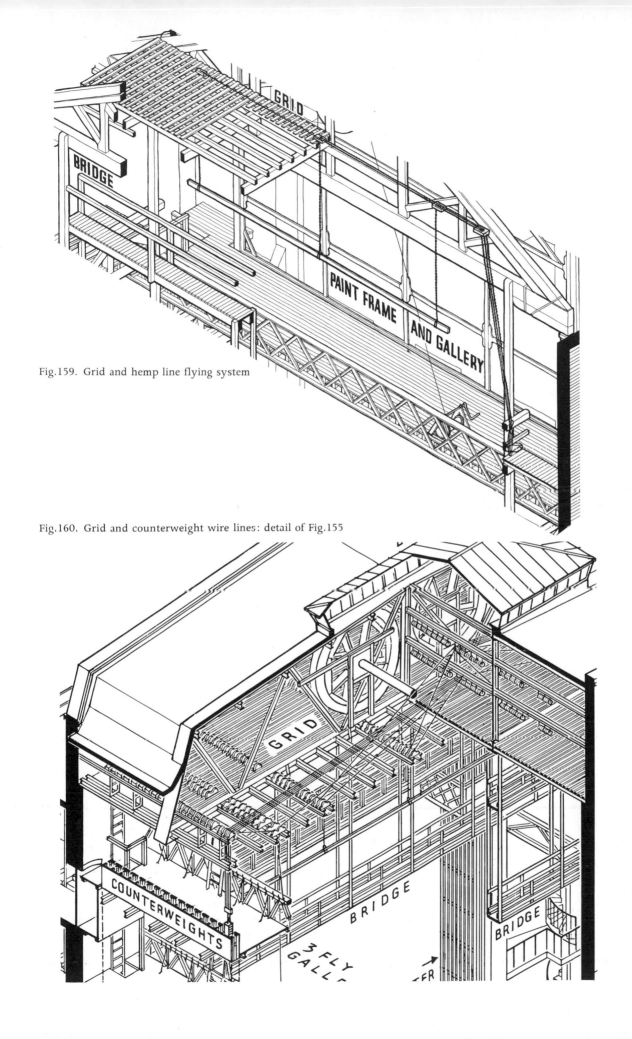

Fig. 159. Grid and hemp line flying system

Fig. 160. Grid and counterweight wire lines: detail of Fig. 155

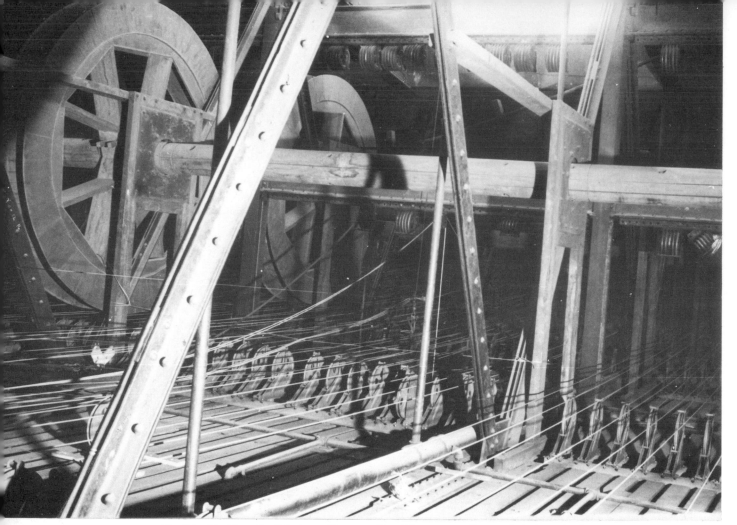

Fig.161. The New English Opera House: grid, with master pulleys and timber wheels

who had only to operate the single working line controlling the movement of both batten and counterweight.

> 'By carrying all the counterweight wires and working lines into the middle of the gridiron over the centre pulleys . . . the use of the "long and short line" is obviated: the two counterweight wires farthest from these centre pulleys are therefore of the same length, and it is evident that the two lines at the ends of the battens exercise an equal strain.'[42]

Mr Dando would also seem to have 'invented' a further device, in this instance a 'thunder run', very similar to that already described in the roof (fig.79) of the Theatre Royal, Bristol. Although Dando's thunder run does not seem to have survived, an excellent example of the period may still be seen on the prompt side fly gallery at Her Majesty's Theatre (figs.169, 171).

The iron trusses of the roof were of a mansard shape, and the roof was crowned by a smoke flue, now required by the authorities. In 1894, Woodrow was to comment that opinions still varied as to the construction of the roof over the stage. One theory still suggested was that the roof should be of wood, so that on burning the failure of the roof would itself provide a huge flue to the fire. Woodrow, however, suggests that the roof should be fire-resisting and that 'the smoke flues over the stage demanded by the municipal regulations should be made sufficiently large to carry off the smoke by the up-draught'.[43] The increased provision for the storage of scenery in the flying space above the stage, and the greater weight and size of scenic items which it might be required to fly, of necessity placed greater loads on the roof trusses spanning the stage, and it is perhaps as well that iron and steel began to replace timber in these areas. Woodrow reminds us that the roof truss over the Royal English Opera House stage had a span of 70 ft. in length, and 'in addition to supporting the roof itself, also carries the gridiron floor' which in this instance was also of iron and from which depended 'the weight of the great masses of scenery and, standing on the gridiron floor, the usual machinery found in the rigging-loft of a theatre'.[44]

In the interests of safety from fire all the window frames were of steel, and the doors, with the exception of the entrance doors which were of mahogany, were of steel and asbestos millboard. Provision was made for extinguishing a fire by incorporating a large tank of water over the ceiling of the stage. Ventilation was no longer left to take care of itself. Instead, air was forced in to the building by fans, and could be heated or cooled as required. It was led by ducts to various parts of the auditorium where its inflow could be regulated by valves. Further ducts were provided for the removal of the vitiated air, which terminated in an exhaust fan in the auditorium roof. The building was heated by steam coils, and lighted by electricity provided by 'three special designed boilers of the locomotive type, and dynamos with all the latest improvements. One half of the working plant is equal to provide for the full requirements of the house, calculated to be between 2,000 and 3,000 lights.'[45] With standby equipment for use in emergencies, gas was no longer considered necessary, and no provision was made for it in the building.

Fig.162. The New English Opera House: timber

It would seem that no accommodation was provided here for making and painting scenery, and little space was provided for its storage. This was in line with the changing pattern whereby

> 'so much of the scene-painters' and carpenters' work which used to be done in the theatre is now done by the scene-painter in his own painting-room, and by the carpenter in his own workshops away from the theatre, it has been found unnecessary to provide rooms for these purposes in our modern play-houses on such a scale as was necessary in the past . . . Another improvement in theatrical matters is that nowadays a large stock of scenery is never kept on the premises. In the West-end theatres pieces are played which are intended for, even if they do not have, long runs. In the outlying theatres travelling companies fill the bill, and bring with them their own scenery. The consequence is that large scene docks and stores are not wanted. The valuable space can be used by the architect to better advantage.'[46]

In America it was by now considered that a theatre should be subdivided into a number of different cells, each separated by walls carried above the roofs. In a paper read by C. J.

Hexamer in 1892[47] these divisions are suggested as follows: '1. A fire-proof auditorium . . . 2. A stage building . . . 3. A fire-proof building for dressing rooms, 4. A fire-proof storage room for scenery, properties, &c, with fire-proof doors.' The wall above the proscenium opening should be carried on an iron girder, above which should be built a relieving arch, capable of taking the wall loading if, or when, the girder collapsed. If it was not required to square off the top of the proscenium opening, then the iron girder could be omitted. Mr Hexamer also dwelt on the necessity for separating the understage areas from the auditorium, and quotes the example of the Academy of Music (presumably in Philadelphia) where he recommended that a wall be built up and finished with cement level with the stage floor. He recommended that the fire-curtain should be 'of real asbestos, not half-cotton, with an interior network of strong, woven, pliable wire to give it tensile strength, and should slide in iron grooves, at least 6 in. deep, on both sides of the stage, securely bolted into the masonry of the proscenium wall'.

He further suggests that each separate part of the building should have its own exits, as should each part of the auditorium, that every exit should be separated from any other, and that all such corridor exits must widen out as they approached the open air. All doors should open outwards. Seating must be in short lengths, the rows of seats 'being tightly screwed to the floor' and limited by aisles. On the question of seating Woodrow mentions a German seat 'the back of which falls, and the seat rises when the occupant gets up, thus leaving gangways at right angles to the curtain'.[48] It may seem strange that with the new regulations regarding fire escapes, it should still be possible to block the gangways with folding seats, yet the continued use of flap seats in the centre gangway of the pit seating at Drury Lane is noted in reports of December, 1892, and February, 1894, and in April, 1894 it is recorded that 'The flap seats were approved by the Committee 30 April, 1890.'[49]

Hexamer recommended the use of electric light, with separate circuits to stage and auditorium, and deplored the continued use of gas, with its many naked flames, and also of coal-oil, which he claimed was still in use 'in our country and Western theatres'. If fire broke out, then a constant supply of water must be at hand in the form of a tank 'the bottom at least 10 ft. above the highest sprinkler, holding at least 5,000 gallons'. This should be prevented from freezing by passing one of the steam-pipes for heating through it. In addition to the sprinklers, there should also be numerous fire-hydrants, connected to the system, as in many areas the pressure of the city water supplies was not sufficient to raise the jets to the upper levels of the theatre.

It is of interest that in recommending that the stage and workshops be protected by such a sprinkler system, he also says: 'if there is an attic above the auditorium, this also, should be fully equipped with an approved system of automatic sprinklers'. Here he is, perhaps, alluding to the protection of such areas in existing buildings. He quotes an underwriters' report which sets out at length their various requirements; these included such items as an electrical warning system to the local fire station, the provision of a special fireproof dock, where all scenery not in use on the stage might be stored, and the impregnation of all items

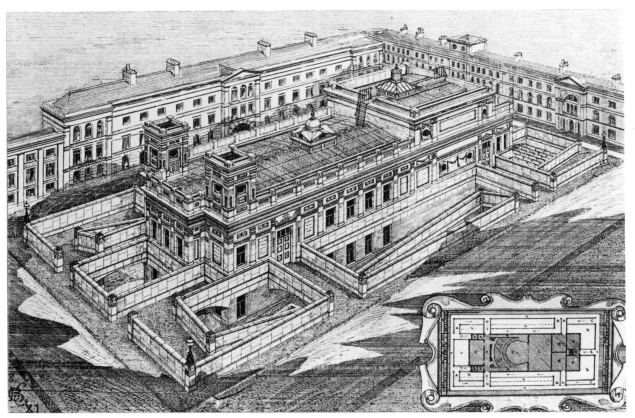

Fig.163. J. G. Buckle's Model Safety Theatre

of scenery with fire-proofing substances. On this latter point, however, he comments: 'Laws making the treatment of scenery in new theatres compulsory (as in New York) have not been successful. Although the ''stock'' scenery of a new theatre must be impregnated before the playhouse is allowed to be opened, the travelling companies, with each piece, bring in materials which have not been treated, and which may cause a fire.' In this country it was not until 1904 that the London County Council adopted their Theatre Committee's recommendations regarding non-inflammable scenery, and the use of louvres, sprinklers, etc.[50]

Hexamer touched on one main point regarding fire precautions, which was also found desirable in this country, and that was the need to separate such buildings as theatres from the surrounding properties. Ideally, it is suggested, this should be achieved by placing the building on an open site, but in this instance it was recommended that theatres should front on to 'broad streets not less than 60 ft. wide, with wide open spaces on both sides not less than 20 ft.-30 ft. would be better'. On this point Woodrow, speaking in 1892,[51] pointed out that on the continent, where theatres were state-aided, regulations existed for their isolation: 'In Austria, theatres holding more than 600 persons must be perfectly isolated', and in St Petersburg and Italy the requirements were the same. In Brussels and Paris, theatres

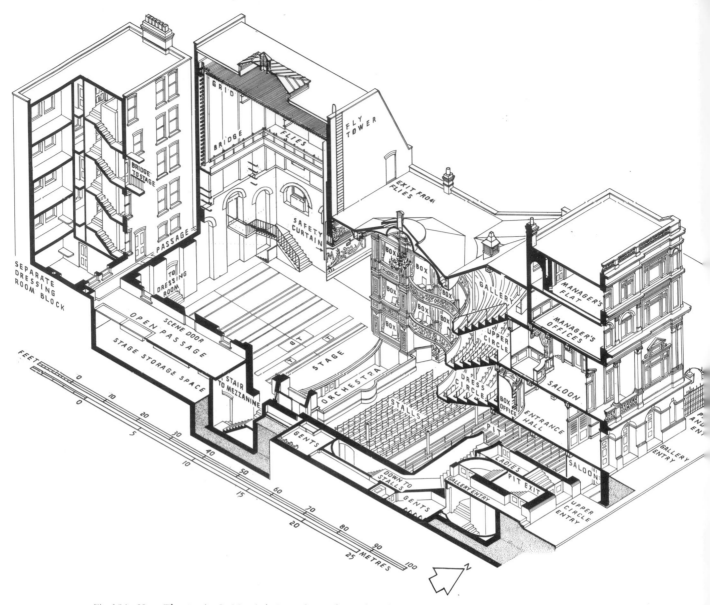

Fig.164. New Theatre in St Martin's Lane (now the Duke of York's), Walter Emden, 1892: scale reconstruction

must be separated by open spaces or brick walls. In New York 'the front must be on a public way, and open spaces at least 8 ft. wide must be left on both sides, from the line of the proscenium wall, the full length of the auditorium', in the manner already improved on in Emden's St Martin's Lane Theatre (fig.164). In this country, however, such perfect isolation as was required on the continent was seldom achieved, although the Royal English Opera House and the Shaftesbury Theatre were so planned on open island sites. In general the theatres being built now occupied situations similar to those required in New York, with passageways down either side, or all round, the building. Woodrow further pointed out the advantages, earlier proposed by Buckle in his 'Suggestions for a Model Safety Theatre' (fig.163)[52] of sinking the theatre into the ground. Buckle suggested that 'the *ground-line* should be nearly equidistant between the pit and gallery levels',[53] and said that 'the safest theatre in the event of a panic would be one in which the public had to rush *up* staircases into the street rather than *down*. HENCE THE GALLERY, AND NOT THE PIT, SHOULD BE ENTERED FROM THE STREET LEVEL'. At the time of writing Buckle was able to point to the Criterion Theatre as approaching most nearly to these conditions. He placed his ideal theatre in an open 'moat', permitting fenestration even to the floor levels below ground, and the towers shown on the illustration had a practical purpose in housing water tanks, thus providing a maximum head of water.

That Buckle's suggestions were recognised to be of value is indicated by the ability of Woodrow to be able to say of the Savoy, the Lyric, the Garrick, and the Cranbourne Street – Daly's – and St Martin's Lane – Duke of York's – theatres, all recently built, or in the process of building, that 'In all these cases it will be observed that a limit to the height of the building is obtained by sinking the pit below the level of the pavement, thus placing the back of the dress circle on a level with the street'.[54] When Daly's Theatre was opened the whole of the area – the pit – was described as lying lower than the roadway,[55] with the main tier at the entrance vestibule level, so that the highest seat was no more than 40 feet above street level, and the lowest 15 feet 6 inches below. Not only did this arrangement permit more direct egress from the varied parts of the theatre to the street, but it brought the upper sections within the then limited heights to which the fire brigades could elevate the water from their hoses. Experiments quoted by Buckle[56] suggest that 30 to 35 feet high would have been a good throw obtainable in only a few parts of London from the natural pressures supplied by the various water companies, and that this was a maximum height that could be approached on their fire-escapes. Woodrow particularly condemned the practice of including 'shops or cafés as part of the scheme, on the ground floor of a theatre',[57] as not only would they occupy space better given over to exits, but would provide additional fire hazards to those inherent in the theatre structure.

Woodrow's point of view regarding theatre design is very clear:

> 'It is . . . the duty of the architect to design his Building so as to reduce the chances of panic to a minimum, and one of the chief provisions to this end is short and un-obstructed exits. Everything in and about a theatre should tend to make an audience have confidence in their own security, and give them a feeling that, should anything happen, they would be able to help themselves without causing injury to others.'[58]

He suggests that people will naturally tend to leave a building by the door they entered, but where there is symmetry of design, they may well use another door corresponding to that by which they came in.

> 'Thus, where there is a pit entrance on the one side, a pit exit will now be found on the other; where there is a gallery staircase on the right, a gallery staircase is on the left, and so on for each tier, or division of the audience, as seen in the Shaftesbury Theatre (fig.150c). Every such division is provided with two separate exits leading directly into the street.'[59]

Emden's design for the New Theatre in St Martin's Lane, 1891-2, known also as The Trafalgar, and now as The Duke of York's, is a particularly good example of the realisation not only of his theories, but also of those of Woodrow. Although the site is in a very built-up area, the theatre itself (fig.164) was isolated from the surrounding buildings by passageways some 9 feet wide, into which the numerous exits emerged – an arrangement which was felt to be an improvement on an island site, where the rumble of traffic would be heard on all sides of the theatre. The dressing rooms were built in an entirely separate block beyond the rear passage, beneath, and above which they were connected to the stage. Bathrooms and wash basins, with hot and cold water, were to be provided.

The whole theatre was erected of fireproof construction, and here steel replaced iron. Like the Royal English Opera House (fig.155), the roof and ceiling over the auditorium were designed in a single skin of steel and concrete, and the roof over the stage, with sloping sides over the fly galleries, was constructed in a similar manner. The omission of rooms over the auditorium resulted in a change in the external appearance of theatres in that the 'fly tower' was now to be seen dominating the auditorium.

> 'For the protection of the public, beyond the fireproofing of the building, the auditorium will be dominated by hydrants and the stage by sprinklers, while the act-drop, which will be of new construction, will form a protective fire-screen between the stage and the auditorium.'[60]

Double entrances and exits were arranged from all parts of the house, together with fire escapes from the flies and upper portions of the stage. The dress circle (fig.165) was now at street level, with pit and stalls below, and the upper circle and gallery above, thus reducing the distances which any member of the audience had to traverse to reach the street. Electricity replaced gas in this theatre, but the latter was installed as a standby in case of failure of the electricity system. The theatre was ventilated, as would be expected, by 'extracting heated and vitiated air by exhausts, allowing sufficient fresh air to pass into the building through shafts arranged in the side walls'.[61]

Ingenuity was needed in the placing of payboxes in relation to entrances and exits, not only for the safety of the public, but in the interests of the management. Much of the nightly takings of a house could be dissipated unnecessarily in payments to a multiplicity of attendants, money-takers and check-takers, and on this point it is perhaps worth recalling the ingenious arrangement seen in the little theatre at Richmond in Yorkshire (fig.101), where all entrances were controlled by the single pay-box. Woodrow suggested in 1892 that 'some houses have proved failures because they have been too expensive to work, have required too many attendants, money-takers, and check-takers, and have not held enough "money" to pay the weekly salary list'.[62]

Barriers for controlling the entry of crowds, particularly at pit and gallery, were now replaced by narrow entry ways to the pay boxes, permitting the passage of only one person at a time, but so arranged that the full width exit way bypassed this box passage. Such an

Fig.165. New Theatre, St Martin's Lane, O.P. stage boxes at dress circle level

arrangement may be seen at Daly's Theatre (fig.167a), while at Her Majesty's (fig.169), movable hinged screens made a similar arrangement possible. These narrow entry ways encouraged the formation of queues, and canopies were now needed to protect the queue (fig.166) from the weather, as has been earlier noted at Covent Garden (p.221). The possible beginning of the system of camp-stool queueing may be noted in Woodrow's comment on 'the lady who took up her stand, or rather her camp-stool, at the Lyceum pit-door at 10 in the morning for admission to the first night of "Henry viii".'[63]

The need to make provision for a multiplicity of exit stairs led to some ingenious planning, such as might be seen at the Gaiety, and also at Drury Lane (fig.188), where the gallery and upper circle stairs ascend one above the other within the same containing walls. It was now recognised that long flights of stairs were dangerous, but too few steps were equally bad: 'there should not be more than twelve or less than three. Single steps, or steps at half landings are certain stumbling blocks.'[64] It goes without saying that there should be no winders, and that the going should be even throughout the whole flight. Woodrow reminds us that the regulations in London 'do not permit of any other stone staircase being erected than solid square steps supported by brickwork at both ends'.[65] While there is obviously sense in this arrangement, it was pointed out by some that the total enclosure that resulted could increase

Fig.166. The Queue

Fig.167. Daly's Theatre, Spencer Chadwick, 1893. (a) narrow entrance to the pit pay box and the wide exit

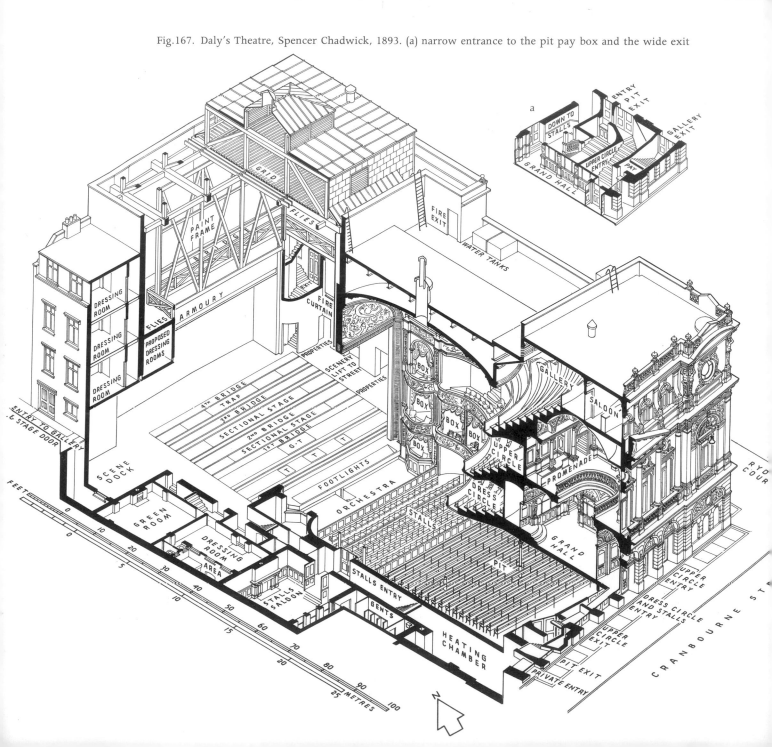

a sense of panic, in that a crowd might be halted without being able to understand the reason for the stoppage. The use of open arches providing support for the steps, and permitting a view through to the flight beyond, was suggested as one possible solution, and the Grand Stair in the Royal English Opera House (fig.155) was cited as an example.

Daly's Theatre, opened in 1893, was designed by Spencer Chadwick to seat some 1,500 persons. As has already been noted (p.265), the theatre was entered at dress circle level, the pit and stalls being sunk below ground level (fig.167). There were 150 stalls seats approached by stairs and corridors from the Grand Hall above. As usual the stalls were separated by a low partition from the pit benches, with their entrance and exit at the rear direct from the street above. The dress circle, with 141 seats, was arranged on a flat canti-levered arc directly facing the stage, with three boxes on either side infilling the space between circle front and proscenium wall. Above, the upper circle, set slightly back from the front of the dress circle, was arranged on a semi-circle, with one box on either side. The front row of the gallery again conformed to the semi-circle with arms stretching forward to the roofs of the boxes, this encircling bench, and the one behind, being separated from the rest of the gallery by a low partition, and the remaining benches being arranged on a flat arc facing the stage.

'Everything has been done to admit of the possibility of the theatre being emptied in the smallest possible time, the exits being provided in excess of those required by the L.C.C. There are no less than twelve exits, two each from the stalls, dress circle, upper circle, pit, gallery, and stage, and the whole building could, in emergency, be cleared within three minutes.'

These exits are arranged in the manner suggested by Emden and Woodrow, being sym-metrically placed on either side of the auditorium.

'The stage will be among the largest in London, being 60 ft. by 40 ft., with a pro-scenium opening 31 ft. by 32 ft. It is to be divided from the auditorium by a fire-resisting curtain of double thickness of asbestos cloth enclosed in an iron frame, and the scene-dock, property and other rooms connected with the working of the stage, will be separated by fire resisting doors . . . The building will be constructed entirely of fire-resisting material, all ironwork being encased in concrete, and it will be fitted with a thorough system of hydrants . . . The ventilation and system of warming the theatre has been carefully considered. In addition to the main ventilating system through a large lantern light fitted with louvres and exhaust placed in the roof over the stage, there are to be two smaller exhausts in the main building, and the retiring and dressing rooms for artistes on each level are also to be provided with outside ventilation and light.'[66]

The above description suggests that the regulations, first of the Metropolitan Board of Works, and later of the L.C.C., were by now having their effect on theatre design, not wholly, however, without pressure from the authorities. A Select Committee of the House of Commons reported in 1892 that credit for 'the vast improvement in the structure of London theatres during recent years has been mainly due to the zealous efforts, first, of the Metropolitan Board of Works, and afterwards of the London County Council, working through the Theatres Committee'.[67] In spite of the claim noted above regarding ventilation and lighting of the dressing rooms at Daly's, the plans submitted for approval in June, 1891,[68] showed that it was proposed to use the enclosed space beneath the O.P. fly gallery to house three dressing rooms with no windows at all. A pencilled note on the drawings: 'These dressing rooms to be removed see letter 9th July 1891' and further notes regarding the filling in of the proposed door openings in the side wall of the stage to these rooms and to the fly gallery above, indicate the need which still existed for the controls necessary to implement the regulations.

Similar spaces, beneath the P. side fly gallery and a rear bridge for use by the scenic artist, were designated on the drawings as 'Armouries'. The stage itself was still subdivided into opening sections, as shown on the reconstruction (fig.167), with cuts for carpet and pipes at the front, and four bridges and two sectional stages behind. In between were a number of narrow openings, presumably sloat cuts, but here named 'sinks'. The designs submitted for approval[69] show an elaborate internal decorative scheme, but a much simpler scheme was finally adopted, at least for the auditorium (fig.168).

Fig.168. Daly's Theatre, showing simplified decorative scheme finally adopted

12 The traditional picture-frame theatre

When Her Majesty's Theatre was rebuilt by C. J. Phipps for Beerbohm Tree, and opened on 28th April, 1897, the site was developed not only as a theatre, but also as a hotel. Unlike the architects of subsidised continental theatres, Phipps had to 'satisfy the requirements of the typical theatrical speculator, who primarily demands the greatest accommodation in a limited space at as low a cost as possible'.[1] Although no attempt had been made to sink the pit below the level of the streets, the house was so designed that there were two separate staircases and exits to each part. 'The staircases to the upper tiers are of the uniform width of 4 ft. 6 in., those to stalls and dress circle 6 ft., formed of concrete, with a rise of only 6 in., no flight having more than twelve steps.'[2] In spite of the rear of the pit being at street level, the uppermost seats in the theatre are no more than 45 feet above the street.

The proscenium opening was some 33 feet in width, and here is seen a return to the formal proscenium area, flanked by giant Corinthian columns, enclosing between them three private boxes on either side (figs.169,170). The columns support an arched ceiling, but there is no projecting stage, and the orchestra pit curves forward from the base of the near-stage columns. Beyond this area the auditorium opens out to a total width of some 69 feet, and with an overall depth of only 60 feet from the stage front to the rear wall of the pit, it is 'remarkable for width in proportion to depth, the curve of the galleries on plan being designed as flat as possible; this promises good results, as the distance from the stage to the audience is appreciably diminished'. All the seats, with the exception of the proscenium boxes, now faced the stage, an arrangement made possible by a similar use of cantilevers to that previously noted at the Royal English Opera House, 'with iron cantilevers and joists, . . . filled in with concrete; on this are built brick risers and the tiers formed of concrete'.[3]

A feature which Sachs particularly commended was the treatment of the gallery, which had 'an open and spacious appearance as seen from below, owing to the considerable height between the balcony and the ceiling'.[4] Here he was presumably referring to the upper circle and amphitheatre, which together form the second circle within the body of the house, from which the gallery itself was separated only by a cross gangway, and a rise of some 6 feet.

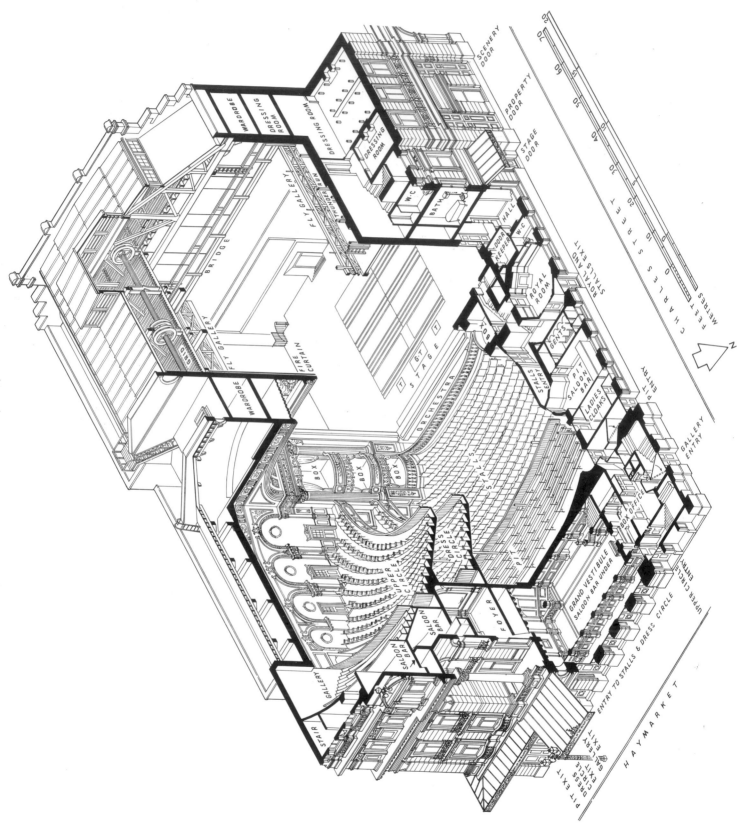

Fig.169. Her Majesty's Theatre, Haymarket, C. J. Phipps, 1897: scale reconstruction based on drawings in the G.L.C. collection and drawings of the same date

Labels within the figure:

WARDROBE
DRESSING ROOM
DRESSING ROOM
BRIDGE
FLY GALLERY
THUNDER RUN
SCENERY DOOR
PROPERTY DOOR
STAGE DOOR
DRESSING ROOM
W.C.
BATH
FLY GALLERY
FIRE CURTAIN
DOOR KEEPER
HALL
W.C.
ROYAL ROOM
ROYAL AND STALLS EXIT
GRID
STAGE
ORCHESTRA
GENTS
STALLS ENTRY
PIT SALOON BAR
LADIES CLOAKS
PIT ENTRY
WARDROBE
BOX
BOX
BOX
STALLS
PIT
PIT
GALLERY ENTRY
UPPER CIRCLE
DRESS CIRCLE
BOX OFFICE
FOYER
GRAND VESTIBULE
SALOON BAR UNDER
SALOON BAR
SALOON BAR
STAIR
GALLERY
ENTRY TO STALLS & DRESS CIRCLE
UPPER CIRCLE ENTRY
DRESS CIRCLE EXIT
PIT EXIT
GALLERY EXIT
HAYMARKET
CHARLES STREET
FEET
METRES
N

Fig.170. Her Majesty's Theatre: interior

The upper circle and amphitheatre together contained ten rows of armchairs, the gallery some five rows of benches. The dress circle and family circle below at first tier level together had eight rows of chairs, and were approached by a flight of stairs in the main entrance hall. The ground floor was here subdivided three ways, with a new feature, the orchestral stalls, at the front, the pit stalls behind, and at the rear, cut off by a partition, the six rows of pit benches. The two forms of stalls together occupied eleven and a half rows of armchairs.[5] Once again the problem of bypassing the occupants of the pit led to a descent by the stalls audience to a special foyer below the entrance hall, from which they could make their way to entrances near the front of the stalls area. Exits from stalls and pit led directly to Charles Street on the right of the auditorium. We read that 'The theatre was designed for an audience divided into five separate classes', each having 'two distinct ways out, opening into different streets'.[6]

In view of the comments recorded earlier regarding the need to economise on the staff

Fig.171. Her Majesty's Theatre:
prompt-side fly gallery with
thunder run on left

controlling pay boxes, Phipps's arrangement here receives high praise from Sachs, which it rightly deserves, the box office being so placed that every section of the audience may purchase tickets from different sides of the same room (fig.169). The stage is enclosed by solid walls which separate it from the five floors of dressing and other rooms on the Charles Street frontage. It is separated from the auditorium by two cross walls, spaced to the 9 feet width of the proscenium unit. Both these walls are carried above the roofs of stage and auditorium, and at higher level the space between is filled by the wardrobe. The use of a fire-proof curtain is recorded,[7] made of a light iron frame faced on either side with asbestos, and filled with slag wool. Sachs, writing in 1897, mentions that in 1892 'when the new County Council regulations were published . . . only 5 London theatres had fire-resisting curtains'.[8] These he thought to be the Court, the Lyric, the Prince of Wales, Terry's, and the Shaftesbury (figs.150,172).

Timber queen-post roof trusses spanned both stage and auditorium, those over the stage carrying an open timber grid floor at a height where the width conformed to the open space between the fly galleries below. This gave a free height of some 60 feet from stage to grid,

MODERN THEATRE STAGES; FIRE-RESISTING CURTAINS.

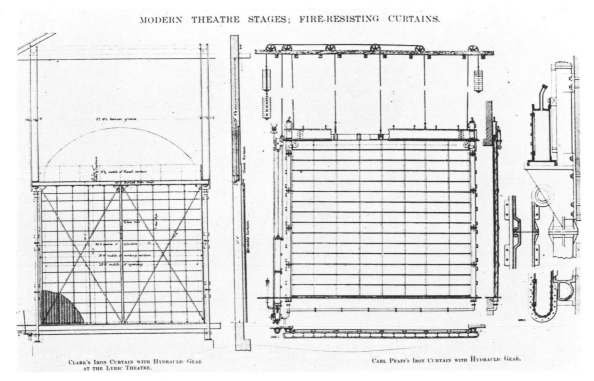

CLARK'S IRON CURTAIN WITH HYDRAULIC GEAR
AT THE LYRIC THEATRE.

CARL PFAFF'S IRON CURTAIN WITH HYDRAULIC GEAR.

Fig.172. Fire-resisting curtains

sufficient to permit the hydraulically operated fire curtain to be raised in one piece above the proscenium opening, and for the flying of scenery without folding or rolling. The roof over the auditorium was of wood with a fibrous plaster ceiling.

The drawings submitted for approval show the usual raking floor to the stage, but it was decided to make a drastic change here and build it flat. Although the raking stage had its birth in the perspective needs of the early Renaissance stages (p.18), its retention at this time was thought to be due to 'the height of the "float" of the footlights, which was liable to hide the feet of the performers': the use of electricity made it possible for the footlights to rise no more than two or three inches above the stage, and as a result the need for the slope is no longer there. It is of interest to note that the raking stage is now criticised for producing the very effect for which it was originally introduced: 'as the perspective effect of a rising stage is always unfortunate'.[9] The removal of the sloping stage was, however, largely conditioned by the changing scenic needs: while the wing and shutter system was in operation with all the scenic movement parallel to the front of the stage, the raking stage was no hindrance, but with scenery set obliquely to or up and down on the stage, difficulties were encountered which required it to be specially built, with the bottom rails cut to conform to the slope of the stage. The use of wheeled trucks, too, was rendered unnecessarily difficult – I have, myself, had the unpleasant experience of a run-away truck ploughing its way across a whole line of footlights. In a paper read to the Society of Arts in April, 1898, Sachs told his audience, which included Bernard Shaw:

'such a step as that recently taken by Herbert Beerbohm Tree at Her Majesty's Theatre was of greater importance than is generally understood, for he introduced into this country for the first time a flat stage, and its use has simplified everything in connection with stage mechanism. The sloping stage has always been a hindrance to those who desired to adopt some mechanical power for the working or the handling of the scenery. The sloping stage always added to the first outlay for any innovation of this description. The flat stage has been tried and used successfully on the Continent for a considerable time, and in the United States it has for years been a popular improvement in every modern theatre. Nevertheless, the prejudice and ridicule with which Beerbohm Tree's idea of introducing the flat stage into London first met was almost astounding, and even after its advantages had been recognised there are many who would attribute any mishap, even of the most trivial kind, that might occur on the stage of Her Majesty's Theatre to the absence of the usual slope.'[10]

In all other respects, however, the stage conformed to the old-fashioned system. It was

'arranged to slide away in sections. . . . Each so-called "cut" or section of the floor, ranging from 6 inches to 3 feet wide, is formed of narrow widths of boarding resting in rebate on joist; on a wedge being removed, the end of the section drops into a groove below, and is drawn off by cords underneath the side of the stage, the scenes or platforms then being hoisted through the space thus left by means of ropes wound on large drums'.[11]

Much of this equipment is still to be seen *in situ* beneath the stage (figs. 133, 136).

The theatre was lit throughout by electricity, not supplied now from their own system, but provided by three different companies to avoid any chance of failure. Ventilation was mechanical, 'fresh air being drawn in by fans worked from the engines in the basement, and filtered before entering the house, and foul air drawn out by similar fans through the cupola on the roof'. The air was intended to be kept 'at a uniform temperature of 62 deg. all through the summer and winter'.[12]

Attempts to replace the wooden machinery by metal date from as early as March 1840, when the Royalty Theatre was equipped with machinery designed by R. M. Stephenson.[13] This was intended to be worked by a single man, but needed a horse to put it into noisy movement. If the change from wood to metal was slow, the change from manual to mechanised power was even slower. On the continent, however, mechanical power was being experimented with, and an early use of steam power to activate the stage traps was incorporated in the old Opera House in Vienna, but the motive power most widely used was hydraulic. This was featured in the Asphaleia stage which was incorporated in the Buda-Pest Opera House, opened in 1881, and in the Halle Theatre in Germany, designed in a competition held in 1883.[14] In a prospectus issued in 1882 the Asphaleia stage was described as being 'so arranged as to open in every possible direction and that without any special preparation being necessary. Every trap goes right across the stage, and is in this direction divided into three parts. Each one of these parts rests on the plunger of an hydraulic press.'[15] (figs.173a,b). These traps, which in practice in the two theatres mentioned, follow very closely on the contemporary pattern of stage divisions seen in the traditional theatres, were capable of being both raised and lowered, singly or in any combination. In addition they could be rotated at an angle, or set at a slope to the stage floor.

The standard stage promoted in the prospectus was described as having two sliders between the trapped sections of the stage 'through which a whole scene can be raised to any required height. Besides these there runs down each side of the stage from front to back, a similar slide, through which wings can be erected. Thus it is possible to raise up from below the stage into view of the audience a complete scene representing a room.'[16] The flying mechanism of the Asphaleia stage is described as being very simple, capable of being moved anywhere, not only in straight lines, but also in curves or in any direction required.

The Asphaleia stage made use of a further feature: the enclosing panorama, which was described as

'a continuous cloth scene, on which there is painted a sky, called the horizon (fig.173a) which runs round the back of the stage and both sides, as far forward as the second grooves, and in order to produce the effect of an unbroken surface the corners are rounded off very gently and carefully, by which arrangement the eye of the spectator is not brought up by the wings, but he can look away out to the right and to the left'.[17]

This cloth could be used as an enclosing stationary sky cloth, or it could be used as a painted panorama to display differing aspects of the sky, which could 'be made to change its nature during the playing of a scene, if necessary to the action of the play'. It is claimed, however, that such a 'horizon' cloth was first used at the Vienna Karl Theatre, and later at the Old Burg Theatre as early as 1873. Indeed Sachs comments[18] that the Asphaleia stage was

'in reality . . . only to a great extent . . . a clever combination of the most modern improvements of the time, carefully collected from all parts of the continent and then adapted for a special purpose.

'. . . the purpose of the "Asphaleia" syndicate was to construct everything of metal work, in order to minimise the inflammability of the stage. Secondly, to make every part of the stage floor moveable, and, what is more, to allow a section of the floor to move above or below stage floor level at will, to enable the stage floor and sections of it to slope in any direction, and to give it the greatest possible elasticity. Next, the syndicate aimed at dispensing entirely with manual labour, and permitting every-

Fig.173. The Asphaleia stage
   (a) traps and 'horizon'

(b) traps

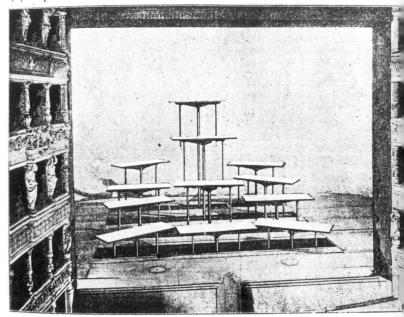

thing to be worked from one point only and regulated by a single mechanic. It also had great ambitions as to scenic effect, and the dangling border, the angular wing, and the straight back cloths, were very wisely done away with to make room for the curved horizon and more artistic set pieces. The realisation of the artistic ideals put forward were, I am glad to say, found not only practicable but also highly effective, yet as regards the mechanical ideals – such as the idea of one man at a keyboard working the whole of the stage machinery for a large opera – this was found neither economic or reliable.'[19]

An example of continental developments may be seen in the equipment of the Buda-Pest Opera House (fig.174). Here the horizon was some 50 feet high, with the bottom hung some 6 feet above the stage to permit the passage of actors beneath. The total length of the horizon was over 450 feet, with the vertical rollers some 72 feet apart. The cloth was hung on wires, and was worked by winches from the second fly gallery. The entire horizon could be wound on to one of the rollers, so as to permit the use of the back-stage area, or the whole horizon be raised *in situ* to permit a clear height of some 25 feet beneath. The gridiron was supported on five secondary girders set parallel to the proscenium opening, and these in turn were supported on two lattice girders set up and down stage, 104 sets of 3 wires each being arranged one behind the other on the gridiron floor, each set running over four pulleys and connected to 36 small hydraulic rams. 'The whole of the hydraulic rams are worked from a set of levers on two switchboards in the front part of the stage, where there is a small raised gallery fitted for the mechanic.'[20] This system was criticised by the resident engineer, who found that the control of the movement of cloths by a single mechanic was not practicable, it being necessary to keep a close eye on them, which was not possible from the mechanic's gallery. The problem was augmented by the need to hang additional cloths in the flying space to offset the resonance of the iron stage, resulting in very crowded conditions at this point, which increased the risk of cloths fouling one another and of catching fire.

A further criticism of the Buda-Pest stage was the high cost of the original installation of machinery, and the subsequent rapid depreciation of its value. The use of mechanisation certainly permitted the movement of heavier pieces of scenery, but hardly speeded up the operation, as it took some three minutes to raise a section through its full height.[21] Similar equipment was introduced on the stage of the Auditorium Building in Chicago, which was some 70 feet by 110 feet by 95 feet high, with a floor divided into sections, all of which could be moved jointly or separately in a vertical plane to 'create variations and gradations of level of stage floor almost instantaneously in any direction, up, down or oblique, for any part of the stage floor'.[22] The system used here was, however, an improvement on the Asphaleia system, and is said to have been quicker in action. The various sections could be raised from 12 to 15 feet above stage level.[23]

Nevertheless, in spite of these mechanical improvements, much of the standard form of scenery continued to be used, with scenes sinking beneath the stage, and cloths being flown by machinery rather than raised by hand. It was claimed by the Asphaleia company that this machinery would reduce costs by re-placing stage hands, but a single machinist received as much pay for his more complicated work as the redundant stage hands, and it still took as many men to attach a cloth to the new machinery as to the ropes and battens of the old system.

There had always been an element of danger in the use of the old timber traps, especially when a trap was 'sent up' with an actor in position before the flap in the stage floor had been removed, thus crushing the actor between the trap and the stage. When the trap was worked by machinery the actor had 'no power to ease or stop its movement, whereas in the old system of counterweights some effort exercised by the actor may relieve the force of the mishap'.[24] Further criticisms were made of the vibration caused by the machinery, and the bad acoustics associated with the iron stages, but probably the most important criticisms were made by Herr Rudolph of the Vienna Opera House, who pointed out that the principle of the system of traps was wrong as it required the stage manager to arrange the scenes according to the stage, rather than the stage in accordance with the scene. This was a point

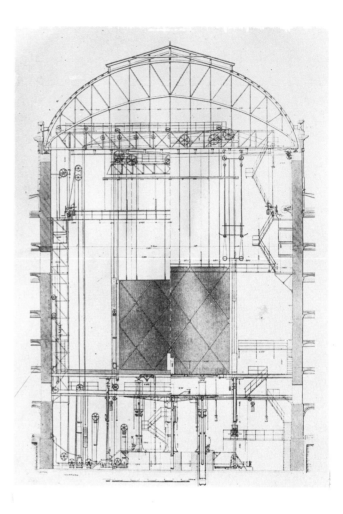

Fig.174. Buda-Pest Opera House:
section across the Asphaleia stage

of view which indicates a complete break with tradition, and a new approach to the art of scenic design, which up to this time was almost entirely conditioned by the traditional arrangement of the stage machine except where this had been ignored, and temporary rostra and other scenic pieces had been set across the traps and bridges. Sachs pointed out that it would hardly be worth installing a system like the Asphaleia stage in a London theatre, where 'a run of 100 nights, or more, is to be expected',[25] although it might be of value at Covent Garden, which followed the pattern of the continental theatres with their nightly change of play and the consequent need for a rapid change of scene, particularly as regards the use of varying stage levels.

Sachs underlines the current attitude to stage design when he tells us that in the theatres of the past there was 'no thought of illusion, none dreamed of trying to make the audience think they were not in a theatre. The theatrical was the antithesis of the natural. . . . Actor and scene-painter must, above all, alike so labour that the audience shall forget that they are within the four walls of a theatre.'[26] If this high degree of realism was to be obtained on the stage then the old ways would eventually have to go, to be replaced with new and more efficient methods of changing the scene with ease and speed. But old habits die hard, and although new ideas were introduced they still went largely hand in hand with the old.

Little of this, however, was to find its way to Britain. As one of the audience at Sachs' lecture to the Society of Arts put it, the conditions here

'were entirely different, on the continent there was State or municipal aid for the manager who endeavoured to provide plays artistically; here there was nothing of the kind. Theatre building took its initiative in the speculative architect, who, having found a suitable site, next found a speculative capitalist, who looked simply for a good return on his investment, and always had before his eyes the authorities at Spring-gardens, who might step in at any moment and require an expenditure of £3,000 or £4,000 on matters which they had not before deemed necessary. For theatres in London, the improvements Mr. Sachs had described were hardly required, and the other class of theatres were the suburban or provincial houses, which were confined to six-night runs of plays sent on tour already equipped with most of their scenery; and these theatres, even if they had these appliances, could not use them because of the stage manager who travelled with the scenery of the plays, and was a most appalling person.'[27]

Nevertheless some small improvements were made. After the Lyric Theatre was erected in 1888 to the designs of C. J. Phipps, five sets of bridges, constructed by Messrs Clark and Bunnet, were installed 'supported by hydraulic rams and placed towards the rear of the stage proper. . . . Four of the "bridges" may be termed "bridges" proper, for they only rise to stage level, but a fifth and larger "bridge" can be taken 10 ft. above this level.'[28]

In 1896 two large lifts, hydraulically operated, were installed at Drury Lane.[29]

'The machinery for these two bridges was ordered in Austria, and put up by a London firm. Each bridge measures 40 ft. by 7 ft. 6 in., and they can be raised to nearly 12 ft. above stage floor level, whilst the fall under the stage is, I believe, 9 ft. The two bridges adjoin one another, and are only divided from each other and from the surrounding floor by a so-called "cassettenclappen" which is fixed to the slab of the bridge. The appliances sent from Austria have been adapted for the so-called "sea-saw" movement under the direction of Mr. Brown'[30] (fig.175).

As far back as March, 1882, attention had been called to the fact that the whole of Drury Lane

'was in one fire risk, and it was recommended that a solid wall of masonry should be built from the foundations to a height of 20 ft. above the roof so as to separate the stage from the auditorium, all necessary openings between stage, orchestra and dressing

Fig.175. Drury Lane: the stage in 1898, showing in front the two hydraulic lifts, and behind the two electric bridges

rooms to be furnished with iron doors and the stage opening with a heat proof curtain or screen of an approved kind'.[31]

And in July of the same year a notice was served under the Metropolis Management and Building Acts Amendement Act, 1878, requiring a proscenium wall but not a fire proof curtain. The proscenium wall was presumably built prior to 1887, when a further report noted that 'an iron door is wanted at the prompt side to complete the fireproof separation of the stage and the auditory'.[32]

In 1894 the L.C.C. was reporting that there was no fire-resisting curtain, and that the 'underside of the sixpenny gallery is formed of wood, canvas and plaster'. As a result we read of 'the removal of all inflammable materials from the walls, ceiling of tiers, &c, and their replacement with fire-resisting materials',[33] and of the resolution of the 23rd May to do away with the 6d., or upper, gallery (fig.116).[34] By May, 1898, a fireproof curtain had been fixed and was in working order, and the proscenium wall was made fireproof throughout.[35] In the same year electric lighting was installed, and Edwin O. Sachs was called in to prepare plans for electrifying the stage equipment. The stage floor was to be

'divided into six large sections, (it would appear, however, that only the four described here were actually installed at this time) on two of which hydraulic power has already

Fig.176. Drury Lane: *right,* the plungers of the hydraulic lifts, *left,* the lattice structure of one of the electric bridges

been temporarily tried' [i.e. on the two central ones]. 'The first sections to be worked by electricity were the fifth and sixth, i.e. those most distant from the auditorium. These are the sections completed up to date. . . . Each section measures 40 ft. by 7 ft. 6 in., and forms an independent whole. The idea is to raise the stage floor above the stage to the extent of 12 ft., and to lower below it to the extent of 8 ft., for the purposes of scenic effect. . . . By a combination of sections working at different levels the most varied effects can be obtained (figs.175,176), and it is of course possible to couple two or more sections together for a specific purpose. Each section of the stage now takes the form of a platform resting on a lattice work "bridge", the "bridge" being suspended by wire cables, part of the weight being taken up by counterweights, whilst the difference and any load is moved by a winding gear driven by an electric motor.'[36]

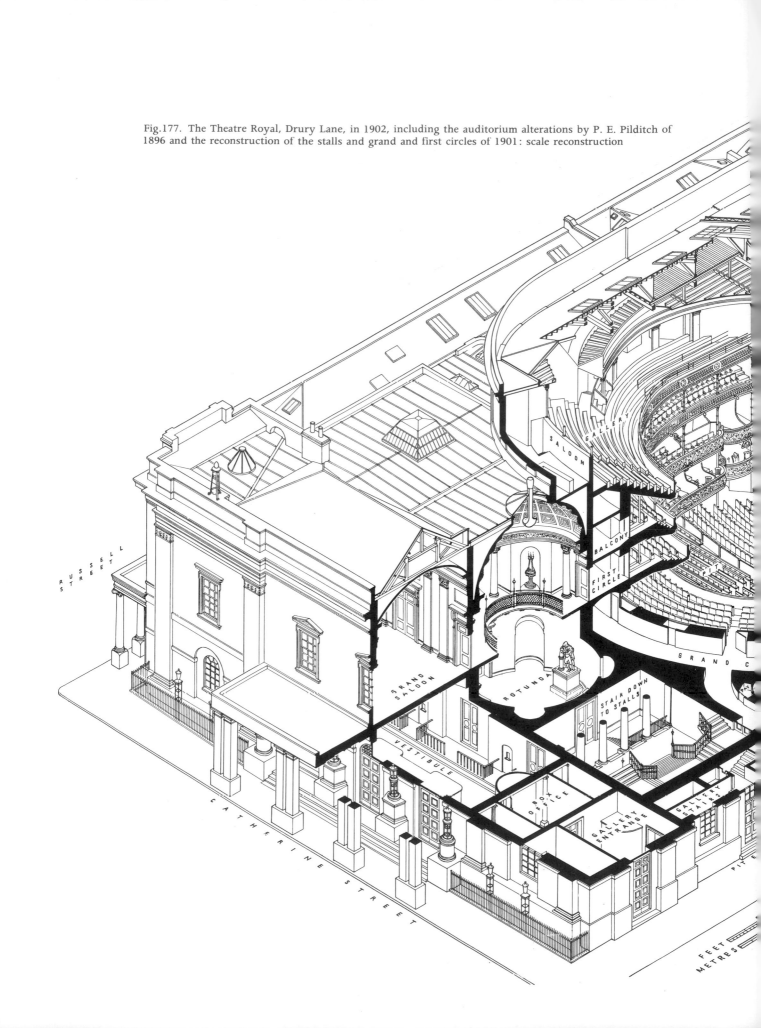

Fig.177. The Theatre Royal, Drury Lane, in 1902, including the auditorium alterations by P. E. Pilditch of 1896 and the reconstruction of the stalls and grand and first circles of 1901: scale reconstruction

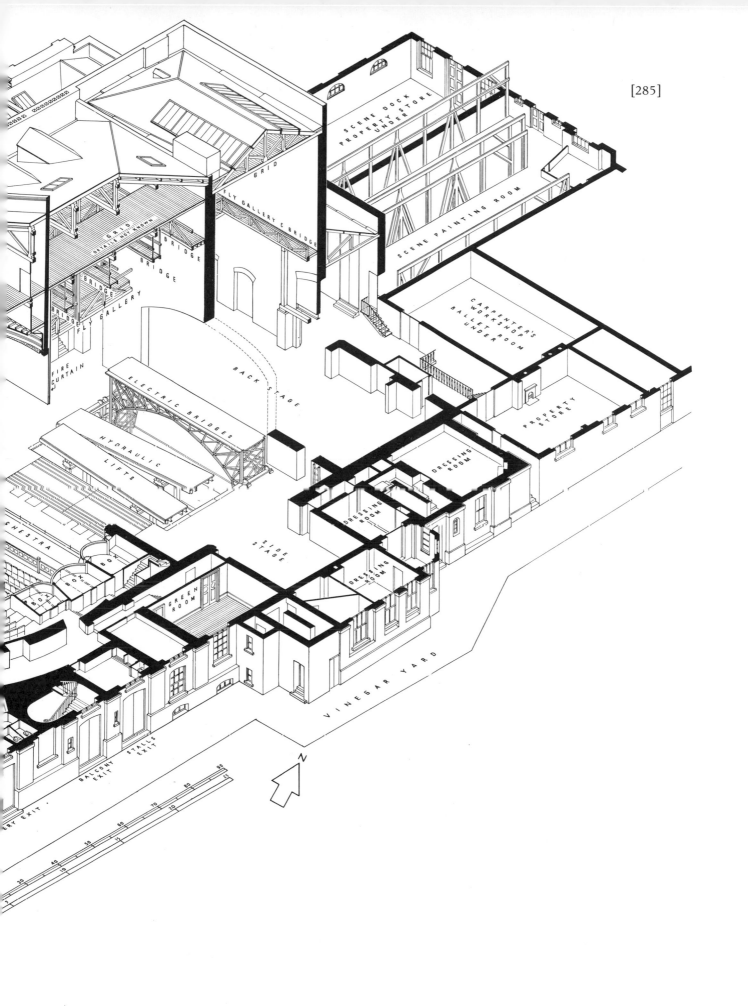

SCENE DOCK
PROPERTY UNDERSTORE

SCENE PAINTING ROOM

CARPENTER'S WORKSHOP
BALLET ROOM UNDER

GRID

FLY GALLERY & BRIDGE

GRID

PROPERTY STORE

STAGE MACHINERY ROOM

BRIDGE

BRIDGE

BRIDGE

FLY GALLERY

BACK STAGE

FIRE CURTAIN

ELECTRIC BRIDGES

DRESSING ROOM

HYDRAULIC

DRESSING ROOM

LIFTS

SIDE STAGE

DRESSING ROOM

ORCHESTRA

BOX

BOX

BOX

GREEN ROOM

VINEGAR YARD

GALLERY EXIT

BALCONY EXIT

STALLS EXIT

N

30 40 50 60 70 80 90

During this year it was also proposed to remove 'all carpenter's work and the wardrobe stores from the working parts of the house'[37] and new buildings were erected the following year at the rear of the existing building (fig.177) containing 'a carpenter's shop, a wardrobe store, a ballet room, and a paint room'[38] connected by a roofed corridor alongside the rear wall of the theatre. In 1901 further alterations were put in hand, including the removal of the private boxes at pit level to enable this area to be brought into line with development else-where, extending the pit to the full width of the auditorium beneath the Grand Circle. The pit was now subdivided between nine rows of pit stalls, and what amounts to seventeen rows of pit seats, separated from each other by a partition; it was still approached by the same entrances as previously, but it now became necessary to provide a means of access for the occupants of the stalls from the main entrance. This was achieved by introducing stairs in the vestibule to the right of the Rotunda, leading down to a new corridor beneath that which already surrounded the pit (fig.177). Stairs in the corridor then led up beneath the pit en-trances to the stalls level, connecting at this point with exits on either side of the building. At some previous date the family boxes at Grand and first circle levels had been removed, but now both circles were reconstructed with steelwork and columns, and advanced some 4 feet nearer the stage to permit additional seating to be installed: six rows in the former, and seven in the latter. At first circle level only the seven centre bays projected to the new line of the Grand Circle below, the sides being stepped back by one row. In July, 1901, it is also recorded [39] that the flies were being altered, but not with fire-resisting materials, and it is possible that the trusses strengthening the flies (p.195) were removed as a part of this operation.

Although the Local Government Act, 1888, placed the responsibility of licensing authorities regarding buildings for stage plays on the County and County Councils, Drury Lane, as a Patent theatre, required no licence.[40] As the granting or witholding of a licence was the only means of control by which the L.C.C. could insist on the provision of safety requirements, it is not surprising that this theatre was now found to be deficient in many respects, and in 1904 the L.C.C. presented a report formulating 144 'alterations necessary to bring the theatre as far as practicable up to the standard required for a modern place of public entertain-ment',[41] in accordance with the regulations made by the Council in July, 1901. The matter was taken to arbitration, and 111 of the requirements were upheld. As a result further major alterations (fig.178) were put in hand by Pilditch, which involved

'the removal of the wooden balcony, gallery and ceilings, and the substitution of steel, concrete, and non-inflammable plaster. The cantilever system has not been adopted, and the overhanging structures are supported on solid steel columns, as this plan was used when the lower tiers were reconstructed. In addition the gallery has been pro-vided with fresh exits, and four new stone staircases, instead of the two old spiral ones, have been put in. The proscenium opening is also undergoing considerable decorative changes (fig.179). On the other side of the curtain the alterations are of a

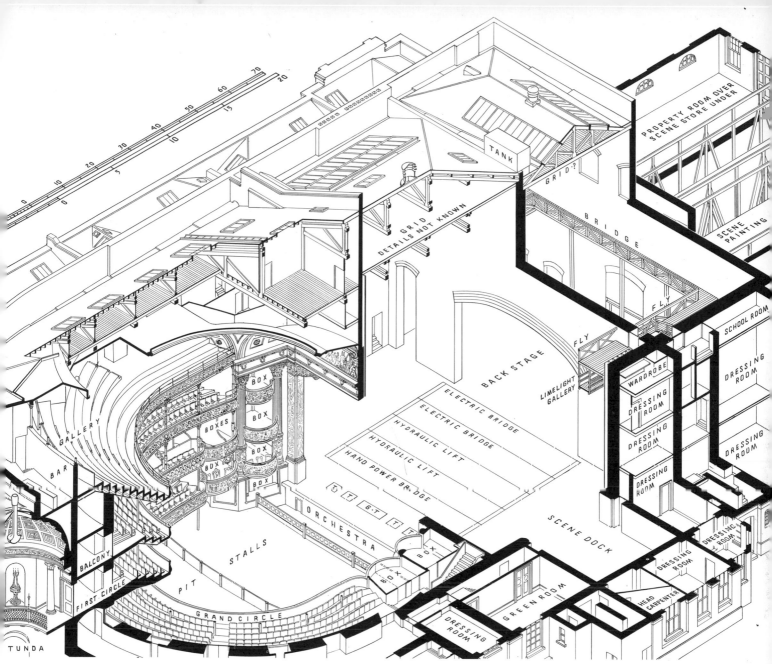

Fig.178. The Theatre Royal, Drury Lane, P. E. Pilditch, 1904: scale reconstruction based on drawings and photographs in the G.L.C. collection

still more extensive character. The stage has been rebuilt from basement to roof. The stage itself, which was of wood, is now of steel, with teak boarding; there are new flies of steel, and a new grid from which the scenery cloths are suspended; and they will be worked by new wire ropes, instead of hemp, running in steel channels with counterweights.'[42]

The existing bridges had been retained, and an additional 'hand powered bridge' had been installed in front. A grave trap and four corner traps – seen for the first time on the drawings prepared for these alterations[43] – were presumably retained from earlier times, possibly, even, from the original Wyatt stage.

Fig.179. Drury Lane: auditorium after the alterations of 1904

Sachs' main achievement in the modernisation of the British stage, however, was at Covent Garden, where he completely reconstructed the stage. In 1899 he was appointed to be general technical adviser 'on all matters architectural and mechanical'[44] to this theatre. Various alterations were put in hand that year in the front of house, mainly concerned with the improvement of the safety and sanitary facilities. Backstage a large 'wing' store was formed to ease the change of scenes, and a 'full installation of electric light[45] in four colours – white, red, blue and yellow' was carried out. At this time the open portico above the *porte cochère* was filled in with a smoking lounge. It was, however, in the following season that the main alterations were put in hand. These necessitated the complete gutting of the stage area 'so that nothing of the old stage from "gridiron" to cellar' remained, with the exception of the two raking fly galleries. The existing roof over the stage was raised, in a similar manner to that of the Leicester Theatre Royal, some 20 feet, to permit the insertion of a new gridiron to carry a 'Brandt patent counterweight system' so that it would be possible to hang the scenery for three operas at a time, balanced by weights. A new patent extract ventilator was incorporated in the rebuilt stage roof. The scene docks, on either side of the stage, were remodelled, one being equipped with a 28 feet high opening to the street, another having several floors for the storage of 'planned scenery, such as rocks, groups, &c'[46] and a new scenery store for 'cloths' was formed beneath the rear stage area.

The front of the stage was cut back to the proscenium wall, and the space gained was taken up by the orchestra pit, leaving room for additional stalls seating. The proscenium wall, built up in 1882, was raised to the new roof level. 'The opening of the stage towards the auditorium had to be equipped with an enormous fire-resisting curtain', and the earlier wall separating the under-stage area from the orchestra pit having been removed, "a strong party-wall [was] built from stage level downwards into the cellar'.[47] Footlights edged the stage, and there was a carpet cut on the line of the false proscenium. The new stage (fig.183) was flat, and at the front there was a trapped area so subdivided that portions of it could be used as a grave trap or as corner traps. Beyond this the stage was divided into five 8 feet wide sections, each of which contained a bridge and a 2 feet wide flap through which scenery could be raised or lowered. The first two bridges could be raised 6 feet above, or lowered 8 feet below, the stage, and were constructed on two levels so that sections could be raised or lowered as minor platforms or traps. The remaining three bridges could be raised 9 feet, or lowered 8 feet. All the bridges were worked electrically, as were the traps in the rear stage leading to scene stores below stage level. Each section was equipped with a pair of chariots, with wing ladders to support both wings and lights (figs. 180–1).

Above the stage each of the eight sections was reflected by a set of ten lines to take borders and cloths. In addition each section had provision for an electric light batten, and a wooden lattice girder to which heavy items of scenery could be attached. Each set of wire lines ran over iron pulleys on the grid to a counterweight system against the side wall, which could be worked by one man either from fly gallery or stage level. The property room, which until now occupied the traditional position in the roof space, was moved to a new floor built above the remodelled rear wing, which now contained dressing rooms and 'all modern sanitary arrangements'.[48] Hydraulic lifts were installed to serve the wardrobe and tailoring departments on the upper floors.

The gas chandelier was replaced by the present double ring of electric pendant lights, and a heating and ventilating system was introduced. 'By adopting the Plenum system and doing away with the large chandelier which acted as an outlet in former years the existence of draughts will no doubt be diminished. The fans for the ventilating system are electrical.'[49]

The main changes to the front of house at this stage (fig.182) were in the pit. The previous subdivision of this space was now removed, following the trend earlier introduced by the Bancrofts in further alterations to the Haymarket, carried out by Phipps in 1880, when they decided to 'abolish the pit and fill the whole of the ground floor of the house with high-priced seats'.[50] The former pit stalls had been approached down steps on either side from the corridor providing access to the first tier of boxes. The new arrangement made use of the central rear entrance which had previously given access only to the pit. This was now altered, and a new wide corridor surrounded the whole pit area, from which this entrance, and two new entrances immediately adjoining the orchestra pit, could be approached. A direct exit to Hart – now Floral – Street was also provided. The spaces earlier occupied by the pit stall entries were filled by two additional boxes.

Fig.180. Covent Garden: the stage in 1901

While the advantages of sinking theatres into the ground (p.264) to reduce the escape distance from the gallery to the street were accepted, it was nevertheless pointed out that they were only achieved at extra cost, occasioned by the additional waterproofing necessitated by the greater amount of basement work involved. However, even if these higher costs were accepted, it might not always be possible to sink the building to a greater depth than some 15 feet below ground level, or even less if the public sewers were not that deep, as it was necessary to drain the lower levels 'direct to the sewer'. These restrictions were mentioned in a paper read to the Architectural Association in December, 1903,[51] and in the same paper the author, H. T. B. Spencer, directed the greater part of his discourse to a discussion of the problems of auditorium design which he saw mainly as the difficulties of incorporating within a single space the many differing areas needed to house the various classes of society who were to be accommodated in the theatre. Earlier (p.174) we noted Wyatt's preoccupation with the problems of separating the prostitutes and their potential clients from the rest of the audience, but among the respectable members of the audience a whole range of variations from private to family boxes, dress circles to upper circles, has been noted, and even among the 'gods' the divisions of slips, amphitheatre, gallery stalls and gallery, all marked variations in price and comfort. The complications of theatre design which these many sub-divisions, each with its own duplication of exit stairs and passageways, presented is well illustrated by Spencer when he too considered the problems created when the once unified pit was subdivided to include orchestral stalls: 'the stalls people, who will enter from the main thoroughfare, have to get past the pit

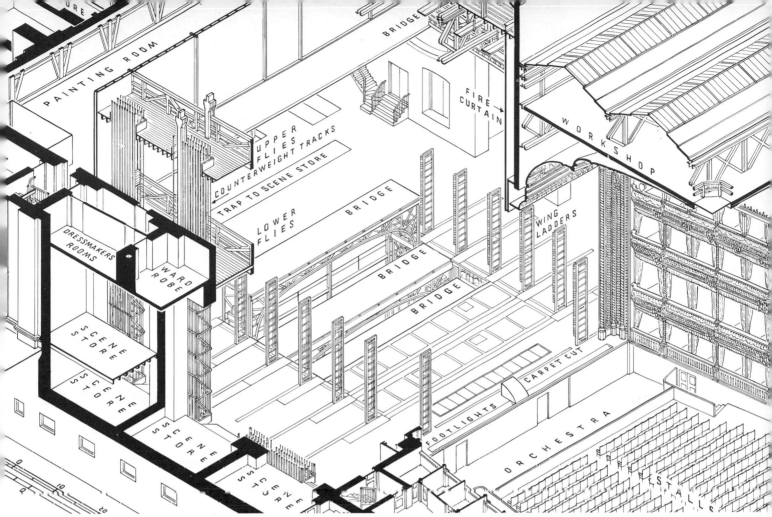

Fig.181. Covent Garden: the stage in 1901: detail of Fig.182

folk to their seats not far from the proscenium, while the occupants of the pit will generally have to be admitted and seated somewhere between the two points'. The current attitude to the classes is well illustrated by the difference between 'people' and 'folk', but the real social comment lies in the fact that while the folk sit on benches separated from the people in their armchairs only by a low partition across the area, they must keep to their segregated area, and on no account may they mix, at least until they have turned the corner outside the theatre, and even then the stalls people will most probably have entered straight into their carriages on the main street, to be conveyed safely home still unpolluted.

Since, however, the stalls people are of the same social order as those in the dress circle, or private boxes, they could share the same foyer and retiring rooms. In this case it was considered advisable to keep the dress circle as near to street level as possible, thus permitting the stalls people to by-pass the pit folk by ascending any stairs to the dress circle foyer, making their way round the dress circle corridors, and descending by stairs adjoining the proscenium opening, to their orchestral stalls at the front of the area. A similar arrangement was noted earlier at the Theatre Royal, Leicester. Alternatively, it is suggested that by keeping 'the pit back low down, and the dress circle back as high as possible' it would be possible to provide a mezzanine-level corridor providing exclusive access from the entrance crush-hall direct, by a short flight of steps, to the stalls seats.

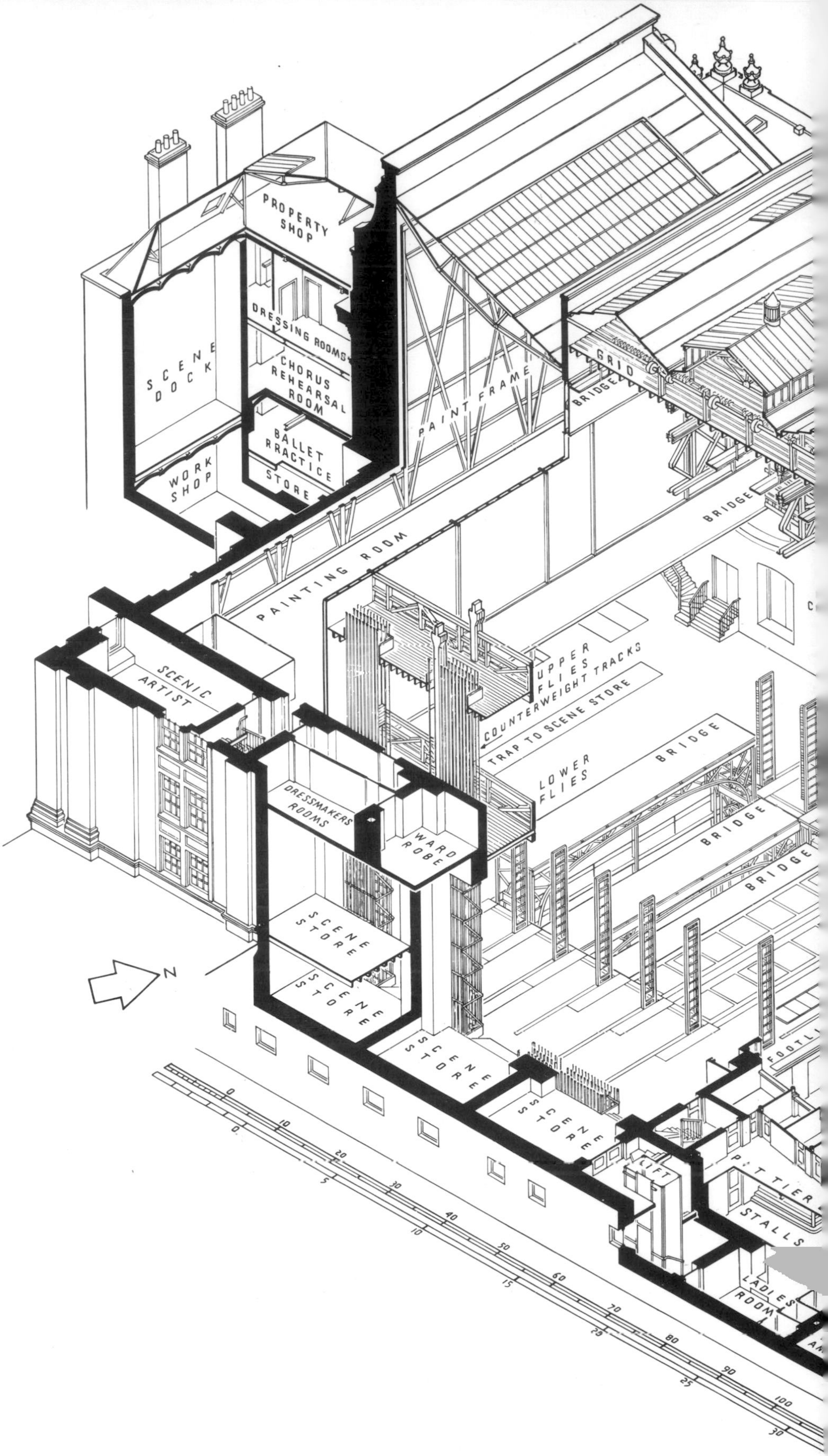

PROPERTY
SHOP

DRESSING ROOMS

SCENE
DOCK

CHORUS
REHEARSAL
ROOM

BALLET
PRACTICE

PAINT FRAME

GRID

BRIDGE

WORK
SHOP

STORE

BRIDGE

PAINTING ROOM

SCENIC
ARTIST

UPPER
FLIES

COUNTERWEIGHT TRACKS

TRAP TO SCENE STORE

LOWER
FLIES

BRIDGE

DRESSMAKERS
ROOMS

WARD
ROBE

BRIDGE

BRIDGE

N

SCENE
STORE

SCENE
STORE

SCENE
STORE

SCENE
STORE

FOOTLI

LIFT

1st TIER

STALLS

LADIES
ROOM

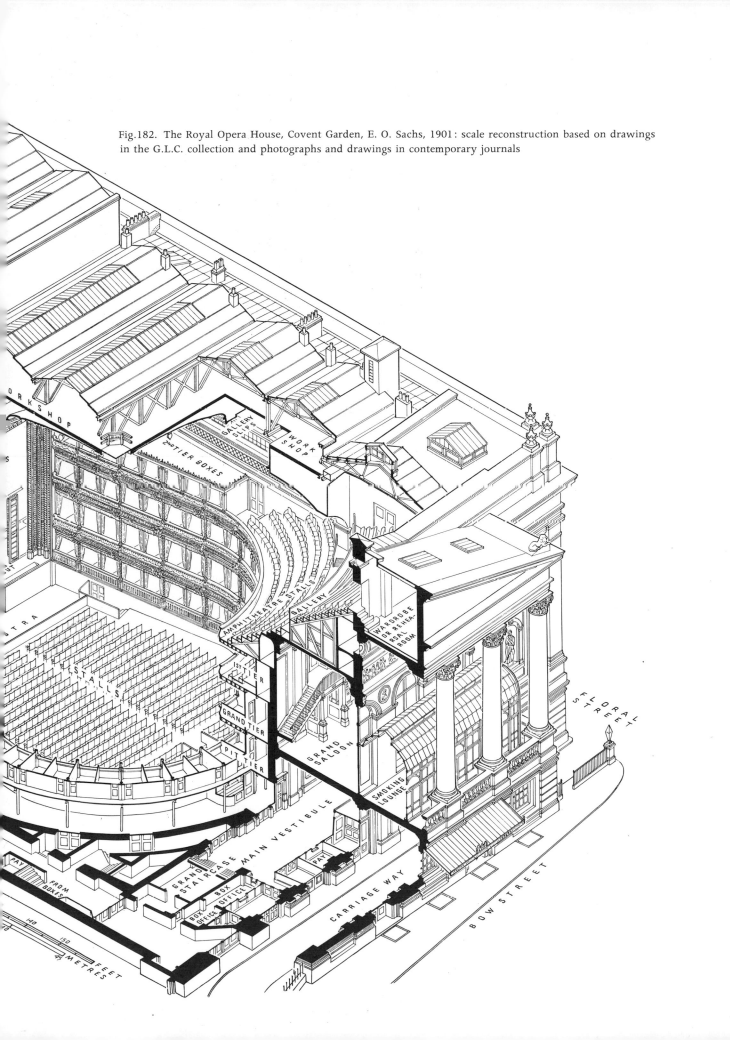

Fig.182. The Royal Opera House, Covent Garden, E. O. Sachs, 1901: scale reconstruction based on drawings in the G.L.C. collection and photographs and drawings in contemporary journals

Fig.183. Covent Garden: *upper left*, paint room; *extreme left and centre*, counterweight tracks; *right*, front curtain and proscenium opening

These examples serve to indicate the complications of planning which the class-conscious structure of the period inflicted on theatre design, problems which were further complicated by the repetitious provision of saloons, foyers, lavatories, and cloakrooms required by each area.

> 'In some houses you get almost the same class of people in both the stalls and the dress circle, and perhaps to some extent in the "upper circle", and, therefore, there is no object in not permitting them the common use of the foyer and saloon. But in other theatres the stalls would be patronised by a set as distinct from that in the dress circle as the latter is from the upper circle, and, therefore, each has to be separately catered for.'

So we see that these complications vary according to the area in which the theatre is situated. Spencer says that it might be possible to replace the unreserved pit by cheap reserved seats 'approached through the same entrance as the stalls', but his thoughts on the subject appear to have little social significance and to be largely conditioned by questions of economy in the simplification of theatre design.

It was to the continent that one had to look for simplified auditorium design based on ideas of social equality, which led to the construction, as early as 1887, of the Peoples' Theatre in Worms (fig.184.a.b.), created to 'promote the spirit of community by assisting the spectator to see his neighbour near him'. Boxes were largely dispensed with so that there should be no feeling 'of exclusion or privilege with regard to view or position'.[52] The higher-priced seats were in the middle of the house, their only difference being that they were more comfortable – those members of the audience who occupied them were still sitting in the midst of their fellow tradesmen. There were in fact some fourteen boxes arranged around the rear wall of the auditorium, with a narrow gallery of seats all round the walls at the upper level, but the main body of seats was arranged in a fan-shape on a single slope, with twenty-six rows of seats extending the full width of the auditorium, and exits leading direct from the ends of the front fourteen rows through doors into enclosing lounges and escape stairs. Such an arrangement was, however, unlikely to have found favour in Britain. Sachs makes a compelling contrast between continental and British theatres at this time. He says:

> 'no more striking demonstration can be afforded of the difference in requirements of theatre-building than a comparison of Continental ideas on the subject with those prevalent in England. In this country, with but few exceptions, the Private Theatre is governed in its requirements by investors, or ambitious actors, who cater for the pleasure of sensation-seekers, among a people practically devoid of any feeling for architecture.'[53]

As a result, the arrangements already noted in the Royal English Opera House and at Her Majesty's are typical of the accepted pattern, providing for two or three tiers arranged on a slight curve facing the proscenium opening. Unlike the Worms theatre, where all the members of the audience might see one another, here

> 'It is not necessary to give a sumptuous view of the stalls and orchestra from the body of the tier: in fact, you cannot do that without setting the centre of the curve further back, and so diminishing the seating area. But, with no extra depth of auditorium at your disposal, it is possible to get more seats in a tier as such described than if the more familiar horse-shoe or semi-circle be used, with the great advantage that each seat commands a full view of the stage.'[54]

The main aim, therefore, would seem to be to include as many seats as possible within the building, and to this end the rows were more closely spaced than was the case in the Worms theatre, where the space between them was sufficient to permit gangway access across the full width of the auditorium to the exit doors on either side. In the discussion following Spencer's talk a speaker noted that 'Ground rents were enormous, so the planning of the seating had to be largely a matter of returns from the financial point of view. The crowding of seats, therefore, was not always attributable to the bad planning of the architect, but to pressure from the managers. This also accounted for the smallness of crush-rooms, saloons, etc.'[55]

[296]

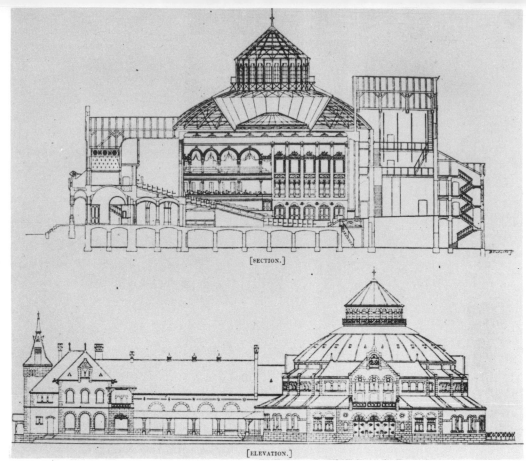

(a) section and elevation

Fig.184. The People's Theatre, Worms, Otto March, 1887

(b) ground plan

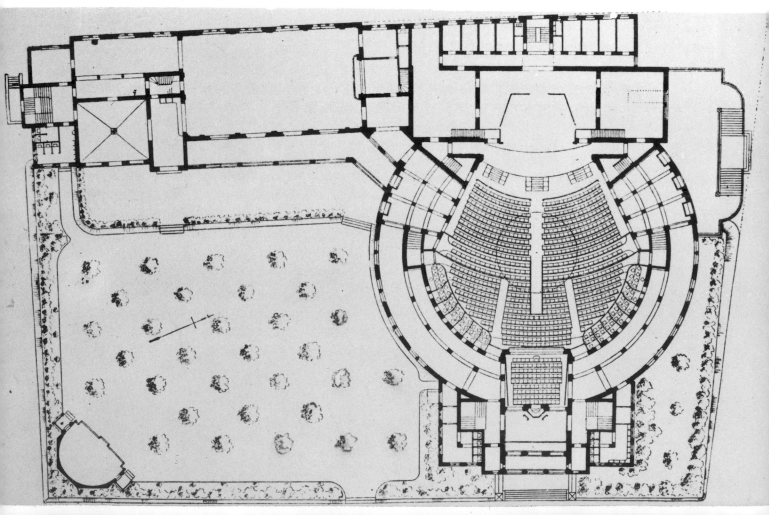

Spencer had little to say about the stage apart from mentioning that where 'limelight is likely to be used fireproof chambers must be provided for the tanks, with direct ventilation through an external wall'. Accommodation was to be provided for the resident engineer and his assistants, as well as the stage carpenter, who should have an office and a workshop, which must be 'fireproof chambers with iron doors, and ventilated through an external wall'. The stage manager required a room communicating directly with the stage, together with a room for the orchestra, and possibly one for the conductor. While a property room was necessary, there was no longer any need to make provision for a scenic artist, and the scenery and properties not needed for the current production should be stored elsewhere away from the theatre.

The stage at Drury Lane was reconstructed in its present form following a fire which broke out at 4.00 a.m. on the 25th March, 1908.[56] The stage area, above stage level, was burnt out (fig.185), but, the fire curtain being lowered at the time, the auditorium was only 'slightly damaged by water'. In the rebuilding which resulted, the opportunity was taken to remove the central arched cross-wall, which no longer served any good purpose, and to provide a clear space of 80 feet deep by 79 feet wide. The stage walls were raised some 20 feet to permit a new steel grid (figs.186–7) to have a clear height above the stage of 70 feet. Both roof and grid were now supported on six steel lattice girders spanning the width of the stage. The scenes were hung from a new counterweight system, with wire lines set at approximately 1 foot centres; in addition there were four timber wheels and barrels (fig.127) set on the centre line of the stage, and a number of hemp lines tied off to cleats on the fly gallery. In the roof there was a 30 feet square skylight, arranged to act as a smoke vent in case of fire.

A new fire curtain was installed 'with improvements, including the buffers to insure it descending gradually and evenly, and stopping without any jar, and the water sprinkler, which is placed immediately behind the curtain, so that in the event of a fire it automatically discharges a continuous stream of water on the back of the curtain to keep it cool'.[57] The fly galleries were, as was suggested by Buckle and Hexamer, supported on lattice girders on their outer edges, spanning the full 80 feet depth of the stage, with a limelight gallery hung beneath the floor, and above, hanging from the grid, there was a loading gallery for the counterweights on either side.

At stage level the electric and hydraulic bridges had survived the fire, but an additional electric bridge now replaced the grave and corner traps at the front of the stage. It is, however, an interesting reflection that all this expensive equipment, in full working order, is today hidden below a later stage surface. It would appear as though Herr Rudolph's comments regarding the limitations imposed by the fixed positions of the bridges and elevators were valid, and on this point Irving Pichel was to say in the 1920s that these devices 'are deadening, and divert effort from the true end of all experiment and advance in the Theatre. There is no doubt in my mind that the sort of theatre that wants to be built is one in which the machinery is reduced to a minimum – efficient, controllable, but never controlling the sort of work that must be done on the stage.'[58] Earlier he notes that 'scenery is of two types,

Fig.185. Drury Lane: roof of stage after fire of 1908, showing grid and counterweight pulleys still in position

pieces that are suspended from ropes . . . and pieces that stand on the floor'.[59] By 1949 it was possible to read that the need for apertures in the stage floor 'formerly considered essential . . . has almost entirely died out'.[60] As a result of the alterations Drury Lane is now seen to represent the ideal picture-frame stage in which a maximum area of stage floor is provided, together with a side dock for the storage of scenery required in the current production, and with fully mechanised facilities for the raising of scenery above the stage, suspended from the counterweighted wire lines of the flying system.

In 1911 the entrance vestibule, saloon and grand staircases, were all modified and re-decorated,[61] but it was not until 1921 that the management put in hand a complete rebuilding of the auditorium (fig.188), which was to bring the theatre into line with the new pattern of auditoria design, seen in the Royal English Opera House and Her Majesty's. In these altera-tions the old auditorium and massive circular walls were completely removed, but the existing roof was retained intact until 1952, when the timber trusses were amputated, and the remaining sections, carrying roof and ceiling, were supported by a series of new steel trusses.[62] Within the remaining shell a new auditorium was constructed with three canti-levered tiers directly facing an enlarged proscenium opening, from which they were sep-arated, on either side, by two groups each of seven boxes. These boxes were raised to a sufficient height to enable the ends of the orchestra pit and the stalls seats to extend beneath. The stalls were no longer divided from the pit by a partition, the new division being no more than a cross gangway, and the pit benches were replaced by chairs. The amphitheatre benches, too, were replaced by individual seats in what was now called the Balcony.

Fig.186. Drury Lane: grid and lantern light

Spencer had noted that 'in the general distribution of seats above the ground floor, theatres are classed as two-tier or three-tier houses, three tiers being the limit allowed by the L.C.C. Sometimes the top or gallery tier is not constructed over the upper circle, but at the back of it, and somewhat raised above it',[63] as was done at Her Majesty's. Drury Lane was therefore working, with its three tiers, to the maximum permitted by the regulations. All the tiers were raked at a sufficient slope to enable each member of the audience to have a clear view of the stage over the heads of the row in front. At the back of the Grand Circle were seven roomy boxes, so arranged that these too had a clear view over the heads of the Grand Circle audience. 'The floors to all the circles and galleries as well as to the boxes, are constructed in reinforced concrete, the whole of which were laid on the Self-Sentering expanding metal process, which was also used for the flat roof.'[64] The portion of auditorium directly related to the side boxes was roofed with a flat arch, the remainder rising to a higher level where it was finished with a flat ceiling. The proscenium opening had now been

Fig.187. Drury Lane: grid from stage, with counterweight tracks and loading gallery

widened from 37 feet 6 inches to 42 feet 6 inches to fit in with the new design, and as a result the fire curtain had also to be enlarged. As is only to be expected, each separate part of the auditorium was now provided with duplicate escape stairs direct to the open air.

In spite of the late date of the rebuilding, the same problems persist, in that it was still felt necessary to make provision for the 'stalls people' to approach their seats from the main entrance hall by way of two flights of steps, which now led down through the ground floor of the Rotunda to a stalls foyer and cloakrooms, and thence to passages and stairs leading up through the remaining vestiges of the earlier curved auditorium walls to entry doors providing access to the rear of the orchestra stalls. The same doors were also used as emergency exits opening directly to the open air on the south side. True to tradition, the 'pit folk' had their own entry and pay box opening off Vinegar Yard and leading direct to the rear of the pit, an exit in Russell Street being provided in a corresponding position on the opposite side of the house.

The Grand Circle, being the best part of the house, was still approached by the two Grand Staircases, which remained on either side of the Rotunda, with the Grand Saloon situated over the entrance hall. Exits from either side of the front of the Grand Circle led back through corridors to the half-landings of the Grand Staircases. The first circle audience mixed with the upper circle in their ascent, as far as the Grand Staircase landings, where an individual flight on either side led up to the rear of the circle. Additional exits midway on either side led direct to the open air, by way of the earlier balcony stairs now adapted to this purpose. The balcony had two sets of stairs designed (p.267) with the two flights arranged one above the other in the same brick shaft. Each has its own entry and pay box, the one leading to the upper part of the tier, the other to the lower, front, portion. The balcony bar was retained in a similar position to the earlier arrangement, set within the one remaining portion of the circular outer wall of the earlier auditorium. During these alterations the whole theatre was ventilated by a balanced Plenum system, which blew washed and heated fresh air into the building, and extracted the vitiated air at high level through outlets situated on the roof.

It was now claimed that:

> 'As far as the means of entrance and exit are concerned, Drury Lane, it may, without fear of contradiction, be asserted is surpassed by no other London theatre. Large as the house is it can be emptied within a very few minutes, and the mere idea of congestion has been placed outside the limits of possibility. Every seat in the building is a modern tip-up upholstered armchair, while ample knee room and wide gangways replace the somewhat confined accommodation of the old building.'[65]

As a result of these alterations, Drury Lane may also be seen to represent an excellent example of what today is called a traditional 'picture-frame' theatre (fig. 189), with its stage viewed through the opening in the proscenium wall. This 'orthodox "picture-frame" stage' could still be described in 1961 as 'the type of stage that is in almost universal use in the

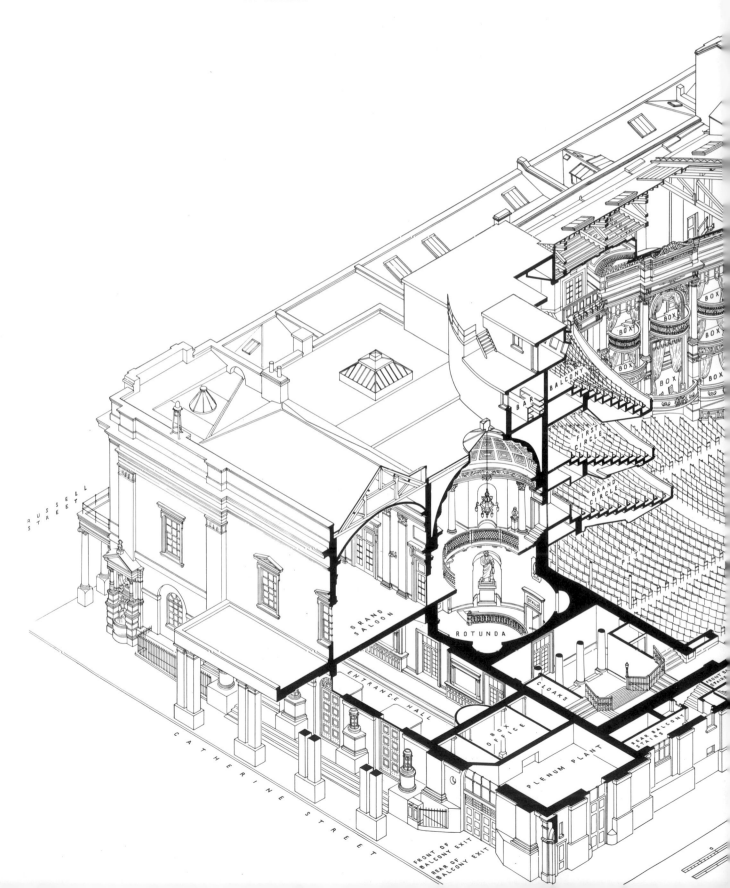

Fig.188. The Theatre Royal, Drury Lane in 1958–9, with stage as rebuilt in 1908 and auditorium as redesigned in 1921–2: scale reconstruction

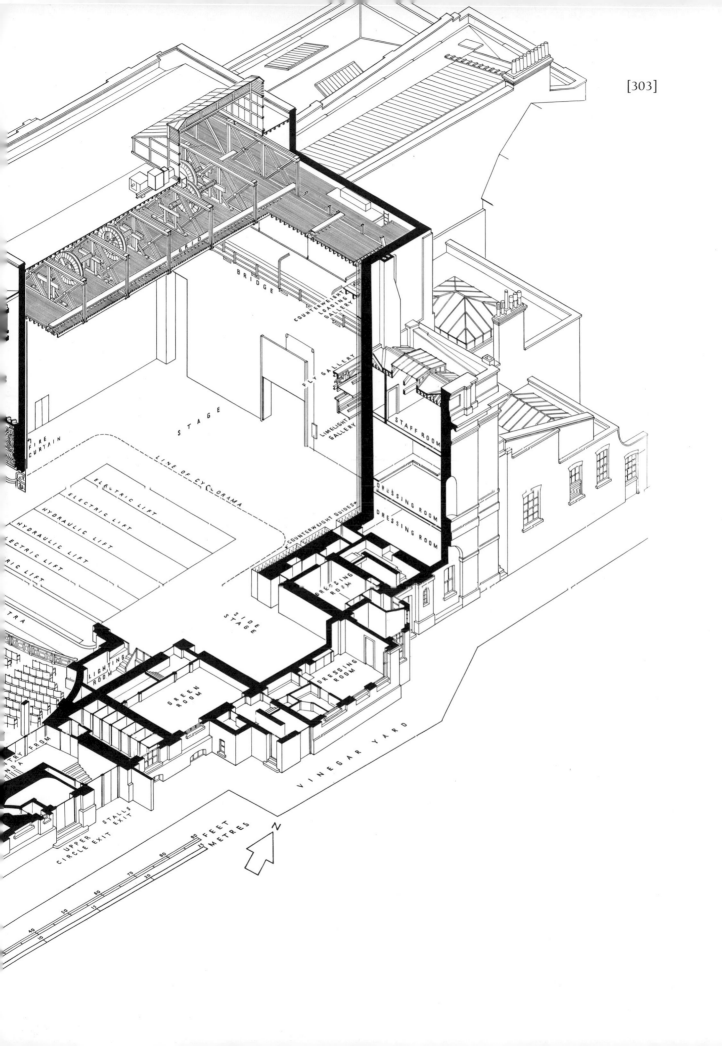

FIRE CURTAIN

GRID

BRIDGE

COUNTERWEIGHT LOADING GALLERY

FLY GALLERY

LIMELIGHT GALLERY

STAFF ROOM

DRESSING ROOM

DRESSING ROOM

STAGE

LINE OF CYCLORAMA

ELECTRIC LIFT

ELECTRIC LIFT

HYDRAULIC LIFT

HYDRAULIC LIFT

ELECTRIC LIFT

ELECTRIC LIFT

COUNTERWEIGHT GUIDES

DRESSING ROOM

SIDE STAGE

DRESSING ROOM

ORCHESTRA

LIGHTING ROOM

GREEN ROOM

DRESSING ROOM

ENTRY FROM VERANDA

VINEGAR YARD

UPPER CIRCLE EXIT

STALLS EXIT

FEET

METRES

N

British Theatre',[66] but it is also as a reaction against this formal arrangement that many new theatre forms have evolved, the prototypes for which were in many instances being proposed, or even built, concurrently with the later buildings described here.

Although we speak of the traditional picture-frame theatre, this can now be seen to have been a comparatively recent innovation in the development of the playhouse as a whole. It is only just a century and a half since the actor was pushed – protesting – through the frame to accord with a particular theory based on the importance of the stage picture, a move, however, which conformed to the need to subdivide the fire-risk of theatres into smaller and more compact compartments. Safety requirements, involving additional financial expenditure, had to be forced on reluctant managements, and their reaction is well summed up in the remarks quoted earlier regarding the authorities at 'Spring-gardens, who might step in at any moment and require an expenditure of £3,000 or £4,000 on matters which they had not before deemed necessary.' It is enlightening to ponder on the conditions regarded, both by management and public, as acceptable prior to the enforcement of the regulations: narrow and winding stairs, blocked gangways, hinged seats of minimum dimensions, ceilings of board and canvas, and an almost total lack of ventilation.

Present demands for completely free uninhibiting spaces in which to experiment with new forms of theatrical expression must take into account that many of the limitations of existing theatres are in fact essential features necessary to protect an assembled audience from the dangers of fire and panic. Electricity may have replaced the naked flame on stage and in the auditorium, but the recent fire at The Maltings has demonstrated that the dangers are still present. This study has indicated the features of the developing playhouse directly relevant to the expression of the theatrical art, as well as those brought into being by conditions no longer apposite to modern needs. But in developing any new theatrical forms it would be as well to bear in mind E. A. Woodrow's dictum that 'It is the duty of the architect to design his building so as to reduce the chances of panic to a minimum.'

The picture-frame theatre was evolved for a particular form of naturalistic production which in many respects remains valid today, but changes in social conventions, and the new forms evolved by modern playwrights requiring a return to a closer relationship of actor and audience, suggest that further changes are inevitable. The needs of spectacle are not, however, easily set aside, 'for they have therein devils and devices, to delight as well the eye as the ear'. Throughout theatrical history the scenic device is present, and will not lightly be dispensed with even though, with modern mechanics and lighting, the form may be differently presented. To the relationship of audience to actor must be added that of the scene, with all the attendant problems of directional relationship that this involves, and which were apparent even in the architectural environment of the late Elizabethan playhouses.

Fig.189. Drury Lane: auditorium after alterations of 1921–2

Notes to the Chapters

The following abbreviations have been used:

EES G. W. Wickham, *Early English Stages*
ES   E. K. Chambers, *The Elizabethan Stage*
MS   E. K. Chambers, *The Medieval Stage*
SL   *The Survey of London*
SS   *Shakespeare Survey*
TN   *Theatre Notebook*

CHAPTER 1

1. [p.1] Allen-Brown, *The History of the King's Works*, i, 2–3, fig. 1

2. [p.1] Arnott, 'The origins of Medieval Theatre in the Round', *TN*, xv, 84–7; Freeman, 'A Round Outside Cornwall', *TN*, xvi, 10–1; Holman, 'Cornish Plays and Playing Spaces', *TN*, iv, 52–4; Ordish, *Early London Theatres*, 18, 20

3. [p.1] Nicoll, *The Development of the Theatre*, 50, fig. 56; Chambers, *MS*, ii, 52–4

4. [p.2] Nicoll, *The Development of the Theatre*, figs. 61, 62

5. [p.2] Wickham, *EES*, i, 159–60

6. [p.3] Chambers, *MS*, ii, 80–2

7. [p.4] Nicoll, *The Development of the Theatre*, 53. Nagler; *Sources of Theatrical History*, 45–7

8. [p.4] Altman, *Theater Pictorial*, Pls. 56, 57, 58; Gascoigne, *World Theatre*, figs. 63. pl. x

9. [p.4] Altman, op. cit., pl. 64.; Gascoigne, op. cit. fig. 87

10. [p.4] This arrangement as illustrated could well result from the artist's difficulties in tackling the subject of complete enclosure of the central area by both audience and mansions.

11. [p.4] Southern, *Medieval Theatre in the Round*, 56; Schmitt, 'Was there a medieval Theatre in the Round? A Re-examination of the evidence', Pt. I, *TN*, XXIII, 130–42; Pt. II, *TN*, XXIV, 18–25

12. [p.4] Southern, *Medieval Theatre in the Round*, 18

13. [p.4] Ordish, *Early London Theatres*, 17

14. [p.4] Ibid., 21

15. [p.6] Leacroft, *The Buildings of Ancient Greece*, 30–3; Bieber, *The History of the Greek and Roman Theater*, figs. 491–2, 500, 507

16. [p.6] Leacroft, *The Buildings of Ancient Rome*, 14, 18 – see figs; Arnott, op. cit., 84–7; Wickham, *EES*, ii, 165f

17. [p.6] Wickham, *EES*, i, 51f

18. [p.7] Sharp, *A Dissertation on the Pageants or Dramatic Mysteries*, Harl. *MSS* 1948, fol 48. 17–8. Ascribed to Archdeacon Rogers, but compiled by his son, David: see, Salter, *Medieval Drama in Chester*, 54.

19. [p.7] Salter, Ibid, 59f

20. [p.7] Cameron and Kahrl, 'The N. Town plays at Lincoln', *TN*, XX, 61–9

21. [p.7] Wickham, *EES*, i, 172–5

22. [p.7] Streit, *Das Theater*

23. [p.7] See illustrations of two-storeyed mobile Spanish *autos* of the 17th century in Gascoigne, *World Theatre*, figs. 66, 67

24. [p.7] Salter, op. cit., 68; Langdon, H. N. 'Staging of the Ascension in the Chester Cycle', *TN*, XXVI, 53–60

25. [p.7] Wickham, *EES*, i, 95

26. [p.7] Hartley, *Life and Work of the People of England*, pl. 18; Fry, *The Greater English Church*, 24 – see fig. A 'Wind rope and a locker to the wind; a man to "tend" it, – sometimes three men.' Mentioned in Sharp, op, cit., 47

27. [p.8] In a similar manner the prohedria adjoining the orchestra of the Hellenistic theatre at Priene were duplicated at a higher point in the cavea when a raised stage was added.

28. [p.8] Wickham, *EES*, i, 155

29. [p.9] Chambers, *MS*, ii, 138, 360

30. [p.9] Laver, *Isabella's Triumph*, pls. 5, 6

31. [p.9] Wickham, *EES*, i, 172

32. [p.10] Craik, *The Tudor Interlude*, 2

33. [p.10] Ibid., 10

34. [p.10] Ibid., 19

35. [p.10] Chambers, *ES*, i, 150–1

36. [p.11] Wickham, *EES*, i, 208–9

37. [p.12] Ibid., 218

38. [p.12] Chambers, *ES*, i, 162–3

39. [p.12] Per Palme, *The Triumph of Peace*, 114

40. [p.12] Welsford, *The Court Masque*, 143

41. [p.12] Two banqueting houses, one 'the long house' or 'disguising house', were decorated by Holbein for the reception of a French embassy at Greenwich in 1527. Chambers, *ES*, i, 15, n. 4; Chambers, *MS*, ii, 189

42. [p.12] Chambers, *ES*, i, 175

43. [p.12] Paterson, 'The Stagecraft of the Revels Office during the Reign of Elizabeth' (Revels documents 1908, 202) in Prouty, *Studies in the Elizabethan Theatre*, 36

44. [p.12] Campbell, *Scenes and Machines on the English Stage during the Renaissance*, 112. Paterson, op. cit., 36–7

45. [p.12] Welsford, op. cit., 182

46. [p.12] Chambers, *ES*, i, 226–7, n. 6

47. [p.13] Nichols, *The Progresses and Public Processions of Queen Elizabeth*, i, 163, 166–7; Boas, *University Drama in the Tudor Age*, 91–3

48. [p.14] Campbell, op. cit., 107

49. [p.14] Prouty, op. cit., 46

50. [p.14] Wickham, *EES*, ii, 222

51. [p.15] Kernodle, *From Art to Theatre*, fig. 12

52. [p.15] Kernodle, op. cit., fig. 18

53. [p.15] Southern, 'A 17th Century Indoor Stage', *TN*, IX, 5, pl. 2

54. [p.15] Vitruvius, *The Ten Books of Architecture*, V.

55. [p.16] Kernodle, op. cit., 163

56. [p.16] Bibliothèque de l'Arsenal, *MS* 664, illustrated in Sonrel, *Traité de Scénographie*, pl. VIII

57. [p.16] Serlio, *Tutte l'opere d'architettura et prospettiva*, 1545. An edition of 1619 in the possession of the Royal Institute of British Architects was owned by Inigo Jones and Sir John Thornhill, and annotated by John Webb.

58. [p.18] Campbell, op. cit., 33

59. [p.18] The plan, published in Campbell, op. cit., fig. 34, from the English edition of 1611, shows doors at the end of the raised platform – C; that illustrated by Chambers, *ES*, IV, 357, does not.

60. [p.18] It has been suggested by some authorities that the rectangular boundary to the plan represents the margin of the original woodcut, and not the walls of a room. Serlio is, however, concerned here with the setting up of a temporary theatre within the bounds of an existing hall which may not of necessity have doors in the same positions in all instances. See Campbell, op. cit., 33.

61. [p.19] Southern, 'The Houses of the Westminster Play', *TN*, iii, 46–52

62. [p.19] Campbell, op. cit., 83

63. [p.19] Campbell, op. cit., 84; Chambers, *MS*, II, 196, 215

64. [p.19] Campbell, op. cit., 102

65. [p.19] Hall's *Chronicle* (1809), 735; quoted in Campbell, op. cit., 84, n. 2; also Welsford, op. cit., 144

66. [p.20] Southern, 'The Houses of the Westminster Play' *TN*, iii, 47; see also Chambers, *ES*, II, 72

67. [p.20] Chambers, *ES*, I, 227–8, n. 2

68. [p.21] Lawrenson, *The French Stage of the Seventeenth Century*, fig. 86

69. [p.21] Chambers, *ES*, I, 177

70. [p.22] Nicoll, *Stuart Masques and the Renaissance Stage*, 56

71. [p.22] Per Palme, op. cit., 114–5

72. [p.22] B. M. Harl. *MS* 293f.217, quoted in *SL*, XIII, 117

73. [p.22] *Royal Historical Society Transactions*, 2nd ser. ix, 236, quoted in *SL*, XIII, 118

74. [p.22] Campbell, op. cit., 110

75. [p.22] Per Palme, op. cit., 115

76. [p.23] *Wren Society*, XI, pl. viii

77. [p.23] Sekler, *Wren and his place in European Architecture*, 181; Stratton, 'The Westminster Dormitory', *The Builder*, 7 June, 1902, 559–63

78. [p.24] R. S., 'The Houses of the of the Westminster Play', *TN*, III, 46–52

79. [p.24] Wickham, *EES*, i, xli

CHAPTER 2

1. [p.25] Wickham, *EES*, I, 184

2. [p.25] Chambers, *ES*, I, 270–2

3. [p.25] Wickham, 'players at Selby Abbey, Yorks, 1431–1532', *TN*, XII, 46

4. [p.25] Chambers, *MS*, II, 188

5. [p.25] Kelly, *Notices illustrative of the Drama and other Popular Amusements at Leicester*, 15

6. [p.25] Hardy, 'Elizabethan Players in Winslow Church', *TN*, XII, 107

7. [p.25] Kelly, op. cit., 16

8. [p.25] Wickham, *EES*, I, 243

9. [p.26] Ibid., II, 184, 333

10. [p.26] Chambers, *ES*, III, 40–1

11. [p.26] Wickham, *EES*, II, 104

12. [p.26] Chambers, *ES*, II, 379–83

13. [p.26] Chambers records that Exeter had 'a regular theatre' as early as 1348, and also the building of a 'Game House' in Gt. Yarmouth by the Corporation in 1538–9, and its leasing to one Robert Copping on the understanding that he should permit players to perform plays or interludes there. Chambers, *MS*, II, 190, n. 1

14. [p.26] Ordish, *Early London Theatre*, 32

15. [p.27] Chambers, *ES*, II, 496; Sarlos, 'Development and Decline of the First Blackfriars Theatre' in Prouty, *Studies in the Elizabethan Theatre*, 145

16. [p.27] Sarlos, op. cit., 156; Armstrong, 'The Elizabethan Private Theatres. Facts and Problems', Society for Theatre Research Pamphlet, VI, 5
17. [p.27] Sarlos, op. cit., 159
18. [p.27] Sabbattini, *Practica di Fabricar scene e machine ne' theatri*, I, 68; Lawrenson, op. cit., 26–7
19. [p.28] Chambers, *ES*, II, 535. Chambers claims 1596 for the emergence of the practice of sitting on the stage.
20. [p.28] Eccles, 'Martin Peerson and the Blackfriars', *SS*, XI, 104
21. [p.29] Sarlos, op, cit., 170f
22. [p.29] Ibid., 172–3
23. [p.29] Ibid., 169
24. [p.29] Yates, *Theatre of the World,*
25. [p.29] Hodges, *The Globe Restored,* 171
26. [p.29] See footnote 75, p. 310
27. [p.29] Wickham, *EES*, II, 137, 171
28. [p.29] Chambers, *ES*, II, 392–3
29. [p.29] Wickham, 'The Privy Council Order of 1597', *The Elizabethan Theatre,* 21–44
30. [p.29] Ordish, op. cit., 35, 60
31. [p.29] Hartnoll, *The Oxford Companion to the Theatre,* 677
32. [p.30] Shapiro, 'The Bankside Theatres: Early Engravings', *SS*, I, pl. vi
33. [p.30] Ibid., pl. viiiA
34. [p.30] Chambers, *ES*, II, 406
35. [p.30] Ibid. 407–8
36. [p.30] Wickham, *EES*, II, 309
37. [p.30] Chambers, *ES*, II, 409
38. *SS*, I, pl. ix
39. [p.30] Ibid., pl. vii
40. [p.30] Chambers, *ES*, II, 413
41. [p.30] Nagler, *Sources of Theatrical History,* 116–17; Whalley, 'The Swan Theatre in the 16th Century', *TN*, XX, 73, pls. 3, 4
42. [p.32] Chambers, *ES*, II, 365
43. [p.33] Hodges, 'The Contract for Building the Hope Theatre 1613', *The Globe Restored,* 191–3
44. [p.33] Ordish, op. cit., 156
45. [p.34] Hodges, *The Globe Restored,* 187–90
46. [p.35] Idem, 'de Witt again', *TN*, V, 32–4, pls. 1, 2
47. [p.35] Wickham, *EES*, II, 306. The Heavens had presumably been an essential piece of scenic equipment dating from the medieval provision for Christ's ascension (p.7).
48. [p.35] Hodges, 'A Seventeenth-Century Heaven', *TN*, VI, 59–60, pls. 1, 2
49. [p.36] Chambers, *ES*, II, 208
50. [p.37] Audience seated at the extreme ends of the Festival Theatre in Stratford, Ontario, experience a similar loss of relationship with the actor when he performs in the immediate vicinity of the 'tiring house façade', and the projecting balcony likewise obscures the actors from their audience on the opposite side of the house; see photograph, Leacroft, 'Actor and Audience', Pt. I, *RIBA Journal,* LXX, No. 4, fig. 10, 145–55 For more detailed information regarding the numbers, behaviour and composition of the audiences, see: Harbage, *Shakespeare's Audience,* 19–116
51. [p.37] Chambers, *ES*, II, 366
52. [p.37] Bentley, *The Jacobean and Caroline Stage,* VI, 141–3
53. [p.38] Shapiro, 'The Bankside Theatres, Early Engravings, *SS*, i, pl. XIII, Shapiro, 'An original drawing of the Globe Theatre', *SS*, ii, 21–3, pls. XI, XII
54. [p.39] Chambers, 'Stowe's Annales', *ES*, II, 419
55. [p.40] Henslowe Papers, 116, reproduced in Harrison, *Introducing Shakespeare,* 106–7
56. [p.40] Wickham, *EES*, II, 318
57. [p.40] Speight, *William Poel and the Elizabethan Revival,* 86
58. [p.40] See also Chambers, *ES*, III, 74–82, for examples of actors entering the stage from differing places and sides.
59. [p.40] Reynolds, *The Staging of Elizabethan Plays at the Red Bull Theatre,* 130f

60. [p.40] Hosley, 'The Discovery Space in Shakespeare's Globe', *SS*, XII, 35–46

61. [p.40] See reconstruction: Leacroft, *The Buildings of Ancient Greece*, 32–3

62. [p.40] Chambers, Florio, 'Dictionary' (1598) *ES*, II, 539, n. 2

63. [p.40] Ibid., III, 79

64. [p.41] Adams, *The Globe Playhouse; its Design and Equipment,*

65. [p.41] Chambers, *ES*, III, 114, n. 1

66. [p.41] Ibid., III, 117; Armstrong, 'The Elizabethan Private Theatres. Facts and Problems', *Soc. for Theatre Research Pamphlet*, VI, 10

67. [p.41] Hodges, *The Globe Restored*, 58, 64; Chambers, *ES*, III, 92–4

68. [p.42] Chambers, *ES*, II, 542, n. 4; ibid., III, 91. Pepys mentions the 'musique-room' at the Red Bull which he visited on 23rd March, 1661. Wheatley, *The Diary of Samuel Pepys*, i, 338

69. [p.42] Armstrong, 'The Elizabethan Private Theatres', *Soc. for Theatre Research Pamphlet*, VI, 3f

70. [p.42] Chambers, *ES*, II, 513

71. [p.42] Bentley concludes that it was at the upper level (Bentley, op. cit. 5), as does Hosley in 'A Reconstruction of the Second Blackfriars', in Galloway, *The Elizabethan Theatre*, 74–88).

72. [p.42] Nagler, op. cit., 135

73. [p.42] Armstrong, 'The Elizabethan Private Theatres', *Soc. for Theatre Research Pamphlet*, VI, 7

74. [p.42] Hotson, *Commonwealth and Restoration Stage*, 98; Bentley, op. cit., 47–77

75. [p.42] Rosenfeld, 'Unpublished Stage Documents', *TN*, XI, 92–6; Bentley, op. cit., 86–115; Professor Langhans suggests that a drawing on a map of 1706 showing a rectangular courtyard theatre could be Salisbury Court. If, however, the theatre was in fact adapted from an old barn as noted by Miss Rosenfeld then this attribution seems unlikely. Langhans, 'A

Picture of the Salisbury Court Theatre', *TN*, XIX, 100–1, pls. 9, 10

76. [p.42] Hotson, *Commonwealth and Restoration Stage*, 108–9.

77. [p.43] Armstrong, 'The Elizabethan Private Theatres. Facts and Problems', *Soc. for Theatre Research Pamphlet*, VI, 6

78. [p.43] Chambers, *ES*, II, 556

79. [p.43] Armstrong, 'The Elizabethan Private Theatres', *Soc. for Theatre Research Pamphlet*, VI, 16

80. [p.43] *Historia Histrionica*, 1699; The Blackfriars, Cockpit and Salisbury Court 'had Pits for the Gentry, and Acted by Candlelight'; quoted in Nagler, op. cit., 162.

81. [p.43) Hotson, *Commonwealth and Restoration Stage*, 109

82. [43] Reynolds, op. cit., 6. See also footnote 68 above.

83. [p.44] Wickham, *EES*, II, 306

84. [p.45] Professor Nicoll suggests that the strip of yard on either side of the Swan stage was not particularly advantageous to the audience; a further reason for putting this space to more practical use as a part of the stage. Nicoll, 'Passing over the Stage', *SS*, XII, 47–55

85. [p.45] Dekker, *The Gull's Horne Booke*. Evidence for five entries at the Blackfriars after 1608 suggests a Palladian style façade with a central opening. Wren, R. M., 'The Five-entry Stage at Blackfriars', *Theatre Research*, VIII, 130–8; quoted in Freehafer, 'Inigo Jones's Scenery for *The Cid*', *TN* XXV, 84–92

86. [p.46] Chambers, *ES*, II, 539, n. 1

87. [p.47] R. M.'s *Micrologia*, 1629, quoted by Reynolds, op. cit., 98

88. [p.47] This may be an answer to Reynolds' problem (ibid., 117) concerning a character who speaks of the doors as being all unlocked, when only 'the right is supposed to lead to the street and is the only one, therefore, to be locked'. In speaking of double doors one uses the

plural to refer to what is in fact only one doorway.
89. [p.47] Chambers, *ES*, III, 75
90. [p.48] Nicoll, 'Passing over the Stage', *SS*, XII, 51
91. [p.48] Reynolds, op. cit., 10
92. [p.50] Nicoll, 'Passing over the Stage', *SS*, XII, 51
93. [p.50] Chambers, *ES*, II, 442–3

CHAPTER 3

1. [p.51] Chambers, *ES*, III, 375–7; Per Palme, *The Triumph of Peace*, 145
2. [p.51] Campbell, *Scenes and Machines on the English Stage during the Renaissance*, 165–7
3. [p.52] Ibid., 168
4. [p.52] Nicoll, *Stuart Masques and the Renaissance Stage*, 57–8
5. [p.52] Campbell, op. cit., 169.
6. [p.52] Nicoll, *Stuart Masques and the Renaissance Stage*, 63; Campbell, op. cit., 186–7; Chambers, *ES*, I, 228, 233
7. [p.53] Nicoll, *Stuart Masques and the Renaissance Stage*, 69
8. [p.53] Campbell, op. cit., 172–3; ibid., 70–1
9. [p.54] Per Palme, op. cit., 115, fig. 8
10. [p.55] Busino, 'Anglopotrida', *VP* XX, 110, quoted in Chambers, *ES*, I, 202, n. 5
11. [p.56] Wood, *The History and Antiquities of the University of Oxford*, II Bk. 1, 408–9, quoted in Bentley, *The Jacobean and Caroline Stage*, V. 1191
12. [p.56] Summerson, *Inigo Jones*, 29
13. [p.56] Per Palme, op. cit., 115
14. [p.56] Inigo Jones is referred to in the Warrant for *Florimene* as 'Mr Survayer to cause the Hall at Whitehall to bee furnyshed with Scaffolds, degrees, etc., against the Pastorall on the King's birthday'. Public Record Office, L.C. 5/134, p. 78 quoted in *SL*, XIII, 50.

15. [p.56] Palladio, *Second Book of Architecture*, ch. X, pl. xxviii
16. [p.57] Per Palme, op. cit., 117; *SL* XIII, 119
17. [p.57] Shute, *The First and Chief Groundes of Architecture*, Folio. vi, viii
18. [p.57] *SL*, XIII, 120
19. [p.58] Hotson, *The First Night of Twelfth Night*, 70, n. 1
20. [p.58] Southern, 'Observations on the Lansdowne MS No. 1171', *TN*, II, 6–19, pls. 4, 8, 9, 12; Southern 'Inigo Jones and Florimene', *TN*, VII, 37–9, pls. 1–8
21. [p.60] Southern, *TN*, II, pl. 5
22. [p.60] Ibid., VII, pl. 6
23. [p.60] Ibid., pls. 3, 4
24. [p.60] Boswell, *The Restoration Court Stage, 1660–1702*, 40, 169
25. [p.60] Ibid., 29–30
26. [p.60] *SL*, XIII, 51, quoted from P.R.O., Works, 5/7; for a description of the Hall see p. 47
27. [p.61] Per Palme, op. cit., 152, n. 2
28. [p.62] Lansdowne, 9v–10. B. M. 7/6225
29. [p.62] Bentley, *The Jacobean and Caroline Stage*, VI, 286–7
30. [p.63] Wheatley. *The Diary of Samuel Pepys*. VI, 40, 29th October, 1666. This was on the occasion of Pepys' first visit to the new playhouse erected in the Great Hall in Whitehall in 1665. See also Sabbattini's comments on the audience (p. 27).
31. [p.63] Nicoll, *Stuart Masques and the Renaissance Stage*, figs. 78–9
32. [p.64] Southern, *Changeable Scenery*, pl. 24
33. [p.64] Boswell, op. cit., February, 1670/1, 250, February, 1678/9, 261; Hartnoll, *Oxford Companion to the Theatre*, 465

CHAPTER 4

1. [p.66] Peccati, *Collana Storica Sui Monumenti Gonzagheschi di Sabbioneta. Il Teatro Olimpico*,

2. [p.69] Campbell, *Scenes and Machines on the English Stage during the Renaissance*, 53

3. [p.70] Simpson and Bell argue that the first set is in fact a copy of Webb's draw ing by a foreign subordinate of Jones'; Simpson and Bell, *Designs by Inigo Jones for Masques and Plays at Court*, 27. James Lees-Milne in *The Age of Inigo Jones*, 164, suggests that Jones had 'set Webb to copy and vary by way of exercise' his drawing, presumably at the time when Webb first joined his uncle's office.

4. [p.70] Keith, 'A Theatre Project by Inigo Jones', *Burlington Magazine*, XXXI, No. 174, 105–11, pls. iii, iv

5. [p.70] Ibid., No. 173, 61–70

6. [p.73] Wickham, *EES*, II, 177. Since this reconstruction was prepared an article discussing these drawings has appeared, see Rowan, 'A Neglected Jones/ Webb Theatre Project, Part II: A Theatrical Missing Link', in Galloway, *The Elizabethan Theatre*, II, 60–73

7. [p.73] Strong, *Festival Designs by Inigo Jones, International Exhibitions Foundations*, pl. 104

8. [p.73] King, 'Staging of Plays at the Phoenix in Drury Lane, 1617–42', *TN*, XIX, 146–66. Richards, 'Changeable scenery for plays on the Caroline Stage', *TN*, XXIII, 17

9. [p.73] Wickham, 'The Cockpit recon- structed', *New Theatre Magazine*, VII, No. 2, 26–35; Rowan, 'The Cockpit-in- Court', *The Elizabethan Theatre*, 89–102; *SL*, Pt. III, XIV

10. [p.74] Keith, 'John Webb and the Court Theatre of Charles II', *Architectural Review*, LVII, No. 2, 49–55

11. [p.74] Boswell, *The Restoration Court Stage, 1660–1702*, 239

12. [p.74] Ibid., 24

13. [p.75] Keith, 'John Webb and the Court Theatre of Charles II', *Architectural Review*, LVII, No. 2, 49–55. Keith

incorrectly gives these dimensions as 8 feet 6 inches and 6 feet.

14. [p.75] Ibid, pl. 10

15. [p.76] Ibid., pl. 8

16. [p.76] Wickham, 'The Cockpit recon- structed', *New Theatre Magazine*, 32

17. [p.78] Hotson, *Commonwealth and Restoration Stage*, 37

18. [p.78] Ibid., 13

19. [p.78] Ibid., 43. Freehafer, 'The Formation of the London Patent Com- panies in 1660', *TN*, XX, 6–30

20. [p.78] Hotson, ibid., 168

21. [p.78] Freehafer, op. cit., 7, 8

22. [p.78] Reyer, *Les Masques Anglais* quoted in Hotson, *Commonwealth and Restoration Stage*, 149–50

23. [p.78] Ibid.

24. [p.79] Hotson, *Commonwealth and Restoration Stage*, 156–7

25. [p.79] Freehafer, op. cit., 8–9

26. [p.79] Hotson, *Commonwealth and Restoration Stage*, 119

27. [p.80] Wheatley, op. cit. I, 268. II, 137

28. [p.80] Hotson, *Commonwealth and Restoration Stage*, 207

29. [p.80] Summers, *Playhouse of Pepys*, 103

30. [p.80] Hotson, *Commonwealth and Restoration Stage*, 123

31. [p.80] Langhans, 'The Vere Street and Lincoln's Inn Fields Theatres in Pictures', *Educational Theatre Journal*, XX, No. 2, 171–85

32. [p.81] Scanlan, 'Reconstruction of the Duke's Playhouse in Lincoln's Inn Fields, 1661–1671', *TN*, X, 48–50. Langhans, 'Notes on the Reconstruction of the Lincoln's Inn Fields Theatre', *TN*, X, 112–4

33. [p.81] Ibid.

34. [p.82] *BM Add. MS.*, 20, 726, No. 1, quoted in *SL*, XXXV, 30, n. 5

35. [p.82] Summers, *The Restoration Theatre*, 30–3. A record of the Duke's visit by Lorenzo Magalotti.

36. [p.82] Wheatley, op. cit., III, 108. VIII, 1. There was a similar disorder recorded on 1 July 1664. IV. 138

37. [p.82] Ibid., III, 156, 12th June, 1663. Visit to see alterations: v. 235, 19th March, 1666

38. [p.83] Langhans, 'Pictorial Material on the Bridges Street and Drury Lane Theatre', *Theatre Survey*, VII, pl. 7, 80–100; *SL*, XXXV, pl. 1b

39. [p.83] Langhans, ibid., pl. 8

40. [p.83] Hotson, *Commonwealth and Restoration Stage*, 291–2

41. [p.83] *The New Theatre Royal, Drury Lane, Then and Now*; Hartnoll, *Oxford Companion to the Theatre*, 201

42. [p.83] Summers, *The Restoration Theatre*, 125; Hartnoll, ibid.

43. [p.84] All Souls, Wren Collection, IV, No. 81; *SL*, XXXV, 40–1; Langhans, 'Pictorial Material on the Bridges Street and Drury Lane Theatre', *Theatre Survey*, VII, 80–100

44. [p.84] The same possibility is suggested in *SL*, XXXV, 41. The Great Hall was converted into a permanent theatre in 1665, under the supervision of John Webb, but this design could have been a sketch for an earlier investigation into the possibilities of converting the hall, or, if by Wren, a later variation.

45. [p.85] Ibid.

46. [p.85] Hotson, *Commonwealth and Restoration Stage*, 233

47. [p.85] Langhans, 'The Dorset Garden Theatre in Pictures', *Theatre Survey*, VI, No. 2, 134–46

48. [p.86] Hotson, *Commonwealth and Restoration Stage*, 233

49. [p.86] Southern, *Changeable Scenery*, 185

50. [p.86] Summers, *Restoration Theatre*, 127

51. [p.86] Letter of 22 April 1966 to the author

52. [p.87] *Voyage d'Angleterre, 1676*, quoted in Nagler, *Sources of Theatrical History*, 203

53. [p.87] Summers, *Restoration Theatre*, 30

54. [p.87] Behn, *The Court of the King of Bantam,* quoted in Summers, *Restoration Theatre*, 33

55. [p.87] Gent, *The Play-House*; Satyr, *Poems on Affairs of State*, II, 375–7 quoted by Summers, *Restoration Theatre*, 277. Summers notes further versions to be found in a *Pacquet from Parnassus*, 1702, B. M. Harl. MSS 7315s.267

56. [p.88] Avery, 'A Poem on Dorset Garden Theatre', *TN*, XVIII, 121–4

57. [p.88] Summers, *Restoration Theatre*, 239, 246

58. [p.88] Hotson, *Commonwealth and Restoration Theatre*, 177–9

59. [p.88] Ibid., 187–9. Van Lennep, *The London Stage, Pt. 1*, XXXIV, also quotes Mrs Pepys as attending 'a play at the New Nursery, now established in the Vere Street Theatre,'

60. [p.88] Hotson, op. cit., 189–194

CHAPTER 5

1. [p.89] Newsletter, 27 January 1671–2, quoted by Summers, *Restoration Theatre*, 82; Hotson, op. cit., 253

2. [p.89] *Wren Society*, XII, pl. 81

3. [p.89] Bell, 'Contributions to the History of the English Playhouse', *Architectural Record*, XXXIII, 359–68

4. [p.89] *Stow's Survey of the Cities of London and Westminster*, I and II as corrected by John Strype; Summers, *Restoration Theatre*, 276, pl. 9

5. [p.89] Langhans, 'Pictorial Material on the Bridges Street and Drury Lane Theatres', *Theatre Survey*, VII, pl. 11

6. [p.89] *SL*, XXXV, 32

7. [p.89] 'Deed of 23 March 1673–4', *Shakespeare Society Papers*, IV, 147f

8. [p.89] *SL*, XXXV, pl. 5b

9. [p.91] *An apology for the Life of Mr Colley Cibber written by himself* 339–40

10. [p.91] *The Public Advertiser*, 30 September 1775, quoted in *SL*, XXXV, 46

11. [p.92] Mission, *Memoirs and Observations in his Travels over England*, 219–20

12. [p.92] Adam, *The Works in Architecture of Robert and James Adam*, II, Set V, pl. vii

13. [p.92] Sir John Soane's Museum, Adam Collection, XIV, No. 17

14. [p.92] Ibid., No. 16; see *SL*, XXXV, pl. 10b

15. [p.92] Sir John Soane's Museum, Adam Collection, XXVII, No. 85; see *SL*, XXXV, pl. 11a

16. [p.93] *SL*, XXXV, 44

17. [p.93] Southern, 'Concerning a Georgian Proscenium Ceiling', *TN*, III, 6–12, figs. 1–5

18. [p.94] Leacroft, 'Wren's Drury Lane', *Architectural Review*, CX, 43–6

19. [p.94] *SL*, XXXV, pl. 7

20. [p.95] *Public Advertiser*, 30 September 1775

21. [p.96] Wilkinson, *Memoirs of his Own Life*, IV, 91

22. [p. 97] *A Tale of a Tub* quoted Avery, *The London Stage*, Pt. 2, vol i, xlv.

23. [p.98] 'The Retirement of Rich', *Tatler*, IC, quoted by Summers, *Restoration Theatre*, 239

24. [p.98] Summers, *Restoration Theatre*, 54

25. [p.98] Ibid., 59

26. [p.98] Ibid., 60

27. [p.99] Hartnoll, *The Oxford Companion to the Theatre*, 463

28. [p.99] Book 1, figs. 72–7. For comment on the use of Slanting Wings on the English stage, see: *TN*, XII, 105

29. [p.99] *SL*, XXIX, 223, 225

30. [p.99] *Daily Courant* 20 July, 1705, quoted in Jackson, *London Playhouses, 1700–1705*, vol. VIII, 302

31. [p.99] *SL*. XXIX, 224

32. [p.99] Dumont, *Parallèle de Plans des Plus Belles Salles de Spectacles d'Italie et de France*, pl. 21. According to Mr John Harris, of the RIBA, although the book is dated 1774, the *Parallèle de Plans* accompanied part of Dumont's *Receuil* dated 1764.

33. [p.102] *SL*, XXX, pl. 27a

34. [p.102] Cibber, *An Apology for the Life of Mr Colley Cibber*, 257–260

35. [p.102] Southern, *Changeable Scenery*, 183f; see *SL*, XXX, pl. 27a

36. [p.103] Croft-Murray and Philips, 'The Whole Humors of a Masquerade', *Country Life*, 672–5

37. [p.103] Ibid.

38. [p.104] Ibid., pl. 1

39. [p.107] *SL*, XXXV, 86

40. [p.107] Ibid.

41. [p.107] *The aily Advertiser* quoted in *SL*, XXXV, 86

42. [p.107] *Covent Garden Inventory*, quoted in Nagler, *Sources of Theatrical History*, 352–6

43. [p.109] *SL*, XXXV, 87. In a riot of 1763 'The rashness of the rioters was so great, that they cut away the wooden pillars between the boxes, so if the inside of them had not been iron, they would have brought down the galleries on their heads'. Whitty, 'The Half-price Riots of 1763', *TN*, XXIV, 25–32

44. [p.110] Lawrence, *Old Theatre Days and Ways*, fac. 174; *SL*, XXXV, pl. 41c

45. [p.110] *Covent Garden Inventory*, loc. cit.

46. [p.110] *SL*, XXXV, 86

47. [p.110] *Covent Garden Inventory*, loc. cit.

48. [p.110] Ibid.

49. [p.110] Rosenfeld, 'Theatres in Goodman's Fields', *TN*, I, 48–50; Kennedy-Skipton, 'Notes on a Copy of William Capon's plan of Goodman's Fields Theatre', *TN*, XVII, 86–9. Thomas Odell actually obtained Letters Patent from George II to erect a theatre, later rescinded. Scouten, *The London Stage. Pt. 3*, vol. I. xlviii.

50. [p.110] Eddison, 'Capon and Goodman's Fields', *TN*, XIV, 127–32

51. [p.112] Edwards, 'The Theatre Royal, Bristol', *Archaeological Journal*, IC, 123f

52. [p.112] Barker, 'The Theatre Proprietors' Story', *TN*, XVIII, 79–91

53. [p.112] *Theatre Order and Divend Book*, 6 November, 1764, quoted by Miss Barker in a letter to the author, 8 September 1967

54. [p.112] *Felix Farley's Bristol Journal*, 24 November 1764, quoted by Edwards, op. cit.

55. [p.112] Ibid.

56. [p.114] Edwards, op. cit.

57. [p.114] Southern, 'The Winston MS and Theatre Design', *TN*, I, 93–5

58. [p.114] Barker, *The Theatre Royal, Bristol. The First Seventy Years*, 3

59. [p.114] *Memoirs of Richard Smith, cir. 1838–40*, R. Smith Collection, Bristol Reference Library

60. [p.116] Bingham, *A Celebrated Old Playhouse*, 11–12

61. [p.116] Southern, *The Georgian Playhouse*, fig. 13

62. [p.116] le Grice, *New Theatre Royal, Norwich, its past history and present story*, 4–5

CHAPTER 6

1. [p.118] *SL*, XXXV, 33

2. [p.118] Covent Garden Inventory, loc. cit.

3. [p.118] Hartnoll, *Oxford Companion to the Theatre*, 464

4. [p.119] Wilkinson, *Memoirs of his own Life*, IV, 109–14

5. [p.120] Davies, *Memoirs of the Life of David Garrick*, I, 377–8

6. [p.121] *SL*, XXXV, fig. 3, pl. 7

7. [p.122] Ibid., 48

8. [p.124] 1778 survey drawing

9. [p.124] *SL*, XXXV, pl. 6 and fig. 2,

10. [p.124] Ibid., 46, n. 21

11. [p.125] Ibid., 47

12. [p.125] Davies, op. cit., 366

13. [p.126] Victor, *History of the Theatres of London and Dublin. From the year 1730 to the Present time*, I, 96, 99

14. [p.127] Oulton, *The History of the Theatres of London*, I, 114

15. [p.128] Undated press cutting; quoted in *SL*, XXXV, 48

16. [p.128] Eddison, 'Capon, Holland and Covent Garden', *TN*, XIV, 17–20, pls. 1, 2, 5a. Before its enlargement the theatre held 2,180 people: boxes, 729: pit, 367; first gallery and slips, 700; upper gallery, 384. Stone, *The London Stage*, pt. IV, vol. 1, xxx. After the reconstruction it held about 2,500 seated spectators. Hogan, *The London Stage*, Pt. V. vol. 1, xliii.

17. [p.128] Saunders, *A Treatise on Theatres*

18. [p.128] *SL*, XXXV, 89

19. [p.129] Ibid., 89

20. [129] *The Morning Chronicle*, 24 September 1782, quoted in *SL*, XXXV, 89, n. 7 – A ventilator is mentioned as having been installed in the roof during these alterations, Hogan, op. cit., liii

21. [p.129] *SL*, XXXV, pl. 42b

22. [p.129] Ibid, pl. 41c

23. [p.132] *SL*, XXX, pl. 27b

24. [p.132] Ibid., XXIX, 231

25. [p.133] Ibid., XXX, pl. 32b

26. [p.133] Feltham, *The Picture of London for 1806*, 259–61, quoted in *SL*, XXIX, 239–40

27. [p.133] *The Times*, 16 January 1815, quoted in *SL*, XXIX, 240

28. [p.134] Boaden, *Memoirs of the Life of John Philip Kemble Esq.*, II, 65

29. [p.134] Ibid., 39

30. [p.134] Wilkinson, T., op. cit., IV, 91

31. [p.134] Boaden, *Memoirs of Kemble*, II, 39

32. [p.134] Ibid., 41–2

33. [p.135] Wilkinson, T., op. cit., IV, 91f

34. [p.135] Saunders, op. cit., 75, pl. 6, fig. 4

35. [p.135] Donaldson, 'New Papers of Henry Holland and R. B. Sheridan (1) Holland's Drury Lane, 1794', *TN*, XVI, 90–6; Stroud, *Henry Holland*, 118

36. [p.135] Eddison, 'Capon, Holland and Covent Garden', *TN*, XIV, 17–20, pls. 3, 4

37. [p.135] Boaden, *Memoirs of Kemble*, II, 182

38. [p.135] Oulton, op. cit., II, 116
39. [p.135] Hogan, op. cit., xlix
40. [p.136] Ackerman, *The Microcosm of London*, I, 212
41. [p.136] *The Public Advertiser,* September 1792 quoted in *SL*, XXXV, 91
42. [p.136] Oulton, op. cit., II, 116
43. [p.137] Ibid., II, 116f
44. [p.138] Ibid.
45. [p.138] Ackerman, op. cit. As this account includes a description of the upper gallery introduced later, the colour may also refer to a re-decoration.
46. [p.138] Oulton, op. cit.; *The Public Advertiser,* September 1792, quoted in *SL*, XXXV, 92
47. [p.138] Oulton, op. cit.
48. [p.138] *SL*, XXXV, pl. 45a
49. [p.138] *The Public Advertiser,* quoted in *SL*, XXXV, 93, n. 10
50. [p.138] Ackerman, op. cit., I, 212
51. [p.138] Boaden, *Memoirs of Kemble*, II, 183
52. [p.139] Ackerman, op. cit., I, 212
53. [p.139] Boaden, *Memoirs of Kemble*, II, 376
54. [p.139] Troubridge, 'Theatre Riots', *Studies in Theatre History*, 376
55. [p.139] Brayley, *Historical and Descriptive Account of the Theatres of London*, 15
56. [p.139] Donaldson, op. cit., 92

CHAPTER 7

1. [p.140] *SL*, XXXV, 37
2. [p.140] Boaden, *Memoirs of Kemble*, II, 482
3. [p.140] Donaldson, 'New Papers of Henry Holland and R. B. Sheridan (1) Holland's Drury Lane, 1794', *TN*, XVI, 91
4. [p.140] Holland's own account, MS quoted in *SL*, XXXV, 49
5. [p.140] Wilkinson, 'Londina illustrata, II', *Theatrum illustrata*, quoted in Carter, 'The Drury Lane Theatres of Henry Holland and Benjamin Dean Wyatt', *Journal of the Society of Architectural Historians*, XXVI, No. 3, 200–16
6. [p.141] Holland MS, loc. cit.
7. [p.141] Prepared in 1811 by William Capon, illustrated in Carter, op. cit., *SL*, XXXV, pls. 15, 16a, 16b, 16c, 17a, 17b, 17c; also a plan and two sections, Sir John Soane's Museum, Drawer XXXVIII, i, pls. 34, 35, 36
8. [p.141] Oulton, op. cit., II, 135
9. [p.141] Boaden, *The Life of Mrs Jordan*, I, 261. Although no architectural precautions had been included in 'Old Drury' against fire, the management were clearly aware of the need to make adequate provisions. 'Each night the manager regularly posted several persons, with a "General Inspector" in charge, whose "proper business" was to set all the lights and lamps in and about the playhouse "in large *Candlesticks* and on broad *Stands* made of Tin, in so safe a manner, that should any *Candle* swail and fall out of its Sockets, no danger would attend it." In addition, the theatre possessed "Large Cesterns of Water above Stairs and below, and *Hand-Engines* . . . always ready." Furthermore, the "*Carpenters, Scene-Men* and *Servants* were employ'd in such Numbers . . . and disposed in such Order" that "upon the first Appearance of the least *Spark* of *Fire*, it cannot but be instantly seen and extinguished." Not only that, but every "light in the whole *Theatre* being so plac'd, that it is in the View of some of the *Servants*," and if any "false Alarm" be uttered in any part of the theatre, the spectators should not "inconsiderately throw themselves into Disorder and Confusion, since the House cannot be subject to the least *Danger* from *Fire* on that Side where the Audience sit, as no Light is placed there, that can possibly occasion it." In addition, the "Walls are of such a thickness and such a space between, that no Fire could reach any part of the *Theatre* in several Hours." The report concluded with the point that a "Report of Fire within the House, can

only proceed from Pickpockets, or some other ill-designed Persons".' *The Craftsman*, 4 November 1727, quoted in Avery, *The London Stage*, Pt. 2, vol. 1, 1.

10. [p.141] Donaldson, op. cit., 93–4
11. [p.144] Boaden, *The Life of Mrs Jordan*, I, 250
12. [p.144] Oulton, op. cit., II, 137
13. [p.144] Boaden, *The Life of Mrs Jordan*, I, 250. Note the different use of the term 'slips', which was normally applied to the open side spaces at gallery level.
14. [p.144] *SL*, XXXV, 57
15. [p.146] Ibid., frontispiece
16. [p.146] Ibid., pl. 18a
17. [p.146] Boaden, *The Life of Mrs Jordan*, I, 250
18. [p.146] Holland MS, loc. cit., 50
19. [p.148] Ibid., 49–50
20. [p.148] Ibid., 54
21. [p.149] Ibid.
22. [p.149] Boaden, *The Life of Mrs Jordan*, I, 254
23. [p.149] Boaden, *Memoirs of Kemble*, II, 102
24. [p.149] Ackerman, *The Microcosm of London*, I, 229
25. [p.149] See *SL*, XXXV, pl. 25c
26. [p.149] B.M. Add. MS. 31972–5, quoted in Southern, *Changeable Scenery*, 245. Southern quotes this reference as evidence that wings of decreasing height were no longer to be used; if, however, the upper grooves were all of one height, and the stage at the same time sloped up, then the wings accommodated in the grooves would in fact decrease in height towards the rear of the stage.
27. [p.151] Oulton, op. cit., II, 135
28. [p.151] B.M. Collection of Memoranda, VII, pressmark C 120hl, quoted in *SL*, XXXV, 56, n. 41
29. [p.151] Stroud, *Henry Holland*, 122: ref. to E. G. Saunders, Carpenter, 120
30. [p.151] Ackerman, op. cit., 229
31. [p.151] It is to be presumed that Vol. 12 was written after 1808, and that these references are therefore to Holland's Covent Garden.

32. [p.153] *Rees's Cyclopaedia*, XII, pl. ix, fig. 1
33. [p.154] Ibid., pl. x, fig. 1
34. [p.154] Dumont's method of indicating the side wings on his plan (fig. 72), seems to indicate cuts for carriages rather than sets of bottom grooves. Rider, *A General History of the Stage*, 73; Hitchcock, *An Historical View of the Irish Stage*, I, 116; both quoted by Southern, *Changeable Scenery*, 213–4. 'paid on 26 February 1714 for "6 pound of new Rope for the Scene frames in the Celer at 8d per pound;"' Avery, *The London Stage*, Pt. 2. vol. 1. lxiv
35. [p.155] *Rees's Cyclopaedia*,
36. [p.155] Donaldson, op. cit., 92–3, n. 3. Hogan, op. cit., XLII gives a capacity of nearly 2,300
37. [p.155] Boaden, *Memoirs of Kemble*, II, 428–9. Mrs Siddons, however, refused to 'strain her voice unnaturally. She does not choose to make the sacrifice, and preserves her excellence with the near, whatever she may lose to the remote.' Hogan, op. cit., XLIV
38. [p.155] Cumberland, *Memoirs*, quoted by Nagler, *Sources of Theatrical History*, 408
39. [p.156] Dibdin, *History & Illustrations of the London Theatres*, 51n
40. [p.156] Boaden, *Memoirs of Kemble*, II, 454
41. [p.156] Boaden, *The Life of Mrs Jordan*, II, 225
42. [p.156] Ibid., 220
43. [p.156] Rosenfeld, 'The XVIII Century Theatre at Richmond', *York Georgian Society Occasional paper*, No. 3
44. [p.158] 'Oddfellows Hall, Loughborough, *TN*, I, 75–7, pls. 1, 2
45. [p.160] Leacroft, 'The Remains of the Theatres at Ashby-de-la-Zouch and Loughborough', *TN*, IV, 12–21, pls. 6, 7, figs. 1, 2, 3; Leacroft, 'The Remains of the Fisher Theatres at Beccles, Bungay, Lowestoft and North Walsham', *TN*, V, 82–7, pls. 1, 2

46. [p.164] Wilkinson, *Memoirs*, IV, 108–9
48. [p.164] Boaden, *The Life of Mrs Jordan*, I, 237f. Screwing in: 'The pit doors appear, for this purpose, to have been furnished with large screws' Hogan. op. cit., XXIV

CHAPTER 8

1. [p.166] Wyatt, *Observations on the Design for the Theatre Royal, Drury Lane*. Wyatt comments on his use of the term Proscenium. 'The term ''Proscenium'' has, in this Country, by common acceptance, become synonimous with the frontispiece of the Stage-opening; and as its literal analysis will admit of that application, I shall, in the following pages, use it in that sense, although it bore a different signification among the Ancients.
2. [p.167] Boaden, *Memoirs of Kemble*, II, 548
3. [p.170] Oulton, *A History of the Theatres of London*, I, 228–31
4. [p.170] Lawrence, *The Elizabethan Playhouse and other Studies*, 184
5. [p.170] Nicoll, *The Development of the Theatre*, 159
6. [p.172] Southern, 'The Picture-Frame Proscenium of 1880', *TN*, V, 59–61
7. [p.172] Boaden, *Memoirs of Kemble*, II, 548
8. [p.173] Oulton, op. cit., 228–31
9. [p.173] *SL*, XXXV, pl. 32a
10. [p.174] *Leigh's New Picture of London*, 1819, quoted in *SL*, XXXV, 64
11. [p.174] Bloch, *Sexual Life in England*, 490
12. [p.175] Drawings dated February 1810, R.I.B.A. Collection; see *SL*, XXXV, pls. 22, 23
13. [p.177] Sir John Soane Museum, drawing collection, drawer XXXVIII, i, pls. 13–27; see *SL*, XXXV, pls. 24, 25
14. [p.177] Sir John Soane Museum, loc. cit., pls. 28, 32
15. [p.177] Wyatt, op. cit., pls. iii–vii
16. [p.177] Ibid., pl. ix

17. [p.177] Boaden, *Memoirs of Kemble*, II, 487
18. [p.177] Ibid., 490
19. [p.177] Ibid.
20. [p.179] Boaden, *Memoirs of Mrs Siddons*, 339
21. [p.179] Ackerman, *The Microcosm of London*, III, 262
22. [p.179] Ibid.
23. [p.179] Boaden, *Memoirs of Kemble*, II, 490
24. [p.180] Dibdin, *History & Illustrations of the London Theatres*, 29
25. [p.181] Ibid.
26. [p.181] Ibid., pl. i
27. [p.181] Contant, *Parallèle des principaux théâtres modernes de l'Europe et des machines théâtrales françaises, allemandes et anglaises*, pls. 32, 33
28. [p.181] Dibdin, op. cit., 31
29. [p.184] Ibid., pl. 3
30. [p.184] Barry, 'On the Construction and Rebuilding of the Italian Opera House, Covent Garden', *R.I.B.A. Transactions*, X, 64
31. [p.184] *The Builder*, 15 March 1856, 138–9
32. [p.184] Boaden, *Memoirs of Kemble*, II, 514
33. [p.185] Ibid., 539
34. [p.185] Donaldson, 'New Papers of Henry Holland and R. B. Sheridan (1) Holland's Drury Lane, 1794', *TN*, XVI, 93
35. [p.185] *The Times*, 10 September 1810, quoted in *SL*, XXXV, 96
36. [p.185] *The Times*, 8 September 1812, ibid
37. [p.185] Dibdin, op. cit., pls. i, ii, iii
38. [p.186] Ibid., 27–8
39. [p.186] Boaden, *Memoirs of Kemble*, II, 490
40. [p.186] Brayley, *Historical and Descriptive Accounts of the Theatres of London*, 20
41. [p.186] Byrne, 'Stage Lighting', *Oxford Companion to the Theatre*, 466
42. [p.187] Dibdin, op. cit., 30
43. [p.187] Shaw-Taylor, *Covent Garden*, 29
44. [p.187] *The Builder*, 28 November 1846, 570
45. [p.187] Ibid., 10 April 1847, 165–6
46. [p.187] Ibid., 17 April 1847, 182
47. [p.187] Dibdin, op. cit., pls. i, ii

48. [p.187] National Building Record
49. [p.187] B.M., Dept. of Prints and Drawings, Vol. 10, Nos. 351–2; see *SL*, xxxv, pls. 58a, 58b
50. [p.188] *The Builder*, 10 April 1847, 165–6
51. [p.189] Ibid.
52. [p. 189] Ibid.
53. [p.190] Ibid. Heating in earlier theatres had been provided by the occasional fireplace (pp. 158, 207). In 1767 there is mention of a 'warming machine' at Covent Garden – Stone, *The London Stage*, Pt. 4, vol. i, xxxiv –, and in 1796 'an elegant fire-place was introduced into the Royal Stage Box' at this theatre – Hogan, *The London Stage*, Pt. 5, vol. i, liii. Before 1762 boxes built on the stage at Drury Lane 'were ceil'd . . . to prevent the Ladies catching cold', and Garrick's alterations to the first gallery placed the seats 'so neighborly together that they keep people warm in a cole (sic) winter's night especially at the upper end.' – Stone, ibid. xxxv. In cold weather thick clothing was the order of the day for audience and actors alike. A poem of 1776, 'The Best Way to Keep a Theatre Warm', tells us: "Experience hath told That a well crowded playhouse can never be cold." – Stone, ibid., xxxv–vi.

The main problem, however, was how to ventilate the usually overheated auditorium without admitting blasts of cold air (pp. 125, 129, n.20 p.316, 237).
54. [p.190] Ibid., November 1846, 570
55. [p.191] Ibid., 15 March 1856, 138
56. [p.191] Emden, 'Theatres', *The Architect*, 31 March 1883
57. [p.191] Sachs, 'Modern Theatre Stages', viii *Engineering*, 8 May 1896, 594
58. [p.191] Ibid.
59. [p.191] Lloyds, *Practical Guide to Scene Painting*, 74
60. [p.192] Harcourt, *The Theatre Royal, Norwich, The Chronicles of an Old Playhouse*, 24–5

61. [p.193] *The Builder*, 2 October 1847, 465; drawings of the building suggest, however, that the first two dimensions should read respectively, 56 and 63 feet; Dibdin, op. cit., pls. ii, iv, v; Contant, op. cit., pls. 38, 39
62. [p.193] Dibdin, op. cit., 61n. Hogan claims the Haymarket of 1843 as the first theatre to have backs to the pit seats. Hogan, op. cit., xlviii
63. [p.193] Dibdin, ibid.
64. [p.193] Ibid., 62, n
65. [p.194] Ibid., pl. ii
66. [p.194] Contant, op. cit., pl. 39
67. [p.194] Ibid., pl. 38
68. [p.194] Dibdin, op. cit., 64
69. [p.194] Ibid., 65
70. [p.194] Ibid., pl. iv
71. [p.195] G.L.C. Theatre drawings collection
72. [p.195] *The Builder*, 5 February 1859, 87–8. Attempts had been made in the past to control crowds, by limiting the numbers admitted to the theatre, as is recorded for the Haymarket on 16th April, 1792 or by the use of barriers. After an accident involving fifteen persons trampled to death on the stairs leading to the pit passage of the same theatre on 3rd February, 1794, 'The manager did, however, have a bar, probably borrowing the idea from the Opera House across the way, fixed to the head of the stairs, with a servant standing by it who would admit the playgoers one by one.' Hogan, op. cit., xxix–xxx
73. [p.196] *The Builder*, ibid.

CHAPTER 9

1. [p.197] Egan, *The Life of an Actor*, 175
2. [p.198] *The Builder*, 10 January. 1863, 26; *Western Daily Mercury*, 14 June 1878, 3; 18 June 1878, 3
3. [p.199] 'Theatre Royal, Plymouth. The Improvements', *Western Daily Mercury*, 15 August 1861, 2

4. [p.199] *The Public Buildings in the West of England as designed by John Foulston, F.R.I.B.A.*
5. [p.201] Sachs, 'Modern Theatre Stages', VII, *Engineering*, 24 April 1896, 539
6. [p.201] Ibid., VIII, 8 May 1896, 593
7. [p.201] Ibid., IV, 28 February 1896, 276
8. [p.202] Ibid.
9. [p.202] Wilkinson, *Memoirs of his own Life*, III, 257
10. [p.202] *Western Daily Mercury*, 15 August 1861, 2
11. [p.203] Leacroft, 'Theatre Machinery', *Architectural Review*, CXVI, 113–14
12. [p.203] *Leicester Journal*, 9 September 1836
13. [p.203] Ibid. (see footnote 62, p. 319)
14. [p.203] Ibid., 19 September 1873
15. [p.204] *Minute Book of the New Theatre*, 24 May 1850, Leicester Museum Archives
16. [p.204] *Leicester Journal*, 9 September 1836
17. [204] For further details and additional drawings of this theatre see Leacroft, 'The Theatre Royal Leicester, 1836–1958', *Transactions of the Leicester Archaeological and Historical Society*, XXXIV, 39–52
18. [205] *Minute Book*, 23 February 1872
19. [205] *Leicester Journal*, 19 September 1873
20. [205] *Minute Book*, 11 November 1891
21. [p.205] Ibid., 2 April 1874
22. [p.206] Ibid., 23 February 1883
23. [p.206] Ibid., 26 May 1881
24. [p.206] Ibid., 29 September 1908
25. [p.206] Ibid., 27 March 1913
26. [p.207] *Leicester Journal*, 19 September 1873
27. [p.207] *Minute Book*, 4 March 1918
28. [p.207] *Leicester Journal*, 9 September 1836
29. [p.207] Ibid. 19 September 1873
30. [p.208] *Minute Book*, 9 February 1853
31. [p.208] Ibid., 21 February 1865
32. [p.208] Sachs, 'Modern Theatre Stages IV', *Engineering*, 28 February 1896, 271–6
33. [p.210] Buckle, *Theatre Construction and Maintenance*, 31
34. [p.212] Sachs, 'Modern Theatre Stages IV', loc. cit.
35. [p.216] Ibid.
36. [p.216] Contant, op. cit., pl. 27
37. [p.218] Sachs, 'Modern Theatre Stages VIII', *Engineering*, 8 May 1896, 593–5
38. [p.219] *Minute Book*, 21 February 1865

CHAPTER 10

1. [p.220] 'Paper read at the R.I.B.A. by E. M. Barry', *The Builder*, 11 February 1860, 85–7
2. [p.220] Ibid.
3. [p.220] Ibid.
4. [p.221] G.L.C. Theatre drawings collection
5. [p.221] *The Builder*, 22 May 1858, 345–7
6. [p.221] Ibid., 2 April 1859, 235–6
7. [p.221] Ibid., 24 April 1858, 274
8. [p.221] Ibid., 14 May 1858, 510–11
9. [p.225] Ibid., 18 February 1860, 102–3
10. [p.225] Ibid., 11 February 1860, 85–7
11. [p.225] Ibid., 22 May 1858, 345–7
12. [p.226] 'A French Survey of English Theatres', *The Builder*, 1 June 1867, 381–2
13. [p.227] *The Builder*, 18 February 1860, 102–3
14. [p.227] Ibid.
15. [p.227] Ibid.
16. [p.227] Ibid., 15 May 1858, 326
17. [p.228] Ibid.
18. [p.228] Ibid.
19. [p.228] Ibid.
20. [p.228] Ibid. 18 February 1860, 103
21. [p.228] Ibid., 25 April 1863, 291–2
22. [p.228] *Building News*, 14 May 1858, 510–11
23. [p.229] *The Builder*, 11 February 1860, 85–7
24. [p.230] Ibad., 18 February 1860, 102–3
25. [p.230] Ibid., 1 June 1867, 381–2
26. [p.230] G.L.C. Theatre drawings collection
27. [p.230] *The Builder*, 11 November 1882, 632
28. [p.232] *SL*, XXIX, 244
29. [p.232] *The Builder*, 28 November 1868, 872

30. [p.232] Phipps, 'History and arrangement of Theatres', *The Builder*, 25 April 1863, 291–2

31. [p.232] *The Builder*, 23 January 1875, 82

32. [p.233] Ibid., 23 September 1876, 935 ·

33. [p.233] *Building News*, 11 December 1857, 1294

34. [p.233] *The Builder*, 2 August 1862, 556

35. [p.233] Phipps, 'History and arrangement of Theatres', *The Builder*, 25 April 1863, 291–2

36. [p.233] Ibid.

37. [p.233] *The Builder*, 10 October 1857, 585

38. [p.234] Ibid., 5 September 1957, 516

39. [p.234] Ibid., 24 April 1858, 273–4

40. [p.234] Emden, 'Theatres', *Architect*, 24 March 1883, 196–8

41. [p.236] *Building News*, 25 March 1892, 430

42. [p.236] Harker, *Studio and Stage*, 45

43. [p.237] Penley, *The Bath Stage*, 34, 49. See footnote 53, p. 320

44. [p.237] Emden, op. cit.

45. [p.237] Ibid.

46. [p.237] Emden, 'Theatres', *Architect*, 31 March 1883, 212–3

47. [p.238] Ibid.

48. [p.238] Ibid.

CHAPTER 11

1. [p.239] Southern, 'Scenery at the Book League', *TN*, v, 35–8, pl. 10

2. [p.239] Armstrong, 'Madam Vestris: A centenary appreciation', *TN* xi, 11–8

3. [p.239] Ibid.

4. [p.240] Buckle, *Theatre Construction and Maintenance*, 31

5. [p.240] Sachs, 'Modern Theatre Stages vi', *Engineering*, 10 April 1896, 459–61

6. [p.240] Ibid., v, 13 March 1896, 333–5

7. [p.240] Ibid., i, 17 January 1896, 71–2

8. [p.242] Ibid., iii, 14 February 1896, 205–7; see also Sachs, 'Stage Mechanism', *Journal of the Society of Arts*, 22 April 1898, 512–28

9. [p.243] Buckle, op. cit., 32. The 'First revolving stage in Europe' in the Residenz theater, Munich, was fully equipped with bridges and cuts. See Fuerst and Hume, *Twentieth Century Stage Decoration*, fig. 17

10. [p.244] Buckle, op. cit., 33

11. [p.245] Ibid., 35

12. [p.245] Ibid., 34–6

13. [p.245] Birkmire, *The Planning and Construction of American Theatres*, 93–8

14. [p.245] Buckle, op. cit., 28–30

15. [p.247] Sachs, 'Modern Theatre Stages xxvii', *Engineering*, 12 March 1897, 331–2

16. [p.247] Directors' Annual Report, Theatre Royal, February 13th, 1889. Author's collection

17. [p.247] *Minute Book of the New Theatre*, October 1887, Leicester Museum Archives

18. [p.247] Directors' Annual Report, ibid.

19. [p.249] Sachs, *Modern Opera Houses and Theatres*, i, 42–3 and pls.

20. [p.249] Ibid., 35–7

21. [p.249] G.L.C. Theatre drawings collection

22. [p.251] Ibid.

23. [p.251] Enthoven collection, V. & A. Museum

24. [p.251] L.C.C. Theatres and Music Halls Committee Presented Papers 1888–1903

25. [p.251] Ibid.

26. [p.251] See plans and sections prepared by J. Emblin Walker in April 1908, G.L.C. Theatre drawings collection, and *The Builder*, 10 October 1908, 279

27. [p.252] Sachs, *Modern Opera Houses and Theatres*, i, 35–7

28. [p.252] *Building News*, 9 January 1891, 64

29. [p.252] Woodrow, 'Theatres, xxxii', *Building News*, 19 January 1894, 76–8

30. [p.254] Ibid.

31. [p.255] Ibid. xxxiii, 107–10

32. [p.255] L.C.C. Theatres and Music Halls Committee Presented Papers, letter of 19 March 1903

33. [p.255] L.C.C. Theatre drawings AR/TH. 456

34. [p.255] Sachs, *Modern Opera Houses and Theatres*, i, 35–7

35. [p.255] *Building News*, 25 March 1892, 427–30; Sachs, 'Modern Theatre Stages XI', *Engineering*, 3 July 1896, 3–7

36. [p.255] L.C.C. Theatres and Music Halls Committee Presented Papers, 25 June 1890

37. [p.256] Sachs, *Modern Theatre Stages*, XI

38. [p.256] Ibid.

39. [p.256] *Building News*, 6 February 1891, 194–5; *The Builder*, 14 February 1891, 126–7

40. [p.256] Sachs, 'Modern Theatre Stages, XI', *Engineering*, 3 July 1896, 3–7

41. [p.258] Ibid.

42. [p.260] Ibid.

43. [p.261] Woodrow, 'Theatres, XXXIII', *Building News*, 26 January 1894, 107–10

44. [p.261] Ibid., XXXIV, 23 February 1894, 247–9

45. [p.261] *Building News*, 6 February 1891, 194–5

46. [p.261] Woodrow, 'Some Recent Developments in Theatre Planning', *Building News*, 25 March 1892, 427–30

47. [p.262] Hexamer, 'The Construction and Interior arrangement of Theatres', *Building News*, 15 July 1892, 65–7

48. [p.262] *Building News*, 25 March 1892, 427–30

49. [p.262] L.C.C. Theatres and Music Halls Committee Minutes and Presented Papers: 15 December, 1892. 23 February, 23 April 1894

50. [p.263] *The Builder*, 12 March 1904, 272–3

51. [p.263] Woodrow, 'Some Recent Developments in Theatre Planning', *Building News*, 427–30

52. [p.264] Buckle, op. cit.

53. [p.264] Ibid., 134–5

54. [p.265] Woodrow, 'Some Recent Developments in Theatre Planning', *Building News*, 25 March 1892, 427–30

55. [p.265] Sachs, *Modern Opera Houses and Theatres*, I, 38–9

56. [p.265] Buckle, op. cit., 138

57. [p.265] Woodrow, 'Some Recent Developments in Theatre Planning', *Building News*, 25 March 1892, 427–30

58. [p.265] Ibid.

59. [p.265] Ibid.

60. [p.266] *Building News*, 12 June 1891, 802–3

61. [p.266] Ibid., 27 November 1891, 773 and illustrations including revised elevation; Sachs, *Modern Opera House and Theatres*, I and III. Sachs reproduced the original designs as submitted for approval. The front elevation was completely redesigned to suit the L.C.C. and the freeholder, Lord Salisbury.

62. [p.266] Woodrow, 'Theatres, I', *Building News*, 15 July 1892, 63–4

63. [p.267] *Building News*, 25 March 1892, 427–30

64. [p.267] Ibid. See fig. 6

65. [p.267] Woodrow, 'Theatres', *Building News*, XXXVII, 18 May 1894, 669

66. [p.269] *The Builder*, 14 November 1891, 368

67. [p.270] *Building News*, 15 July 1892, 64 and 19 August 1892, 245

68. [p.270] L.C.C. Theatre Drawings AR/TH. 456

69. [p.270] Sachs, *Modern Opera Houses and Theatres*, I, 38 and pls.; Woodrow, 'Theatres XXXVII', *Building News*, 18 May 1894, 667–70, figs. 2, 2a, 2b; all the drawings included here are of the original designs, later amended, as illustrated by Sachs in the photograph which he reproduces.

CHAPTER 12

1. [p.271] Sachs, *Modern Opera Houses and Theatres*, II, 35

2. [p.271] *The Builder*, 8 May 1897, 421

3. [p.271] Ibid., 13 March 1897, 251

4. [p.271] Sachs, *Modern Opera Houses and Theatres*, II, 35–6

5. [p.273] *The Builder*, 8 May 1897, 421; drawings submitted 10 June 1896, G.L.C. Theatre drawings collection

6. [p.273] Ibid.

7. [p.274] *The Builder*, 13 March 1897, 251

8. [p.274] Sachs, 'Modern Theatre Stages, XXVII', *Engineering*, 12 March 1897, 332

9. [p.275] *The Builder*, 13 March 1897, 251

10. [p.276] *Journal of the Society of Arts*, 22 April 1898, 512–28

11. [p.276] *The Builder*, 13 March 1897, 251

12. [p.276] Ibid. 13 March, 8 May 1897

13. [p.276] Mander and Mitchenson, *The Lost Theatres of London*, 406–9; Southern, *The Victorian Theatre*, 26–7

14. [p.277] Sachs, 'Modern Theatre Stages, XVIII', *Engineering*, 23 October 1896, 513–7; ibid., XIX, 13 November 1896, 600–4

15. [p.277] Ibid., XVII, 25 September 1896, 387–90

16. [p.277] Ibid.

17. [p.277] Ibid.

18. [p.277] Ibid. XVIII, 23 October 1896

19. [p.278] *Journal of the Society of Arts*, 22 April 1898, 520

20. [279] Sachs, 'Modern Theatre Stages, XIX', *Engineering*, 13 November 1896, 600–4

21. [279] Fuerst and Hume, *XXth Century Stage Decoration*, I, 90

22. [p.279] Birkmire, *The Planning and Construction of American Theatres*, 7–8

23. [p.279] Sachs, 'Modern Theatre Stages, XIX', *Engineering*, 13 November 1896

24. [p.279] Ibid., XVIII, 23 October 1896, 513–17

25. [p.280] Ibid., XIX, 13 November 1896

26. [p.281] Ibid., XVII, 25 September 1896, 387–90

27. [p.281] *Journal of the Society of Arts*, 22 April 1898

28. [p.281] Sachs, 'Modern Theatre Stages', *Engineering*, XXIX, 9 April 1897, 463

29. [p.281] *Journal of the Society of Arts*, 22 April 1898; *The Builder*, 12 September 1896, 216

30. [p.281] Sachs, 'Modern Theatre Stages, XXIX', *Engineering*,

31. [p.282] Capt. Shaw's Report, Metropolitan Board of Works Report, MBW 2396/1035

32. [p.282] L.C.C. Theatres and Music Halls Other Presented Papers, 27 September 1887

33. [p.282] *The Builder*, 12 September 1896, 216

34. [p.282] L.C.C. Theatres and Music Halls Committee Presented Papers 23 May 1894

35. [p.282] Ibid. 20 May 1898

36. [p.283] *The Builder*, 17 December 1898, 566

37. [p.286] Letter from P. Pilditch of 13 October 1898, L.C.C. Theatres and Music Halls Committee Presented Papers

38. [p.286] *Building News*, 12 May 1899, 658

39. [p.286] L.C.C. Theatres and Music Halls Committee Presented Papers 5 July 1901

40. [p.286] *Manual of Safety Requirements in Theatres and other places of Public Entertainment*, Home Office, 90 *The Builder*, 30 January, 1904, 97

41. [p.286] L.C.C. Theatres and Music Halls Committee Presented Papers March 1903, March 1904

42. [p.287] *Building News*, 2 December 1904, 812. The requirements are listed in *The Builder*, 26 March 1904, 337–8

43. [p.287] Drawings dated August 1904, G.L.C. Theatre drawings collection

44. [p.288] *Builders Journal and Architectural Record*, 15 February 1899, 27

45. [p.288] Ibid., 10 May 1899

46. [p.288] *The Builder*, 4 May 1901, 440

47. [p.289] Ibid.

48. [p.289] Ibid.

49. [p.289] Ibid., 24 May 1902, 521

50. [p.289] *Building News*, 25 March 1892, 427

51. [p.290] Spencer, 'Theatre Planning and Construction', *The Builder*, 19 December 1903, 631

52. [p.295] Sachs, *Modern Opera Houses and Theatres*, I, 32–4

53. [p.295] Ibid., 4

54. [p.295] Spencer, op. cit.

55. [p.295] Ibid.

56. [p.297] London Fire Brigade Report, L.C.C. Theatres and Music Halls Committee Presented Papers

57. [p.297] *The Builder*, 19 September 1908, 308–9
58. [p.297] Pichel, *Modern Theatres*, 94
59. [p.298] Ibid., 52
60. [p.298] Bell, Marshall and Southern, *Essentials of Stage Planning*, 29
61. [p.298] *The Builder*, 25 August 1911, 225
62. [p.298] 'The Theatre Royal, Drury Lane, Reconstruction of Auditorium Roof' Architect: Joseph Emberton, *RIBA Journal*, 3rd series, LX, June 1953, 332–3
63. [p.299] Spencer, op. cit.
64. [p.299] *The Builder*, 14 April 1922, 558d
65. [p.301] *The New Theatre Royal, Drury Lane, Then and Now*
66. [p.304] Corry, *Planning the Stage*, 10

Notes on the illustrations

1. a,b) Capitals in the cloister of Monreale Cathedral, 12th c. (Photo: Leacroft.)
2. A medieval performance in a church. Conjectural scale reconstruction based on the nave of Southwell Minster and the capitals (1).
3. The Martyrdom of S. Apollonia.
4. Temporary stage for phylax comedy. Conjectural reconstruction, based on vase paintings (see Bieber, M., *The History of the Greek and Roman Theatre*, Princeton, 1961, figs. 491-2,500,507). From Leacroft, H. & R., *The Buildings of Ancient Rome*.
5. The Pageant of the Shearmen and Taylors' Coventry Corpus Christi play. Conjectural reconstruction.
6. A medieval pageant: conjectural reconstruction showing ascending angel, and trap.
7. Medieval pageants grouped round a raised stage, with raised scaffolding for spectators: conjectural reconstruction.
8. Interior of a medieval hall with a performance of the Christmas play of St George. View from the upper end of the hall towards the screens: conjectural reconstruction.
9. The Great Hall, Penshurst Place. Scale reconstruction including the oriel window, removed in Tudor times.
10. King's College Chapel. The stage erected for the performance of the *Aulularia* of Plautus before Queen Elizabeth I, 1564. Conjectural scale reconstruction.
11. A stage erected against the screens. Conjectural scale reconstruction based on 'The Palace or Senate House' designed and constructed by Garret Christmas for Dekker's *Londons Tempe*, 1629.
12. A city erected against the screens. Conjectural scale reconstruction based on later 14th c. miniatures, and *tableau vivant* from Bruges, 1515 (see figs.9,24,25, Kernodle, G.R., *From Art to Theatre*, Chicago, 1943).
13. Stage settings for the plays of Terence, 1493.
    a) The *Andria*. b) The *Adolphe*. c) The *Heautontimoroumenos*.
14. Sebastiano Serlio's design for a temporary court theatre. Illustration from *Tutte l'opere d'architettura et prospettiva,* 1545.

36. Plan of the Tudor Hall, Whitehall, adapted for the performance of the pastoral *Florimene* by Inigo Jones, 1635. (By courtesy of the Trustees of the British Museum.)

37. The interior of the Tudor Hall during the performance of *Florimene*.
Conjectural reconstruction.

38. The Tudor Hall, Whitehall, arranged for the production of *Florimene*, 1635. Conjectural scale reconstruction based on the drawings contained in the B.M. Landsdowne Ms. No. 1171, and the Chatsworth Collection; see Walpole & Malone Society's *Designs by Inigo Jones for Masques and Plays at Court,* vol. xii, 1925, nos 243-6, 249, 250-1.

39. The Tudor Hall, Whitehall, *Florimene*. Detail of the stage area.

40. Unidentified plan for a mask. Lansdowne 9v-10, B.M. 7/6225.
(By courtesy of the Trustees of the British Museum.)

41. The Theatre of Pompey, Rome, 55 BC. Detail from the great model of Ancient Rome, Museum of Roman Civilization, E.U.R., Rome. (Photo: Leacroft.)

42. The Teatro Olimpico, Vicenza, Andrea Palladio, 1580.
a) the frons scenae, with three-dimensional perspective vistas b) general view of stage and auditorium. (Photos: da Edizione L. Chiovato, Vicenza.)

43. The Teatro Olimpico, Vicenza. Backstage view of the permanent scenery designed by Vincenzo Scamozzi, 1585. (Water colour by the author.)

44. The Teatro Olimpico, Sabbioneta, V. Scamozzi, 1588.
Scale reconstruction based on an original drawing by Scamozzi.

45. Theatre design by Inigo Jones on the theme of Palladio's Teatro Olimpico.
(Reproduced by courtesy of the Provost and Fellows of Worcester College, Oxford.)

46. Theatre design by Inigo Jones. Scale reconstruction based on 45.

47. Unidentified theatre by Inigo Jones. Catalogued as pls. 7b,c, The Barber-Surgeon's Hall. a) elevation b) plan c) cross-section through auditorium d) cross-section through stage, showing frons scenae. (Reproduced by courtesy of the Provost and Fellows of Worcester College, Oxford.)

48. Unidentified theatre by Inigo Jones.
Scale reconstruction based on the original drawings, (47a,b,c,d.)

49. Interior of the unidentified theatre. Perspective reconstruction.

50. Unidentified theatre. Detail of the reconstruction.

51. The Cockpit-in-Court, Inigo Jones–John Webb. Converted to a theatre in 1629-30. Altered in 1660. Original drawings by John Webb. a) detail plan and elevation of stage and frons scenae b) general plan of building, with impressed lines strengthened to indicate their nature and position. (Reproduced by courtesy of the Provost and Fellows of Worcester College, Oxford.)

52. The Cockpit-in-Court, Inigo Jones. Conjectural scale reconstruction based on the original drawings (51a,b.), on Hendrik Danckert's painting of Whitehall, 1747. Scenery designs in the Chatsworth collection nos 371-2-3.

53. The interior of the Cockpit-in-Court. Perspective reconstruction.

54. The Cockpit-in-Court. Detail of scale reconstruction.
55. The stage for *The Siege of Rhodes* at Rutland House, John Webb, 1656.
    a) section. b) plan.
56. The first Theatre Royal, Drury Lane, 1663. Scale reconstruction based on Morgan and Ogilby's *London*, 1681-2. Site plans noted under 63.
57. Unidentified theatre design. Possibly an adaptation of the Tudor Hall, Whitehall. Wren collection, vol. iv, no. 81. (Reproduced by courtesy of the Warden and Fellows of All Soul's College, Oxford.)
58. Unidentified theatre design. Scale reconstruction based on 57.
59. The Dorset Garden Theatre, 1671. The proscenium stage and scenic vista. Illustration to Settle's *The Empress of Morocco*, 1673.
60. Longitudinal section through a playhouse by Sir C. Wren. Wren collection, vol. ii, no. 81. (Reproduced by courtesy of the Warden and Fellows of All Soul's College, Oxford.)
61. Design for the ceiling to the Theatre Royal, Drury Lane, Robert Adam 1775. (Reproduced by permission of the Trustees of Sir John Soane's Museum.)
62. The Bowling Green House, Wrest Park, *c.* 1740. Restoration of the portico columns around supporting post. (Photo: Leacroft.)
63. The Theatre Royal, Drury Lane, Sir C. Wren, 1674. Conjectural scale reconstruction based on the longitudinal section (60). The Adam ceiling (61). Site plans of 1778 in the Greater London Record Office (see pls. 6,7, *Survey of London*, vol. xxxv.)
64. The Theatre Royal, Bristol. View of the passage at the rear of the side boxes showing, on right, the staircase built into the thickness of the wall. (Photo: Leacroft.)
65. Interior of the Theatre Royal, Drury Lane, 1674.
    Perspective reconstruction based on 63 and 81.
66. *The Beggar's Opera*, William Hogarth.
    View with audience seated on either side of the stage.
67. A theatre in the continental manner by Andrea Pozzo, 1692. Scale reconstruction based on Pozzo's original illustrations.
68. The Queen's Theatre in the Haymarket, Sir J. Vanbrugh, 1704-5. Conjectural scale reconstruction based on Dumont's drawings (69). A water-colour in the Burney Collection, B.M., and a property plan of 1777 (see pls. 24a,27a, *Survey of London*, vol. xxx.). An engraving by Hogarth (70), and the description by Colley Cibber.
69. The Queen's Theatre, Haymarket, in 1764. Plan and section illustrated by C. P. M. Dumont, *Parellèle de Plans des Plus Belles Salles de Spectacles d'Italie et de France*, pl. 21. In this engraving both plan and section were incorrectly reproduced by Dumont reversed left to right. (Courtesy of Bristol University Library.)
70. *Masquerades and Operas*, William Hogarth, 1724. Detail of the signboard. (Reproduced by permission of the Warburg Institute.)
71. The Queen's Theatre, Haymarket, after the alterations of 1707-8. Conjectural scale

reconstruction based on the Dumont drawings (69). Kip's *Bird's Eye View of London.* Capon's view of the Haymarket frontage (see pl. 25a, *Survey of London*, vol. xxx).

72. The Theatre Royal, Covent Garden, Edward Shepherd, 1731-2. Plan and section, illustrated by C. P. M. Dumont, op. cit. pl. 20. In this engraving the plan was incorrectly reproduced by Dumont reversed top to bottom. (Courtesy of Bristol University Library.)

73. The Theatre Royal, Covent Garden, Edward Shepherd, 1731-2. Scale reconstruction based on Dumont's drawings (72). The frontispiece to *Harlequin Horace*, 3rd edition, 1735, and information quoted on 86.

74. The Theatre Royal, Covent Garden. Detail of reconstruction.

75. Goodman's Fields, Edward Shepherd, 1732. Reconstructed plan by William Capon.

76. The Theatre Royal, Bristol, James Paty, 1764-6. The theatre as it was prior to the alterations of 1948. Scale reconstruction based on drawings prepared in 1942-3 by J. Ralph Edwards, FRIBA, and a personal survey by the author.

77. The Theatre Royal, Bristol. The auditorium in 1943. (Author's collection.)

78. The Theatre Royal, Bristol. The gallery prior to the alterations of 1948. (Courtesy of the Bristol University Arts Faculty Photo Unit.)

79. The Theatre Royal, Bristol. Detail of scale reconstruction.

80. The New Theatre, Richmond, Surrey, Saunders, 1765. a) The stage from the auditorium b) auditorium from stage. (Author's collection.)

81. Interior of the Theatre Royal, Drury Lane, Robert Adam, 1775. Engraving published in *The Works in Architecture of Robert and James Adam.*

82. Interior of the Theatre Royal, Drury Lane, with figures corrected in accordance with Adam's scale section, vol. 27, no. 85, Adam collection, Sir John Soane's Museum.

83. The Theatre Royal, Drury Lane, Robert Adam, 1775. Scale reconstruction based on the information noted (63). The engraving of the Bridges Street frontage published in *The Works in Architecture of Robert and James Adam. The School for Scandal* engraving of 1778. Information quoted on 82.

84. The Theatre Royal, Drury Lane. Detail of scale reconstruction.

85. Interior of the Theatre Royal, Drury Lane, Greenwood and Capon, 1783. (National Monuments Record: Crown Copyright.)

86. The Theatre Royal, Covent Garden, J. I. Richards, after the alterations of 1782. Scale reconstruction based on plans prepared by William Capon. Plans published by G. Saunders in his *Treatise on Theatres.* Plan of *c* 1808 in the Crace collection, B.M., and an interior view by Rowlandson (see pls. 42b, 45a, *Survey of London*, vol. xxxv).

87. The King's Theatre, Haymarket, M. Novosielski, 1790. Superimposed plans of the old and new Opera House. (Reproduced by courtesy of the Trustees of Sir John Soane's Museum.)

88. The Theatre Royal, Covent Garden, plan and section. Henry Holland's proposals for remodelling the 1731-2 building in 1791.

89. The Theatre Royal, Covent Garden. The auditorium as altered prior to the opening of

the season on the 15th Sept. 1794. Engraving from R. Wilkinson's *Theatrum Illustrata,* 1825, vol. ii.

90. The Theatre Royal, Covent Garden, longitudinal section. Henry Holland's proposals for remodelling the 1731-2 building in 1791.

91. The Theatre Royal, Drury Lane, Henry Holland, 1794. View of the intended design. (Reproduced by courtesy of the Victoria and Albert Museum.)

92. The Theatre Royal, Drury Lane, Henry Holland, 1794. Scale reconstruction based on plans prepared in 1811 by William Capon. A plan and sections by H. Holland, pls. 34-5-6 drawer 38. set 1, Sir John Soane's Museum. Interior views by Edward Dawes, Rowlandson and Pugin, W. Capon (94), R. Wilkinson (96). Exterior views and plans by Capon. Plan of 1806 (95). Preliminary designs prepared by B. Wyatt for his theatre, see 106.

93. The auditorium of the Theatre Royal, Drury Lane, H. Holland, 1794.
Detail of reconstruction.

94. The Theatre Royal, Drury Lane. Unfinished interior view by William Capon, 1805, including the alterations of 1794 and the proscenium doors. (Reproduced by courtesy of the Trustees of Sir John Soane's Museum.)

95. The Theatre Royal, Drury Lane. Plan at dress circle level. Published 15th April, 1806. (Courtesy of the Theatre Collection, The New York Public Library, Astor, Lenox and Tilden Foundations.)

96. Interior of the Theatre Royal, Drury Lane, including the proscenium doors. Engraving by Robert Wilkinson, published 27th Sept. 1820. (Courtesy of the National Monuments Record: Crown copyright.)

97. The stage of the Theatre Royal, Drury Lane, H. Holland, 1794.
Detail of scale reconstruction.

98. Rees's *Cyclopaedia,* 'Dramatic Machinery', 1800, pls. ix,x. Right: Plan and section of a typical stage. Left, top: Wings and carriages as used at Covent Garden.

99. 'A Startling Effect', The Grave Trap. Illustration by George Cruickshank to the *Memoirs of Joseph Grimaldi.* (Author's collection.)

100. Wing carriage, Manoel Theatre, Valetta, Malta. Measured and drawn by the author.

101. The Theatre, Richmond, Yorks, 1788. Scale reconstruction based on survey drawings prepared by the author.

102. The interior of the Theatre, Richmond, Yorks. Conjectural reconstruction.

103. The Theatre, Richmond, Yorks. Drawings prepared for the restoration of the pit in 1949. a) Section with stage to left b) Plan with stage to right.

104. Interior of the Theatre, Richmond, Yorks, during restoration of the pit and understage areas in 1949. (Water colour by the author.)

105. Saunders' Ideal Theatre, 1790. Scale reconstruction based on pls. 11,12 of *A Treatise on Theatres.*

106. The Theatre Royal, Drury Lane, Benjamin Wyatt, 1811. Scale reconstruction based on Wyatt's preliminary designs, drawer 38, set 1, pls. 13-27, Sir John Soane's Museum. Detail sections of stage, drawer 38, set 1, pls. 28, 32 (108). Drawings of the finished theatre as illustrated in *Observations on the Design for the Theatre Royal, Drury Lane*, pls. iii-xii. Exterior views from the Enthoven collection, Victoria and Albert Museum. Interior view of 1813 (see pl. 32a, *Survey of London*, vol. xxxv). The four corner traps and the grave trap have been based on information obtained from drawings of the theatre dated Aug. 1904, G.L.C. Theatre drawings collection.

107. a) Plan of the Haymarket Theatre, John Nash, 1820. Illustration to Brayley, E. W., *Historical and Descriptive Accounts of the Theatres of London*. Print dated 1826. b) Interior of the Haymarket Theatre in 1825. Pl. 2, Dibdin, C., *History and Illustrations of the London Theatres*, London, 1826. For this theatre Nash used the rectangular pattern of pit and boxes in contrast to the, by now, more generally accepted horseshoe form. (Both illustrations by courtesy of the Guildhall Library.)

108. The Theatre Royal, Drury Lane. Cross-section through the stage by Benjamin Wyatt, including details of the wing carriages. Drawer 38, set 1, pl. 32. (Reproduced by permission of the Trustees of Sir John Soane's Museum.)

109. The Stage of the Theatre Royal, Drury Lane, B. Wyatt.
Detail of the scale reconstruction.

110. The Theatre Royal, Covent Garden, Sir Robert Smirke, 1809 Plan of the theatre incorporating the basket boxes.
A. The Stage. BB. Recesses for Scenes. C. Manager's Room. DD. Women's Dressing Rooms. E. Men's Dressing Rooms. F. Store Room. G. Stage Manager's Room. H. Green Room. I. Royal Saloon. K. Ante Room. L. King's Box. M. The King's Staircase. N. Entrance Hall. O. Principal Box Staircases. P. Entrance to Boxes. Q. Lower Gallery Staircase. R. Bar for Refreshments. S. Saloon. T. Vestibule. U. Stairs to Lower and Upper Galleries. Pl. xv. Brayley, E. W., *Historical and Descriptive Accounts of the Theatres of London*, London, 1833, (Courtesy of the Guildhall Library.)

111. Interior of the Theatre Royal, Covent Garden in 1810. *The Covent Garden Journal*, vol. ii. (Reproduced by courtesy of the Trustees of the British Museum.)

112. The Theatre Royal, Covent Garden, Sir R. Smirke. The theatre in 1824, including the alterations made prior to that date. Scale reconstruction based on pls. i-vi, Dibdin, C. *History and Illustrations of the London Theatres*, 1826, (drawings dated 1824.). Undated plan, Crace Maps. Portfolio xviii, sheet 49 (see pl. 52a, *Survey of London*, vol. xxxv). Plan (110). Pls. 32-3-4, Contant, C. *Parallèle des Théâtres*, plates possibly prepared in 1838. Measured drawing of the roof over the theatre, RIBA drawings collection. Exterior and interior views (see pls. 49a,b.50a.51b.54a,b.55b. *Survey of London*, vol. xxxv). Interior (113). Post-fire sketches, drawings and photographs.

113. Interior of the Theatre Royal, Covent Garden in 1825. Pl. vi. Dibdin, C. *History and Illustrations of the London Theatres*. (Courtesy of the Guildhall Library.)

114. Covent Garden Theatre after the fire of 1856.

115. The auditorium of the Royal Italian Opera House, Covent Garden, B. Albano, 1847. *The Builder*, 10th April, 1847, p. 170.

116. The Theatre Royal, Drury Lane, S. Beazley, 1822-3. Scale reconstruction based on pls. ii, iv, v, Dibdin, op. cit. Pls. 38, 39, 40, 41, Contant, op. cit. Interior views, (117, 118). Views of alterations (119), and *The Builder*, 2nd October, 1847, p. 471. Plan of the 1st tier (see pl. 30a. *Survey of London*, vol. xxxv). A set of plans and sections by S. Beazley, drawer 38, set 1, pls. 1-12, Sir John Soane's Museum.

117. Interior of the Theatre Royal, Drury Lane, 1825. Pl. vi, Dibdin, op. cit.

118. Interior of the Theatre Royal, Drury Lane on the 1st October 1842. (Reproduced by courtesy of the Victoria and Albert Museum).

119. The Stage of the Theatre Royal, Drury Lane, during alterations. Upper grooves may be seen attached to the underside of the fly galleries, and two gas lengths are suspended above the stage. (From the Theatre Collection, New York Public Library. Astor, Lenox and Tilden Foundations.)

120. 'The Gallery – powerful attraction of talent.' From Pierce Egan. *The Life of an actor*. (Author's collection.)

121. 'The Benefit Night – A beggarly account of Empty Boxes.' From Pierce Egan. *The Life of an Actor*. (Author's collection.)

122. The Theatre Royal, Plymouth, John Foulston, 1811. Scale reconstruction based on the illustrations to *The Public Buildings in the West of England* as designed by John Foulston.

123. The stage of the Theatre Royal, Plymouth. Detail of the reconstruction.

124. Prompt side fly gallery and machinery. The Theatre Royal, Plymouth. Detail of reconstruction.

125. The Theatre Royal, Bath. Barrels on the prompt side fly gallery. Measured and drawn by the author, 1954.

126. The Theatre Royal, Bath. a) Detail of drum and shaft. b) Details of driving wheel c) Detail of pulley block. Measured and drawn by the author, 1954.

127. The Theatre Royal, Drury Lane, drum and shaft on the grid. (Photo: Leacroft.)

128. The Theatre Royal, Leicester, William Parsons, 1836. The theatre after the alterations of 1873. Scale reconstruction based on drawings by James Barradale, 1888, and survey drawings prepared by the author and students of the Leicester School of Architecture.

129. The gallery of the Theatre Royal, Leicester, after the alterations of 1888. Illustrating the padded steps typical of many galleries. (Crown copyright.)

130. The stage & machinery of the Theatre Royal, Leicester. Measured & drawn by the author.

131. The Theatre Royal, Bristol. Mezzanine floor and corner trap. (Photo: Leacroft.)

132. The Theatre Royal, Bristol. Bridge at mezzanine level. (Photo: Leacroft.)

133. Her Majesty's Theatre, Haymarket. Stage cellar and underside of bridge with driving

drum. (Photo: Leacroft.)

134. The Theatre Royal, Leicester. Detail of sliders and paddles. a) Slider closed b) Slider dropped ready to slide under fixed side stage. Measured and drawn by the author.

135. The Theatre Royal, Bristol. Centre: Two sloat-cut paddles in vertical position. Beyond, a wider bridge paddle with its handle missing. (Photo: Leacroft.)

136. Her Majesty's Theatre, Haymarket. View across the mezzanine floor with, left – a bridge with double-handled paddle. Centre – bridge and double-handled paddle. In the foreground – motivating winches. (Photo: Leacroft.)

137. The Theatre Royal, Leicester. Details of sloats and sloat cuts. a) Constructional detail of sloat. b) Detail of sloat and bridge cuts: 1) sloats 2) sloat sliders 3) bridge sloat 4) fixed side stage 5) paddle. Measured and drawn by the author.

138. The Theatre Royal, Leicester. Upper scene grooves. a) Constructional detail b) Grooves with extension piece raised for use with side wings c) Grooves with extension piece lowered for use with flats. (Photos: Ronald Hunt, AIIP.)

139. E. O. Sachs' English Wooden Stage. a) Section across stage. b) Section on centre line of stage c) Plan at stage level d) Plan at mezzanine level. 'Modern Theatre Stages', no. x, 28th February, 1896, *Engineering*, p. 271-6.

140. The Theatre Royal, Leicester, after the alterations of 1888. Upper right – scene painter's bridge. Centre – catwalks across the stage for the use of the scene riggers. Bottom left – proscenium opening and upper scene grooves attached to the lower fly gallery. (Photo: Ronald Hunt, AIIP.)

141. The Theatre Royal, Leicester. Scene painting bridge and paint-frame with scenery in position. (Photo: Ronald Hunt, AIIP.)

142. The Theatre Royal, Leicester. Conjectural backstage view.

143. Royal Italian Opera House, Covent Garden, E. M. Barry, 1858. Scale reconstruction based on L.C.C. survey drawings dated 1882. Pls. 35-6-7, Contant, op. cit., section, plan and views, *The Builder*, 22nd May, 1858; 2nd, 16th April, 1859. Elevations of original design (see pls. 60a.b., 61a. *Survey of London*, vol. XXXV). View of the Bow Street frontage, *The Builder*, 24th October, 1857. Plans, sections and details, RIBA Transactions, 1st series, vol. 10, 1859-60, pp. 54-5. Four corner traps and a grave trap have been omitted from this drawing owing to lack of visual evidence as to their exact position.

144. Interior of the Royal Italian Opera House, Covent Garden.
The Builder, 22nd May, 1858.

145. Royal Italian Opera House, Covent Garden. Detail of the proscenium frame. (Photo: Leacroft.)

146. Royal Italian Opera House, Covent Garden. Scene painting room with the smaller paint-frame on right. (Photo: Leacroft.)

147. Royal Italian Opera House, Covent Garden. The roof space over the auditorium. (Photo: Leacroft.)

148. Her Majesty's Theatre, Haymarket.

a) Plan of the 1790 theatre. Designed by Novosielski; reconstructed 1796 by Marinari; further altered in 1799, 1818 and 1866. Burnt 6th December 1867. A. Dressing rooms. B. Gallery entrance, and stairs to amphitheatre, and amphitheatre stalls. C. Stage entrance. D. Housekeeper. E. Treasury. F. Manager's room. G. Box Office. H. Royal Entrance. I. Committee-room. J. Entrance to stage. K. Omnibus boxes. L. Stairs to flies.

b) Plan of the 1868-9 theatre. Designed by Charles Lee. A. Stairs to amphitheatre. B. Stairs to amphitheatre stalls. C. Stairs of communication between tiers of boxes. D. Cheque-taker. E. Soldiers' room. F. Acting manager's room. G. Conductor's room. H. Royal entrance and stairs. I. Open areas. J. Box Office. K. Manager's room. L. Treasury. M. Waiting-room. N. Stage entrance. O. Scenery entrance. P. Green room. Q. Dressing room. R. Stairs to stage. S. Stairs to dressing-rooms and carpenter's shop. T. ditto. U. Stairs to stalls. V. Stairs to pit. W. Waterclosets etc. X. Stairs to pit tier of boxes. Y. Stairs to flies. *The Builder,* 12th December, 1868.

149. The Theatre Royal, Leicester. View of the auditorium showing the full-width Pit, and the cantilevered extension to the front of the Dress Circle. (Crown copyright.)

150. The Shaftesbury, Mr Lancaster's Theatre, Shaftesbury Avenue, E. J. Phipps, 1887. a) Cross-section through auditorium b) Cross-section through stage c) Plan at Upper Circle level. Greater London Record Office, Theatre Plans 124/5,9.

151. Typical stage setting and scenic construction of 1896. Sachs, E. O., 'Modern Theatre Stages,' no. v, *Engineering,* 13th March, 1896, p. 333.

152. The Theatre Royal, Leicester. The stage and stage machinery after the alterations of 1888. Scale reconstruction based on a survey by the author.

153. The Theatre Royal, Leicester. Hemp lines for flying scenery, descending from the grid and tied off to cleats on the upper fly gallery. (Photo: Ronald Hunt, AIIP.)

154. The Theatre Royal, Leicester. a) View from the stage end of the theatre showing the continuous roof over the whole building, prior to 1888 b) The theatre from a diagonally opposite view, showing the fly tower raised above the stage in 1888. (City of Leicester Museum and Art Gallery).

155. The New English Opera House, T. E. Collcutt and G. H. Holloway, 1891. Scale reconstruction based on drawings in the Greater London Council theatre drawings collection, dated November 1888, June 1890, January 1918, June 1947. Drawings for a fire curtain, April, 1903. Reconstruction of gallery, April, 1908. Plans and sections, *Building News*, 6th February, 1891. Details of stage, *Engineering*, 3rd July, 1896. Drawings and photograph, E. O. Sachs, *Modern Opera Houses and Theatres*, vol. 1. Author's survey.

156. Interior of the New English Opera House. From the opening night brochure. (Courtesy of the Victoria and Albert Museum.)

157. New English Opera House. Detail of reconstruction illustrating the construction of the cantilevered circles.

158. New English Opera House. The stage and stage machinery. Detail of reconstruction.

159. The Theatre Royal, Leicester. Detail of the grid and hemp line flying system.

160. New English Opera House. Detail of the grid and counterweighted wire lines.

161. New English Opera House. View of the grid, with disused master pulleys at upper level, and timber wheels. (Photo: Leacroft.)

162. New English Opera House. Original timber counterweight tracks. (Photo: Leacroft.)

163. J. G. Buckle's Model Safety Theatre. (Author's collection.)

164. New Theatre in St Martin's Lane, now the Duke of York's, Walter Emden, 1892. Scale reconstruction based on drawings in the G.L.C. theatre drawings collection, dated 15th July, 1891; 9th April, 1892; 1st July, 1892; 11th, 14th, 17th October, 1892. Illustrations in the *Building News*, 12th June, 27th November, 1891. Illustrations to E. O. Sachs, *Modern Opera Houses and Theatres*, vol. 1.

165. Interior of the New Theatre in St Martin's Lane, now the Duke of York's. View of the O.P. stage boxes at Dress Circle level. (National Monuments Record. Crown copyright.)

166. 'The Queue,' from Pierce Egan, *The Life of an Actor*. (Author's collection.)

167. Daly's Theatre, Spencer Chadwick, 1893. Scale reconstruction based on drawings in the G.L.C. theatre drawings collection dated 25th June, 1891; March, 1916. Plans and sections from *The Builder*, 14th November, 1891. Interior view (168).
a) Detail of the Cranbourne St–Ryder Court corner, showing the narrow, one at a time, entrance to Pit pay box, and wide exit.

168. Interior of Daly's Theatre. Architect's sketch showing simplified decorative scheme finally adopted. (Courtesy of the Victoria and Albert Museum.)

169. Her Majesty's Theatre, Haymarket, C. J. Phipps, 1897. Scale reconstruction based on drawings in the G.L.C. theatre drawings collection dated 10th June, 1896; January, 1922. Exterior view from *The Builder*, 8th May, 1897. Drawings and photographs, E. O. Sachs, *Modern Opera Houses and Theatres*, vol. 11. Author's survey.

170. Interior of Her Majesty's Theatre. Based on a photograph in E. O. Sachs op. cit.

171. Her Majesty's Theatre. Prompt side fly gallery looking towards the proscenium wall, with hemp lines on right and thunder run on left. (Photo: Leacroft.)

172. Fire-resisting curtains. E. O. Sachs, 'Modern Theatre Stages', no. xxviii, *Engineering*, 26th March, 1897, p. 393.

173. The Asphaleia stage. a) 'Asphaleia' Traps and the 'Horizon'. b) 'Asphaleia' Traps as photographed from a model. E. O. Sachs, 'Modern Theatre Stages,' no. xvii, *Engineering*, 25th September, 1896, figs. 224-5, p. 389.

174. Buda-Pest Opera House. Section across the Asphaleia stage. E. O. Sachs, 'Modern Theatre Stages', no. xix, *Engineering*, 13th November, 1896, fig. 236, p. 605.

175. The Theatre Royal, Drury Lane. The stage in 1898, showing in front, the two hydraulic lifts, and behind, the two electric bridges installed in 1896 and 1898 respectively. (Courtesy of the Victoria and Albert Museum.)

176. The Theatre Royal, Drury Lane. The underside of the lifts and bridges. Right, the

prompt side plungers of the hydraulic lifts. Left, the lattice structure of the foremost of the two electric bridges. (Photo: Leacroft.)

177.   The Theatre Royal, Drury Lane. The theatre in 1902, incorporating the auditorium alterations by P. E. Pilditch of 1896, and the reconstruction of the stalls, and grand and first circles of 1901. The hydraulic lifts of 1896; the electric lifts and fire curtain of 1898; the carpenter's shop, wardrobe store, ballet room and paint room of 1899; and the reconstructed flies of 1901. Scale reconstruction based on drawings in the G.L.C. theatre drawings collection dated December 1902. Photographs of the stage of 1898 (175) in the Enthoven Collection, Victoria and Albert Museum, and *The Sketch*, 27th April, 1898.

178.   The Theatre Royal, Drury Lane, P. E. Pilditch, 1904. Scale reconstruction based on drawings in the G.L.C. theatre drawings collection dated August, 1904. Post-fire photographs (185) in the G.L.C. Photograph Library (© G.L.C. 1973).

179.   Auditorium of the Theatre Royal, Drury Lane, after the alterations of 1904. (Courtesy of the Manager, Theatre Royal, Drury Lane.)

180.   The Royal Opera House, Covent Garden. The stage in 1901, with electrically operated lifts and three wing ladders with lights attached. *The Builders Journal and Architectural Record*, 22nd May, 1901.

181.   The Royal Opera House, Covent Garden, 1901.
The stage, detail of the reconstruction (182).

182.   The Royal Opera House, Covent Garden, 1901, E. O. Sachs. Scale reconstruction based on drawings in the G.L.C. theatre drawings collection. Drawings for proposed proscenium wall, October 1882. Drawings by E. O. Sachs, February 1899, July 1900. Survey drawings, October 1921. Plan and section in *The Builder*, 1st June, 1901. Photographs (180) and plan, *The Builders Journal*, 22nd May, 1901. Photographs of the stage area in *The Sketch*, 3rd, 24th April, 1901.

183.   The Royal Opera House, Covent Garden. The stage. Upper left: the paint room (146) with main paint-frame lowered to stage level. Extreme left and centre: counterweight tracks. Right: Front curtain and proscenium opening. (Photo: Leacroft.)

184.   The People's Theatre, Worms, Otto March, 1887. a) Section and elevation b) Ground plan. *The Building News*, 14th December, 1894.

185.   The Theatre Royal, Drury Lane. The roof of the stage after the fire of 1908, showing the grid of 1904 and counterweight pulleys still in position. (... 1971. Greater London Council, Photograph Library.)

186.   The Theatre Royal, Drury Lane. The grid and lantern light. (Photo: Leacroft.)

187.   The Theatre Royal, Drury Lane. The grid viewed from the stage, with prompt side counterweight tracks and counterweight loading gallery. (Photo: Leacroft.)

188.   The Theatre Royal, Drury Lane. The theatre in 1958-9, incorporating the stage as rebuilt by P. E. Pilditch after the fire of 25th March, 1908, and the auditorium as redesigned by J. E. Walker, F. E. Jones and R. Cromie in 1921-2. Scale reconstruction

based on survey drawings in the G.L.C. theatre drawings collection, dated 1958-9. The present working stage plan. Author's survey.

189.   The Theatre Royal, Drury Lane. The auditorium after the alterations of 1921-2. (National Buildings Record, Crown Copyright.)

Bibliography

ACKERMAN, R., *The Microcosm of London*, vols i-iv, facsimile edition (London, 1904).

ADAM, R. and J., *The Works in Architecture of Robert and James Adam*, vol. ii (London, 1779).

ADAMS, J. C., *The Globe Playhouse: Its Design and Equipment* (Cambridge, 1942).

ALLEN-BROWN, R., *The History of the King's Works*, vol. i (H.M.S.O., 1963).

ALTMAN, T. P., *Theater Pictorial* (California, 1953).

ARMSTRONG, W. A., *The Elizabethan Private Theatres, Facts and Problems,* Society for Theatre Research Pamphlet no. 6, (1957-8).

– 'Madam Vestris: A Centenary appreciation', *T.N.* ii, pp. 11-18.

ARNOTT, P. D., 'The Origins of Medieval Theatre in the Round', *T.N.*, xv, pp. 84-87.

AVERY, E. L., 'A Poem on Dorset Garden Theatre', *T.N.* xviii, pp. 121-4.

– *The London Stage*, Pt. 2, vol i, (Illinois, 1960).

BARKER, K. M. D., 'The Theatre Proprietor's Story', *T.N.* xviii, pp. 79-91.

– *The Theatre Royal, Bristol. The First Seventy Years* (Bristol, 1963).

BARRY, E. M., 'On the Construction and Rebuilding of the Italian Opera House, Covent Garden', *R.I.B.A. Transactions*, vol. x, p. 64, (1859-60).

– Paper on Covent Garden read at the Royal Institute of British Architects, *The Builder*, pp. 85-7, (11th February, 1860).

BELL, H., 'Contributions to the History of the English Playhouse', *Architectural Record*, vol. xxxiii, pp. 359-68, (1913).

BELL, S., MARSHALL, N., SOUTHERN, R., *Essentials of Stage Planning*, (London, 1949).

BENTLEY, G. E., *The Jacobean and Caroline Stage*, vii vols. (Oxford, vol. v, 1956, vol. vi, 1968).

BIEBER, M., *The History of the Greek and Roman Theater* (Princeton, 1961).

BINGHAM, F., *A Celebrated Old Playhouse* (London, 1886).

BIRKMIRE, W. H., *The Planning and Construction of American Theatres* (New York, 1896).

BLOCH, T., *Sexual Life in England* (London, 1965).

BOADEN, J., *The Life of Mrs. Jordon*, 2 vols. (London, 1831).

– *Memoirs of the Life of John Philip Kemble, Esq.*, 2 vols. (London, 1825).

– *Memoirs of Mrs. Siddons*, 2 vols. (London, 1827).

BOAS, F. S., *University Drama in the Tudor Age* (Oxford, 1914).
BOSWELL, E., *The Restoration Court Stage, 1660-1702* (London, 1932).
BRAYLEY, E. W., *Historical and Descriptive Accounts of the Theatres of London* (London, 1833).
BUCKLE, J. G., *Theatre Construction and Maintenance* (London, 1888).

Builder, The
(COVENT GARDEN)
    28 November, 1846, p. 570
    10th April, 1847, pp. 165-6
    17th April, 1847, p. 182
    15th March, 1856, pp. 138-9.
    24th October, 1857, pp. 610-1
    24th April, 1858, p. 274
    14th May, 1858, pp. 510-11
    15th May, 1858, p. 326
    22nd May, 1858, pp. 345-7.
    2nd April, 1859, pp. 235-7
    16th April, 1859, pp. 268-9
    11th February, 1860, pp. 85-7
    18th February, 1860, pp. 102-3
    25th April, 1863, pp. 291-2
    1st June, 1901, pp. 537-40
    11th November, 1882, p. 632
    1st June, 1901, pp. 537-40
    4th May, 1901, p. 440
    24th May, 1902, p. 521

(DALY'S)
    14th November, 1891, p. 368

(DRURY LANE)
    2nd October, 1847, p. 465
    15th March, 1856, pp. 138-9
    5th February, 1859, pp. 87-8
    12th September, 1896, p. 216
    17th December, 1898, p. 566
    26th March, 1904, pp. 337-8
    2nd December, 1904, p. 812
    19th September, 1908, pp. 308-9
    25th August, 1911, p. 225
    14th April, 1922, p. 558.

(THEATRE ROYAL, PLYMOUTH)
    10th January, 1863, p. 26

(THEATRE ROYAL, BIRMINGHAM)
    23rd September, 1876, p. 935

(NEW ENGLISH OPERA HOUSE)
    14th February, 1891, pp. 126-7
    10th October, 1908, p. 379

(HER MAJESTY'S)
    28th November, 1868, p. 872
    12th December, 1868, pp. 911-2

Builders Journal and Architectural Record, (COVENT GARDEN) 15th February, 1899, p. 27, 10th May, 1899, p. 209, 22nd May, 1901, p. 303-5

Building News
(COVENT GARDEN)
    14th May, 1858, pp. 510-11.

(DRURY LANE)
    12th May, 1899, p. 658
    2nd December, 1904, p. 812.

(DUKE OF YORK'S)
    12th June, 1891, pp. 802-3
    27th November, 1891, p. 773

(NEW ENGLISH OPERA HOUSE)
    9th January, 1891, p. 64
    6th February, 1891, pp. 194-5

CAMERON, K. and KAHRL, S. J., 'The N. Town Plays at Lincoln', *T.N.* xx, p. 61ff.

CAMPBELL, L. B., *Scenes and Machines on the English Stage during the Renaissance* (London, 1923).

CARTER, R., 'The Drury Lane Theatres of Henry Holland and Benjamin Dean Wyatt', *Journal of the Society of Architectural Historians*, vol. xxvi, no. 3, pp. 200-16 (October, 1967).

CHAMBERS, E. K., *The Elizabethan Stage*, iv vols (Oxford, 1923).
  – *The Medieval Stage*, 2 vols. (Oxford, 1903).

CIBBER, C., *An Apology for the Life of Mr. Colley Cibber written by himself* (London, 1740).

CONTANT, C., *Parallèle des principaux Théâtres modernes de l'Europe et des machines théâtrales françaises, allemandes et anglaises*, (1859).

CORRY, P., *Planning the Stage* (London, 1961).

CRAIK, T. W., *The Tudor Interlude* (Leicester, 1958).

CROFT-MURRAY, E. and PHILIPS, H., 'The Whole Humors of a Masquerade', *Country Life*, pp. 672-5, (2nd September, 1949).

CUMBERLAND, R., *The Memoirs of Richard Cumberland* (London, 1806).

DAVIES, T., *Memoirs of the Life of David Garrick, Esq.* 2 vols. (London, 1808).

DEKKER, T., *The Gull's Horne Booke* (1609).

DIBDIN, C., *History and Illustrations of the London Theatres* (London, 1826).

Directors' Annual Report, Theatre Royal (13th February, 1889).

DONALDSON, I., New Papers of Henry Holland and R. B. Sheridan. (1) 'Holland's Drury Lane, 1794', *T.N.*, xvi, p. 91ff.

DUMONT, C. P. M., *Parallèle de Plans des Plus Belles Salles de Spectacles d'Italie et de France* (1774).

ECCLES, M., 'Martin Peerson and the Blackfriars', *Shakespeare Survey*, vol. xi, p. 104ff. (Cambridge, 1958).

EDDISON, R., 'Capon and Goodman's Fields Theatre', *T.N.*, xvii, pp. 86-9.
  – 'Capon, Holland and Covent Garden', *T.N.*, xiv, pp. 17-20.

EDWARDS, J. R., 'The Theatre Royal, Bristol', *Archaeological Journal*, vol. 99, p. 123ff.

EGAN, P., *The Life of an Actor* (London, 1825).

EMBERTON, J., 'The Theatre Royal, Drury Lane, Reconstruction of Auditorium Roof'. Architect: Joseph Emberton, *R.I.B.A. Journal*, 3rd serics, LX, June, 1953, pp. 332-3.

EMDEN, W., 'Theatres', *The Architect*, pp. 196-8, 24th March, 1883; pp. 212-3, 31st March, 1883.

FOULSTON, J., *The Public Buildings in the West of England as Designed by John Foulston, F.R.I.B.A.* (London, 1838).

FREEHAFER, J., 'The Formation of the London Patent Companies in 1660', *T.N.*, xx, p. 6.
  – 'Inigo Jones' scenery for *The Cid*', *T.N.*, xxv, 84–92.

FREEMAN, A., 'A Round Outside Cornwall', *T.N.*, xvi, p. 10.

FRY, C., *The Greater English Church* (London, 1943-4).

FUERST, W. R. and HUME, S. J., *Twentieth Century Stage Decoration*, 2 vols. (London, 1928).

GALLOWAY, D., *The Elizabethan Theatre* (Ontario, London, 1969).

– *The Elizabethan Theatre*, II (Ontario, London, 1970).

GASCOIGNE, B., *World Theatre,* (London, 1968).

G.L.C. Theatre Drawings Collection.

GRICE, E. C. LE, *New Theatre Royal, Norwich. Its past history and present story* (Norwich).

HARBAGE, A., *Shakespeare's Audience,* (New York, 1941).

HARCOURT, B., *The Theatre Royal, Norwich. The Chronicles of an Old Playhouse* (Norwich, 1903).

HARDY, W. LE, 'Elizabethan Players in Winslow Church', *T.N.*, xii, p. 107.

HARKER, J., *Studio and Stage* (London, 1924).

HARRISON, G. B., *Introducing Shakespeare* (London, 1939).

HARTLEY, D., *Life and Work of the People of England*, 2 vols. (London, 1931).

HARTNOLL, P., *The Oxford Companion to the Theatre* (Oxford, 1951).

HEXAMER, C. J., 'The Construction and Interior Arrangements of Theatres', *Building News*, 15th July, pp. 65-7 (1892).

HITCHCOCK, R., *An Historical View of the Irish Stage* vol. i. (Dublin, 1788).

HODGES, C. W., 'A Seventeenth Century Heaven', *T.N.* vi, pp. 59-60.

– 'de Witt again', *T.N.* v, pp. 32-4.

– *The Globe Restored* (London, 1953).

HOGAN, C. B., *The London Stage*, Pt. 5, vol. i (Illinois, 1968).

HOLMAN, T., 'Cornish Plays and Playing Spaces', *T.N.* iv, pp. 52-4.

Home Office, *Manual of Safety Requirements in Theatres and other Places of Public Entertainment* (London, 1934).

HOSLEY, R., 'A Reconstruction of the Second Blackfriars': see Prouty, G., pp. 74-88.

– 'The Discovery-Space in Shakespeare's Globe', *Shakespeare Survey 12*, pp. 35-46 (Cambridge, 1959).

HOTSON, L., *Commonwealth and Restoration Stage,* (Harvard, 1928).

– *The First Night of Twelfth Night* (London, 1964).

JACKSON, A., 'London Playhouses, 1700-1705', *The Review of English Studies,* viii.

KEITH, W. G., 'A Theatre Project by Inigo Jones', *Burlington Magazine*, vol. 31, no. 174, pp. 105-11.

– 'John Webb and the Court Theatre of Charles II', *Architectural Review*, vol. lvii, 2, pp. 44-55 (1925).

KELLY, W., *Notices Illustrative of the Drama and other Public Amusements at Leicester* (London, 1865).

KENNEDY-SKIPTON, L., 'Notes on a Copy of William Capon's Plan of Goodman's Fields Theatre', *T.N.* xvii, pp. 86-9.

KERNODLE, G. R., *From Art to Theatre,* (Chicago, 1944).

KING, T. J., 'Staging of Plays at the Phoenix in Drury Lane, 1617-42', *T.N.* xix, pp. 146-66.

LANGDON. H. N., 'Staging of the Ascension in the Chester Cycle', *T.N.* xxvi, pp. 53-60.

LANGHANS, E. A., 'A Picture of the Salisbury Court Theatre', *T.N.* xix, pp. 100-1.

— 'Notes on the Reconstruction of the Lincoln's Inn Fields Theatre', *T.N.* x, pp. 112-4.

— 'Pictorial Material on the Bridges Street and Drury Lane Theatres', *Theatre Survey*, vol. vii, pp. 80-100, (1966).

— 'The Dorset Garden Theatre in Pictures', *Theatre Survey*, vol. vi, no. 2, pp. 134-46, (November, 1965).

— 'The Vere Street and Lincoln's Inn Field Theatres in Pictures', *Educational Theatre Journal*, vol. xx, no. 2, (May, 1968).

LAVER, J., *Isabella's Triumph* (London, 1947).

LAWRENCE, W. J., *Old Theatre Days and Ways* (London, 1935).

— *The Elizabethan Playhouse and other Studies*, 2 vols. (Stratford-on-Avon and New York, 1912).

LAWRENSON, T. E., *The French Stage of the Seventeenth Century*, (Manchester, 1957).

L.C.C. Theatres and Music Halls Committee Presented Papers

LEACROFT, H. and R., *The Buildings of Ancient Greece* (Leicester, 1966).

— *The Buildings of Ancient Rome* (Leicester, 1969).

LEACROFT, R., 'Actor and Audience', pts. i, ii, *R.I.B.A. Journal*, vol. 70, nos. 4, 5, (April, May, 1963).

— 'Theatre Machinery', *Architectural Review*, vol. cxvi, no. 692, pp. 113-4 (August, 1954).

— 'The Theatre Royal, Leicester, 1836-1958', *Transactions of the Leicester Archaeological and Historical Society*, vol. xxxiv, pp. 39-52, (1958).

— 'The Remains of the Fisher Theatres at Beccles, Bungay, Lowestoft and North Walsham', *T.N.* v, pp. 82-7.

— 'The Remains of the Theatres at Ashby-de-la-Zouch and Loughborough', *T.N.* iv, pp. 12-21.

— 'Wren's Drury Lane', *Architectural Review*, vol. cx, pp. 43-6, (July, 1951).

LEES-MILNE, J., *The Age of Inigo Jones* (London, 1953).

Leicester Journal, 9th September, 1836, 19th September, 1873.

LENNEP. W. van, *The London Stage*, Pt. 1, (Illinois, 1945).

LLOYDS, F., *Practical Guide to Scene Painting* (London, 1875).

MANDER, R. and MITCHENSON, J., *The Lost Theatres of London* (London, 1968).

Minute Book of the New Theatre, Leicester Museum Archives, 24th May, 1850, 9th February, 1853, 21st February, 1865, 23rd February, 1872, October, 1887, 11th November, 1891, 4th March, 1918.

MISSON, H., *Memoirs and Observations in his Travels over England*, translated Ozell, J. (1719).

NAGLER, A. M., *Sources of Theatrical History* (New York, 1952).

NELSON, M., 'Inspection of Theatres', *The Builder*, pp. 87-8, (5th February, 1858).

NICOLL, A., *The Development of the Theatre*, 5th ed. (London, 1966).

— *Stuart Masques and the Renaissance Stage*, (London, 1937).

— 'Passing over the Stage', *Shakespeare Survey*, vol. 12, pp. 47-55 (Cambridge, 1959).

NICHOLS, J., *The Progresses and Public Processions of Queen Elizabeth*, 3 vols (1823).

ORDISH, T. F., *Early London Theatres*, (London, 1894).

OULTON, W. C., *The History of the Theatres of London*, 2 vols. (1796).

– *A History of the Theatres of London*, 3 vols. (1817-18)

PALLADIO, A., *I Quattro Libri dell'Architettura*, (1570).

PALME, PER, *The Triumph of Peace*, (London, 1957).

PATERSON, M., 'The Stagecraft of the Revels Office during the reign of Elizabeth', see Prouty, G. pp. 1-52.

PECCATI, G., *Collona Storica sui Monumenti Gonzagheschi di Sabbioneta. Il Teatro Olimpico* (Mantua, 1950).

PENLEY, B. S., *The Bath Stage* (London, 1892).

PHIPPS, C. J., 'History and Arrangement of Theatres', *The Builder*, pp. 291-2, 25th April, 1863.

PICHEL, I., *Modern Theatres* (New York, 1920-5).

POZZO, A., *Rules and Examples of Perspective Proper for Painters and Architects* (London, 1707).

PROUTY, G., *Studies in the Elizabethan Theatre* (U.S.A., 1961).

Public Advertiser, 30th September, 1775.

REES, DR A., *Cyclopaedia, or universal Dictionary of Arts, Sciences and Literature* (1803-1819).

REYNOLDS, G. F., *The Staging of Elizabethan Plays at the Red Bull Theatre* (Oxford, 1940).

RICHARDS, K. R., 'Changeable Scenery for plays on the Caroline Stage', *T.N.* xxiii, 6-20.

RIDER, E., *A General History of the Stage* (1749).

ROSENFELD, S., 'The XVIII Century Theatre at Richmond', York Georgian Society, Occasional Papers, 3 (1947).

– 'Theatres in Goodman's Fields', *T.N.* i, pp. 48-50.

– 'Unpublished Stage Documents', *T.N.* xi, pp. 92-6.

ROWAN, D. F., 'The Cockpit-in-Court'; see Galloway, D., *The Elizabethan Theatre*, pp. 89-102.

– 'A Neglected Jones/Webb Theatre Project, Part II; A Theatrical Missing Link', in Galloway D., *The Elizabethan Theatre*, ii, pp. 60-73.

SABBATTINI, N., *Practica di Fabricar scene e machine ne' theatri* (Ravenna, 1637-8).

SACHS, E. O., 'Modern Theatre Stages', nos. i-xxx, *Engineering*, 17th January, 1896-23rd April, 1897.

– 'Stage Mechanism', *Journal of the Society of Arts*, 22nd April, 1898, pp. 512-28.

SACHS, E. O., and WOODROW, E., *Modern Opera Houses and Theatres*, 3 vols. (1896-8).

SALTER, F. M., *Medieval Drama in Chester* (Toronto, 1955).

SARLOS, R. K., 'Development and Decline of the First Blackfriars Theatre'; see Prouty, G., pp. 139-178.

SAUNDERS, G., *A Treatise on Theatres* (London, 1790).

SCHMITT, N. C., 'Was there a Medieval Theatre in the Round?', *T.N.* xxiii, pp. 130-42.

SCOUTEN, A. H., *The London Stage*, Pt. 3. vol. 1, (Illinois, 1961).

SEKLER, E., *Wren and his Place in European Architecture* (London, 1956).

SERLIO, S., *Tutte l'opere d'architettura et prospettiva*, (1545).

Shakespeare Society Papers, 'Deed of 23 March 1673-4', IV, 147f. (London, 1849).

SHAPIRO, A., 'The Bankside Theatres: Early Engravings', *Shakespeare Survey*, 1, pp. 25-37, (Cambridge, 1948).

– 'An original drawing of the Globe Theatre', *Shakespeare Survey*, 11. pp. 21-3.

SHARP, T., *A Dissertation on the Pageants or Dramatic Mysteries,* (London, 1825).

SHAW, CAPTAIN, Captain Shaw's Report, *Metropolitan Board of Works Report*, MBW 2396/1035.

SHAW-TAYLOR, D., *Covent Garden* (London, 1948).

SHUTE, J., *The First & Chief Groundes of Architecture* (London, 1563).

SIMPSON, P., and BELL, C. F., *Designs by Inigo Jones for Masques & Plays at Court* (Oxford, 1924).

The Sketch, Drury Lane, 27th April, 1898, Covent Garden, 3rd April, 1901, 24th April, 1901.

SMITH, R., *Memoirs of Richard Smith, cir. 1838-40*, R. Smith Collection, Bristol Reference Library

Society of Arts, *Journal of the Society of Arts*, 22nd April, 1898.

SONREL, P., *Traité de Scénographie* (Paris, 1943).

SOUTHERN, R., *Changeable Scenery* (London, 1952).

– 'Concerning a Georgian Proscenium Ceiling', *T.N.* iii, pp. 6-12.

– *The Georgian Playhouse* (London, 1948).

– 'The Houses of the Westminster Play', *T.N.* iii, pp. 46-52.

– 'Inigo Jones and Florimene', *T.N.* vii, pp. 37-9.

– *Medieval Theatre in the Round* (London, 1957).

– 'Observations on the Lansdowne Ms. no. 1171', *T.N.* ii, pp. 6-19.

– 'The Picture-Frame Proscenium of 1880', *T.N.* v, pp. 59-61.

– 'Scenery at the Book League', *T.N.* v, pp. 35-8.

– 'A Seventeenth Century Indoor Stage', *T.N.* ix, p. 5.

– *The Victorian Theatre* (Newton Abbot, 1970).

– 'The Winston MS and Theatre Design', *T.N.* i. pp. 93-5

SPEIGHT, R., *William Poel and the Elizabethan Revival* (London, 1954).

SPENCER, H. T. B., 'Theatre Planning and Construction', *The Builder*, p. 631ff, 19th December, 1903.

STONE. G. W., *The London Stage*, Pt. 4, vol. i, (Illinois. 1962).

STRATTON, A., 'The Westminster Dormitory', *The Builder*, 7th June, 1902. pp. 559-63.

STREIT, A., *Das Theater* (Vienna, 1903).

STRONG, R., *Festival Designs by Inigo Jones* (International Exhibitions Foundation, 1967-8).

STROUD, D., *Henry Holland* (London, 1966).

SUMMERS, M., *The Playhouse of Pepys* (London, 1935).

– *The Restoration Theatre* (London, 1934).

SUMMERSON, J., *Inigo Jones* (London, 1966).

Survey of London, The, Greater London Council. (Vol. xiii, 1930; vol. xiv, 1931; vols. xxix, xxx, 1960; vol. xxxv, 1970).

Theatre Notebook, A Quarterly Journal of the Society for Theatre Research.

TROUBRIDGE, SIR ST V., *Theatre Riots, Studies in Theatre History* (Society for Theatre Research, 1952).

VICTOR, B., *The History of the Theatres of London & Dublin from the Year 1730 to the Present Time*, 2 vols. (1761).

VITRUVIUS, *The Ten Books of Architecture*, tr. M. H. Morgan (New York, 1960).

WELSFORD, E., *The Court Masque* (Cambridge, 1927).

Western Daily Mercury, 15th August, 1861, 2; 14th June, 1878, 3; 18th June, 1879, 3.

WHALLEY, J. I., 'The Swan Theatre in the 16th Century', *T.N.* xx, p. 73.

WHEATLEY, H. B., *The Diary of Samuel Pepys*, vols. i-viii, (London, 1923).

WHITTY. J. C., 'The Half-price Riots of 1763', *T.N.* xxiv, pp. 25-32.

WICKHAM, G. W., 'The Cockpit Reconstructed', *New Theatre Magazine*, vol. 7, no. 2.

– *Early English Stages* (London, Vol. i, 1959, vol. ii, 1963).

– 'Players at Selby Abbey, Yorks, 1431-1532', *T.N.* xii, p. 46.

– 'The Privy Council Order of 1597'; see *The Elizabethan Theatre* pp. 21-44, (Ontario, 1969)

WILKINSON, R., *Londina Illustrata*, 11, *Theatrum Illustrata*, (London, 1825).

WILKINSON, T., *Memoirs of his own Life* (Vols. i-iv, 1790).

WOOD, A À, *The History & Antiquities of the University of Oxford* (1796)

WOODROW, A. E., 'Some Recent Developments in Theatre Planning', *Building News*, 25th March, 1892, p. 430ff.

– 'Theatres', nos. i-xlvii, *Building News*, 15th July, 1892-28th December, 1894.

Wren Society, vols. xi, xii (Oxford, 1934-5).

WYATT, B. D., *Observations on the Design for the Theatre Royal, Drury Lane* (London, 1813).

YATES, F. A., *Theatre of the World* (London, 1969).

Index